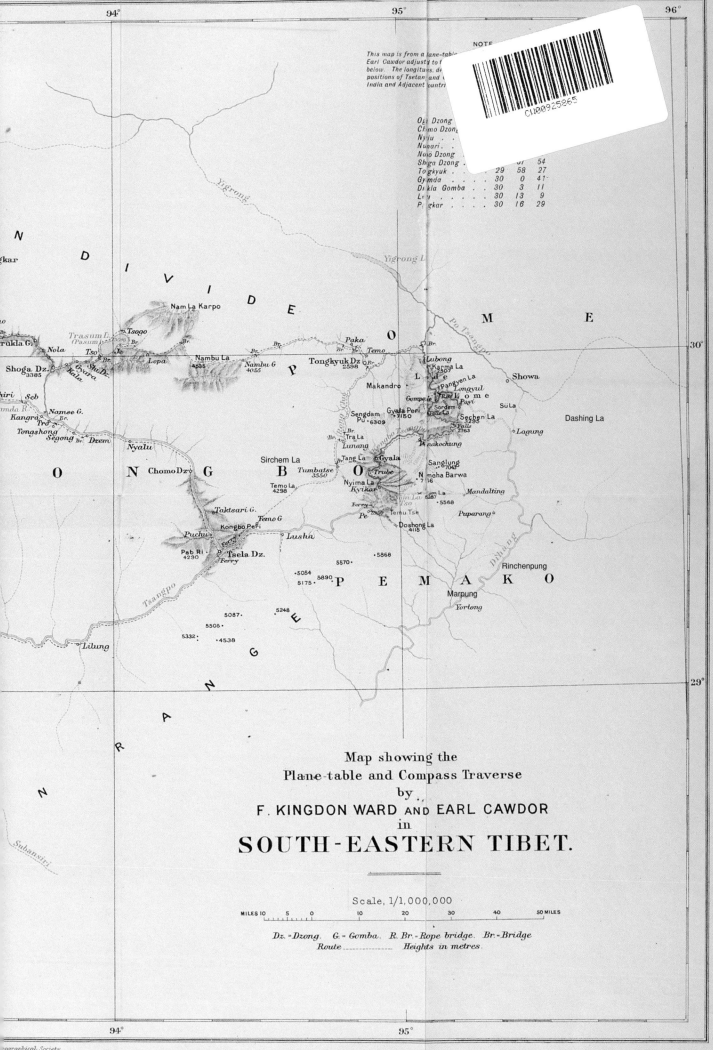

NOTE
This map is from a lane-table...
Earl Cawdor adjusts to f...
below. The longitudes, de...
positions of Tsetan and ...
India and Adjacent countri...

O..t Dzong			
C..mo Dzon..			
Ny..u			
Nunari			
Na..o Dzong			
Shiga Dzong		..7	54
To gkyuk	29	58	27
Gy..mda	30	0	41
D..kla Gomba	30	3	11
L..y	30	13	9
P..gkar	30	16	29

Map showing the
Plane-table and Compass Traverse
by
F. KINGDON WARD AND EARL CAWDOR
in
SOUTH-EASTERN TIBET.

Scale, 1/1,000,000

MILES 10   5   0   10   20   30   40   50 MILES

Dz.=Dzong.   G.=Gomba.   R.Br.=Rope bridge.   Br.=Bridge
Route ....   Heights in metres.

Frank Kingdon Ward's
Riddle of The

TSANGPO
GORGES

Frank Kingdon Ward's
Riddle of The
TSANGPO GORGES

Retracing the Epic Journey of 1924-25 in South-East Tibet

ORIGINAL TEXT BY FRANK KINGDON WARD, ED. KENNETH COX
ADDITIONAL MATERIAL BY KENNETH COX,
KENNETH STORM, JR. AND IAN BAKER

GARDEN • ART • PRESS

British Library Cataloguing-in-Publication Data
A catalogue record for this book is available from the British Library

Printed in China for Garden Art Press, an imprint of The Antique Collectors' Club Ltd.,
Woodbridge, Suffolk

Frontispiece: Rainbow Falls and *Rhododendron ramsdenianum*

The Antique Collectors' Club

Formed in 1966, the Antique Collectors' Club is now a world-renowned publisher of top quality books for the collector. It also publishes the only independently-run monthly antiques magazine, *Antique Collecting*, which rose quickly from humble beginnings to a network of worldwide subscribers.

The magazine, whose motto is For Collectors–By Collectors–About Collecting, is aimed at collectors interested in widening their knowledge of antiques both by increasing their awareness of quality and by discussion of the factors influencing prices.

Subscription to Antique Collecting is open to anyone interested in antiques and subscribers receive ten issues a year. Well-illustrated articles deal with practical aspects of collecting and provide numerous tips on prices, features of value, investment potential, fakes and forgeries. Offers of related books at special reduced prices are also available only to subscribers.

In response to the enormous demand for information on 'what to pay', ACC introduced in 1968 the famous price guide series. The first title, *The Price Guide to Antique Furniture* (since renamed *British Antique Furniture: Price Guide and Reasons for Values*), is still in constant demand. Since those pioneering days, ACC has gone from strength to strength, publishing many of today's standard works of reference on all things antique and collectable, from *Tiaras* to *20th Century Ceramic Designers in Britain*.

Not only has ACC continued to cater strongly for its original audience, it has also branched out to produce excellent titles on many subjects including art reference, architecture, garden design, gardens, and textiles. All ACC's publications are available through bookshops worldwide and a catalogue is available free of charge from the addresses below.

For further information please contact:

ANTIQUE COLLECTORS' CLUB

www.antiquecollectorsclub.com

Sandy Lane, Old Martlesham
Woodbridge, Suffolk IP12 4SD, UK
Tel: 01394 389950 Fax: 01394 389999
Email: info@antique-acc.com
or
Eastworks, 116 Pleasant Street - Suite 18,
Easthampton, MA 01027, USA
Tel: 413 529 0861 Fax: 413 529 0862
Email: info@antiquecc.com

Contents

Foreword to the 2001 edition   8
    Jean Rasmussen (formerly Jean Kingdon Ward)

Introduction to the 2001 edition   10
    Kenneth Cox

Acknowledgements   13

Preface to the 1926 edition   15
    Frank Kingdon Ward

Introduction to the 1926 edition   16
    Sir Francis Younghusband

i. Frank Kingdon Ward and the plant-hunters of China and the Himalaya   17
    Kenneth Cox

ii. The exploration of the Tsangpo Gorges to 1924   26
    Kenneth Storm, Jr.

iii. The Thousand-Petalled Lotus: Tibetan visions of the Tsangpo Gorge   48
    Ian Baker

THE RIDDLE OF THE TSANGPO GORGES **by Frank Kingdon Ward**   65
    ed. Kenneth Cox

I   Overview of the Geography and Peoples of Tibet   66

II   Over the Himalaya   73

III   Tsangpo, the Mysterious River   82

IV   A Botanical Reconnaissance   90

V   The Land of the Blue Poppy   100

VI   The Paradise of Primulas   112

VII   In the Rhododendron Fairyland   126

VIII   Pemakö: The Promised Land   145

IX   In the Assam Himalaya   161

X   A Journey to the Lost Lake   171

XI   The Crisis at Drukla Monastery   182

XII   Autumn Colours   190

XIII   The Gorge of the Tsangpo   201

XIV   In the Heart of the Himalaya   212

XV   The 'Falls of the Brahmaputra'   222

XVI   Christmas in Tibet   237

XVII   Winter on the Plateau   248

XVIII   Through Bhutan to India   260

XIX   The People of South-east Tibet *by Lord Cawdor*   268

XX   House and Home in South-east Tibet *by Lord Cawdor*   275

iv. The exploration of the Tsangpo Gorge region from 1925   280
    Kenneth Storm, Jr. and Kenneth Cox

v. The Tsangpo Gorges in the 21st Century   314
    Kenneth Cox

Author biographies   330

Bibliography   330

Index   332

Foreword to the 2001 Edition

Jean Rasmussen (formerly Jean Kingdon Ward)

My husband Frank Kingdon Ward died over forty years ago and there are few alive today who knew him, so it may be of interest to say a bit about the kind of man he was.

His father was a mycologist, frequently visited and consulted by fellow scientists, and Frank, in his boyhood and youth, met many of them, heard tales of places remote from Cambridge and Englefield Green and was fired with the desire to see such places for himself. In due course he did indeed visit, for example, the Malayan rain forest – but only very briefly – in 1909 on his way to China where he had secured a post as schoolmaster at the Shanghai Public School. Frank did not long remain a schoolmaster as a matter of months after arriving in China he joined an American zoological expedition as a botanist.

Frank's expeditions took place over a period of forty-five years. Inevitably, some years were fallow while he worked up his plant collections in England and wrote up his latest journey. But always further commissions for expeditions arose. Frank had a marvellous memory, learned quickly in the field, and each time brought back seed from the autumn harvest of several hundred 'garden plants'. These were beautiful plants such as rhododendrons which he reckoned had a good chance of thriving in Britain – not, alas, on the chalk downs where I now live, but in parts of Scotland, Ireland, Wales, the Lake District, Cornwall and a few other selected areas noted for their acid soil.

A very fine yellow rhododendron was named *R. wardii* after him. This he found near Atunze (now Deqin) in 1911, in the Tibetan part of China. It is still a favourite with gardeners who exhibit at the annual Rhododendron show in Vincent Square, London.

Of the more unusual plants discovered by Frank, I would pick out *Lilium arboricola* from the Triangle, North Burma which, most unusually, grows only as an epiphyte high up in great forest trees. It is a 'martagon' lily, pale green with contrasting brick red anthers and with a delicious scent of nutmeg. Alas, in Britain it flowered only once, at the Liverpool Botanic Garden, and is now almost certainly lost to cultivation. Frank had a good eye for lilies. *L. wardii*, another 'martagon', is named after him. Its discovery is documented in this book. In 1946 he found the beautiful bell-shaped Manipur Lily (*Lilium mackliniae*) which I will return to presently.

Our living conditions on plant hunts could vary very greatly. Bamboo huts called *bashas* were always very comfortable and so were our tents. Not large, but big enough for two safari camp beds, with deep pockets along the walls and stores boxes useful as tables – well, one table – there wasn't room for more.

The fixed daily routine began with a cup of tea and breakfast, followed by changing the herbarium presses and getting the damp paper spread out to dry on bamboo racks over the cookhouse fire. In the rains it was often necessary to change the presses twice a day, which meant a lot of tedious hand-drying of plant paper, sheet by sheet, on the part of our two servants, and by good-natured porters when we were on the move. They and the paper were well and truly kippered by the smoky fire of wet wood!

It was always Frank who wrote up the botanical notes, in a beautifully legible hand that scarcely varied in forty-five years. But I eagerly took over the plant-pressing. A 'chore', some might say, yet for me this daily routine was an endless delight that never, never grew stale. After 'doing the presses' we'd go out on a plant hunt, locally if at our base camp, or else on the day's march from 'A' to 'B'. The pace was pretty slow. You cannot properly observe your surroundings if you gallop along at more than 2-2½ miles per hour. Frank was most meticulous in observing, remembering and writing up the day's plants, often with details recorded in his diary about the local people, tribal customs, geographical observations and so on.

Frank was tough. On his early expeditions I don't think he really cared what he ate or when. Still less did he bother about health and medicine. Before I expanded greatly the contents of our medicine chest Frank boasted that he took with him only quinine, iodine, a 'starter' and a 'stopper'. Well, he got away with it, more or less anyway, though after one or two of his early expeditions he came out a physical wreck.

He had quite a good ability to pick up a smattering of useful languages and could bargain with Chinese muleteers and shop keepers when required. Some of his Tibetan servants chose to go with him more than once and our Tangkhul Naga cook wanted to stay with us too.

Though quite a clubbable man, Frank was never happier than when he was in the field engaged in his chosen profession of plant hunting. The rewards of plant-hunting were so great – in the field anyway – that I don't recall Frank missing anything much from the world of Europe. (*I* did though – for me the lack of music was the one really severe deprivation.) The greatest reward that we ever had together happened on what was my first expedition and Frank's seventeenth. On 5 June 1948 we walked twenty-five miles in order to see a particular lily in flower on Mount Sirhoi Kashong in Assam in North-east India, and were totally overwhelmed by the sight of a vast grass slope absolutely solid pink with thousands upon thousands *of Lilium mackliniae*. In a state of pure ecstasy we floated up to the top of that marvellous mountain, which generously produced yet another sensational experience for us, when, growing against black rocks that set it off to perfection, we came upon a most unusual and very rare pale lilac Primula (*P. sherriffiae*), previously found once only in Bhutan by George and Betty Sherriff. Nothing could have been more unexpected and for several moments time froze. We were both speechless. Literally. Set against months of monsoon rains, such ravishing moments go a long way to even up the score.

One thing about Frank that never ceased to amaze me was, of all things, his choice of profession – or rather, his sticking to it for the best part of half a century! Twice he had the opportunity to settle down into a more routine botanical job – once at the end of a not very successful expedition, and again after his outstandingly successful 1924 journey to the Tsangpo Gorge of South-east Tibet. Both offers were considered, but both were turned down. I would guess that one of the factors he may have considered was the fact that a desk job would release him from the recurring ordeal of his phobia for 'airy situations'. Such situations are ten-a-penny in the kind of country where the best rhododendrons, primulas and meconopsis grow, and each time for Frank was a nightmare: I have seen his face chalk white as he stepped out on to an almost non-existent track with a 2,000ft. drop down to the river below. He said not a word, and I marvelled then (as indeed I do still) that anyone with such a phobia of heights could continue for decades in his chosen profession of plant hunter in the high mountains of Asia. That called for sustained courage of a high order indeed.

He might well have died in harness – indeed he might – and no one would have thought that anything but fitting, but in fact he died, aged seventy-two, in London. At the time we were fully engaged in planning yet another plant-hunting expedition to the mountains of what would now be called Vietnam.

Frank's innumerable plant introductions still give untold delight to garden lovers in their millions and, to judge from frequent references to him in the current gardening and botanical press, Frank and his life's work will be remembered for a long time to come.

Introduction to the 2001 Edition

Kenneth Cox

The Riddle of the Tsangpo Gorges, published in 1926, describes what was undoubtedly Frank Kingdon Ward's most ambitious and successful expedition of the many he made in the course of a long career as a plant-hunter. Several of the Kingdon Ward books have been reprinted but for some reason this one has remained out of print for many years, and the few copies which have changed hands have commanded very high prices. Recent years have seen a resurgence of interest in the Tsangpo Gorge area, from Chinese scientists, foreign explorers, plant hunters, canoeists and mountaineers.

David Burlinson, founder of Exodus, a British adventure travel company, spent many years trying to obtain permission from the Chinese authorities to take an expedition into the Tsangpo Gorges region. A small American expedition managed to visit the area in April 1986, but it was rather too early in the year and it proved impossible to cross the Doshong La due to snow. Kenneth Storm, Jr. and Ian Baker began exploring the gorge in 1993. Following David's reconnaissance in autumn 1994, David Burlinson and Kenneth Cox led an expedition in 1995 which crossed the Doshong La and several other passes in the area. *Riddle of the Tsangpo Gorges* was the only 'guidebook' available and it was fascinating to be able to match Kingdon Ward's descriptions of the rhododendron 'Orange Bill' and the blue poppies to these plants *in situ*. In 1996 we returned to the area and met Kenneth Storm and Ian Baker who were on their way back from exploring the gorge. Over a few beers, a large amount of information was exchanged, and I mentioned an idea I had been considering – to republish *Riddle of the Tsangpo Gorges*. Not surprisingly this book was Ken and Ian's 'bible' too. It was apparent that between us we had travelled through almost all the places the Ward book describes and that we had photographs to illustrate most of the plants and much of the scenery. In many ways very little has changed in the intervening years and it seemed to be a magnificent opportunity to draw attention to a little known region, to celebrate Kingdon Ward's achievement and to share our passion for the mountains, people and flowers of south-east Tibet.

Jean Rasmussen, Frank Kingdon Ward's widow, was delighted to hear of our endeavour. Once we had had the copyright returned to her, and found a publisher, it was a matter of co-ordinating the various strands of the project. When republishing a historical work, there are always dilemmas as to what to change for a new edition. The inclusion of metric measurement was one obvious addition. But other aspects are more problematic.

There is no doubt that, for their time, Frank Kingdon Ward and the Earl of Cawdor were relatively enlightened and broad-minded. But the white, Anglo-Saxon, male assumptions prevalent in their day are considered far from 'politically correct' today. Some of their comments would now be considered downright offensive. Tribal people and the Tibetan officials he describes are often judged with an inescapable sense of white superiority which would nowadays be considered racist. After much reflection, I have left the text largely unaltered, censoring only a few of the most unacceptable comments. I have also added the chapter sub-headings.

The taxonomy of plants is a both a fascinating subject and a controversial one. There have been many attempts to classify plants over hundreds of years, and there has always been a great deal of disagreement. Many of the plants described in *The Riddle of the Tsangpo Gorges* were new to science and had not yet been described (in Latin) at the time the book was published, soon after Ward returned to England. Ward therefore uses a combination of nicknames such as 'Orange Bill' and approximations such as 'the lacteum' to refer to plants (in these examples rhododendron species) to which he cannot yet give Latin names. Many of these names have been left in the text but the most up-to-date nomenclature has been added. For example 'Coals of Fire' is changed to 'Coals of Fire' (*R. cerasinum*). If Ward's specific name has been changed to something else, his name is placed within square brackets: *Meconopsis cawdoriana* becomes *M. speciosa* [*M. cawdoriana*], for example. Where the taxonomy has changed but the epithet remains (reduced from a species to a subspecies for example) I have used the most recent taxonomy: *Primula ninguida* changed to *P. macrophylla* var. *ninguida*. Many more details on taxonomic matters are given in the captions to the photographs.

The text is punctuated with collector's numbers. These numbers are assigned to pressed Herbarium specimens and to seed collections. The following is an example from Kingdon Ward's field notes from the expedition:

K.W. 6257 (later identified as) *Rhododendron keysii*. Pemakö. from 9,000-10,000ft 24/10/24 (date of collection). Slim shrub to 8-10ft high, in thickets on the southern slopes of the valley...capsules small in large trusses...leaf surface with close set small scales...'

The collector's number is a very useful reference point, both for the taxonomist and for keeping accession records of plants growing in botanical gardens and private gardens. Many plants grown from seed from the 1924-25 expedition can still be traced if the collector's number has been recorded.

The rules concerning the italicisation of Latin names has changed somewhat since Ward's day. Ward places binomials (genus and species) such as *Rhododendron wardii* in italics, but refers to Genera alone (Primula, Meconopsis...) in roman script with an initial capital letter. In order to retain consistency, I have followed this practice in the new chapters and in the captions.

Taxonomists tend to fall broadly into two categories, somewhat disparagingly but pithily described as 'splitters' and 'lumpers'. Splitters tend to describe a large number of new species using a minimum number of, or not particularly significant characters. In contrast, lumpers reduce the number of species by amalgamating those under one name which they consider are simply variations on a theme. It is true to say that the broad direction of present day taxonomy is towards lumping, but there are still trends in both directions. The changes and disagreements in taxonomy of many of the plants are discussed in the captions to the photographs.

In Kingdon Ward's day, rhododendrons were classified into groups known as 'series' which contained a number of related species. When the huge Genus *Rhododendron* was revised at Edinburgh and elsewhere from 1970 onwards, a more hierarchical system of classification was adopted with the groups of related species renamed 'sections' and 'subsections'. A similar system is used to classify the genus *Primula*. In most cases the term 'series' has been left in the Kingdon Ward text, while the captions tend to carry the more modern term 'subsection'.

Kingdon Ward, like many explorers of his time, painstakingly measured altitudes throughout his journey and in all weathers by taking boiling points. In returning to China and Tibet with more modern tools of measurement, we find that Ward is much more accurate than many of his contemporary explorers such as Joseph Rock who tended to exaggerate altitudes. I have given approximate equivalents in metres to Ward's readings in feet, but have converted more accurately for important measurements such as the heights of mountains and passes.

Chinese and Tibetan names cause considerable confusion in the inconsistent way that the sounds are transliterated into roman script. There are often several different spellings for the same word, so I have largely retained Kingdon Ward's spellings of place names. The following are some of the equivalent spellings typically used on Chinese produced maps and in modern guidebooks:

PLACE NAMES

Kingdon Ward's spelling	*Modern and other spellings*
Abor	Adi
Doshong La	Dozhong La
Gyala Peri	Jiala Peri, Gyala Pelri
Gyamda	Chiang-t'a
Medok	Medog
Menling	Mi-lin
Mönba	Mompa
Namcha Barwa	Namchak Barwa
Nyangtri	Lin-chih, Nyingchi
Pasum Tso	Passum Tso, P'a-san Hu
Payi	Bayi, Bayu, Bayul, Payu, Payul
Pemaköchung	P'i-ma-k'uo-ts'un
Pome	Bome, Pomed
Putrang La	Podrang La
Tongkyuk Dzong	Tongjuk
Trube	Tripe
Trulung	Pylung
Sirchem La	Serkhyem La
Tumbatse	Tang-pa-tse
Yarlung Tsangpo	Parlung Tsangpo, Yarlung Zangbo

GLOSSARY of TIBETAN TERMS

Chu:	stream or small river
Chorten:	sacred monument
Dzong:	fortress, castle
Dzongpön/Tsongpön:	Government official
Gompa:	monastery
La:	pass
Po:	large river
Rong:	valley
Thang:	plain
tsampa/tsamba:	roasted barley flour, the staple food of Tibet
Tso:	lake

PHOTOGRAPHERS

AC:	Anne Chambers
FKW:	Frank Kingdon Ward
IB:	Ian Baker
JC:	Jack Cawdor
JR:	June Ross
KNEC:	Kenneth Cox
KR:	Keith Rushforth
KSJ:	Kenneth Storm, Jr.
OT	Oken Tayeng
PC:	Peter Cox
RR:	Ralph Rynning
WK	William Kidd

Acknowledgements

Kenneth Cox

There are many people who have contributed greatly to the long process of getting this project off the ground and seeing it to fruition. Jean Rasmussen has been unstinting in her support for the book and has contributed a fine foreword. The Dowager Countess Cawdor has allowed us to republish the chapters and photographs by Lord ('Jack') Cawdor, as well as providing a photograph of him. Edward Arnold (publishers) Ltd allowed the rights of the book to revert to Jean Rasmussen so we could republish it. Diana Steel, Primrose Elliott and Brian Cotton at Antique Collectors Club who shared my vision for a lavishly illustrated book and have seen the project through from contract to publication. Lastly my wife Jane Bradish-Ellames for her help on the contract, her expert proof reading and for keeping me going through many months of work on this project. I would like to thank all three of my co-authors whose intrepid journeys through the gorge over seventy years apart have made this book possible.

Peter Cox, Anne Chambers, Keith Rushforth, June Ross and Hugh McAllister for the loan of their fine slides to the book. The Royal Geographical Society allowed a search of their Kingdon Ward archives and gave permission to reprint numerous black and white pictures. Every effort has been made to trace the copyright holders of all other original material reproduced in this book. Many people have helped greatly over the years in identifying plants which we have found in South-east Tibet. Those who have been most invaluable are Peter Cox, Anne Chambers, Chris Sanders, Graham Rugman, Keith Rushforth and Hugh McAllister, all of whom have been to Tibet and who are great experts in their various fields. Amongst those who have helped identify specimens and pictures at home are: John Richards, Henry Noltie, Eona Aitken, Dr. Philip Cribb, the late George Smith and David Chamberlain who looked out lots of important specimens for me. Roy Vickery allowed me to look up specimens at the British Museum and Lourdes Rico was a great help at the Herbarium at Kew. Anne Chambers has given generously of her time with correcting aspects of botanical nomenclature and proof reading captions.

David Burlinson from Exodus is a great Tibetophile and it is mainly his persistence in the face of bureaucracy, and arrest, which allowed us to get into the Tsangpo Gorges region. The key person on the ground in Tibet has been our good friend He Hai who has obtained permits and negotiated our way out of numerous brushes with authority. We could not have survived either without our Nepali crew, led by our sirdar Tsering. (who said after his second crossing of the Doshong La that he would not make a third one under any circumstances as the weather was so depressing) and his staff. We would all like to thank our Tibetan drivers, guides and porters.

Acknowledgements 2007 Edition

Kenneth Cox

George Schaller, Dan Janzen and Daniel Taylor of Future Generations, Peycom Ringu, Claire Scobie, Oken Tayeng, Omak Apong, Bill Kidd, Mike Searle, Dale Vrabek for a detailed archive on the Tsangpo floods of 2000.

Acknowledgements
Ian Baker

In compiling a religious history of the Tsangpo Gorge region, many Lamas both within and outside Tibet have been extremely generous with their knowledge. I would especially like to thank Bhakha Tulku Rinpoche of Pome, Khamtrul Rinpoche, Tulku Pema Wangyal, Jedrung Rinpoche of Tezu, Lama Rinchen, Jigme Rinpoche, Namkha Rinpoche, Lama Topgye, Lama Konchok Wangpo, Kawa Tulku as well as numerous other Tibetan yogis and yoginis who saw in the wilds of Pemakö, a doorway to exalted vision.

Acknowledgements
Kenneth Storm, Jr.

A shared passion for wilderness, the Tibetan people, botanical wonders, and sacred geography is part of the rich legacy of western exploration to the Tsangpo Gorges/Pemakö over the past hundred years. Each explorer has stood on the shoulders of those who have gone before, often acknowledging their gratitude personally – Bailey and Morshead to Kintup; Kingdon Ward and Lord Cawdor to Bailey; Ludlow and Sherriff to Kingdon Ward. One of the great pleasures of my own travels to the gorges has been the opportunity to extend that same obligation to Frank Kingdon Ward's widow, Jean Rasmussen. A seasoned explorer herself, Jean graciously welcomed me at the Royal Geographical Society on a visit to London after our second expedition, and from then on we have corresponded regularly. No journey has been complete without a 'phone call or exchange of letters describing our recent travels in Frank's footsteps to the same wild places she too loves so deeply. It has been a privilege to hear first hand of those long seasons in the field with Frank, searching the hillsides for beauty, and to see one of her husband's finest books back in print.

To Ian Baker and Hamid Sardar who revealed to me the wonders of the sacred geography of Pemakö. Ours has been a friendship nurtured by many extraordinary journeys through trackless wilderness and along pilgrim trails. Through their vision I have come to understand that all true explorers to Pemakö are 'pilgrims' at heart.

To other fellow travellers who have shared the journeys, especially – Jill Bielawski, Eric Manthey, and Geng Zuanru who accompanied Ian and me on our first expedition (1993); Ralph Rynning who revealed the enchanting bird-life of the gorges (1996); Jenny M. for the story of the 'Red Lily' (1997); Gil and Troy Gillenwater who shared with me that marvellous view from the cliffs above Rainbow Falls to the 'new' falls beyond (1997). To Jean-Pierre Burg for his notes on the geology of the region.

To our Tibetan guides and porters who shared our adventures, trusted us with their 'stories', and were always ready with a helping hand – especially Sherab, Jyang, and Bullock. Thanks also to Pemba, Dawa and the rest of our Sherpa team for their many kindnesses. To Kenneth Cox – without his untiring efforts and enthusiasm this book would not have been possible.

Preface to the 1926 Edition

Frank Kingdon Ward

In 1923, through the kindness of the Indian and Tibetan Governments, I obtained permission for myself and one companion to visit Tibet for the purpose of collecting plants. Much of Tibet being a semi-desert, the scene selected was the south-east corner where most of the big rivers which rise in Tibet squeeze their way through the mountains to the sea. Of the botany of this region, at the extreme eastern end of the Himalaya, practically nothing was known.

I laid my plans before the Government Grant Committee of the Royal Society, and the Trustees of the Percy Sladen Memorial Fund, and these two bodies financed me. Lord Cawdor, who was then up at Cambridge, and who was interested in Ethnology, and other branches of Natural Science, volunteered to accompany me; and we left England in February, 1924.

It is with great pleasure that I acknowledge the kind assistance of many friends. Personally my first tribute is due to my companion, Lord Cawdor, for his splendid co-operation throughout a trying journey, and I am further indebted to him for two interesting chapters, and for permission to reproduce several of his excellent photographs. Much of the success of the journey was due to his skill, ingenuity and patience.

Major F.M. Bailey, Political Officer, Sikkim, who was instrumental in obtaining for us our passport, gave us most valuable advice and assistance; and to our friends in Gyantse, Mr. David MacDonald (British Trade Agent), Major J.H. Hyslop, Captain J.E. Cobbett, and Mr. F. Ludlow, we owe many pleasant hours spent on the roof of the world.

F.K.W.
London, 1926.

Introduction to the 1926 Edition

Sir Francis Younghusband, K.C.S.I., K.C.I.E.

Captain Kingdon Ward is happy in his vocation and happier still in his choice of the field in which to fulfil it. His object in life is to collect plants. And not merely dried plants suitable for the herbarium, and to be described in mechanical fashion in the dead language of Latin, would he collect, but living seeds also – seeds of the most beautiful plants and most suited to our English gardens so that beauty upon beauty might be added to our already lovely land. This is Captain Ward's vocation.

And where in the world could he have chosen a better ground for accomplishing his object than in the Himalaya and in that part of the Himalaya where India touches China, where Indian plants intermingle with the rich flora of China, and where the climate is not so dissimilar to England but what our clever gardeners might be able to make them grow in English and Scottish gardens.

So Captain Kingdon Ward, with his companion Lord Cawdor, go off to that wonderful region where the Tsangpo of Tibet cuts its way clean through the Himalaya and emerges on to the plains of India under the name of Brahmaputra. And here in the mountains and the gorges, both in the full flowering season of the year and in the harvest time of seeds, he revels in fulfilling his vocation. And the titles alone of the chapters describing his adventures fill us with envy of the opportunities he had made for himself. "The Land of the Blue Poppy" – how we would love to see that land of hope and glory! "The Paradise of Primulas" – what flower lover would not wish that this is the heaven that destiny has in safe reserve for him! "In the Rhododendron Fairyland" – what fairy would ever want a more glorious land in which to disport herself than among the delicate bells of the red and crimson, the mauve and white and yellow rhododendrons of the Indian Himalaya and of the Chinese borderlands.

Let it not be imagined, though, that such joys are come by without toil. No joy worth having ever is. It has to be won. And Captain Kingdon Ward won his at the cost of long journeying over the bleak and wind-swept uplands of Tibet, and afterwards of steep climbs in rain and mist and sleet on the mountain-sides which hemmed in the terrific gorges. It was hard and strenuous work. It was no matter of strolling out and picking a few flowers as the spirit moved him. He had to bear in constant remembrance that the opportunity he had now made he might never be able to make again. He must make the most of it while he had it. In that brief flowering season when plants burst into sudden life and quickly pass away again he must not let a single chance slip by. However disinclined he might be on a day of pouring rain when it is either hot and steamy or chilly with the approach of snow, he must descend to the gorge or climb to the pass. And however exhausted he might be, on his return he must note carefully for each plant the conditions in which he saw it growing so that the gardener at home might reproduce as near as he could these conditions and give the seeds which Kingdon Ward had subsequently to collect a chance of maturing and the plant of properly thriving.

And then would come the supreme difficulty of adequately describing the plant itself and its flower. How could anyone less than a Reginald Farrer accomplish so delicate a task? Any lover of flowers would be longing for the genius to describe the rare glories which he had seen about him so that those at home might share with him his enjoyment. But how describe the innumerable forms? How describe the different shades of colour? To some extent this may be done by comparison with other natural objects – with the colours of precious stones or of the sky or of fruits, etc. But there is the ever-present difficulty. And we must give the poor plant collector our sympathy as we see him doing all he can to communicate his pleasure to us and we must play our part and go out half way to meet him.

In that mood we must approach this record of a man's effort to enrich the beauty of his native land and give pleasure to his fellows.

i
Frank Kingdon Ward
and the plant hunters of China and the Himalaya
Kenneth Cox

Rhododendron fortunei, Onosma hookeri, Clethra delavayi, Pleione forrestii. These are just a handful of the hundreds of plants from China and the Himalaya named after the European plant hunters who 'discovered' them. Of course the concept of 'discovery' is somewhat problematic as most of the plants were already well known to the inhabitants of the areas where they were found, and many of them were already used for medicinal purposes.

The list of collectors whose names are most often commemorated in the Latin epithets of the plants they collected includes Fortune, Hooker, Delavay, Wilson, Forrest, Kingdon Ward and Rock. These collectors operated between 1843 and 1950, a period which saw the gradual opening up of the Himalaya, China and Tibet to western exploration. The new plants were brought back in the form of pressed specimens and seed collections. The pressed specimens gathered on these expeditions were sent to herbaria at botanical institutions in the west for naming, while the seed was distributed to botanical gardens, nurseries and private individuals who sponsored the plant hunters in the field. It soon became apparent that many of the plants from mountainous regions from above approximately 3,000m (10,000ft.) were ideally suited for cultivation outdoors in Britain, much of northern Europe and favourable parts of North America.

This period could be called 'the golden age of the plant hunter' since so many of what have become our commonest hardy garden plants were introduced from the Sino-Himalayan region during this time. Examples include magnolias, Pieris, rhododendrons, Meconopsis, primulas and lilies. It is no coincidence that so many of the plant hunters were British, as this era coincided with Britain's greatest influence as a colonial power. Prior to 1850, several explorers including Nathaniel Wallich and Dr William Griffith had introduced plants from the more accessible parts of the Himalaya, but it was the two collectors, Robert Fortune in China and Joseph Hooker in the Himalaya, who were the first to introduce really significant numbers of new plants to the west.

Fortune was sent to the Orient in 1843 by the Horticultural Society (of London) following the signing of the Treaty of Nanking in 1842 which brought a degree of stability to China. He was given extremely precise and detailed orders: 'to collect seeds and plants of an ornamental or useful kind, not already cultivated in Great Britain.' A number of specific plants were mentioned, 'The peaches of Pekin…the plants that yield tea…the double yellow roses…Peonies with blue flowers, Camellias with yellow flowers, if such exist…the azalea from Lo-fou-shan….' He was also instructed to bring back soil samples. Interestingly, the yellow Camellia (*C. chrysantha* and several other species) has only recently been introduced to the west, over 140 years later.

Joseph Hooker's explorations in Nepal and Sikkim in 1847-51 yielded extensive and well-distributed seed collections. Spectacular displays of Primula, Rhododendron, Meconopsis, Magnolia and other plants were soon to be found in major British gardens and new plants commanded premium prices. The successes of the Fortune and Hooker introductions revealed the potential of the Sino-Himalayan region as a major source for garden plants and it was obvious that as most of China was still unexplored, there would be many plants yet to be discovered. The years between 1855 and 1885 saw fewer introductions, partly due to the 1860 Anglo-French War with China. However, during the last ten to fifteen years of the nineteenth century, Russian explorers such as Przewalski, French missionaries such as Delavay and David, and English collectors such as Maries and Gill were active in China. There was said to be an astonishing total of 2,800 missionaries at work in China during the 1890s and a surprising number seemed to have spent more time plant collecting than proselytising. Many thousands of specimens reached herbaria in Paris, London, Boston and St Petersburg where botanists set about describing the thousands of hitherto unknown plant species. These herbarium specimens consisted of a dried and pressed plant or part of a plant, mounted, numbered, labelled and accompanied by a description of habit and habitat. Some idea of the scale of this botanical endeavour can be seen in the statistics: the French missionary and plant collector Jean Marie Delavay alone collected over 200,000 herbarium specimens in China during the last two decades of the nineteenth century. It is estimated that Delavay discovered approximately 1,500 species of plants new to western science, many of which were named after him.

Despite the huge number of new plants discovered, the missionaries sent back mainly specimens rather than seed, and it was not until the early years of the twentieth century that large numbers of the newly discovered plants were introduced to the West by dedicated seed collectors. Ernest Wilson, then a twenty-three year old teacher of botany, was sent to Sichuan in 1899 by Sir Harry Veitch of the then well-known nursery firm of James Veitch and Son, principally to seek out and introduce the handkerchief tree *Davidia involucrata*. This tree had been discovered earlier by one of the French missionaries, Abbé Jean Pierre David. Another of the missionaries, the Irish Augustine Henry, had sent some of his many dried specimens to Kew where Sir Harry Veitch had been much excited by them. The Veitch Nursery had a long history of financing plant hunters including William and Thomas Lobb who introduced many plants from North and South America. Both Veitch and A.K. Bulley (Ward's first sponsor) corresponded with several of the missionaries. It was Augustine Henry who offered to assist Veitch in sending a collector out to China and this led to Wilson's appointment. Wilson's 1899 expedition was a great success: seeds of the Davidia and several other significant plants were successfully collected and introduced, and Wilson was to return to China in 1903, 1907 and 1910. Another of the most important collectors, Scotsman George Forrest, was sent to Yunnan in 1904 and returned a further six times until his early death in the field in 1932.

The scale of introductions during this period was unprecedented both in the number of species discovered and the volume of seed collected. It is clear that only a tiny fraction of the seed sent from China at this time was ever raised to maturity. Many plants needed expert handling and specialist knowledge which was not yet available. In addition, some genera were largely neglected in the rush to bloom the first introductions of then fashionable plants such as new species rhododendrons. The early years of the twentieth century witnessed a revolution in gardening tastes due to both the new plant introductions and to the influence of garden writers such as William Robinson who championed woodland gardening. A number of wealthy landowners such as J.C. Williams, Lionel de Rothschild, Lord Aberconway and others sponsored plant hunting expeditions. They or their gardeners raised large quantities of Chinese seed, landscaping their expanding woodland gardens in a 'natural' style, with ponds, streams, ravines and meandering paths, in imitation of Chinese hillsides, into which they planted the exciting new Magnolias, Rhododendrons, Azaleas, Camellias, Meconopsis and other Asiatic plants.

Frank Kingdon Ward on a horse.
This picture appears to have been taken in China, on an earlier expedition.

Frank Kingdon Ward 1885-1958

After Wilson and Forrest, the next significant collector to reach China was Frank Kingdon Ward. He was born in Withington, Lancashire in 1885 and ten years later his father was appointed to the Chair of Botany at Cambridge. Frank was evidently inspired by his father's work and in turn chose to read Natural Sciences at Cambridge. Due to financial constraints, following his father's early death in 1906, Frank Kingdon Ward's degree was completed in two (rather than the normal three) years and he immediately accepted a job as a teacher in Shanghai. During periods of leave from this post he explored parts of Java and Borneo and in 1909 when the opportunity arose to join an expedition to central and western China, primarily for the purpose of studying animals, Kingdon Ward was quick to accept this offer. It was during this expedition that he managed to collect his first herbarium specimens which he sent to Cambridge University. His classroom days were almost over.

Kingdon Ward's first employment as a professional plant collector was provided by A.K. Bulley, a Liverpool cotton magnate and keen plantsman. Up until 1910 Bulley had employed George Forrest as his collector in China but Forrest had been headhunted by J.C. Williams of Caerhays Castle in Cornwall who appointed him to seek out new rhododendron species. Bulley looked around for a replacement and approached Ward after a recommendation from Professor Bailey Balfour at The Royal Botanic Garden, Edinburgh. Though concerned by Ward's relative lack of experience, Bulley wrote to Ward in China asking him to undertake an expedition to Yunnan in late 1910. George Forrest, now of course an experienced plant hunter, made it plain that he guarded his collecting 'patch' jealously and insisted that Kingdon Ward steer clear of his collecting areas. When the two men met in Lijiang in 1913, Forrest offered Ward little advice and no encouragement and was scathing about Ward's inexperience. Perhaps this meeting was in part responsible for Ward's particular determination to reach Tibet later that year, an attempt that was to end in failure. In the years to follow, Ward was to prove Forrest's judgement wrong and even during his first serious plant-hunting trip, Ward's stamina and tolerance of extreme hardship was evident. The 1910 expedition from Dali to Atunse (Deqin) was to prove eventful and included an often recounted incident where Ward was lost for several days on the Litiping with no food and only a single cartridge in his shotgun. The bird he shot with it, at near point blank range, was blown to bits, and he ate the remains raw. Even in his first book *In the Land of the Blue Poppy* which covers this expedition it is clear that, despite a lack of botanical expertise, Kingdon Ward was already addicted to his new life of explorer and plant hunter.

'Bulley's [1910] letter decided my life for the next 45 years' Kingdon Ward wrote many years later in his book *Pilgrimage for Plants*. Ward's first years as a plant-hunter were not easy and not particularly successful. A.K. Bulley was disappointed by Ward's seed hauls compared to those of his predecessor George Forrest. Ward's unofficial and unsuccessful attempt to get to Tibet in 1913 was a drain on Bulley's finances and gave little reward in terms of plants. It almost cost Ward his job. He made amends in 1914 by moving his focus to Burma where, despite incessant rain, almost continuous fever, an injured foot and a steady supply of leeches, he managed to discover some fine new plants. During the First World War, Ward enlisted in the Indian army and rose to the rank of captain, returning to Burma in 1919 on a further expedition where he spent a few days with Reginald Farrer and Euan Cox (Kenneth Cox's grandfather) at Hpimaw. After an expedition to China in 1921, Ward returned to Britain and later that year married Florinda Norma-Thompson with whom he had two children, Martha and Pleione. The well-connected Florinda introduced Ward both to his publisher, Jonathan Cape, and to his important patron and sponsor, Lady Londonderry.

It is generally considered that the 1924-25 Tsangpo Gorges expedition, covered in this book, was Kingdon Ward's finest achievement. It was successful both in terms of pure exploration and in the discovery and introduction of new plants, and the expedition gained Ward considerable celebrity in Britain and elsewhere. Of the plants introduced from the expedition, the blue poppy *Meconopsis betonicifolia* is the most famous but other notable discoveries and introductions included: *Rhododendron cinnabarinum* ssp. *xanthocodon* Concatenans Group ('Orange Bill'), *R. lanatoides, R. venator, R. montroseanum, R. parmulatum, R. leucaspis, Primula florindae, P. cawdoriana, Cotoneaster conspicuus,* and *Berberis calliantha*.

In 1926 and 1928 Ward returned to Burma. On the latter expedition, he introduced the magnificent *Rhododendron macabeanum* from Mt. Javpo in Assam. During the 1930s Ward made several more expeditions to Tibet, Burma and India. The 1935 expedition from Assam into Tibet, via Tsari, east along the Tsangpo retraced some of the ground of his 1924 journey such as the passes around the valley of the Rong Chu and the route north to Pasum Tso. Ironically the Tibetan sector of this expedition was technically illegal: neither Kingdon Ward nor any of his party was able to read the letter in response to his request for permission to enter the country, so he travelled ever further into Tibet hoping to find an interpreter. In the event the letter was never examined by officials during the journey and it was not until it was translated on his return to India that he realised that his request to enter Tibet had been refused.

During the Second World War, Kingdon Ward made good use of his specialist

Rhododendron wardii on the Doshong La.   **KNEC**
Named after Frank Kingdon Ward, this is one of the most widely grown yellow-flowered rhododendron species and it has been used in the breeding of most larger growing yellow hybrids. *R. wardii* is extremely variable and its distribution stretches from Muli in southern Sichuan to southern Tibet near the Bhutan border. Its nearest relative, *R. campylocarpum* (ssp. *campylocarpum*), is the Himalayan equivalent, occurring in Nepal, Sikkim, Bhutan and the southern slopes of the Himalayan range in south-east Tibet. On the Doshong La the two species meet at the tree line on the north side of the pass and a whole range of intermediate forms occur. The two species are easily separated when in flower by examining the glands on the style. These are present along the length of the style in *R. wardii* and to less than half the length in *R. campylocarpum*. The form shown here is a fine pure yellow unmarked form (Cox and Vergara 9548).

knowledge of northern Burma working for the Special Operations Executive, establishing safe corridors for downed allied airmen escaping the Japanese. After the war, he worked to locate crashed aircraft used on 'the Hump' (the nickname given to the relief flights ferrying food from India to China over Burma). Frank and his first wife had divorced in 1938; the relationship had always been strained as Frank spent so much of his time away on long expeditions. In 1947 he married Jean Macklin when she was twenty-five and he sixty-one. Despite the difference in age, their marriage was very happy and in the field they were to make a good team. In 1948 Frank and Jean made the first of six expeditions together. This was the first time Ward had a genuine plant-hunting partner who shared his love of plants and who would willingly contribute to the laborious work of collecting, pressing and recording plant material. Ward often acknowledges Jean in his later writings, and he was delighted to be able to name one of his favourite discoveries, the Manipur lily *Lilium mackliniae* (discovered in 1946) after her.

In 1950, during an expedition to the Burma-Tibet border, Jean and Frank survived the Assam Earthquake which, at 8.6 on the Richter scale, was then one of the most powerful ever recorded. They were only twenty-five miles from the epicentre in Rima

Frank Kingdon Ward. A photograph taken towards the end of his life.

but, probably due to the fact that they were under canvas, they managed to escape unhurt. Ward's last expeditions at the age of seventy to seventy-one in 1956-57 were to Burma and Sri Lanka. A year later, he was still planning a further expedition to Vietnam when he fell ill while having a lunchtime drink with Jean in a London pub and died on Easter Sunday 8 April 1958.

In a long life of plant collecting, Kingdon Ward made over twenty expeditions to Yunnan, Burma, Tibet, India and Sri Lanka. He covered thousands of lonely miles, suffered a great deal from illness, disease (including malignant tertiary malaria) and accidents and fought to overcome or ignore his fear of heights, rope bridges and snakes. Unlike most of his fellow collectors, who left much of the work to their local staff, Ward did most of the collecting and pressing work himself. He left a legacy of over twenty books, most describing his expeditions. Compared with the rather turgid prose of most of Ward's fellow plant hunters (the exception being Reginald Farrer who gilded every possible lily), Ward's writing is lively, often poetic, and full of incident as well as packed with detailed background information. He learned several languages, was well versed in, and fascinated by, geology and had a great curiosity for the customs of the people he lived amongst even if, today, some of his remarks can only be considered patronising, if not racist.

It is hard to be precise about how many plant species Frank Kingdon Ward discovered and introduced. Some of the hundred or so rhododendron species he was credited with have been subsequently downgraded taxonomically ('lumped' or 'sunk' where they are considered to be merely variations on species described earlier). But many of his rhododendron introductions are still widely grown, none more so than the one named after him, *R. wardii*. Some Kingdon Ward introductions such as the blue poppy *Meconopsis betonicifolia* and *Lilium mackliniae* are first class garden plants, as Ward guessed they would be, while others are mainly prized by collectors and connoisseurs. Many beautiful plants, especially amongst the Primula species, proved to be difficult to cultivate and survived only a short time in western gardens (again Ward usually knew when this would be the case). And, thankfully for us, he even left one or two plants for those who have followed him to discover and introduce. In his book *Plant-Hunting in China,* my grandfather Euan Cox, who knew him well, gives his insight as to what really drove Frank Kingdon Ward:

> As Ward once wrote, it is his profession to collect seeds and herbarium material, but the real work of exploration is his hobby. He is and always has been much more than a great plant collector. He tells me that he is prouder of the Gold Medal of the Royal Geographical Society and the Livingstone Medal of the Scottish Royal Geographical Society than of his three gold medals for horticulture.

The last word in this short biography is left to Frank Kingdon Ward himself who discusses his motivations as a lifelong plant-hunter in his book *Pilgrimage for Plants*:

> I should find it difficult now to give any one simple reason…the pleasure and the pride gradually increased…I can only suppose that some element of romance must have also lain behind it. Plant hunting has always seemed to be a romantic occupation – and romance must be a part of life, or people would not cling to it so irrationally, even when the pursuit of it gives so much unease. …no sooner was one journey finished… 'thank heavens *that's* over!' and assured myself, 'never again' than all the troubles and difficulties fell away, were forgotten…and I began to long for the hills again.

Jack Cawdor, the 5th Earl of Cawdor.
This picture was found at Cawdor Castle and may have been taken in Tibet. Lord 'Jack' Cawdor died in 1970.

Kingdon Ward and Cawdor

Contemporary travel writing tends to tell us as much about the writer as what he or she is writing about. In contrast, in the travel writings of the 1920s the facts of the journey are considered enough, while emotions and feelings are largely kept in the background. Ward and Lord Cawdor set out into the unknown on a long and very arduous expedition in 1924–25, but *The Riddle of the Tsangpo Gorges* contains little detail of the relationship between the two men. And despite being married for only a year before setting out on the 1924 expedition, Kingdon Ward's wife Florinda only merits a mention in the text when *Primula florindae* is named after her.

Ward often travelled alone and seemed quite happy to do so, but on the course of his many journeys he had several companions. Only H.M. Clutterbuck (known as 'Buttercup') who travelled with Ward in 1928 seems to have become a close friend, while on his later expeditions Ward was accompanied by his wife Jean. Travelling in extreme conditions inevitably causes a certain amount of friction between the participants, as Kingdon Ward acknowledges in his diary:

> If two chaps like us…go into the blue for a year, they are bound to have words until they settle down.

Ward's companion in 1924, Lord Cawdor, was a young Scottish aristocrat who partly financed the expedition. The 'Cawdor' name is one of Scotland's oldest titles: Macbeth, in Shakespeare's play of the same name – which was based on historical fact – , has several titles including 'Thane of Cawdor'.

From Ward's narrative, we learn that Cawdor is put in charge of transport and the medical chest, that he is sometimes ill and dispenses a great deal of medicine. From his chapters in *Riddle of the Tsangpo Gorges* we can read Cawdor's observations on Tibetan life. Ward acknowledges Cawdor in the foreword and a handful of plants collected on the expedition were named in Cawdor's honour. Ward's biographer, Charles Lyte, gained access to the expedition diaries of both Kingdon Ward and Cawdor and managed to piece together some telling details of the inevitable tensions between the two men. The relationship was evidently rarely close and often rather stormy. By 1924 Ward was a veteran traveller, used to discomfort and dirt, and he mocked the much younger Cawdor's preference for cleanliness. Despite Ward's disapproval, Cawdor determined to try to have a bath at least once a week.

Cawdor was not impressed by the standard of much of the food on the expedition, particularly bemoaning the time they ran out of curry which was used to flavour the rather monotonous local fare. In his diary he rather comically pines for the school boy favourite 'plum duff'. Despite Cawdor's complaints, this was in fact one of the best equipped of Ward's many expeditions. They carried hampers from Fortnum and Mason in London full of 'special treats' such as jam, baked beans, sardines, coffee, tea, paté, cakes and chewing gum. Worried about the possible difficulty in obtaining food deep in the Tsangpo Gorge, they purchased a sheep at Gyala which Cawdor christened 'Homeless Horace'. It is unclear how far along the arduous route through the Gorge the unfortunate animal struggled before being killed and eaten.

Cawdor found Ward's meticulousness as a plant-collector infuriating, and considered the pace unbearably slow. Cawdor's frustration can be seen in his diary entries:

> It drives me clean daft to walk behind him – stopping every 10 yards and hardly moving in between – in the whole of my life, I've never seen such an incredibly slow mover – if I ever travel again I'll make damn sure its not with a botanist. They are always stopping to gape at weeds…'

and later:

> I'm bound for God knows how long to wander this damned country with a man who can only shuffle along like a paralytic – I could forgive W most things if only he could walk – though, evidently, God never intended him to be a companion to anyone!

Ward's own diaries reveal his reaction to an outburst of frustration from Cawdor:

> I irritated Cawdor who had a bad night and was feeling unwell from the effects of the last few days: and he went straight in at the deep end. Smoothed him down.

There is no doubt the constant hardship and lack of companionship depressed Cawdor greatly. He envied Ward's ability to communicate with those around him in local languages. At one of his lowest points, he writes in his diary:

> I think the chief reasons for my present discontentment are firstly my sickness which completely kills what pleasure there is in life, secondly my lack of knowledge to do justice…to the opportunities available (in other words I am a failure!) and thirdly the feeling of being utterly cut off from the ones one cares for.

Meanwhile, there were also times when Kingdon Ward evidently suffered from something close to depression, causing him to withdraw into himself. Ronald Kaulback, who was Ward's travelling companion in Burma in 1933, describes this side of Kingdon Ward's nature:

> He was…a very difficult man to travel with simply because he could easily fall into total silence which would last for 2-3 days. Not a damn thing. He might say 'good morning' otherwise he would just march along and at the end of the day sit down and have a meal, but nothing, not a word.

Ward was used to and even fond of solitude and silence. In his last book *Pilgrimage for Plants* Ward writes of how much he enjoyed being alone in the mountains:

Primula cawdoriana on the
Temo La.   **KNEC**
This beautiful primula was
named after the Earl of
Cawdor, who accompanied
Frank Kingdon Ward on the
1924-25 expedition. Easily
recognised by the narrowly
tubular corolla with deeply cut
lobes, it was first introduced by
Kingdon Ward and later by
Ludlow and Sherriff. It has
been in cultivation ever since
but has always been a challenge.
In Tibet in early June the first
few flowers are only just
coming out. It must be at its
best in July. A member of
Section Soldanelloides.

There was romance too in the deep silence – not an oppressive menacing silence
but a profound tranquillity. And how marvellously blue – that celestial colour – the
whole world was!

In charge of the medical chest on the 1924 expedition, Cawdor was rather shocked and
disapproving at Ward's readiness to use morphine as an improvised sleeping pill,
considering it little more than recreational use. 'W. seems to regard them as little more
than a tonic….' Cawdor's attitude had softened by the end of the trip when both of
them were using cotton wool soaked in opium to relieve their severe toothache.

Cawdor's diary details an episode concerning 'Cawdor's' rhododendron species. Plant
hunting one day on the Temo La, they found what Ward evidently took to be a new
rhododendron species. Cawdor reports this under the name 'R. cawdorensis,' so
presumably Ward promised to name it after him. When the book *The Riddle of the
Tsangpo Gorges* was published, there was no mention of 'Cawdor's species' and no
rhododendron was named after him. The herbarium specimen of the 'Cawdor'
rhododendron (KW 5759 described as 'lacteum' in the field notes) was later attributed
to the very variable *R. phaeochrysum* and was not new after all. However, in terms of
botanical immortality, all was not lost for Cawdor: in the naming of the delightful and
distinctive *Primula cawdoriana*, discovered on the expedition, he did receive an enviable
tribute to his contribution to the expedition.

Lord 'Jack' Cawdor raised many plants from the seed collected on the expedition
which were planted in the grounds of his home at Cawdor Castle, Nairnshire, Scotland
where some of them can still be found today. Perhaps not surprisingly, Cawdor retired
from the plant-collecting game, and returned to Scotland where he served in the
Cameron Highlanders during the Second World War and rose to the rank of lieutenant
colonel. In later life he served on his local council in Scotland and died in 1970.

ii
The Exploration of the Tsangpo Gorges to 1924:
The Quest for the great Tsangpo Waterfall
Kenneth R. Storm, Jr.

The Yarlung Tsangpo is the great river of Tibet. For over 1600km (1,000 miles), it flows west to east, north of and parallel to the Great Himalaya Range from its source near the slopes of sacred Mount Kailas. Its course roughly follows the boundary that marks the seam between the Indian and Eurasian continental plates. Buckled and folded, the mountains to the south block the moist monsoon winds from reaching the Tibetan Plateau. It is a harsh, desolate landscape of mountain, sand and sky with a mighty river flowing through it. Collecting the glacial waters from the north slopes of the great Himalayan peaks, including Everest, the river spreads out for miles in shallow, braided channels, then plunges through short, rocky gorges. It passes to the south of Lhasa and

FALLS OF THE TSANGPO RIVER.
(*From a Tibetan drawing.*)

Falls of the Tsangpo.
This sketch first appeared in an article by L.A. Waddell in the *Geographical Journal* (1895) and was later published in his book *Lhasa and Its Mysteries* (1905). A Tibetan lama who had travelled on pilgrimage to the falls drew this sketch. It was later identified by Bailey as the 'Falls of Shingche Cho Gye' and located on a side stream flowing into the Tsangpo River, opposite the village of Gyala, at the mouth of the gorge. Bailey believed that this was the falls Kintup described in his Report. It entered Kintup's report through an error in transcription as a 150ft. (45m) waterfall on the Tsangpo River, a short distance below Pemaköchung. Only after Kintup was interviewed by Bailey after his return from the 1913 expedition was he able to correct the mistake. Or was it a mistake? Could this be the 'sacred' Hidden Falls of Dorje Pagmo, located just below Frank Kingdon Ward's Rainbow Falls? Waddell describes the setting: 'Their height is estimated at about 70 feet, and they are enveloped, as shown in the picture, by clouds of mist and spray, and the cliffs are covered by subtropical vegetation, and tiger lurk in the neighbourhood.'

continues to the east for another 480km (300 miles), seeking a course to the sea through the mountains.

For much of the last half of the nineteenth century, an intense debate raged as to what happened to the Tsangpo River where it disappeared from the map in south-eastern Tibet. In a narrow gap, about 320km (200 miles) wide, four of the major rivers of Asia descend from the Tibetan plateau confined in great gorges – the Yangtze, the Mekong, the Salween, and the Irrawaddy. Some were convinced the Tsangpo was a tributary of one of these rivers. On the plains of Assam three more rivers unite to form the Brahmaputra – the Lohit, the Dibang, and the Dihang. Others suspected that the Tsangpo River bent sharply to the south and plunged wildly through the heart of the Himalayas to emerge as one of these rivers. And if it did indeed bend to the south abruptly somewhere in south-eastern Tibet, by what tremendous passage did it make its descent?

Far to the east of Lhasa the Tsangpo is still a gentle river flowing at more than 3050m (10,000ft.) above sea level. Yet, just over 240km (150 miles) below, in Assam, the Dihang or Brahmaputra River flows out of the Abor Hills at 150m (500ft.) above sea level. If indeed the Tsangpo and Dihang were one and the same, geographers speculated that somewhere along its course there was room for a waterfall or series of falls perhaps to rival Victoria in Africa or Niagara in North America – a new wonder of the world. The logical way to find out was to travel north up the Dihang from British territory in Assam.

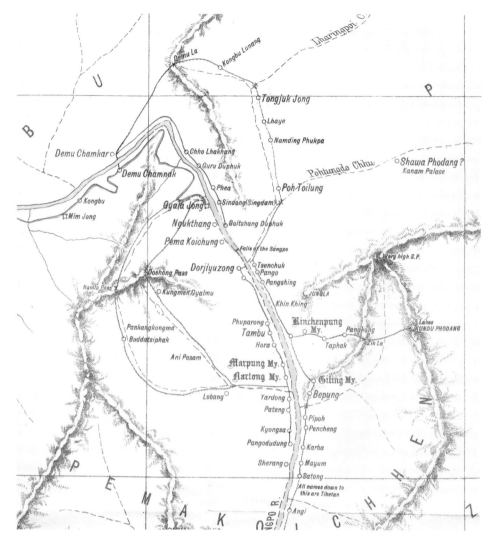

Kintup's Map.

This is 'Kintup's map' drawn by Col. Tanner from information 'supplied by K.P. in 1886–1887.' It was published in 1889 to accompany Kintup's Report, Dehra Dun. The 'Falls of the Sangpo' appear on a map for the first time. Many of the place names correspond with the names of today.

Early attempts to force a way upstream ended a short distance into the foothills. Fierce tribes such as the Abor and Mishmi zealously guarded their homeland, ambushing and killing trespassers, while the rugged, impenetrable jungle terrain turned back even the most determined explorers. If an attempt to follow the course of the river were to be made, it would have to be from Tibet. Nothing short of a journey along the entire course of the Tsangpo from the Tibetan Plateau to the plains of India, in Assam, could solve the mystery.

The Pundits: The Indian Explorers of the Himalaya

In the later half of the nineteenth century Tibet was as isolated from the outside world as almost any country on earth. The Tibetans successfully guarded their borders from foreign intrusion, which frustrated the empire-building British in India in particular. The Tibetans themselves believed that their sacred Tsangpo was the same river as the Brahmaputra and there were tales of sacred waterfalls presided over by powerful deities located in the deep gorges along the river's course. What the British wanted was empirical evidence, not myths and legends, and they devised an ingenious plan to carry it out. The Survey of India recruited and trained Tibetan speaking natives of the Himalayan region to cross surreptitiously into Tibet and survey along carefully designed routes, on journeys that often lasted months and even years. Travelling in disguise as pilgrims or merchants, these so-called Pundits counted each step along the way on the

The Namcha Barwa massif at Pemaköchung.   **KSJ**

The Tsangpo River sweeps around a bend beneath an amphitheatre of great peaks at Pemaköchung. The Pundit explorer Kintup reached here in 1881. The small monastery, now in ruins, was situated in a valley on the right bank of the river. (Hidden beyond the dark, forested hill on the right.) It was here that Kintup said the Tsangpo 'falls over a cliff…from a height of about 150 feet', confirming hopes of finding a large waterfall along the course of the Tsangpo River deep in its gorges. In 1913, F.M. Bailey and Henry Morshead reached the fabled spot to find only a 30ft. falls. Bailey later questioned Kintup about the falls and learned that an error had been made in the recording of his report – the 150ft. falls was on a side stream, not the main river.

prayer beads they carried (modified from the sacred number of 108 beads to 100 to help make counting easier). In prayer wheels they spun as they walked, they concealed their notes, prismatic compasses, and thermometers (used to measure the boiling point of water to determine the elevation of the passes they crossed). Known often by initials such as 'A.K.', 'K.P.', and 'G.M.N.' to disguise their identity in official British reports, they were entirely on their own beyond the frontiers of India. These intrepid men risked their lives while mapping in remarkable detail the length and breadth of Tibet.

Information brought back by the Pundits began to lift the veil of mystery from the Tsangpo River in south-eastern Tibet and at the same time intensified excitement about the possibility of finding a large waterfall hidden somewhere deep in its gorges. In 1878 the first attempt to follow the river down to the plains of India began from the Tibetan town of Tsetang. Nem Singh, known by his code name 'G.M.N.', was directed to follow the river as closely as possible, all the way to Assam. Travelling with him, as an assistant, was a tailor from Sikkim named Kintup.

Kintup's First Journey

Below the town of Tsetang, little was known about the character of the Tsangpo. The broad valley that characterises the river in its middle course is more constricted to the east, alternating between wild, barren gorges and narrow valleys. Gradually, the dry climate of the Tibetan Plateau gives way to a more humid world. Forests of pine and birch appear on the slopes above. In places the mountains shoulder in on the river, forcing the traveller to leave it on long, fatiguing climbs before rejoining further below. When the wind blows, dust obscures the valley and great sand dunes flank the sides of the gorge.

One can only imagine the prospect that confronted the travellers as they followed the Tsangpo eastward. Directly athwart the river's course rise two of the most magnificent mountains in all the Himalayas. A long banner of wind-blown snow sweeps from the 7757m (25,446ft.) pyramidal summit of Namcha Barwa. To the north, just 21km (13 miles) away, looms the snow-hooded peak of Gyala Peri, 7287m (23,901ft.) high. Approaching this barrier, the river's current picks up speed and breaks into rapids, then slides north along the base of Namcha Barwa. The snow-sculpted heights now loom directly above, so close you can feel the icy chill off the great glaciers sweeping down the face of the mountains. Then the improbable happens. The Tsangpo swings back to the east, pools, and then darts directly between these great peaks to begin one of the world's most dramatic encounters between river and mountain.

In 1878, Nem Singh and Kintup reached the village of Gyala, at the mouth of the great gorge, but went no further. From there they retraced their route back to India, having advanced geographic knowledge of the river's course some 400km (250 miles) below Tsetang and closing the unexplored 'gap' to a little over 160km (100 miles). What lay beyond, as the river plunged into that awful gorge between those icy mountains, could only be imagined.

Back in India, Captain Harmon of the Survey of India was less than satisfied by the information Nem Singh brought back. He had stood at the threshold of the gorge but had secured no reliable information about what lay beyond. Meanwhile, at the Royal Geographical Society, Robert Gordon, a member of the Public Works Department in Burma, resurrected the theory that the Tsangpo connected with the Irrawaddy. Harmon himself had recently travelled to Assam and measured the volume of water discharged from each of the three rivers. The Dihang, the westernmost tributary of the Brahmaputra, was clearly the largest and his choice for the link with the Tsangpo. Still, Harmon knew that unless he had direct proof linking the two rivers the controversy would rage endlessly. He decided to press forward with another plan that, if successful, would conclusively put the matter to rest.

In 1880 Harmon dispatched yet another pair of explorers into the field. Once again they were to follow the river as far as they could but this time they had an alternative plan. If they were prevented from following the river as far as India, the men were ordered to cut and mark a number of logs and launch them into the river at regular intervals. Far below on the plains of Assam, at a prearranged time, Harmon planned to station observers along the river to watch for the logs sweeping down on the flood. Already there had been reports of pieces of wood bearing Tibetan markings found in the Brahmaputra. If the rivers were one and the same he would have his own proof. It was an ingenious plan and one likely to work if everything went according to schedule.

Little did Harmon realise in the summer of 1880, as he prepared to send those two men off into the unknown, that he was launching one of the most extraordinary journeys of Himalayan exploration. It would be more than four years before anything would be heard from the expedition. Then, one man would return to tell a remarkable story.

Kintup's Second Journey

Although he was illiterate and uneducated, there must have been something in Kintup's character that prompted Harmon to select him again for such a rigorous journey. Perhaps he had told Harmon stories he had heard himself of the place called Pemakö, the 'land that opens like a lotus'. Pilgrims had penetrated this wild, mysterious world for many years, following instructions in secret guidebooks kept by monks describing a powerful, 'hidden land', a place of refuge in times of trouble. Perhaps Kintup was

The wooded cliffs of the
Tsangpo gorge.   FKW

aware of the recent travels in the lower gorge of a Mongolian Lama named Serap
Gyatso who described a fascinating sacred landscape of mountains, lakes and forests and
the perils of travel there. Or maybe he was also fascinated by rumours of sacred
waterfalls located somewhere deep in the gorge. This time Kintup was sent with a
Chinese lama and they were to travel together as pilgrims. The journey went wrong
almost from the start. The lama became entangled in a four-month affair with the wife
of their host at a village along the way. Kintup restored the honour of the aggrieved
husband by paying him compensation and hurried the lama out of town. It wasn't until
March of 1881 that they reached Gyala, perhaps just in time for the yearly pilgrimage
to the small monastery of Pemaköchung, four days' journey into the gorge.

Years later, after Kintup's account had been transcribed and published, this small out-
of-the-way place, an Asian 'ultima thule', became the subject of endless speculation and
discussion in geographic circles throughout Europe. The monastery was an insignificant
structure rising on a small hill amidst a dense forest laced with streams. In the spring
and during frequent rains a swamp infested with leeches and insects surrounds it. On
clear days, however, the view from the monastery is magnificent. The Tsangpo swings
around a bend beneath an amphitheatre of jagged peaks and glaciers thrown off the
north face of the Namcha Barwa massif. Pemaköchung is more than 5km (3 miles)

Marpung Monastery, where Kintup spent four months.   **IB**
At the monastery of Marpung, Kintup was saved from his pursuers by a benevolent lama who bought him for fifty rupees. Based at this monastery, Kintup worked as a tailor and made several pilgrimages into remote parts of Pemakö until he was freed by the present abbot's great-grandfather. The present abbot is shown here flanked by two younger lamas wearing ritual masks of Garudas, or celestial hawks. These masks are worn in religious dramas analogous to the Mystery Plays of Medieval Europe.

directly below Namcha Barwa and Gyala Peri, in the deepest river gorge in the world. But Pemaköchung would soon find a place in the imagination of the West for another reason. Kintup reported that a short distance away the Tsangpo 'falls over a cliff called Sinji-Chogyal [Singche Chögye] from a height of about 150 feet [45m]. There is a big lake at the foot of the falls where rainbows are always observable.' This brief comment, recorded in the official report compiled from his oral account long after his return, kindled visions of a large waterfall. Here at last, it seemed, was the great natural wonder along a major river in Asia geographers had dreamed of finding. It would be more than thirty years, however, before the next explorer would return for another look.

Below the monastery a low, cone-shaped peak stands above the bend of the river, remote and unreachable across the raging Tsangpo. To the Tibetans this peculiarly shaped mountain is the home of a fierce protector deity who guards the approach to the rugged, mysterious gorge below. No one travelled beyond this point, Kintup was told. Reluctantly, Kintup and the lama retraced their steps to Gyala and climbed out of the gorge to the north, hoping to skirt the impassable section below Pemaköchung and rejoin the river further downstream. Little did Kintup realise that his own odyssey was just beginning. They crossed a pass (probably the Tra La) above Gyala, arriving at the *rong,* a broad, forest-bound meadow surrounded by mountains, with a river, the Rong Chu, running through it. In early May, when Kintup passed through the upper valley, it was a bleak place, still more or less locked in winter, but in just a few weeks the valley would be ablaze with wild flowers. In 1924 Frank Kingdon Ward and Lord Cawdor would establish a base camp here at the village of Tumbatse for five months. They would call the valley 'The Paradise of Primulas'.

Travellers in Tibet were often required to secure passports from a local village headman, called a *Dzongpön*, before proceeding from one area to another. At a bridge where the Rong Chu joins a larger stream the lama and Kintup were stopped at a check post that marked the boundary between Tibet and the independent kingdom of Pome, to the east. While the lama left with the guard to obtain permission in the nearby village of Tongkyuk, Kintup remained behind and hid his three compasses and pistol. Four days later the lama returned with the passport and they were housed with the *Dzongpön's* servants and given food for the journey ahead. Unexpectedly, the village headman now demanded that Kintup turn over one of his three compasses and the pistol. Kintup had been betrayed. A few days later, on the pretext of attending to business, the lama departed saying he would return in two or three days. That was the last time Kintup saw him. Kintup waited two more months working as a tailor for the *Dzongpön* of Tongkyuk before realising he had been sold into slavery. He bided his time, waiting for an opportunity to escape, which finally came in the spring of the following year – 1882.

The lower Tsangpo Gorge begins south and east of where the Po-Tsangpo River joins the Yarlung, or main Tsangpo River, at the top of what is today called the Great Bend. Mönba people emigrated from the region east of Bhutan and settled in the immediate area of the confluence and in villages downstream almost a century before Kintup arrived. They brought with them their Buddhist religion and perhaps carried guidebooks to the sacred land called Pemakö. Already, in 1882, pilgrimage routes connected the villages with sacred sites, or *nes,* located throughout the Gorge. It was along these precipitous wilderness tracks, linking small villages and connecting with these sacred sites, that Kintup fled from his captors. Following the course of the river to the south, he traversed high on the flanks of the gorge and crossed the raging Tsangpo several times on treacherous rope bridges. He travelled deeper into a tropical world – a lush rain forest where dangerous animals and deadly snakes lived in the jungle bordering the meagre settlements. In the warmer, lower gorge, interspersed with the Mönba settlements, Kintup passed through villages settled by Lopas. Most had adopted Tibetan Buddhism but many retained vestiges of the animistic beliefs of their tribal relatives, the Abor and Mishmi, living in the jungles to the south.

Kintup was increasinglyly attentive to the sacred landscape around him. His account of the journey reports more on monasteries and pilgrimage routes than on waterfalls and the course of the Tsangpo River. One pilgrimage route led him deep into the wilderness to the east of the river. The journey began from the monastery of Rinchenpung, perched in a beautiful valley high above the town of Medog, in the lower Tsangpo Gorge. To reach it is a climb of more than 915m (3,000 vertical feet) out of the steaming jungle. On top the traveller is greeted by a cooling breeze and the sight of a monastery crowning a low hill. To this day, Tibetans believe this is the very heart of Pemakö and each year small groups of hearty pilgrims wait here for the snow to melt on the mountains to the east before attempting one of the most difficult pilgrimage routes in Tibet. The traveller traverses a wilderness of endless forest, knife-edge ridges, and deep morasses. If he finds the way he reaches a sacred mountain, Kundu Dorsempotrang, reflected in sacred lakes set like jewels below the summit. If the pilgrim loses the way, he can wander for days, exhausted and alone, and may die.

It may have been this devotion as a pilgrim that eventually earned Kintup his freedom. At the village of Marpung, a small settlement that crowns the top of a ridge 610m (2,000ft.) above the Tsangpo, Kintup discovered that men sent by his *Dzongpön* master had come to arrest him and take him back. He fled at once to the monastery and bowed three times before the head lama, explaining his desperate plight. Asked where he was going, Kintup explained that he was on pilgrimage and begged protection. The sympathetic lama agreed to pay 50 rupees to his former master 'for the value of Kintup's life'.

Kintup served the lama for four months and then asked permission to resume his pilgrimage. Recalling his promise to Captain Harmon, he travelled a short distance downstream and cut and marked 500 logs 30cm (a foot) long and hid them in a cave 'where no human foot had yet trodden.' By now the date pre-arranged for the launching of the logs had passed, so Kintup returned to the lama at Marpung for another two months. If he were to complete his mission for Captain Harmon he somehow had to get word back to India and reschedule a date to send the logs down the Tsangpo. And Lhasa seemed his best bet. Leaving the Tsangpo Gorge over the Doshong La, Kintup rejoined his route at the mouth of the gorge, above Gyala. His incredible odyssey had taken him through much of the Tsangpo Gorge and now completely around Namcha Barwa. Kintup could easily be excused if he had turned for home. Instead, this pilgrim/explorer made another long diversion to visit the sacred mountain wilderness retreat of Tsari and its snow-covered Pure Crystal Mountain, and eventually reached Lhasa.

In Lhasa Kintup employed a fellow Sikkimese traveller to compose a letter to the Survey of India via Nem Singh, his companion on his first journey. He wrote:

> Sir, – the Lama who was sent with me sold me to a *Dzongpön* as a slave and himself fled away with the Government things that were in his charge. On account of which the journey proved a bad one; however I, Kintup, have prepared the 500 logs according to the orders of Captain Harmon, and am prepared to throw 50 logs per day into the Tsangpo from Bepung in Pemakoichen, from the 5th to the 15th of the tenth Tibetan month of the year called Chhuluk, of the Tibetan calculation.

With the letter on its way, Kintup hurried back to Pemakö and resumed his role as servant to the Marpung lama. Nine months later, as the new time for the launching of the logs approached, the lama finally set him free, praising Kintup for his devotion as a pilgrim. He returned to his cave and on the appointed day began throwing the logs into the river.

Even with this final act, fulfilling Captain Harmon's directive, Kintup's journey was not over. Perhaps during his long stay at Marpung he had contemplated the possibility of continuing downstream. Standing in the courtyard of the monastery, situated at the end of the long ridge that juts out into the valley, you can follow the course of the Tsangpo to the south, pressed between the folds of lower hills far in the distance. It might be tempting to conclude that the plains of Assam are not far beyond the last range. All the great snow peaks have retreated and only forested hills, covered in dense jungle, seem to intervene. There was a trail of sorts down the river, and more villages, but no one, it seemed, could tell him much about the way. Could he reach India after all? It was worth a try.

For several days Kintup worked his way along the river, where his logs had so recently floated, committing to memory the details of each village he passed. Soon he met people who 'are almost naked, wearing nothing but a wrapper over the lower part of the body. They always carry a sword and bow, and even at night they keep their weapons near them.' The dreaded Abor tribesmen could not be far and the locals were on their guard. Finally, just above a village called Miri Padam, Kintup stopped and retraced his route back up the Tsangpo. By his estimate, he was only 55km (35 miles) from British territory but it was too dangerous to go further. It was not until midsummer of 1884 that he finally reached home after a four-year odyssey.

What became of the logs Kintup so diligently launched on the Tsangpo, hoping to prove once and for all the link between the Tsangpo and the Dihang/Brahmaputra? They presumably floated out into the Brahmaputra and perhaps even to the Bay of Bengal – but unfortunately completely unnoticed. His message signalling the change of dates had gone unheeded. Worse still, by the time of Kintup's return, Captain Harmon had departed India in failing health and died in Italy more than a year before.

When Kintup's dictated report was finally published in 1889 the full scope of his journey, perseverance, and extraordinary powers of observation were revealed. But what caught the imagination was that brief description of a 45m (150ft.) waterfall at Pemaköchung. The idea of a large waterfall stimulated a flurry of excitement and speculation in the years that followed. Not until Frank Kingdon Ward and Lord Cawdor emerged from their incredible journey through the Tsangpo Gorges in January 1925, and later told the complete story in *The Riddle of the Tsangpo Gorges*, would much of the speculation finally be put to rest – for the time being…

Abors with helmets.
This photograph is taken from *Official Account of the Abor Expedition* 1911-1912, Simla, 1913.

India's North East Frontier, 1911

In the heart of tea country far up the Brahmaputra River in Assam, Captain Sir George Dunbar sat down to his nine o'clock breakfast and contemplated the view to the forested hills that bounded his world to the north. All seemed serene and peaceful on that April morning of 1911. Flat bottom steamboats plied the waters of the great river carrying tea to market in Calcutta from plantations along the river. On board the boats, passengers lounged on deck chairs – successful merchants and tea planters seeking relief from the oppressive heat that was already building on shore.

> It was amazing to look from the veranda of my house by the river at the hills that seemed so close across the plain, and to think that, behind the fringe which alone had been penetrated, there were falls to find, and all the wonders that rumour had given an unknown country in the course of 650 years. These astounding features might not exist, but they added a lot of interest to one's speculations.

Dunbar, the commandant of the military police battalion, had spent a long time in the harsh desert world of India's North West Frontier and everything about this new, green world fascinated him. He listened to all the travellers' tales and recorded many of them – fantastic stories of people without necks, Amazons, mountains of solid ruby guarded by yellow snakes. He was reminded of those fabulous creatures drawn on the edges of ancient maps and wondered what facts beyond the hills had spawned those fanciful tales.

George Dunbar's quiet morning reverie ended abruptly when he was handed a telegram from the military post up-river at Sadiya, where Assam's three great rivers, the Dihang, the Dibang and the Lohit, unite to form the Brahmaputra. The news was devastating. Noel Williamson, the political officer at Sadiya, and his travelling companion Gregorson, a tea garden doctor, along with more than forty of their Nepalese carriers, had been killed in the Abor Hills. Dunbar knew Williamson well and could hardly believe the report. Almost single-handedly he had improved the troubled relations with the tribes that lived beyond British India's Inner and Outer Lines, lines of control set up beyond the hills just north of the river to protect the tea gardens and their workers from marauding natives. The fiercest of these were the Abors, an Assamese word meaning 'one who does not submit', and applied to the numerous related tribes living on both sides of the Dihang River. Today, these same proud people prefer to be called by their own name, 'Adis' or 'people of the hills'. In 1909 Williamson led a small party beyond the Outer Line into Abor territory without a military escort, carrying a gramophone and magic lantern to entertain the remote tribes, many of whom had not seen a white man. But Williamson was not just interested in establishing friendly relations with the Abors, he was also tracking those persistent rumours of a large waterfall located somewhere up the river. In 1909 he had heard enough to draw him back two years later – now, presumably, to his death. Dunbar wasted no time commandeering a train and mobilising a relief column in the slim hope of rescue.

While Dunbar was racing to the Abor hills, a tall lanky British officer on leave from his posting in Tibet was ending a journey up the Yangtze River in China and about to begin an overland dash that he hoped would end at the mysterious falls of the Tsangpo. Travelling light and accompanied by his Tibetan servant Putamdu, success was far from certain. China was in political turmoil with the military on the move and he was repeatedly cautioned to turn back.

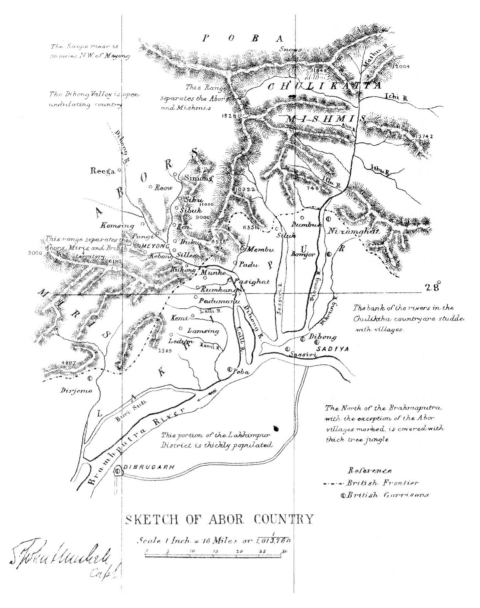

Sketch of Abor Country.

Source: *Report (Topographical, Political, and Military) on the North-East Frontier of India,* by John F. Michell, Calcutta, 1883. This is an early sketch map of Abor and Mishmi country along the Dihang and Dibang Rivers.

F.M. Bailey

The son of a prominent army colonel, educated at Sandhurst, Frederick M. Bailey's appetite for a life of adventure was whetted as a young lieutenant on the Younghusband invasion of Tibet in 1903-1904. Bailey had joined the Bengal Lancers and was soon drawn to India's northern frontier. For years Britain had played a 'Great Game' of imperial chess with Russia in the borderlands beyond their base in India. Fears of direct Russian encroachment in Tibet finally prompted the British to force open the door that had remained closed for so long. Lhasa was occupied with very limited opposition. From a base in central Tibet the British, at long last, had access to explore this vast land so long denied to them. In one grand gesture, before the British left Tibet, three light expeditions were ordered out in different directions. The main expedition, under Captain Ryder, was authorised to follow the course of the Tsangpo east and south all the way down to the plains of India, retracing much of Kintup's journey of twenty years before. Bailey, quickly earning the confidence of Younghusband, was ordered to accompany the second expedition from Lhasa to Peking. A third would travel west, up the Tsangpo Valley. Plans unravelled quickly, however, when word reached Lhasa of an attack on a mail party along the road to India. This news, coupled with long-held government unease over unrest among tribes on the Assam border, prompted Younghusband to consolidate the three expeditions into one. Bailey was reassigned as an interpreter to the joint party and travelled west along the Tsangpo River in winter toward its source near Mt. Kailas. It was Bailey's first real taste of life as an explorer.

Everything about Tibet fascinated Bailey, so it was no surprise that after returning to India he transferred from the Indian Army to the Political Department to accept an appointment as the Trade Agent at the Tibetan town of Gyantse. It was a position he soon learned was only incidentally concerned with trade. He was ordered to observe and report on all activities in the border area. Younghusband himself advised, through Bailey's father: 'He must be all eyes and ears but only as much tongue as is necessary to serve those eyes and ears. He cannot be too careful.' Bailey made the most of the situation, befriending the Panchen Lama, roaming the plateau hunting and collecting, and keeping the British government apprised of the political winds blowing across Tibet.

Bailey read every book written about Tibet, including many which poured off the presses in the wake of the Younghusband Expedition. He studied Tibetan diligently, passing an examination before two masters of the 'Great Game', the Bengali Sarat Chandra Das (immortalised by Kipling in *Kim* as Hurree Chundar Mookerjee) and Pundit U.G., Lama Ugyen Gyatso. The stories of these early Indian explorers fascinated Bailey. Their quiet perseverance and way of travel across the length and breadth of Tibet spoke to him with the force of revelation. 'It seemed to me possible that a single traveller with only one servant who was not dependent on interpreters might succeed in reaching the desired goal without attracting too much attention.' But it was the journey of Kintup along the Tsangpo River deep in its gorges that directly prodded Bailey into a life of exploration. He resolved to some day stand before the fabled falls Kintup described.

Looking back nearly one hundred years, it is sometimes unclear just what motivated Bailey's relentless drive to explore the Tsangpo gorges. Was it the pure exhilaration of exploring unknown territory or was he acting in some official capacity, despatched beyond the frontiers to gather intelligence on Chinese designs on Tibet and India? What makes Bailey the explorer such an enigmatic and compelling figure today is his role as a secret agent in Russia at the end of the First World War. His back-country skills and art of disguise – honed by emulating his heroes, the Pundits, on his travels in Tibet

H. Morshead
and
F.M. Bailey.

and China – were so good that he successfully evaded the Russian Bolsheviks for more than a year in a Central Asia torn apart by revolution. He finally resurfaced long enough to be recruited by his pursuers to look for an elusive British spy – himself – before escaping to a hero's welcome back home.

Bailey's reports, often reserved and understated, belie a careful observer skilled in many disciplines. As a naturalist he collected butterflies, pursued pheasants, and hunted the legendary takin through the mountains of China, Tibet, and Assam. Though not a botanist, he could spot an interesting flower and his name, '*baileyi*', is appended to the scientific names of several species of plants. Whatever Bailey's official capacity, his curiosity and extraordinary determination as an explorer are unmatched. Yet, perhaps it is his impulsiveness that remains his most endearing quality; always working on the fringes of officialdom and then throwing caution to the winds in pursuit of his dream.

When Bailey reached Chengdu in Western China in April 1911 he was handed a telegram from his father in England that read: 'WARN BAILEY MASSACRE SADIYA'. Though troubled by the news, he pressed on westward, traversing all the great river gorges of south-east Asia – the Yangtze, the Mekong, and the Salween. Along the way he was aided by American missionaries and even travelled for a time with two Chinese soldiers, presumably ordered to keep an eye on him. Along the Salween he missed by forty-eight hours another young British traveller just beginning his own career as an explorer – Frank Kingdon Ward. By the middle of June he was in Tibet, beyond the Irrawaddy-Brahmaputra divide.

At Shugden Gompa, near the headwaters of the Po-Tsangpo River, Bailey was within striking distance of his goal and delighted to find himself on the trail of one his heroes, Pundit A.K. or Kishen Singh. Near a lovely lake high on the plateau, Bailey took pride in confirming the accuracy of the Pundit's observation. The position marked on A.K.'s map, derived from counting his steps for hundreds of miles on the outward journey, was four miles north of Bailey's own estimated position. Shooting the stars for latitude that night, Bailey's reading split the difference.

From here it was a relatively straightforward journey downstream to the Tsangpo. Bailey was determined to proceed but forces beyond his control intervened. A war was raging down the valley in the independent kingdom of Pome, to the north of the Tsangpo Gorge. The locals said the Chinese had been routed with more than 300 troops killed and nobody was willing to take him further. With his opportunity of reaching the falls lost, Bailey knew he could still salvage something from his journey by bringing this news of Chinese activity near the Indian frontier back to India. But first he would have to pass through the wild jungles of the Mishmi Hills along the Lohit River to reach Sadiya in Assam. That warning he received from his father now weighed ominously on his mind. If Mishmi warriors had been involved in the 'massacre', he might not get there alive.

The Abor Expedition, 1911-1912
Captain Dunbar's relief column pushed up the Dihang River desperate to find out what happened. 'In all my life I had never seen anything like the gloom of that forest. It was quite impossible to see a couple of yards into it on either side of the narrow winding path.' The night before they had made camp on a sandy island at the mouth of the gorge. The next morning they awoke to find arrows sticking in the sand close to where they slept, the tips smeared with a 'greenish-brown stuff' – poison. Soon they came to a village and the Abors fled into the forest. Cries rang out and three Nepalese porters who had been hunted for several days by the Abors and their dogs, emerged from hiding to tell their story. It was as bad as they feared. Everyone else had been hacked to death, including Williamson and Gregorson. Fearing further ambush, orders came to withdraw and the column beat a hasty retreat down river.

In writing about his own journeys here several years later, Frank Kingdon Ward wryly described the climate of Assam: 'The frivolous might say that there are only two seasons; eight months wet and four months damned wet'. On the verge of the 'damned wet' season, the British began mobilising an expeditionary force. They would wait until the rains subsided in the autumn and then throw their full force against the Abors. But this would be more than just a punitive expedition. The British, long fearful of Chinese advances across their borders, admitted that beyond their own Outer Line and up to the highlands of Tibet was a *terra incognita*. On rare clear days they caught glimpses of the tops of snow peaks far to the north, but they knew virtually nothing about the vast maze of jungle-covered hills that lay between. Attached to the military columns they would send out surveying teams to map the area right up to the distant mountains.

Abor tribesmen.
This photograph is taken from *Official Account of the Abor Expedition* 1911–1912, Simla, 1913.

In late July, his leave running out, Bailey was mired in Mishmi country at the height of the rainy season. To his relief he had learned that it was the Abors, not the Mishmis, who had been implicated in the massacre. Now he had only to traverse gloomy forests and to ford deep streams on his journey down to the plains. All the way he battled leeches, fierce biting flies, truculent porters, and fatigue. Bailey stopped briefly at Sadiya to catch up on news and then hurried on to Calcutta. He was late reporting for duty and docked twenty-one days of pay. Recalling the rebuke more than forty years later Bailey could understand the official displeasure 'but at the age of thirty I felt slightly aggrieved to be reprimanded for what appeared to me a matter for congratulation'. Still, the authorities were eager to have his report about the country they were about to invade and grudgingly acknowledged his contribution by granting his request for a posting to the North East Frontier. The Foreign Secretary thought he 'might be able to do some quietly useful work' there. What must have intrigued Bailey most was one of the goals of the Abor Expedition – 'to explore and survey as much of the country as possible, visiting, if practicable, the "Pemakoi falls" and settling the question of the identity of the Tsangpo and Brahmaputra rivers'.

Following the Younghusband Expedition's opening of Tibet, there was even more fanciful conjecture on the mysterious Tsangpo Gorges. Kintup's report was reprinted on the eve of the expedition and, although acknowledged as important, it was treated with a good deal of scepticism. Thomas Holdich, writing in his book *Tibet the Mysterious*, published in 1906, described the Brahmaputra as 'one great natural highway to Tibet'. With a bold sweep of the imagination he was willing to reduce one of the most impenetrable and unknown places on earth to an easy grade suitable for a Tibetan branch of the Assam Railroad all the way to the plateau. Then, with a flourish of 'Great Game' rhetoric, he shamed his countrymen by suggesting that 'had Russia been in England's position in India, there would have been a right of way, if not a railway, up the Brahmaputra long ere this'. He did admit one possible obstacle – the falls themselves – but these could be skirted and he suggested the place would be an ideal location for 'a spacious hotel for sightseers and sportsmen'. After all, he maintained, 'This prospect is not more visionary than 25 years ago was that of a modern hotel at the Victoria Falls of the Zambezi; or the splendid establishments which will soon overlook the falls of Iguazu…in South America'.

The unbridled optimism of Holdich and others over the prospects of finding an easy route up the Brahmaputra, which may have led directly to Williamson's fatal foray up the Dihang in 1911, was undoubtedly encouraged by the report of two Gurkha surveyors from the Survey of India. In 1901 they reached the village of Kebang, near the place where Williamson's party would be massacred. From a ridge just beyond they looked to the north and described 'an open and undulating' country. They claimed that Gyala, the village near the mouth of the gorge reached by Kintup years before, was visible on a clear day and only ten stages distant.

As a military engagement, the Abor Expedition was not much of a contest. The Abors, armed with bows and arrows, often fled before the advance of British troops. A battalion of Gurkha Rifles was reinforced by more than 3,000 spear-carrying Naga warriors serving as coolies. Mortal enemies of the Abors, the Nagas were not averse to stripping body parts from the dead, including taking human heads as trophies. In the end, Abor defences of pit-traps concealing sharpened bamboo spikes, stone chutes, and brush stockades were no match against the rifle and a mobile, disciplined army. No British troops were killed in action and only a handful of the native Naga fighters died. How many Abors were killed is not known. Resistance ended quickly.

The most important work that first season was carried out by the survey party under Captain Bentinck. Pushing up the Dihang Valley in advance of the main punitive expedition, it was commissioned to carry out the important surveying work, all the way to the 'Falls of Pemakoi', and they expected to get there in the ten marches promised by the Gurkha surveyors. Optimism soon gave way to frustration. The 'open and undulating' country became a nightmare of dense jungle and precipitous ascents and descents. After twenty-four marches up the valley, their supplies running out, they realised they were less than half way to where they suspected Gyala to be. To make matters worse, an immense snowy range of mountains intervened. With a touch of sarcasm, Bentinck began to doubt the veracity of Kintup's account, calling his report 'one of the romances of the Survey of India'. He concluded, 'if there are falls on the Dihang at the place where Kintup saw rainbows, this must be before the river pierces the main range. It may be said in a word that the nearer we got to where the falls ought to be the less was there to be known of them'. Their Abor guides were getting wise too. Although co-operative, they offered to guide them up the valley but demanded that at least three British accompany them. 'One of you' they said, 'will probably die because the country is so bad, and then you will blame us, whereas if three go two may die, but there will still be one to come back and say that it was not our fault'. As the party descended the Dihang, a dejected Bentinck questioned whether further exploration through such difficult country could be carried out with such a large party. It was a lesson Bailey had already learned.

Bailey's Plan

During the autumn and winter of 1911-1912, the punitive expedition under the command of General Bower concentrated on the Abor villages along the lower Dihang River. Bentinck's survey party explored up-river while Bailey, referred to as 'that damn fellow from Simla', was shuttled off to Mishmi territory to keep him out of the way. Secretly he knew that his hopes of reaching the falls depended on a solitary dash to the north, but his orders emphatically prohibited crossing the Tibetan border. Everywhere he went a military escort dogged his steps. 'Quietly useful work' was out of the question and when the heavy rains set in again and field operations came to an end in the spring, he returned to India frustrated.

The following season promised more of the same, another posting to Mishmi country with administrative duties and endless reports to write. This time Bailey took matters into his own hands. He requested (and was granted) an appointment as Political Officer to the expedition instead. Inserted into his orders was a fortuitous clause granting him 'as much scope as possible for the exercise of his talents as regards exploration'. To the ordinary officer, such an order might have invited clarification. To Bailey it could be interpreted as *carte blanche* to operate on the margins of authority. This time his orders did not specifically deny him permission to cross into Tibet, so he assumed permission was implicit. The important point was not to ask.

When Bailey's opportunity arrived it came from an unexpected source. Surveying up a tributary of the Dibang River, deep into the mountains, he came upon a small Mishmi village. Further up the stream, he was told, was another village called Mipi. The trail had reverted to jungle and nobody knew much about the people living there, except that they were Tibetan. Bailey took a small party to investigate. When the party approached Mipi the villagers fled in terror, suspecting they were Chinese soldiers sent to kill them. These Tibetans lived so isolated from the tribes of the lower valleys that news of the British advance had not yet reached here. Bailey calmed them down and over the next month won the confidence of their headman, Gyamtso, who revealed an amazing story.

Bailey was already acquainted with the sacred place called Pemakö and the Tibetan prophecy that spoke of a fertile land and place of refuge in times of persecution. Its location was only vaguely known, lying somewhere deep in the mountain fastness to the north. Now Bailey had stumbled upon a group who had wandered south in search of this 'Promised Land', beyond the borders of Tibet itself, and instead found a veritable hell. Rain fell incessantly and they were plagued by leeches and biting flies. Many became sick, unaccustomed to the low altitude, and they all lived in fear of sudden Mishmi raids. In 1909 most had returned to Tibet, leaving fewer than a hundred who were too weak or too old to travel, defended by a few younger men. It was more than compassion for this beleaguered group of pilgrims, however, that excited Bailey. 'The moment that I had heard of the existence of the Tibetan settlement, the realisation flashed through my mind that here was my chance of getting through to Tibet from the Assamese side'. Bailey questioned Gyamtso about the Tsangpo falls and found that the information matched Kintup's report, but he also learned of the extraordinary natural defences that guarded the approaches to the area. Snow lay deep on the high passes and any journey north was out of the question until late spring. He would have to bide his time until then. 'I hid my own excitement as best I could, because I have found there is a perverse element in human nature that prompts people to put obstacles in the path of anyone who has his heart on something.'

One person Bailey confided in was Captain Henry Morshead. Described by a contemporary as 'small and dark, and hard as nails', Morshead had been assigned to the Dibang Survey with Bailey and almost immediately they struck up a friendship. Morshead's job was to map the terrain along their line of march. This usually involved daily climbs of several thousand feet to the tops of mountains and spurs bounding the valleys, often waiting hours in cloud and rain for a fleeting break in the weather, in order to triangulate on a distant mountain. On one such excursion, from a peak in the Mishmi Hills, he briefly sighted a great snow peak far to the north with another, hooded peak, rising beyond it. Little did he realise that his Political Officer was contemplating a journey to the mountains and that Bailey was about to ask Morshead to join him. 'As soon as I met him he impressed me with his keenness, efficiency and his extraordinary powers of physical endurance. He was my first, and as it proved my only, choice for a colleague, for as soon as I put the idea to him, he leapt at the opportunity.'

In the spring of 1913 the plan began to take shape. With the aide of a third conspirator, Captain Nevill, head of the Mission and the man who would give them political cover with the government in India, Bailey and Morshead stayed on at Mipi after the main expedition left the field for the season. This time Bailey would not be denied. If specific orders came at the last moment ordering them to withdraw, Morshead was to climb a tall hill and light a smoke signal and Bailey would dash off to Tibet alone.

There were two possible routes to the north and Bailey carefully considered both. His Tibetan friend, Gyamtso, asked for a divination from a lama and Bailey was delighted to learn that the oracle had suggested the same route he favoured. For more than a week they would have to traverse a vast, uninhabited wilderness of dark, sombre forests and endless bogs, sealed by two snow-bound passes. If bad weather trapped them between those passes for any length of time they would starve. Gyamtso added to the gloom by telling him of disasters that had befallen two previous parties that had left Mipi too early in the spring. Several had died and the others had crawled out of the wilderness barely alive. Soon another lama came to their aid. He had been treated by a British doctor at Mipi and in thanksgiving had retreated to a cave to meditate and had achieved the ability to mediate with the spirits who control the weather. Asking for the date they would be on the first pass, he promised fine weather – adding that four days later, on the second pass, he would also make it fair. Like Kintup before him and devout pilgrims to Pemakö to this day, Bailey's journey was to begin by appealing to the mercy of the fierce protector deities who guard the Tsangpo gorges.

'Leaving the weather to the lama', Bailey continued preparations, hunting and setting out caches of food up the valley. Finally, at the end of May, he left Mipi with ten porters and three guides, expecting to meet up with Morshead who had departed a day earlier to begin his survey. Before leaving, Gyamtso gave Bailey letters of introduction to present to the headman of the Chimdro Valley, the first inhabited district they would reach – noting that 'Bailey Sahib knows the Dalai and Tashi Lamas' – and asking for safe conduct.

Soon Bailey had another worry on his hands – Henry Morshead. He had not arrived at camp and Bailey suspected he might have had an accident or come down with a recurring fever. Their rations were so tight that if he wasn't found soon, Bailey fretted, 'This heaven-sent opportunity of exploring the gorges was unlikely ever to come our way again'. The next day Morshead reached camp weak with fever after losing his way and spending a rainy night in a cave. But there was another potential problem that began to worry Bailey. In Morshead's exuberance to survey and explore new country he ignored the leeches that plagued the moist, lower elevations. 'I thought at the beginning that this indifference might be a residue of his fever. But later I found this was not the case. When his temperature was indubitably normal, he would stand there covered with leeches and with blood oozing out of his boots as oblivious as a small child whose face is smeared with jam'. Regardless of his reservations over Morshead's apparent disregard for his own health, Bailey had found a travelling companion as determined and untiring as himself.

The Journey Begins – Bailey and Morshead Leave Mipi

Poised at the threshold of the journey he had dreamed about for so many years, it is difficult fully to imagine what this moment meant to Bailey. Much of his life for the past ten years had been a preparation for just this opportunity. Reflecting on his achievement in his book, *No Passport to Tibet*, written in retirement forty-three years later, the delight in that journey of his youth was undimmed. 'We did not carefully plan our routes or seasons; but…we went where and when we could, happy in the knowledge that every place was unknown.'

Even though the lama at Mipi failed to deliver clear weather on the day appointed for crossing the pass, it did not deter the expedition. They marched up the valley into the clouds in the direction where they believed the pass to be, pounded by a heavy rain that 'beat the surface of the snow into slush', and somehow found a way across. On the far side they descended avalanching slopes to the safety of the forest, their porters snow-blind and in pain. For the next several days they hurried through the uninhabited 'no-man's land' between the passes – crossing the trail that Kintup followed as a pilgrim on his visit to the sacred mountain – and then climbed into the snow once again. The entire success of the journey hung on getting over the second pass and down to the warmer, Chimdro valley below. The climb to the summit of the pass went well, but on the other side 'we found what looked like a vision of inferno…We could not see the bottom of the valley. Clouds of dark mist came billowing up obliterating the view. All we saw were steep cliffs in every direction down which, without any firing of gunshots, great masses of snow would break off and avalanche into the mist below.' They tried to descend by the cliffs but were caught in avalanches. Bailey saved himself from a fall by the handle of his butterfly net, while his Tibetan guide, Sonam Chumbi, was swept past him, calling out for salvation to a Buddhist saint, before coming to rest at the edge of a cliff. Finally they descended below the snow line and immediately made a fire and piled it high with fresh fir boughs. Enveloped in the smoky incense, Sonam chanted prayers 'giving thanks for his deliverance'.

The most difficult part of the journey was over and the next obstacle would be diplomatic. The Chimdro River flows into the Tsangpo River from the east deep within its flaring lower gorge. Anxious to reach the Tsangpo itself and pick up Kintup's route of thirty years before, they first had to negotiate with the Tibetans living in the valley for supplies and porters for the onward journey. 'I resolved to put on the bravest show that I could. I sent one of the guides forward to announce to the people of

Chimdro that we had arrived. Since we had no authority to be where we were, our best tactic was to behave as if we had.' While Morshead surveyed up the valley to the east, Bailey boldly marched into a village and presented his letter from Gyamtso to the headman and hoped for the best. Luck was with him. A man came to visit who remembered seeing him on his 1911 journey and when he produced photographs of the Dalai and Tashi (Panchen) Lamas and told the headman that he knew both, all suspicions dissolved. Bailey was invited to a ceremony at the monastery and given the transport they desperately needed.

Trouble on the Way to the Falls

By now, word had spread through the area that a small party from the Abor Expedition was working its way upriver. When Bailey and Morshead reached the Tsangpo, after a march of a few days down the Chimdro, they decided it would be prudent to try to contact the main survey party. They travelled a short distance downstream to Rinchenpung and rested three days at the same monastery where Kintup had lingered on his pilgrimage many years before. With the onset of the summer monsoon just days away, the fierce heat of the gorge was sapping their energy. Even Morshead was beginning to take notice. 'The moist damp heat of the Dihang valley at this time of year is most trying, and combined with the perfect plague of mosquitoes, '*damdims*' [stinging flies], leeches and gadflies would indeed have been almost unbearable were it not for the very excellent quality of the '*marwa*' beer which is brewed here in large quantities.' While waiting for a runner to return with a letter from Captain Dundas of the Abor Survey, they asked everyone they met about the falls further upstream. The information on the falls was sketchy and vague, but Bailey heard much about the prophecy that had brought pilgrims from far and wide to settle in the 'Promised Land' of Pemakö. He also learned of recent military unrest throughout the area. The reports that Bailey had heard in 1911 at Shugden Gompa of fierce battles between Tibetans and invading Chinese forces in Pome, across the passes to the north, indeed proved to have been true. Everyone was on edge.

With no word from the Abor Survey, Bailey and Morshead retraced their route, now under the suspicious gaze of villagers along the way. The mood had noticeably changed since their passage down the gorge just a few days before. A bridge had been removed and they were subtly advised to return the way they had come. The *Nyerpa* Namgye, an official representing the queen of Pome, had been tracking their movements ever since they arrived in the Chimdro Valley. He had sent them an indecipherable letter a few days before from a village farther up the gorge and they were now beginning to wonder if he was not the one responsible for the sudden lack of co-operation. Unwilling to suffer the humiliation of returning to Mipi to face the consequences of an unauthorised expedition, they resolved to push up the river and boldly confront the *Nyerpa* who was now preparing to leave for home. They had hoped to travel right up the gorge, at least as far as the confluence with the Po-Tsangpo River, if not to the falls themselves, but realised this would be impossible if the local people turned against them. Their only hope for success rested in allaying the fears of the government officials of Pome who controlled Pemakö, even if it meant travelling there in person. Should this fail, they would at least get a good look at a portion of the Tsangpo River no westerner had ever seen.

Above the confluence with the Chimdro the valley narrowed. Following a trail high above the left bank of the Tsangpo, they were delighted to be leaving the stifling heat and insects of the lower gorge. They followed Kintup's itinerary as they retraced his route to the north. 'The villages on the opposite bank which we passed fitted in well with Kintup's report. If he remembered these so well four years after he had visited them, we told ourselves that he could hardly have been mistaken about the Great Falls.'

They caught up with the *Nyerpa* at the village of Lagung and the meeting began well. He regaled Bailey and Morshead with tales of victory over the Chinese – boasting seventeen hundred killed – and showed him his cache of seized weapons. Bailey pressed him on the details, saying that he had been told only three hundred had died. 'The *Nyerpa* remarked that it was customary for a defeated enemy to minimise his losses. I agreed and said that the losses were certainly heavy enough to prevent my being allowed to enter Pome, which, I added, had been my desire then as it was ours now.' Bailey was fishing for an invitation to visit Pome but the *Nyerpa* didn't take the bait. Instead, he delivered some surprising news about the rest of the Abor Survey. He had exchanged letters with Captain Dundas and had suggested a route they could take to Gyala, at the mouth of the gorge. The *Nyerpa* was obviously delighted that the survey party had taken his advice and would soon be leaving the lower Tsangpo Gorge. He probably hoped Bailey and Morshead would do the same. But Bailey had other worries on his mind. 'It was news to us that any of the Abor Survey party was trying, as we were, to find the Tsangpo falls…But how long he would keep us hanging around we had no idea, and all the time we had the vision of the Abor Survey party beating us to the falls.'

Bailey and Morshead did not have to wait long. The next day, the *Nyerpa* decided personally to escort them out of the gorge to the village of Showa in Pome where their fate would be decided. It soon became clear that the *Nyerpa* had deep reservations about who they were. The cause of his concern was soon revealed. Apparently Dundas' letters sent to the queen of Pome had been sealed in Chinese envelopes (in order not to alarm the Tibetans with the sight of an English envelope, Bailey learned later) and he had given himself a Chinese title, further confusing the issue. 'It gave us ground for hope that if, when we reached Showa, we could prove that we had nothing to do with the Chinese, we might get permission to proceed.'

The party crossed the snowy range that separates the lower Tsangpo gorges from Pome over a pass called Sü La. Along the way, the *Nyerpa* confessed that he thought the British force moving up the Dihang into Pemakö was actually Chinese. With the Abor Survey turned out of the way, Bailey realised just how perilous their presence here was. The tension was palpable.

> As we approached Showa, I went on ahead of Morshead. I was walking through fields, which were high with wheat, barley and peas, when suddenly there was the noise of a shot behind me.'
>
> 'My God!' I thought, 'have they ambushed Morshead?' I did not know what to do. If they had ambushed Morshead, the next thing they would do would be to shoot me. But there was nothing I could do about that. If they wanted to shoot me, they would.
>
> So I went on, walking past the ruined houses and through the fields, as if nothing had happened, thinking that if I had to die, I had better look as if I didn't expect to.
>
> It was just as well. I found out later that the shot was fired by someone scaring parrots from the crops. If I had gone running to Morshead's assistance, I would have felt such a fool I could never have faced the Nyerpa again.

Now he would have to muster all his skills to convince the government at Showa of his intentions. It was a role Bailey had been preparing for much of his life.

At a meeting with the ministers the following day the suspicious envelopes were produced. At once he understood why his hosts were so upset. The British had made an extraordinary diplomatic blunder. Removing the letters Bailey unfolded them hoping to buy some time and discover a clue to help them press their case. Holding the paper up to the light he examined the watermark and pointed out the letters that matched those in his dictionary. '"Don't you see," I said, "this proves that we are English, not Chinese?" And I went on to demonstrate with the dictionary English words and Tibetan words, repeating over and over again: "This is not Chinese".' Held as prisoners for several days, their fate rested in the hands of these vacillating, war-weary officials. In the end, Bailey's diplomacy carried the day. They were free to go.

It was the turning point of the expedition. The tension and uncertainty they had lived under since leaving Mipi dissolved. Just before departing they finally received the long-awaited reply from the Abor Expedition. One of the letters concluded, 'Whatever happens go everywhere and survey everything you can: we have not staked out any area as a preserve and even if we duplicate bits of work it will make a better map. Above all get to Gyala and the Falls.'

From Showa, Bailey and Morshead travelled slowly down the Po-Tsangpo River through one of the most beautiful of all Himalayan valleys, marred only by the devastation from the recent war. Through forests of pine and giant cypress trees, bordered by flowery meadows, Morshead ranged tirelessly up and down the flanks of the valley, surveying openly. Bailey followed the terraces above the broad sweep of the river stopping now and then to marvel at the exquisite peaks that soared into the Tibetan sky. Rain still fell sporadically, but now they were nearly beyond the reach of the moisture-laden winds blowing up from Assam and of the leeches and insects that had plagued them in the lower gorges for so long. They were on the threshold of the Tibetan Plateau. Bailey crammed his notebooks with observations on everything. No fact – historical, anthropological, or geographic – escaped his notice. When time permitted, he netted butterflies on sunny hillsides and combed the forest searching for rare pheasants.

Bailey and Morshead hoped to follow the Po-Tsangpo River all the way down to its confluence with the Tsangpo into the wild heart of the gorge. From there they would press on upstream in pursuit of the falls. Their plans changed when they discovered that floods had carried away the bridges along that route. Their disappointment was lessened somewhat by the *Nyerpa*'s assurance that there were no large waterfalls on the river from the point where they left it at Lagung to the confluence with the Po-Tsangpo. Instead, they would have to circle around the upper gorges and come at it from above. Now they were back on Kintup's route. Like sacred sites along a personal pilgrimage route, Bailey noted all of the places Kintup passed, including a rock shelter he had slept under after fleeing from captivity. They crossed the bridge near Tongkyuk where Kintup's pistol and compass were seized and then headed up the swift Rong Chu. Bailey had seen many beautiful poppies on his travels, but none finer than a tall blue poppy he saw growing at the margin of the forest. He plucked it and pressed it in his notebook and all but forgot about it. He had other things on his mind. (The poppy was later named *Meconopsis baileyi*.)

To Kintup's Falls and Beyond

By late July Bailey and Morshead were deep within the upper gorge beyond Gyala. Much to their delight they had discovered that the survey party from the Abor Expedition had broken off their journey two weeks before and returned to the lower gorge. The way to the falls lay open before them. For much of their journey up the Tsangpo in the lower gorge their route had kept them far above the raging river. Now, crawling slowly over the great boulders along its banks they felt the full fury of the Tsangpo eating its way deep into the earth. 'The river here is an extraordinary sight, falling in one roaring rapid over which hangs a mist of spray. In places the water is dashed up in waves twenty feet high.' Directly above, often obscured by clouds, loomed the great snow-domes of Gyala Peri and Namcha Barwa. Morshead had glimpsed the summit of Namcha Barwa from the hills above Mipi and now he realised that the second peak he had noticed peaking over its shoulder was an unmapped mountain, Gyala Peri, just thirteen miles beyond with the river flowing between! Their Tibetan guides said the two peaks were the breasts of their goddess Dorje Pagmo – landmarks of a remarkable sacred geography that had so captivated the pilgrim Kintup years before.

Bailey relates the final steps of the journey with a matter-of-factness that must have disguised a deep disappointment. 'After going seven miles we reached a point where the road goes down to the falls which Kintup described. We went a half a mile down to the river and found the fall to be about 30 feet [9m] with very sharp rapids above it, while the whole place was clouded in spray in which Captain Morshead later in the day saw rainbows.' The idea of a large waterfall at Pemaköchung had captivated the world's imagination for nearly twenty-five years. Now, in the duration of a summer's afternoon, it dissolved back into the mists of legend, perhaps, to be found beyond the next bend in the river.

Bailey and Morshead resolved to find out. They followed the trail of takin, powerful buffalo-sized animals related to the musk-ox, through dense thickets of rhododendron and stinging nettles; they climbed thousands of feet to cross sharp, forested ridges; they bridged swift glacier streams. With supplies running out, Morshead turned back while Bailey and a Tibetan made a dash for a sharp bend in the river they could see far in the distance down the narrowing corridors, listening for a roar rising on the breeze from along the unknown river.

Unexpectedly, they came upon a secretive group of Mönba travellers returning to their homes at Payi (Payu, Payul, Bayi, Bayu or Bayul) and Lugu, villages in the lower gorge not far above Lagung where they left the Tsangpo with the *Nyerpa* of Pome. They were the first group in more than twenty years to traverse this portion of the gorge and offered to guide Bailey through. Apparently the Mönbas had second thoughts, for just a day later they abandoned Bailey below unscalable cliffs, throwing down their baggage and retracting the rope ladder they had used to aid their climb. For once, Bailey regretted not having a larger, better-equipped, party with him. 'At this time I was travelling with only a few blankets and one coolie and to their minds was a person of no importance whom it would not be worth while to take any trouble about. Had the party been larger and the Mönbas more impressed by it, I do not think they would have dared to desert as they did.' Before they left, Bailey questioned the Mönbas about the gorge below. 'They said that there was no road, but that they occasionally hunted takin in the neighbourhood and had never heard of any large falls.' Nearly out of food, Bailey hurried back to Pemaköchung and then on to Gyala where he met up with Morshead again.

Now, the pieces of the puzzle began to come together. They crossed the Tsangpo to visit a shrine to the god Shingche Chögye, the same name Kintup had given to the 45m (150ft.) waterfall at Pemaköchung. They were shown a cascading side-stream that attracted a handful of yearly pilgrims, each hoping to get a view of the god chained behind the veil of falling water. 'Some people never see the god at all, others after giving money and burning lamps for several days, while others see him at once. He appears in different colours to different people.' The 'god' was apparently just as elusive as the waterfall they had come looking for. It dawned on Bailey that this small waterfall on an insignificant side stream tumbling into the Tsangpo might have been confused for one on the main river. Had it all been a simple mistake?

Back to India

For years the stories of the Pundits and Kintup's amazing journey had fired Bailey's imagination. Like a pilgrim, he had retraced Kintup's footsteps throughout Pemakö and into the unknown depths of the Tsangpo gorges. It is somehow fitting therefore, that Bailey's quest for Kintup's waterfall should end in a search for Kintup the man.

A few months after returning to India Bailey made an inquiry through a friend in Sikkim to see if Kintup was still alive. Surprisingly, word quickly came back that he had been found, working at his old occupation as a tailor. Bailey sent travel funds and a few days later Kintup arrived in Simla. The young explorer met the old master. Long into the evening they talked, Bailey fresh from the wonder of his journey and Kintup ranging back over a life lived long ago in those same wild places. What stories must have filled the room that night – tales of waterfalls – talk of Pemakö and of pilgrimage to sacred mountains! At Pemaköchung Kintup had seen the same 30ft. waterfall that Bailey and Morshead described – nothing more. The 150ft. waterfall on the Tsangpo River did not exist. As Bailey suspected, a scribe had confused the cascade at the sacred site of Shingche

Chögye at Gyala with the smaller waterfall on the main river at Pemaköchung. Kintup, not being able to read, had never corrected the report.

Later, Kintup went out on a balcony and posed for a photograph. There is a trace of weariness in his eyes. His thinning goatee streams from his chin and wisps of greying hair dangle from beneath his cap. His prayer beads around his neck peek out from the voluminous folds of his *chuba*, perhaps concealing his bowl and prayer wheel. His feet are bare and his massive hands are crossed modestly in front of him, swollen from pulling thread and counting beads – an endless stream of prayers from Pemakö to that moment.

Bailey asked the Indian Government for a small pension 'in recognition of his service to Tibetan exploration' but had to settle for a bonus of 1,000 rupees. It was more than Kintup would ever need: he returned to Darjeeling and died a few months later.

Kintup.
Photograph taken by Sir Gerald Burran. From the frontpiece of *China–Tibet–Assam*, by F.M. Bailey, London, 1945. This is Kintup as he appeared later in life. The photograph was probably taken about the time Kintup was interviewed by Bailey following his return from his exploration of the Tsangpo Gorges in 1913.

Gangtok, Sikkim—March 1924

The arrival of two special guests at the British Residency in Gangtok, Sikkim was greeted with the raucous barking of dogs. From the porch of their rambling, two-storey brick house, the middle-aged Political Officer and his wife welcomed the weary travellers. Soon, they would be off again, bound for Tibet across the passes to the north, but for the next two days they would enjoy the hospitality of their gracious hosts.

For Frank Kingdon Ward and Lord Cawdor this was more than a social call. The man who strode out to shake hands was none other than Major Bailey. In the ten years that had passed since his return from the Tsangpo gorges with Henry Morshead, Bailey's storied life had continued unabated. He was awarded the Gold Medal from the Royal Geographical Society, had been wounded twice at Gallipoli and had eluded the Russian Bolsheviks as a secret agent in Central Asia for more than a year. Recently married, Bailey had settled into the plum government posting on the Tibetan frontier in 1921. As Political Officer, Sikkim, he was the 'gatekeeper' to Tibet and helped secure permission for Kingdon Ward's plant-hunting expedition. Now he presented them with their passports. The two days he spent with his guests must have been a delightful break from mundane official duties. They strolled through the spacious garden of the Residency, pored over maps, and played with the Tibetan mastiffs that Bailey and his wife were breeding for a hobby. For Bailey it was an opportunity to rekindle memories of his journey of 1913 and share his experiences with a younger explorer whose journeys and adventures were the equal of his own.

He briefed them on the routes to the gorge and on people he knew along the way who might prove useful. Also helpful were his suggestions on where to look for promising plants. The blue poppy he pressed in his notebook in 1913 had been named *Meconopsis baileyi* in his honour, but had never been introduced. Bailey told Kingdon Ward where to look for it below Lunang, along the Rong Chu.

In the end, the conversation certainly turned to Kintup and the waterfalls. The hope of finding a waterfall to rival Niagara or Victoria had faded. Still, an unexplored 'gap' of several miles remained after 1913 and Kingdon Ward held out the possibility of yet finding a 'large waterfall of 100-feet or so.' Bailey encouraged them to press the search. Ward and Cawdor agreed to keep an eye out for interesting pheasants, Bailey's great love, and to collect a set of seeds for the Dalai Lama's garden. They would write to each other when they could.

So, on a late March day, Frank Kingdon Ward and Lord Cawdor took leave of F.M. Bailey. They were bound on a journey across a wintry plateau with the prospect of a spring filled with flowery meadows. Beyond beckoned the great gorges along the Tsangpo River. Like Bailey years before, Frank Kingdon Ward was embarking on perhaps the greatest expedition of his life to an area he had once vowed he would 'go there if I die for it, some day'. He would try to solve some of the remaining 'riddles of the Tsangpo Gorges'.

The Thousand-Petalled Lotus:
Tibetan visions of the Tsangpo Gorge
Ian Baker

Ah ho! The great land of Pemakö…strung with rainbows.
In future times, the fortunate will gather here…
A pure realm for the Buddhas of the past, present and future…

Encircled by snow-mountains, rock and jungle
Within lies Padmasambhava's hidden land,
The place for fortunate ones to attain Enlightenment.

-Orgyen Dorje Dranak
Praise to the Sacred Realm of Pemakö

Long before British explorers became interested in the geography of the Tsangpo gorges, the Tibetans envisioned this 'unknown and remote region' as the portal to an earthly paradise. Kingdon Ward acknowledges this indigenous perspective in his chapter, 'Pemakö: The Promised Land', where he refers to Tibetan prophecies describing the area beyond the Doshong La pass as 'a land flowing with milk and honey, where the crops grew of their own accord'.

Mystical texts attributed to an eighth century Buddhist sage named Padmasambhava appeared in Tibet centuries before Kingdon Ward's and Lord Cawdor's historic journey through the Tsangpo gorge. These pilgrimage guides (*ne-yig*) describe Beyul Pemakö, 'The Hidden Land of the Lotus', as 'a celestial realm on earth'. One guide book to Pemakö subtitled *Dispelling Clouds and Increasing Faith* was discovered by a lama named Rigzin Düdrul Dorje (1615-72) in a lake in Pome. 'Just taking seven steps towards Pemakö with pure intention', the scripture states, 'even if one is unable to actually reach [this hidden land], one will certainly be reborn here…A single drop of water or a blade of grass from this sacred place – whoever tastes it will be freed from rebirth in the lower realms of existence.'

Kingdon Ward first encountered Pemakö after crossing the 'rhododendron fairyland' of the Doshong La pass and gazing 'down into a cauldron of whirling mist, through rents in which we could see only snow'. Yet where the intrepid plant-collector ultimately discovered 'a paradise of primulas' and an 'almost inconceivable wealth of flora', Tibetans still experience a land of mysterious and numinous powers. Chögyam Trungpa, a revered lama who later settled in Scotland, escaped the Communist invasion of his homeland in 1959 over the same spur of Namcha Barwa. Encountering disorienting snowstorms like those which had plagued Kingdon Ward and the Earl of Cawdor, Trungpa and his fellow refugees were unfortunately less attuned to Pemakö vegetal riches. Although the sacred texts account for 'hundreds of varieties of trees and thousands of flowers and fruits', the Tibetans passed by edible plants and, in desperation, boiled their yak-leather bags to keep themselves from starving. As Trungpa wrote in *Born in Tibet*:

Our journey now took us through yet stranger country; there were all sorts of trees forming a dense jungle with no level spaces; a tangle of mountains with continual rain and mist. For the first time we saw banana trees, but did not know that the fruit was edible and dared not experiment.

Trungpa referred to the Tsangpo gorge country in his memoirs as a sacred land where 'Tibetans have often come…as hermits and pilgrims to practice meditation'. In a

Looking for hidden crystals.

Local guide Dungle Phuntsok probes cavities in the polished rock for hidden crystals, sacred places exposed by the river.

sermon to his followers as they travelled through this wild and unforgiving land in flight from Tibet's Chinese invaders, he discoursed on the spirit of Buddhist pilgrimage:

> It is fortunate for us that our way is hard and that we are struggling against greater difficulties than the pilgrims of the past, for by this means we shall learn and profit the more from our journey. We should not be thinking only about the enemies threatening us from without. Each moment we should be aware of ourselves and of the forces of destruction that threaten each man from within. If we fail in this, we are indeed putting the spiritual object of our journey in jeopardy; each step along the way should be holy and precious to us.   (Trungpa p. 208)

The Origins of Shangri-La

The first accounts of Pemakö's mist-wreathed valleys were carried over the Doshong La and other passes by Mishmi and Abor tribesmen who traded musk, chillies, tiger pelts, and medicinal plants for Tibetan salt, swords, cooking pots and woven cloth. The half-naked Lopas from the jungles of Pemakö brought stories of abundant game and wild fruits hanging plentifully from the trees.

Rock carving at Gompo Ne.   KSJ

The image of a viper is cut in the rock below a sacred Tibetan inscription. The serpent is honoured in the carving to atone for the inadvertent killing of snakes when the fields are burned and cleared.

By the seventeenth century political pressures within Tibet transformed popular perception of these sequestered lands beyond the snow wall of the Himalayas into visions of a terrestrial paradise and a haven from taxation and religious oppression. The mystical texts which appeared during this period celebrated this region of nearly perpetual rain as a sanctuary where 'all wishes are spontaneously fulfilled'. Inspired by these accounts, charismatic lamas led their followers across the Himalayas into a new and unfamiliar world. As stated in a text entitled *Self-Liberation through Hearing of the Great Blissful Pemakö*:

> Food, drink, and all life's requirements fall with the rain. The happiness and enjoyments here are equal to a god-realm. Even without meditating, anyone who reaches here can attain the state of a Buddha.

Tibetan tradition describes the region of Pemakö and the Tsangpo gorges as the greatest of several *beyul*, or hidden lands – remote Himalayan sanctuaries sealed off from the rest of the world by icy ranges and imbued with rare geomantic and spiritual forces. However, only the most exceptional pilgrims can reach Pemakö's innermost sanctum. A text discovered by the great yogi Dorje Thogme (1746-1797) entitled *Opening the Door to the Hidden Land: Relieving the Heart's Darkness* states unequivocally that:

> The protector spirits will cause perilous circumstances to test the power of your realization. They will assist those who abide by their spiritual commitments (*samaya*) and will punish those unfortunate ones who do not.

James Hilton wrote his immensely popular novel *Lost Horizon* in 1935, less than ten years after the publication of *The Riddle of the Tsangpo Gorges*. Hilton's novel suggests a deep familiarity with the accounts of Pemakö described by Kingdon Ward, Major F.M. Bailey, as well as Kintup in his report to the British Survey of India. Hilton's invention of Shangri-La owes an even greater debt, however, to a little-known novel which was published in the very year of Kingdon Ward's and Lord Cawdor's expedition through the Tsangpo gorge. Talbot Mundy's; *Om: The Secret of the Ahbor Valley,* blends theosophical musings with the account of its hero's journey to a hidden monastery reachable only by a tunnel beneath the Tsangpo River and in direct view of the fabled 'Falls of the Brahmaputra'.

Like a roaring curtain, emerald green and diamond white, blown in the wind, the

Gompo Ne. **KSJ**
Pilgrims climb a notched tree-ladder to traverse a sacred rock outcropping above the river. When the river is in flood this rock is an island cut-off from the mainland.

The 8th century sage Padmasambhava in the dynamic form. IB Padmasambhava is shown here in the dynamic form which he adopted to overcome obstacles to the spreading of Buddhism. This image of the sage who first declared the Tsangpo gorge region as an earthly paradise and hidden sanctuary for the practice of Tantric Buddhism is the central icon at the monastery at Rinchenpung, on a mountain behind Medok-Shing in the lower Tsangpo gorge.

Tsangpo River…tumbled down a precipice between two outflung spurs…The roar [of the falls] came down-wind like the thunder of creation.   (Mundy p. 340)

At the end of the novel, after gazing into the mystical 'Jade of the Ahbor' in which one sees one's 'higher nature shining through the lower', the ageing lama, Tsiang Samdup, disappears into a limestone tunnel above the falls as the young girl who inherits his vision, intones: 'O my Divinity, blend Thou with me…that out of darkness I may go forth in Light.' (Mundy p. 391)

Transformative Journeys
When Kingdon Ward and Lord Cawdor set out from Gyala on their journey through the Tsangpo's inner gorge, they followed a route which Tibetans consider a Buddhist pilgrimage. Perhaps for this reason, the local official insisted that no route existed and initially discouraged the explorers from venturing downstream.

The *Depa*…swore that there was no path, and that no one ever came up through the gorge…Why he was so anxious to conceal from us the fact…that a path through the gorge did exist we could not understand.'

A lama performs a prayer ceremony at Gompo Ne.   KSJ

Pilgrims who journey into Pemakö from the village of Gyala traditionally visit the falls at Shingche Chögye, what Kingdon Ward described as 'a collection of poor little temples clapped against the face of the cliff over which a glacial torrent leaps two-hundred feet into the Tsangpo'. This sacred cataract conceals an image of the lord of death and transfiguration, in which pilgrims acknowledge life's transience at the outset of their journey. Unless this vision of impermanence suffuses one's journey, explained a contemporary Lama, it will not be a true pilgrimage, but rather an expedition based on hope and fear; the subtle impediments to deep spiritual awakening.

As Khamtrul Rinpoche elaborated, the falls at Gyala are a window into a deeper reality, the outer topography supporting what Tibetans call *Danang*, or Pure Vision, in which perceptions of the environment are transformed and exalted. Lamas continually emphasize that the Elysian accounts in the Pemakö *neyig* point less to a literal paradise than

The head Lama of Payi.   IB

Konchok Wangpo, the head Lama of Payi, refers to sacred texts describing the Tsangpo gorge region as the portal to an earthly paradise. Such scriptures inspired generations of Tibetans to leave their homelands and settle in Pemakö's sub-tropical valleys. As Lama Konchok Wangpo declared: 'These texts are the only reason we are here'.

to a landscape supportive of deep inner transformation. Dorje Thogme's revealed text entitled *Relieving the Heart's Darkness* claims that: 'What can be achieved elsewhere in one year [of spiritual practice], can be accomplished here in a single night'.

In 1959, when Khamtrul Rinpoche travelled along the same route followed by Kingdon Ward and Lord Cawdor, he kept a journal of his dreams and visions in which he was guided by ethereal Dakinis to Pemakö's innermost sanctuary – the heart of the Tantric goddess, Dorje Pagmo.

The Body of the Goddess

Early Tibetan chronicles portray the landscape of Tibet as a supine, serpent-hearted demoness. Tibet's earliest Buddhist temples were constructed according to geomantic theory to immobilize different parts of her body. The monastery at Buchu Sengyi Lhakhang in Kongbo which Kingdon Ward visited in 1924 holds down her right elbow. As Buddhism gradually urged Tibetans into a more benevolent view of their surroundings, the landscape was similarly re-imagined. The gorges of the Tsangpo, which had been seen as a gateway to a *terra incognita* lorded over by serpent-worshipping head hunters, was reconfigured as the terrestrial body of the goddess Dorje Pagmo whose sow's head ornament represents the transformation of ignorance to illumination. Specific geographical features in the region of the Tsangpo gorges correspond to the goddess's earthly anatomy. As the texts describe: the soaring peak of Gyala Peri, 'like a pig gazing into the sky', represents her head; Namcha Barwa, 'like an eight-petalled lotus', and the 'jewel-like' Kangla Karpo form her mountainous breasts. Further south, concealed in vast and luxuriant jungles, lie her secret heart-centre and, in a region still not clearly identified, the place of spiritual rebirth in her earthly womb. In this innermost sanctum:

> Day and night have no distinction, since there are always rainbows and shining lights…When you reach here, by drinking the water and eating the fruits and plants, you will be spontaneously absorbed in meditative rapture.

Tibetan Pilgrims.   JC

Abu Lashu, the sacred mountain.   **IB**
At the apex of the Great Bend, the Tsangpo curls around the sacred peak of Abu Lashu where local villagers
perform annual rites in honour of local spirits. This mountain is considered one of the principal 'seats' of Dorje
Traktsen, Pemakö's most important protector deity.

The Tsangpo River is, itself, identified with the Goddess's sinuous spinal column and a
parallel current of transformative energy. To follow the course of the Tsangpo through its
innermost gorges is, according to Tibetan texts, to identify with an exalted image of the
higher self – immanent in the landscape. Although Khamtrul Rinpoche never physically
discovered Pemakö's *sanctum sanctorium*, he was guided by visions through Dorje Pagmo's
terrestrial body and found refuge in India as a spiritual adviser to the Dalai Lama.

Although Kingdon Ward makes no mention of the myth of Dorje Pagmo, Bailey's
book, *No Passport to Tibet,* clearly indicates his awareness of the Tibetans' conception of
the Pemakö landscape. As he wrote in a footnote: 'the two peaks are supposed to be the
breasts of Dorge Pagmo, the Diamond Sow, whose incarnation lives at Samding
Monastery on the Yamdrok Tso'.

With an idealized landscape replacing an earlier one of dread, the gorge which had
been a fearful place of exile – the *ultima Thule* of Tibetan imagination – became a place
of refuge and spiritual renewal. Confronting the mirror of impermanence in the
waterfall at Shingche Chögye at the entry to the gorge, the intrepid pilgrim travels
symbolically through the body of an immanent goddess towards a spiritual rebirth in

Lamas who practise Tantric Buddhism. **IB**
The esoteric Tantric form of Buddhism prevails in Pemakö, practised by lamas with long uncut hair and red and white robes. Some of the lamas from Tashi Jong in north-eastern India fled through the Tsangpo gorge region in 1959 in the wake of the Communist invasion. The principal deity invoked in their religious practices is a form of Dorje Pagmo, the Tantric goddess whose earthly body shapes the Pemakö landscape.

the 'womb' of Pemakö's innermost and still undiscovered sanctuary. For generations of Tibetans, the pilgrimage to Pemakö has represented an inner journey towards spiritual enlightenment, configured as a paradisiacal landscape. During the 1950s a Lama named Kanjur Rinpoche spent five years searching for Pemakö's elusive centre. He ultimately disappeared into a tunnel behind a waterfall through which none of his retinue could follow: a strange echo of the final scene in Talbot Mundy's novel written more than twenty years earlier.

The Tantric deity Vajra Yogini in her form as Dorje Pagmo.   **IB**

Tibetans conceive of the Tsangpo gorges as the terrestrial form of the Tantric deity Vajra Yogini in her form as
Dorje Pagmo, the sow-headed goddess. She is shown here in another of her avatars wielding a bow made from
fragrant flowers.

Sacred Waterfalls

Cawdor and Kingdon Ward slogged through the gorge beyond Pemaköchung seeking a waterfall whose significance lay not in its capacity to induce visions or lead to other realms, but simply in its height. The quest for the fabled 'Falls of the Brahmaputra' had inspired several earlier expeditions, all of which turned back before reaching the innermost depths of the Tsangpo Gorge. Bailey had largely resolved the mistake in Kintup's 1889 report which described a falls of approximately 46m (150ft.) in the vicinity of the monastery at Pemaköchung. Cawdor, like Bailey before him, descended towards 'Kintup's Falls' following a pilgrim's passage through a double-entranced cave paralleling the Tsangpo. Unbeknownst to either of these explorers, the conical peak across the river is revered by Tibetans as the abode of a wrathful spirit named Dorje Traktsen, the guardian of the portals to the innermost gorge.

Kingdon Ward's goal was not to penetrate the mysteries of this metaphysical landscape, but to venture further down river into an area increasingly sacred to the Tibetans. It was in this 'hidden heart of the Himalayas' that Kingdon Ward hoped to discover the lost falls of the Tsangpo. Before leaving Pemaköchung, the monastery's head lama performed a ceremony to ensure their safe passage. As Cawdor recounts in his journal on 22 November:

> When I got back to the temple I found the Walrus…beating the drum and clashing cymbals rather languidly, a whole row of butterlamps, and offerings, consisting of chillies, bannock, turnip, onion and butter on the altar… presumably to ensure a safe passage for us in the gorge.

Further into the journey, having negotiated what Cawdor described as 'particularly pestilential jungle', they camped at a narrow part of the gorge 'hemmed in by river and cliffs'. They little suspected that above them, in Shelkarlungpa, the Valley of the White Crystal, was a sacred three-pillared cave, Drakpuk Kawasum, a gateway to Pemakö's innermost sanctuary – described as a horticulturist's heaven overflowing with magical plants and life-sustaining flowers. Instead, as they ventured through this sacred, if 'rain-sodden' terrain, Cawdor's journal entry on 26 November reveals genuine disenchantment:

> This is without exception the most depressing country I've ever been in. It may grow more weeds per foot than any other country, but what's that to me – blast these showers! I'd sell my soul to see some honest weather again.

Even the plant hunting seemed to get to him:

> After eight months in this infernal country I shouldn't have imagined anyone would wish to see another rhodo again – I'm damned certain I don't!

Cawdor's own orientation towards sacred landscape was suggested early in the journey where, on 21 April, he recounts; 'I sat on my valise in the shadow of the monastery wall and read Addison's critique of *Paradise Lost*.' Above them, but hidden in the mists, was a towering rock citadel called Dorje Pagmo – the goddess's primary residence. Curling around this monolith, the Tsangpo arches back on itself and flows north-west into the most forbidding and, for Tibetans, sacred part of the gorge. Beneath this gneissic pinnacle Kingdon Ward documented Rainbow Falls, which, along with a second falls ten miles further downstream, were the highest that he was able to observe.

Like the Depa who denied the existence of a trail into Pemaköchung, Kingdon Ward's

Opposite.   **IB**

On a ledge above Ward's 'Falls of the Brahmaputra', a lama pacifies local spirits by blowing on a trumpet fashioned from a human thigh bone. Several waterfalls in the Tsangpo's innermost gorge hold religious significance as aqueous 'doorways' to other realms. Lamas maintain that, through proper rites, indigenous protector deities can be coerced into revealing the routes into these paradisiacal spaces hidden in the depths of the gorge.

Mönba guides claimed there was no route through the section of the gorge below Rainbow Falls. He later wrote that the Mönbas were anxious 'to divert our attention from this forbidden land!'. They told him that a sacred text kept at Pemaköchung describes this innermost chasm as concealing a series of seventy-five waterfalls each presided over by a local spirit – 'whether benevolent or malicious is not stated.' Yet instead of forging deeper into the forbidden zone, they began what Kingdon Ward described as the most harrowing ascent of his several decades of Himalayan exploration. Down river, in the area that lies in the shadow of Dorje Pagmo's granite spire – the region of her throat – the Hidden Falls in the Tsangpo's innermost gorge remained concealed from foreign eyes for seventy more years, guarded by devout Buddhist hunters who chant into the night before pursuing their sacred prey through the steep and flowering jungles.

Mystical Plants

When the people of Pemakö meet lamas or make offerings at temples, their first gift is flowers – the beatific emanations of the land itself. Pemakö's innermost valleys are likened to the petals of a blossoming lotus. As stated in *Relieving the Heart's Darkness*:

> Pemakö is shaped like an eight-petalled lotus. In the central pod is the glorious Pemashelri [the Lotus Crystal Mountain], a mandala of all-pervading deities where the activities of enlightened beings are spontaneously accomplished.

The region of the Lotus Crystal Mountain – the closest coordinate for the goddess's heart – is renowned for miraculous mind-altering plants. Padmasambhava's text, *A Clear Mirror for Identifying the Five Special Plants*, describes their uncommon qualities:

> In the centre of Pemakö there are five nectar-bestowing plants. Whoever consumes 'the excellent plant of miracles' will remain free of all disease and attain miraculous powers. One's body will become youthful and one can gain the ability to fly through the sky. Without abandoning the body, you will be able to reach the upper realms…Whoever eats 'the plant of increasing bliss' experiences the inexhaustible union of joy and emptiness…Whoever partakes of 'the plant of purification' dissolves all karmic obscurations and the eighty forms of habitual thought. You will recall countless previous lives. Whoever eats Nyemong Kunchog, 'the plant which severs disturbing emotions', will never think of food or drink…and realization of samadhi will arise spontaneously. These are the supreme plants of the realized adepts. Whoever eats them will release all blockages of the inner energy channels and directly perceive the realms of the Buddhas.'

Another text makes even bolder claims for these uncatalogued species: 'This supreme plant…allows humans, wild animals, and even insects to attain Buddhahood. [Consuming] it will increase ones wisdom and lead to miracles such as leaving imprints of ones feet and hands on solid rock.' Lest one think that collecting these botanical wonders is an easy task, the text clearly identifies the obstacles: 'This excellent plant…will appear instantly to fortunate persons of strong devotion. Those less fortunate whose thought is defiled and those who break their spiritual commitments, for these beings it is invisible!' None the less, the text offers specific instructions for harvesting this 'great king of plants': 'You should approach it slowly like a cat stalking. When you first cut into it, the watery sap should be dropped on the ground. Then comes a milky liquid like a drop of melted butter. This you should consume.'

In my own travels through the Pemakö region, I accompanied a lama from eastern Tibet who was searching for a miraculous herb called Tsakuntuzangpo. He led us through alpine meadows where we feasted on peppery blue flowers (*Codonopsis convolvulacea*) that, although they caused no harm, led neither to mystical visions. At Rinchenpung – the goddess's 'navel centre of great bliss' – a dread-locked yogini from central Tibet was preparing to live for three months on flowers which she had collected

A dread-locked Yogini on pilgrimage to the sacred site of Gompo Ne.　　　　　**IB**
The Yogini rests beside the trail at the Tsangpo's northernmost apex. For centuries, Pemakö has been a haven for spiritual seekers who envision it as the portal to an earthly paradise.

from the surrounding meadows. As a text states…

> In the secret chakra, a place blessed by the wisdom dakinis…bloom pink coloured flowers. The sweet scent of these flowers can induce bliss…Eating them one can survive for years.

At moments Kingdon Ward almost seemed to share elements of this botanical intoxication. When he came upon the species of rhododendron named Scarlet Runner, he stood mesmerized: 'For a moment we just stared at it, drunk with wonder.' Kingdon Ward never explored the medicinal uses of Pemakö's plants, whether the aconite-based poisons used by the Lopas on their hunting arrows or the plants used in the pharmacopoeia of the Tibetan medical tradition, such as the red lily (*L. paradoxum*) which is prized, not for its crimson flower, but for its medically-active root. The plant seeds which Kingdon Ward and Lord Cawdor brought back with them from Tibet were expressly 'to beautify the gardens of England'. The grounds of Cawdor Castle bloom with rhododendron species from the Tsangpo gorges. Several years ago, the present Lady Cawdor planted new exotics to create a 'Paradise Garden' which leads through a symbolic landscape of water and flowering plants.

Landscapes of the Mind
At the height of the British Empire paradise was a place to be created outwardly. For Tibetan Buddhists, paradise is already present, yet veiled by habits of perception. Both visions involve floral metaphors and contribute to understanding the continued lure of the

Tsangpo gorges. As Aldous Huxley wrote in *Heaven and Hell:* 'Preternaturally brilliant flowers…have their place…even in the bejeweled and glassy paradises of the more advanced civilizations…One remembers the lotus of the Hindu and Buddhist traditions, the roses and lilies of the West'. Visionary journeys, plant induced or otherwise, lead beyond the dichotomies of pleasure and pain to a unitary experience often conceived of as 'paradisiacal'. What Wordsworth might have referred to as Pemakö's 'visionary gleam' is ultimately a testament to an idea shared by the Tibetans themselves: 'How the mind of man becomes a thousand times more beautiful than the earth on which he dwells.'

Pemakö's innermost centre, 'the most perfect land of supreme wisdom', is described as a 'thousand-petalled blossoming lotus', referring as much to an inner landscape of the psyche as the outer topography. 'There is not the slightest difference between this place and the pure land of the Buddha Amitabha', a text claims, 'but beings who do not trust in me [Padmasambhava] can never reach this perfect land!' A text entitled *Clear Light,* discovered by Rinchen Riwoche Jedung Pung, further states that: 'To reach this secret place, your meditation and insight should be confident; without any fear or doubt…In order to pass through the tunnel of obstacles, one's behaviour and actions must be impeccable…otherwise the hidden places will never be revealed.'

Kingdon Ward wrote that: 'Most races have their promised land, and such legendary places must necessarily be somewhat inaccessible, hidden behind misty barriers where ordinary men do not go; otherwise people would quickly explore the land and explode the legend.' Yet in Pemakö's dense jungles it is unlikely that the legends of an inner sanctuary on the borderline of mind and landscape will ever be convincingly dispelled. Kingdon Ward had discounted the possibility of a waterfall over 100ft. high but, as it turned out, even so prominent a feature of the gorge had simply been hidden from his sight. No doubt there are further secrets still to be revealed. The gorges remain a haven not only for a wealth of still unknown plants, but for the imagination as well. Blossoming in the deepest forests, the thousand-petalled lotus still waits to be discovered!

For all who journey here as pilgrims, may their vision be purified and all obstacles cleared away! May their lives be filled with joy, and may they gain the highest spiritual attainments (*siddhis*)!'

Guide To Pemakö: The Vajrasattva Palace which Liberates upon Seeing.

Opposite: Two villagers from Payi on pilgrimage to Gompo Ne. **IB**
Gompo Ne is one of Pemakö's principal sacred sites near the confluence of the Yarlung Tsangpo and Po–Tsangpo Rivers. In this 'wilderness of gneissic monoliths', they cut 'lhashing' which Kingdon Ward described as 'long poles, notched into steps, so finely cut that no human being could possibly climb them'. Cutting a notch for each year of their life, these poles establish a link between the pilgrim and the numinous power of the sacred landscape. Placing their ear against a hole in the rock, they listen for sounds of sub-terrestrial dakinis, emissaries of Dorje Pagmo.

Pemakö from the Doshong La. **IB**

Mönba porters descend towards Pemakö over the Doshong La, the pass still heavily covered in snow in late May of 1994. Kingdon Ward and Lord Cawdor visited the Doshong La in June and October of 1924. They descended part way down the valley below, where 'dense thickets of bamboo made progress difficult, and the path was everywhere a black bog'.

THE RIDDLE OF THE
TSANGPO GORGES

BY

CAPTAIN F. KINGDON WARD

Author of "From China to Hkamti Long"
"The Romance of Plant Hunting," etc.

WITH CONTRIBUTIONS BY
THE RIGHT HON. THE EARL CAWDOR

ILLUSTRATED

LONDON
EDWARD ARNOLD & CO.
1926

DEDICATED TO
F. P. ARMITAGE, ESQ., M.A.,
DIRECTOR OF PUBLIC INSTRUCTION, LEICESTER
AND FORMERLY
SCIENCE MASTER AND HOUSE MASTER,
ST. PAUL'S SCHOOL,
BY
AN OLD HOUSE CAPTAIN

CHAPTER I

Overview of the geography and peoples of Tibet

The size of Tibet

I have often observed that no matter how much I read about a foreign land before visiting it, I find by experience that it differs widely from what I expected; it is always fresh, though I had read of it a score of times before. The reason for this seems to me quite simple. When we visit a foreign land for the first time and see for ourselves its scenery, people, vegetation, towns, arts, customs and all else which goes to make up a country, we are moved by quite different emotions to those aroused by reading about it. Our intelligence now seizes on other objects of our own selection, ignoring many to which our attention was previously drawn. More importance is attached to this aspect, less to that. We form new opinions, prejudices, likes, and dislikes. The selective factor which is now active within us, alters our outlook; and the two mental pictures, the one derived from our reading, the other from our experience, by no means coincide. The first was in fact objective; the second is subjective.

In writing this book of travel, therefore, I am fully conscious that a complete presentation of the regions visited is a task beyond my power. All I can strive to do is to convey an illusion – my own illusion, if you like – which nothing short of a visit to the great gorge of the Tsangpo can dispel for the reader; though I am the less troubled on that account when I reflect that few indeed of those who read these lines will ever visit that remote region.

No general description of Tibet can cover the whole; for the country is so vast that, without dissecting it and labelling each part, such description as we can give must necessarily be vague. Yet to classify and to define were to compile an encyclopædia, or at least a gazetteer, which is no part of art. Such a compilation lacks atmosphere; it gains in accuracy only as it loses in elegance; it is indeed a choice between the quick and the dead. And if I myself would produce a work of art, however rough, I must agree to suppress and to extol, to melt the alloy of base facts judiciously with the pure gold of subjective experience, in order to catch the spirit of the land in which we dwelt, while keeping ever before me our object in making the journey.

For it is this spirit of the land which I wish to convey, a spirit of mystery and spaciousness inherent in the very name of Tibet. But first I must prepare a background on which to paint our picture, a solid background of geographical fact; and therein lies the difficulty. At the very outset it is the vastness and emptiness of Tibet which baffles me. How can I describe it? Even to those who have marched across its bleak plains and climbed its rugged mountains, the difficulty remains. If one employs a familiar unit of measurement, such as a square mile, the numbers involved are so great that the mind fails to grasp them. Thus to say that Tibet covers a million square miles has no meaning for us. We cannot comfortably conceive a million – it eludes us by reason of its vague bulk. In trying to focus a million all at once, one resembles an ant looking at a football – most of it is beyond our ken.

If, on the other hand, we employ limited numbers, then the unit of measurement itself becomes so large that we fail to visualise it. We may say indeed that Tibet is seventeen times as large as England and Wales; but we shall be little nearer a real grasp of its size, because of the difficulty we experience in forming a clear conception of the size of Britain. We may evade the difficulty by dealing only with linear measure, and say that Tibet at its greatest length measures 2420km [1,500 miles] from east to west (the distance from London to Moscow, or from London to Constantinople), and at its widest 1290km [800 miles] from north to south (the distance between London and

Wandering Tibetan herds (women), or Drokpa of East Himalayas.   **FKW**
Kingdon Ward writes: 'Necklaces of amber or coral beads. All jewellery is of Tibetan manufacture.' This picture was probably taken on the August journey to Pasum Tso.

Madrid, or London and Trieste). But here again our conception is out of focus, since we must *march* from London to Moscow before we can compare that distance with the length of Tibet. We must go back to the Crusaders, and visualise Europe in those far-off days; for Tibet is still living in the Middle Ages. This we may say at least: that the western peninsula of Europe, from Gibraltar to the Rhine, including all Spain and Portugal, France, Switzerland, and Northern Italy, would fit into Tibet quite comfortably and still leave room over for Britain.

So much for one comparison; and Tibet seems huge indeed. Yet Tibet is but a small part of Asia. It is barely as large as India. It could be dumped down in the middle of Australia, and leave a margin of land all round which would include practically the entire population of Australia; while Brazil could swallow it whole. But the area of Tibet, in whatever terms we express it, conveys no idea of the country itself; indeed, it conveys but an inadequate idea even of its size. For what of the folded mountain chains which pucker, and the river gorges which score, its tortured surface? Much of the country is twisted and furrowed and corrugated to such an extent that the superficial area must be far greater than what can be measured. We cannot estimate it; we must be satisfied to say that it is so.

And this immense country has a population little larger than that of London to-day or of England during the sixteenth century! The population of the largest cities does not approach that of a modern London borough. True, the population is not equally distributed over the country, any more than it is in Britain. About 250,000 square miles – an area roughly twice the size of Great Britain – is uninhabited and uninhabitable. Imagine Great Britain uninhabited, and imagine a man walking from Land's End to John-o'-Groats and back, and you get some idea of what it means in distance to cross Tibet; the conditions are quite another matter. An area the size of another couple of Great Britains is inhabited by the Gypsy population of Tibet, the nomad herds, or Drokpa as they are called; leaving only half the country for settled population. Even so, and admitting a population of 5,000,000 for the rest of the country, we get on the average ten persons, or two households, per square mile. Naturally, a good number of square miles have to get along without their human allowance; and in all parts of Tibet – particularly in the gorge country – it is possible, nay easy, and in fact usual, to travel for several days without seeing a house. And yet we are dull enough to tell each other when we meet by chance in Piccadilly that the world is small! It is our own minds which are small.

Not only is there not a single mile of railway in all that vast region; but to east and north at any rate there is no railway within 805km [500 miles] of the Tibetan border. It is only in the south and west that the Indian railways, following the foot of the Himalaya, approach within 242km [150 miles] of Tibet. But an idea of their distance from it may be better conveyed by reference to the vertical than to the horizontal; for the loftiest of these railways ends 2400m [8,000ft.] below the level of the Tibetan Plateau.

Small wonder, then, that Tibet has captured the imagination of mankind. Its peculiar aloofness, its remote unruffled calm, and the mystery shrouding its great rivers and mountains, make an irresistible appeal to the explorer. There are large areas of Tibet where the foot of no white man has ever trod; mountains, lakes, rivers, monasteries, which he has never seen. But above all, in the most inaccessible and sundered corner, are the bowers and forests, so alien to Tibet. But Tibet is far better known to-day than it was twenty years ago; and though if we were to ask the average educated man to give a short description of Tibet he might reply: 'Tibet is a hilly country with few folk in it, called "lamas,"' yet every intelligent schoolboy has heard of the Tibetan Plateau, possibly even of the Tibetan lakes; and knows too that Everest is in Tibet. Still, every traveller to Tibet has not been to Everest, or even seen it, any more than he has necessarily been to Lhasa. They are not synonymous terms. It is possible to live a year in Europe without either climbing Mont Blanc or visiting Moscow.

Tibet, then, is a 'hilly country,' or more correctly a plateau, elevated from 4300-4900m [14,000-16,000ft.] above sea-level, lower where rivers have scooped out the surface, higher where the crust is buckled into mountain ranges. Four-fifths of the country would answer more or less to that description. But there are, as it were, two Tibets. There is this plateau country including the lake region, called the Chang Tang, and the upper courses of the great Tibetan rivers, where they flow eastwards or south-eastwards in comparatively wide shallow valleys; and there is the little known and far more formidable gorge country comprising the middle courses of these rivers, where, having dug themselves in, they change direction to the south and force the barrier ranges to flow down to the plains of India and China. It is of this latter region that I shall tell – a country of dim forest and fragrant meadow, of snow-capped mountains and alpine slopes sparkling with flowers, of crawling glaciers and mountain lakes and brawling rivers which crash and roar through the mountain gorges; and, where men dwell, of lonely monasteries plastered like swallows' nests against the cliffs, and of frowning forts perched upon rocky steeples, whence they look down on villages clustered in the cultivated valleys at their feet. Such is the other Tibet, a land unknown to the outside world, yet presently to be known by some of the most wonderful flowers ever brought out of the cold heart of Asia. Small as the river gorge country is, compared with the whole area of Tibet, it nevertheless covers some 200,000 square miles, an area equal to that of France and Switzerland combined; and no country in the world is so deeply rent by rivers, so rugged with great mountain ranges, so bristling with high peaks. But of this 200,000 square miles, no more than a tenth is covered with forest.

The geography of the Tibetan Plateau

Tibet, then, must be visualised as a pear-shaped plateau, hoisted from 4300-4900m [14,000-16,000ft.] above sea-level; the narrow end pointing westwards where it adjoins Kashmir and the Pamirs, the broad end abutting on China. The plateau is furrowed with parallel east-and-west troughs, separated by ranges of mountains, and is further ringed about with two great ranges of mountains which, diverging from the Pamir node, stretch eastwards, supporting the plateau between them; that to the north being the Kuen Lun, that to the south, the Himalaya.

At its eastern end, the Himalayan range, after sagging down to lower levels, turns north-eastwards and suddenly rises up in the great spire of Namcha Barwa, which is sliced off abruptly on the east side, forming a gable end overlooking the Plain of Assam. Here the Himalayan range appears to end abruptly. The eastern barrier between Tibet and China is formed by a series of parallel mountain ranges which cut right across those we have described, trending not east and west, but north and south. Beyond them, somewhere in that terrible tangle of mountains which men call the Marches of Tibet, the Himalayan range perhaps emerges, and is continued.

Now if the Himalayan axis were prolonged eastwards without a break towards the Pacific it would sharply separate a rain forest region to the south from a semi-desert region to the north, isolated from the rain-bearing winds which blow up from the Indian Ocean, and watered precariously by the little rain which can find its way over that barrier. But, as we have seen, it is not. But though the moist winds cannot cross the great ranges without being robbed of their moisture, there is still a way through. For note this. Connected with, and separated by the parallel mountain chains just referred to, are several big rivers which, rising in the cold heart of Tibet, set out complacently enough eastwards across Asia. Their sources are hundreds of miles apart and their mouths open on different seas. But all must first escape from the plateau, and all escape through one narrow gateway, which is a breach in the Himalayan axis – the Achilles' heel in that otherwise impenetrable mountain defence which rings Tibet like a wall. Here they are caught and squeezed between two of the mightiest uplifts in the world. The width of this gap, from the dislocated end of the Himalaya, where the Namcha Barwa gable overlooks Assam, to the eastern foot of the Yunnan Plateau, is some 320km [200 miles].

In the extreme east flows the Yangtze and its three tributaries, which together make up the 'four streams' whence the province of Szechuan derives its name. In the west, right under the eaves of the Himalayan gable, is the Brahmaputra, or Tsangpo as it is called in Tibet. Between the Tsangpo and the Yangtze, but closer to the latter, are three other rivers, the Mekong, Salween, and Irrawaddy. A span of 120km [75 miles] covers these last four rivers where they force the mountains.

The consequences of this gap are twofold. It lets out the rivers from Tibet to India and China; it admits the monsoon rains from India into Tibet. The south-west monsoon blowing overland from the Indian Ocean beats against the southern face of the Great Himalayan Range and drops its burden of moisture. It drenches the slopes which face India, and passing on over the line of high peaks, is quickly wrung dry. Consequently, while the southern slopes of the Himalaya are scored with valleys filled with dense forest, the country behind the fighting line is semi-desert. This is the Plateau of Tibet. It is not the cold, but the long period of drought, the scanty summer rainfall, and above all, the dry wind, which is so hostile to plant life.

But the monsoon, though it cannot cross this obstacle without relieving itself of its burden, is quick to find the breach; and striding over the Burma–Assam plain, towards the narrowing mouth of this funnel, forms a bore, which, pushed on from behind and sucked up from in front, rushes furiously through the river gorges. Thus it drenches the country in the neighbourhood of the breach, and the whole of this comparatively narrow gap is jammed with forest, which spreads out fanwise behind the Himalaya and then quickly disappears. But the most of the rain clings close to the Himalaya, rushing up the Tsangpo; for the Himalayan Range is lower here with a vast outwork of foothills, till it suddenly rears up in the mighty peak of Namcha Barwa, standing sentinel over the western side of the breach. As you go eastwards, the fury of the monsoon bore abates, until by the time the Mekong is reached, it has already spent itself.

Tibet then, above the 322km [200 mile] breach, for a depth from north to south of 160km [100 miles] or so, has a very heavy rainfall in summer, and a heavy snowfall in winter. The mountain slopes are covered with dense forest, and above the tree-line, where the snow lies till late in summer, are alps sparkling with flowers for three months in the year.

The lure of Tibet for the traveller

It would appear at first sight that the easiest way into this country behind the wall of the Himalaya would be through the breach, following the river corridors we have described; since it might seem easier to pass through a mountain range than to climb over it. But it is not so. The gorges are deep and narrow, filled with forest, and the rivers quite unnavigable. Moreover, the river gorges are separated from one another by knife-edge ranges. Not till we get far to the east, to the Mekong or the Yangtze, beyond reach of the monsoon, is it profitable, or even possible, to pass through the breach up on to the plateau. But then, to reach the Mekong corridor from the plains, it is first necessary to cross the rain screen and ascend to the Plateau of Yunnan. No, the easiest way to reach the forest lands behind the Himalaya is to cross the barrier ranges east or west of the river gap – in military language, to turn the gap. Having done this one can approach the corridors where they come down from the dry plateau, before the rivers have dug themselves in.

There is another consideration, and that the most important of all. In the dark wet jungles which clothe the southern slopes of the Himalaya and fill the gorges, there is no transport and no food. Villages are few and far between, there are no bridges over the rivers, and no roads, only rough tracks. There is no transport because there is no grazing; there is no food because there is no cultivation – man cannot grapple with the all-devouring jungle; and there is no population because there is no food. It may easily be imagined, therefore, how difficult travel in such a country, with coolie transport, becomes. North of the rain screen, however, on the dry plateau, there is only thin Conifer forest, or none at all. Here are roads, villages, grazing, ample cultivation, and herds of animals. In Western China, on the Yunnan Plateau, mules are used for pack transport; in Tibet, ponies and yak.

I have on previous occasions, entering China from Burma and travelling north-eastwards over the Yunnan Plateau, turned the river gap to the east, crossed the great rain-screen, and reached the forest from that side. But the way is long and arduous, and the great gorge of the Tsangpo, our ultimate goal, so remote and inaccessible, that never had I reached it, though I had penetrated all the other river gorges in the endeavour. Not till we crossed the Sikkim Himalaya, thus turning the river gap to the west, then travelling eastwards across the Tibetan Plateau, were we able to reach the western side of the gap, and see the Tsangpo as it burst round the broken end of the Assam Himalaya. My story, then, is of this journey, and of adventures amongst forest and meadows into which we descended from the bare wind-swept Plateau of Tibet. Of the plateau, which is Tibet as usually understood, I shall have little to say, though we crossed 480km [300 miles] of it to reach our goal; but of the river gorge country, much.

Yak transport crossing the Himalaya: Assam – Tibet.   **FKW**
This was probably taken somewhere on the Tibetan Plateau to the west of the Gorge. The cairn on the crest of
the pass, sometime set with *mani* stones, is kept to the right when passing.

A few words as to our object in making the journey, besides the irresistible lure of geographical discovery. We went to Tibet to collect plants in a region which was an even greater mystery from the botanist's point of view than from the geographer's. We intended to make a collection of dried plants and to collect seed of the most beautiful and suitable garden plants, and so introduce them into Britain, which is the world's temperate garden. Now a glance at the map will show that the parts of Tibet in which our explorations were conducted lie between the parallels of 28° and 30°, that is, in fairly low latitudes. Compare the latitudes of Cairo, Shanghai, California and Florida. These regions indeed lie outside the tropics, but their floras are sub-tropical, and their climates are noted for mild winters and hot summers. Very different is Britain, the extreme south of which lies 20° or some 2260km [1,400 miles] nearer the Pole.

But high altitude in some respects is equivalent to high latitude, and Southern Tibet makes up in altitude what it lacks in latitude; plants from these lofty mountain ranges, if not too close to the Equator, are often, though not necessarily, hardy in Britain, which boasts a wonderful range of climate for so small an area. The number of foreign plants quite commonly met with in this country, growing out-of-doors all the year round, would surprise those who have never given the matter a thought. Even plants which we have long since regarded as typically English – for example, the Horse-chestnut, Lilac, Laburnum, Dahlia, and Chrysanthemum, to mention a few – are aliens; and there are literally thousands more.

The climate and soil of Britain, taking it all round, is probably the most suitable in the world for temperate plants; and the temperate flora of the world is considerable. Of the total land surface of the earth, about half falls within the temperate zone, and a large proportion of the plants found there can be successfully grown in Britain. Besides these, a certain number of arctic or sub-arctic plants are hardy with us, and even a certain number which come from mountains within the tropics; since about a third of the tropical land is sufficiently high to possess a temperate climate. There is no certain guide as to whether a plant will be hardy or not in Britain; trial and error are the ultimate proofs. But experience has shown that plants from moderate latitudes and moderate elevations are hardy, and that those from extreme latitudes and extreme elevations are not. Thus, ruling out the tropics, high or low, and the sub-tropical belt of desert and semi-desert, the Arctic and Antarctic, and their equivalents on very high mountains, we are left with enormous areas of forest, meadow and alpine lands in the Eurasian and American continents.

It is in Tibet, however, that we find not only one of the richest mountain floras in the world, but also the largest unexplored areas; so that we looked forward with the most pleasurable anticipation to the journey, believing as we did that we should make some sensational discoveries. As to whether we did or not, I must leave it to the reader to decide, after having read the book.

Chapter II

Over the Himalaya

The journey from India to Gangtok, Sikkim

We landed in Calcutta on March 5th, 1924, just as the first heat wave of the year broke over Bengal. The thermometer stood at 32°C [90°F] in the shade, and having no desire to linger in the city of dreadful night longer than was necessary, we pushed on our preparations with all speed.

There are many eleventh-hour things to do, however, before one can start on a long journey into the heart of Asia; and when on March 9th we felt justified in leaving Calcutta, we still left behind all our stores which had not yet been cleared by the Customs. There was more work to be done in Darjeeling, in any case, so we removed our headquarters thither, feeling that it would be both less demoralising and less expensive. The train journey from Calcutta to Darjeeling takes only eighteen hours; we left Calcutta on a red-hot afternoon at 4.30 and awoke early next morning for our first sight of the Himalaya, dim in the haze. A long way behind that mighty barrier lay our ultimate goal.

At 6 o'clock in the morning we changed on to the narrow-gauge railway for the 2000m [7,000ft.] climb to Darjeeling. Arrived there we made arrangements for mule transport as far as Phari, the first town on the Tibetan Plateau, and engaged a permanent staff of three men, who knew the hills and could speak both Tibetan and Hindustani; the latter language I can speak sufficiently well. We soon re-christened our men; henceforth they were known as Tom, Dick and Sunny Jim. Tom was *sirdar,* that is, general manager, a title much coveted by mule-contractors and other doubtful scallywags; his chief, indeed his only fault was a fondness for country liquor. Dick was cook, and when Tom left us a month before we got back to India, he took over the duties of *sirdar* as well, and acquitted himself creditably. He was what is called a good general cook, and take him all round he proved invaluable. Sunny Jim was man-of-all-work. He did everything; and he did nothing right, or well. But he was a cheerful idiot, so we gladly put up with his shortcomings. Two rival mule-contractors who desired our patronage, and who called on us simultaneously in order to secure it, came to blows in the street outside our house one morning. As a result we were able to play them off one against the other, and secure a slight reduction in the high cost of transport to Tibet; but once we were in Tibet, transport proved comparatively inexpensive.

We expected to be absent from civilisation for a year, and as we had no means of knowing what facilities we should find for transport and food supplies in the interior the problem of what to take was no easy one. Tents, bedding and camp equipment with clothes, personal property, scientific instruments and collecting outfit accounted for most of our baggage; in addition all our money had to be carried in silver rupees. Of course, had we brought with us food for the whole trip, it would have run to many mule loads, and in view of the possible lack of transport and the expense, we could not risk doing this. Everything, therefore, was cut down to the minimum of reasonable comfort; but there were a number of things, such as oil stoves for our tents, which afterwards we bitterly regretted not having taken.

As for stores, we made a selection of the more indispensable things, together with a few luxuries for birthdays, festivals, chance meetings and emergencies. The foundation consisted of jam, butter, milk, Mexican chocolate, tea, cocoa, coffee, Quaker oats and soup; such things as tinned fish, army rations and bacon were provided in small quantity only. These stores were supplied by Messrs. Fortnum & Mason and packed in six Venesta cases, weighing 27kg [60lb.] each. They arrived in first-rate condition, and being pretty evenly spread over the year, with a special supply for the winter, just made the difference to our otherwise monotonous diet of curry and *chappatties*. In Tibet we reckoned on getting *tsamba* (roast barley flour), butter, milk and yak or goat meat; in the event we also got wheat flour, rice, mutton, and occasionally potatoes, peas, or turnips. The food problem therefore solved itself.

On March 14th we left Darjeeling by road for Tista Bridge away down in the tropical valley, 38km [24 miles] distant. The first 13km [8 miles] we did by motor-car, after which we had to walk and ride. The road, through miles and miles of tea gardens, is picturesque, but monotonous. Arrived at Tista Bridge we found our camp already pitched on the *maidan* outside the village, an evil spot; but the bungalow was occupied. Next day we walked over to Kalimpong Road station, to collect our heavy kit, which had been sent direct by rail from Calcutta; but found that our stores had not yet arrived. We moved the rest of our kit over to the camp by bullock cart, and our mules being ready, we started the same afternoon for Kalimpong, where we arrived at dusk during a terrific thunderstorm. Here we were the guests of Dr. Graham, of the famous Scottish Mission, for a day. There is a cart-road from railhead to Kalimpong and another to Gangtok, the capital of Sikkim, where the Political Officer lives. Tibetan caravans usually come over the Jelep La and halt at Kalimpong, 1200m [4,000ft.] above sea-level, as they do not like going down into the hot Tista Valley, where the men sicken; we however wanted to go to Gangtok to see the Political Officer, so we intended to cross into Tibet by the Nathu La, an alternative pass and a better road. It is not so much used by the Tibetans, however, because Gangtok is over 65km [40 miles] from railhead, whereas Kalimpong is only 16km [10 miles].

On the 17th, therefore, we said good-bye to Dr. Graham, who had very kindly undertaken to receive our stores and forward them to us at Phari or Gyantse; and descending once more into the Tista Valley, we crossed the Sikkim frontier at Rungpo. Here we had to show our Government passes and sign our names in a book; unauthorised persons are not allowed loose in Sikkim now, because once there, it is not difficult to cross the passes into Tibet unobserved and then everybody gets hot and worried. While at Rungpo bungalow, an unexpected visitor, Mr. G.A. Buchanan, turned up, more to our own satisfaction than his. He had just come down from Gangtok in Bailey's car which was to pick us up on its way back from the station and take us on to Gangtok. Unfortunately it had broken down and remained immovable for two days causing Buchanan to miss his train and very nearly his boat.

It is amazing how rumours fly like sparks in India. Buchanan was anxious to send Bailey a wire, telling him what had happened; and we forgathered at the Rungpo telegraph office to help him concoct a suitable message. As a succinct report which covered all the facts and would not cause the owner to be unduly despondent or alarmed, we evolved: 'Carburettor napu, chassis intact.' But before Bailey received that or something like it, he had already received two wires apparently from irresponsible *babus*. The first said: 'Car destroyed at 8th mile,' which was calculated to cause both alarm and despondency; the second said: 'Car smashed, no one hurt,' which at any rate removed all cause for alarm, but left the despondency very much where it was before. Finally, came Buchanan's wire; and it was no small relief to Bailey when two days later the car itself returned under its own steam so to speak. Meanwhile we had to ride and walk the 42km [26 miles] from Rungpo to Gangtok, most of the way under a blazing sun in the valley, though the last 13km [8 miles] through the forest, which also involved a climb of 1500m [5,000ft.], was pleasant enough.

With the Baileys and the journey to Gyantse

We reached the Residency in the evening, and were welcomed by Major and Mrs. Bailey, with whom we spent two delightful days. In 1913 Majors Bailey and Morshead had explored the gorge of the Tsangpo, and it was into the mountains round the knee-bend of that river, where it forces a passage through the Himalaya, that we wished to penetrate. At the beginning we should have to follow much of our predecessors' route, so that Bailey was able to give us valuable information and advice. He also handed to us our passport, which had been specially obtained for us from Lhasa. Thanks to the friendly relations existing between the Indian and Tibetan Governments, and to the influence of Bailey himself with the Dalai Lama, there had been no very great difficulty in obtaining this, though it was of course granted as a favour, the more so as the Tibetan Government had recently been embarrassed by the antics of certain English travellers. Apart from that we were fortunate in our choice of time, the political horizon being clear; and especially so in finding Bailey Political Officer in Sikkim. A distinguished Tibetan explorer himself, he is always willing to do anything in his power to assist other travellers, or would-be travellers, whether in the undertaking of an ambitious expedition, like the Mount Everest Expedition, or a private journey like our own. After seeing the Residency grounds, where Bailey grows a number of interesting plants, many of which he and his wife have themselves collected in Tibet, Sikkim, and Bhutan, and after paying a visit to the Maharaja of Sikkim, who speaks excellent English, we finally started for Tibet on the 21st.

For two days we rode our ponies up through the wonderland of the Sikkim forest and saw with our own eyes the glories so vividly described by Hooker in his *Himalayan Journals;* in 1849 Sikkim was to the world very much what our goal is to-day. Down below we passed by immense trees draped in moss, and supporting huge masses of the white orchid, *Cœlogyne cristata.* Still higher we met with many fine trees of the glorious *Magnolia campbellii* in full bloom; looking down on them from above, one saw as it were thousands of white water-lilies, floating on a rough green sea. Then came scarlet bunches of *Rhododendron arboreum* and under the bamboos, drifts of mauve *Primula petiolaris.* We saw this Primula from 2750-4270m [9,000-14,000ft.], and at every 300m [1,000ft.] ascent it changed in character. As we continued to climb, we noted Rhododendrons *RR. falconeri, grande, barbatum, thomsonii,* and *R. glaucophyllum [glaucum],* in that order (most of them were still asleep, their leaves rolled in tubes and pointing stiffly downwards); a few plants of *R. barbatum* were in flower; the scarlet is even more intense than that of *R. arboreum.* It is perhaps worth mentioning that we saw any number of seedling and sapling rhododendrons by the roadside, as one always does wherever a clearing is made in the forest. Several of them – notably *R. barbatum* – had the under surface of the leaf rich purple, and at an older stage the same species showed a web of hair stretched across, though the mature leaf is bristly, without any continuous coating of wool. At Changu, 3320m [12,600ft.], there is a glacier lake, which was now frozen over, and we spent a cold night at the lonely little bungalow just above the lake. There was hardly a hint of spring here as yet.

On March 23rd we crossed the Nathu La, 4420m [14,500ft.], and entered Tibet; but we were still on the southern slopes of the Himalaya. Not till February 14th, 1925, did we recross the Tibetan frontier into Bhutan. Descending into the Chumbi Valley, we met with better weather and reached Yatung on a bright sunny afternoon the following day. Here we were met by a man sent by Mr. MacDonald, the British Trade Agent, to look after us and escort us to Gyantse. Leaving Yatung, we began the sharp ascent to the Tibetan Plateau. At first the valley of the Ammo Chu was as pleasant as an English May. The steep grass slopes here glowed honey yellow in the lukewarm sunshine, there glimmered with the lilac shadow of *Primula denticulata,* and beyond were dark striped with the rifle-green of pine forest. The barberry bushes shone red like Chinese lacquer, against the turquoise blue sky, and the silver puss tails of the willows glistened at the tips of half-fledged twigs. Passing the old Chinese barracks, now destroyed, we entered the Rhododendron-Juniper forest, and bleak winter shut down on us like night; conditions changed rapidly and it was not till we reached the Tsangpo, a month later, that we saw any further signs of the approach of spring.

The narrow path now became very rocky and the clumsy mules banged our steel boxes against the cliff till their contents rattled. At Gautsa, where we spent the night, the glen was filled with rocks and Rhododendrons, chiefly *R. thomsonii, R. wightii* and *R. cinnabarinum,* all fast asleep; the last-named, however, was looking dejected, as though it had been disturbed before it was time to get up – which it had; for several bushes had poked their flowers out of the buds, and these had been almost immediately destroyed.

On March 26th we emerged from the glen on to the snow-bound plateau and saw the icy pyramid of sacred Chumolarhi, nearly 7400m [24,000ft.] high, poking its head up over a near shoulder. For the next three days we marched parallel to the base of this mountain, with superb views of it from several angles. That afternoon we reached Phari, the first town on the Tibetan Plateau, and the dirtiest and most desolate place imaginable. The *Dzongpön* called on us and stayed till we were quite tired of him; apparently he did not like us very much, for he promised to take delivery of our stores as soon as they arrived from Kalimpong, and send them straight on to Gyantse, but failed to keep his promise. In fact our stores arrived at Phari next day, soon after we left, and as we made only short stages, they might easily have overtaken us on the second or third day out of Phari; but we had to wait a week in Gyantse for them.

We were warned to leave Phari early on the 27th, as we had a 30km [18 mile] march to Tuna, and the wind blows with great violence across the plateau in the afternoon. We did not, however, start very early, and after crossing the Tang La 4600m [15,000ft.] over the main range of the Himalaya on to the plateau proper, we met the wind in force and did not enjoy the long monotonous ride to Tuna. So level is the plateau here and so clear the atmosphere that we could plainly see the tiny village about 20km [12 miles] away, and we wondered why we did not get there sooner; it seemed to get no nearer, though our ponies trotted on mile after mile.

From Tuna to Gyantse is six easy stages, descending very gradually. There are bungalows at every stage, so that however disagreeable the day's march, we were sure of a comfortable night, with a good fire of yak dung and hot soup or tea on arrival. The interpreter kindly sent to our aid by Mr. MacDonald would ride ahead and have everything ready for us, including transport for the next day, when we arrived. We usually walked, as it was too cold to ride; for though by now winter's vicious sting had been withdrawn, the Tibetan Plateau was still very unpleasant; it was all dust and ice and a raving wind which increased in violence throughout the afternoon, to cease suddenly after sunset. Luckily it blew behind us.

How we learnt to hate those endless gravel plains with their thin tufts of herbage and scattered cushions! Everything cowered down behind the stones, or snuggled up tightly to keep out of the ruthless wind. Indeed, crossing the plateau at this season, one might believe that it was a desert, completely devoid of plant life, which only became visible on closer inspection. But during the brief summer, when rain falls for two or three months, and the wind drops, it is astonishing the number of plants which revive. Above 4250m [14,000ft.] there are probably over 250 species of flowering plants to be found hereabouts, some of them, such as the prickly blue poppy (*Meconopsis horridula*), very beautiful. But plants from this sub-arctic region are useless of introduction into Britain; they soon perish in our stuffy atmosphere and damp climate.

Nor were these shrivelled and trembling vegetable carcasses the only indications of life on the plateau; there was actual as well as potential life. On the blue lakes, along whose ice-bound shores we marched for hours, were thousands of birds – bar-headed geese, Brahminy duck, teal, gulls, and others. Tiny picahares scampered in and out of their burrows, which in places honeycomb the ground for miles; and we saw also several common hares. Once a herd of ten *kyang* – the wild ass of Tibet – approached to within a hundred yards of our caravan, and we also saw several graceful gazelle. In a couple of days we had sufficiently accustomed ourselves to the conditions to enjoy the day's march; but the morning start was always a compromise between our desire not to start before the sun was up and our desire to reach our destination before the wind became unbearable. When the sun shone, it was thoroughly enjoyable. Raw and monotonous as the landscape is, these wide, open empty spaces with the thin keen air rushing over them, and the crude generous colouring of earth and sky, beckon man on and on, to investigate and explore and enjoy.

In ages past, great changes have taken place here, and one can clearly trace the effects of a climate which has been gradually growing drier and drier. Lakes have retreated, or

Gobshi, near Gyantse.
FKW

disappeared altogether; glaciers have shrunk back; rivers have dwindled to streams; and
out of the material left high and dry by this general desiccation, wind and frost have
carved new features.

So we marched over the white clay bottoms of ancient lake beds and through dry
glens worn by rivers which had long ceased to flow and beneath great gravel terraces
which marked former water levels, descending gradually, till we came to a long valley;
and this we followed for several days, till clumps of trees appeared again, and houses and
cultivation and huge flocks of sheep and goats grazing.

Here in a grassy bog, where water oozed and remained unfrozen, what should we find
but a tiny rose-eyed Primula starring the dun-coloured hummocks, and gazing up at the
blue dome of heaven as though summer had come again and it had not a care in the
world. *Primula pumilio [P. pygmœorum]* – of the pygmies – is its name and we often saw
pink constellations of this bright little plant during the next fortnight on the plateau.

Gyantse to Tsetang

On April 2nd we reached the wide cultivated plain on which stands the famous city of Gyantse, 4100m [13,500ft.] above sea-level; and being met by more of the Trade Agent's servants, we were led in state to our quarters at the bungalow. We now made the acquaintance of the European population, six in number, including Mr. MacDonald, the British Trade Agent; Major Hyslop, the medical officer; Captain Cobbett, in command of the Agency guard, and Mr. F. Ludlow, in charge of the new Tibetan school. Gyantse stands about half-way between the Indian frontier and Lhasa, being 224km [140 miles] distant from the Holy City by road. It is connected with Lhasa and with India by telegraph, and a postal service is maintained with Lhasa by the Tibetan Government, and with Calcutta by the Indian Government; runners carry the mails to Lhasa and mules carry them to India.

We had to wait a week in Gyantse for our stores, but were by no means idle. Apart from an International Association Football Match between Tibet (represented by Ludlow's School, with such exotic assistance as was afforded by Cawdor, the telegraph babu, and the hospital compounder) and India (represented by Cobbett and his detachment), we played polo during the week (fancy polo at 4100m [13,500ft.]!), and I found time to make an expedition to a neighbouring glen to examine the flora. This is more extensive and varied than might be supposed. There are plenty of trees, chiefly poplar and willow, along the irrigation channels on the plain; away from this water supply, there are only dwarf bushes of *Sophora davidii [viciifolia]* and a few other woody plants such as *Potentilla fruticosa, Rosa sericea,* Hippophae, Caragana, Berberis, and Clematis. But away up in the narrow glens which scar the faces of the low rounded hills are many plants such as Meconopsis, Incarvillea, Gentiana, Aconitum, Didissandra and other alpines; while Irises and a coloured 'Sikkimensis' Primula (*P. waltonii* K.W. 8430) fringe the ditches below, flowering in the summer when the whole plain is green with crops.

I need not describe the town of Gyantse, as it has been done several times before; but we visited the Tibetan trade agent and the bazaar, and the temple, and paid a visit to the great fort, or *dzong,* which was captured by a handful of resolute Gurkhas, led by a young British Officer, when the British Mission was besieged at Gyantse in 1904.

On April 11th, our stores having arrived, we resumed our journey, still following the main road to Lhasa; our friends came to see us off, and it was over ten months before we saw another white man. Two long marches up a very desolate valley brought us to the foot of the Trans-Himalayan, or so-called Ladak Range, which we crossed on April 13th by the Karo La, a pass 4960m [16,200ft.] high. There are no more comfortable bungalows after Gyantse, and our quarters were generally dark hovels, filled with the acrid smoke of a yak-dung fire, and grimy with generations of dirt, accumulated as a protection against the cold. Dour as was the climate, however, we often heard larks singing overhead, and saw rock pigeons, magpies, crows and even hoopoes; partridges too were common, and occasionally we caught sight of wild sheep or *bharal*, as it is called in India.

Descending from the icy passes, we came down to the beautiful Yamdrok Lake, a jigsaw puzzle of sapphire water and honey-coloured rock. At this point we left the Lhasa road and bore due eastwards, skirting the very irregular southern shore of the lake. We were now off the map. As a matter of fact the southern shore of the lake had been surveyed by Captain H.R. Meade in the previous year during a journey he had made through Bhutan and Tibet with Major Bailey; but Meade's map had not yet been published. All this region is very barren, which is not surprising when it is remembered that the lake itself is 4350m [14,350ft.] above sea-level, while the surrounding mountains rise considerably higher.

For three days we marched along the southern shores of the lake, up hill and down dale, with gorgeous views of the sparkling water and the clouds frothing over the snow-crested mountains beyond. There was a certain amount of stunted Juniper on the slopes here and we saw plenty of duck and numerous gazelle. All the wild animals in Tibet, birds as well as beasts, are ridiculously tame, since no one ever molests them. To equalise matters all the tame animals, such as dogs, ponies, and oxen, are wild. In every sheltered bay

Tsetang, on the Tsangpo, looking East.   FKW

nestled a village, guarded by a fort crowning the hill above. Here and there we saw a monastery. Travelling was still unpleasant, because of the bitter wind, and the frequent storms of rain and snow; and in this more populated country we had to change our transport several times each day, which delayed and irritated us. The Yamdrok Lake has withdrawn many of its advanced arms, so that we marched over dry clay bottoms, which in summer are green with grass, though now they formed a hard bare crust. At one stage we rode along the shore of another lake which had been cut off altogether from the main body of the Yamdrok: and isolated. It was snowing and the waves washed mournfully up against the gravel beach. Crossing a ridge, we came down to the big lake again.

On April 17th we reached a village at the south-east corner of the Yamdrok Tso, where a stream flows in through a wide grassy valley. There was more vegetation here than one would ever have expected; grazing for thousands of stock, and on the low hills, crouching juniper bushes, dotted amongst the pale stones like currants in a cake. Hundreds of fat hares lolloped from rock to rock, and herds of yak, sheep and goats nibbled at the brown herbage. We did a long march up this valley on the 18th past several villages, into a bleak rolling country of cheerless bogs. It was dark and snowing when at last we reached Tratsa, a stone village clapped against the side of a stonier hill; our draughty room was filled with the sullen heat and acid smoke of smouldering yak dung, and a film of fine ash covered everything. Looking out after supper we saw the moon shining wanly over a wild and desolate scene, which held out no good prospects for the morrow. However, we started for the pass in fine weather, but long before we reached the summit, called Shamda La, it was snowing hard. Our mixed transport of yak, donkeys, and bullocks advanced slowly in mass formation, the ponies skirmishing round the flanks and keeping them together; the ground was very rough, and it took us several hours to reach the top, where we lost our way in the deep snow. But in the afternoon it cleared up and we descended into a stony cultivated valley which looked to us well wooded, though there were really only a few clumps of trees, including a colony of magnificent old poplars just outside a monastery. At this place, called Chongyechen, we stayed the night and awoke next morning to a short-lived paradise. For two hours we marched down the valley where sparkling streams flowed through green pastures, and birds sang in groves of budding trees; whitewashed houses loomed through a pink mist of almond blossom, and in the fields which floored the wide valley piebald yak pulled wooden ploughs.

'If this is the real Tibet,' I thought, 'what a maligned country it is! Could anything be more charming and peaceful, more full of spring grace and freshness!' Alas! It was but a dream! As we descended, valley and hills grew more and more barren. The streams, sick of trying to keep open a way through the wilderness of gravel belched from the bare hills, sought refuge underground. Cultivation ceased, trees disappeared, and once more plateau conditions were re-established; though as we were still over 3700m [12,000ft.] above sea-level that was not altogether surprising.

Turning the corner of a rocky spur, a great white city came suddenly into view, or so it appeared. It was the monastery of Riudechen, whose villa residences stretched, terrace on terrace, up the hillside; high aloft, crowning the crag, stood a fine old fort, like a Spanish galleon, called Chongyeshö. A stone pillar, with Chinese characters carved on it, stood out in the middle of the gravel plain, and beyond was a Chinese arched stone bridge spanning the river which, however, no longer reached the surface.

After that the valley opened out more and more widely and at the little monastery and village of Chongmoche, where Chortens clustered like Burmese pagodas, trees and cultivation reappeared. Hedges of fragrant *Buddleia* were in bloom – this species often forms small gnarled trees about the size of a hawthorn, and in places were clumps of *Ulmus pumila,* which is by no means a dwarf. At the lower end of the valley, where it opens into the wide Tsangpo Valley, the stream reappeared at the surface and once more we reached green fields; the trees too – willows and poplars – were flushed with green, their varnished yellow and red twigs making a bright display. Beneath them, pale irises were in flower.

It was the evening of April 21st when we reached Netong Dzong, a large village at the mouth of the valley. Here we called on the *Dzongpön,* a friendly capable person in a purple gown and horn-rimmed spectacles, who sent the yak drivers hopping when they grumbled at having to go as far as Tsetang; though customary, it would have been foolish to change transport at Netong, which is barely a mile from Tsetang. So on we went, and turning the corner, saw Tsetang, with its rows of chortens, its monasteries, and houses spread out on a wide terrace above the Tsangpo, with the bare hills all round and clumps of trees in the foreground; though these were quite lost in the immensity of the dead valley.

Atta Ulla Khan, a Ladaki merchant trading in Tsetang, found poor quarters for us in the dirty town where we decided to halt for a day, and look round. We had now almost left the plateau behind us (though the Tsangpo is flowing at an altitude of 3500m [11,500ft.]), and were entering upon the second of the three plant regions into which we may divide Tibet.

The characteristic flora of the plateau has been referred to. Ordinarily there are no woody plants whatever, but there are plenty of alpine flowers belonging to the genera *Androsace, Primula, Meconopsis, Aconitum, Ephedra, Campanula,* etc. Trees and shrubs are found only under exceptional circumstances, and then there is very little variety. Drought is the deciding factor – there is a small summer rainfall, but most of the year the soil is too cold for the roots to function. Next to drought comes wind as a factor; and after that possibly the amount of salt in the soil.

We were now entering regions with a more temperate climate; and though at this altitude the wind still blows, especially in winter, as we travelled eastwards, where the summer rainfall is much heavier, we gradually got into forest country. The temperate forest region is approached through a country with few trees, but fairly rich in shrubs, with many flowering herbs. Of this I shall speak in the next chapter.

While at Tsetang I picked up by the roadside some sprigs of an aromatic-leafed Rhododendron (*R. primuliflorum*), the first I had seen since we left the Chumbi Valley. I was told that the plant grew two or three days' journey distant, and bundles of it were brought in to supply the city censers. Juniper is used for the same purpose, namely the creation of the densest smoke and most pungent smell with the least possible fire. Tsetang is situated on the right bank of the Tsangpo, at an altitude of 3610m [11,850ft.]. It lies almost exactly 80km [50 miles] due south-east of Lhasa, which is reached in four days; but our road lay eastwards, and we had no intention of visiting the holy city.

Rosa sericea **near Tsetang.**   **PC**

The commonest rose species in south-east Tibet and with a huge distribution in north India, Nepal, Burma and China. It is identified by the four- (occasionally five-) petalled flower. All other roses have five petals. Very variable: numerous species have been made synonymous. As with many plant species, this region of Tibet is where Chinese and Himalayan floras meet. Plants occur which match typical *R. sericea* (Himalayan) as well as some closer to var. *omeiensis* (Chinese) – distinguished by the more numerous leaflets and a fleshy fruit stalk. Very adaptable to dry and poor soils, it is a feature of roadsides in many south-east Tibetan valleys. The flowers are used medicinally and the fruits are edible.

Sophora davidii **near Tsetang. PC**

In recent taxonomic re-organisation, *S. davidii* has taken precedence over the more commonly used names *S. viciifolia* and *S. moorcroftiana*. Both blue and white forms occur, blue being more common in south-east Tibet. This member of the legume family is a very tough and adaptable plant occurring in very barren soils, even pure sand, and is often the only woody plant found in such conditions. It could be considered the gorse of the Himalaya.

CHAPTER III

Tsangpo, the Mysterious River

Tsetang to the Lung La

We left Tsetang on April 23rd. It had snowed in the night, but the snow was now melting, and the streets were ankle-deep in slush. Before we started, our Ladaki friend offered to change a hundred-rupee note for Tibetan small change. Having poured out from a leather bag a mixture of coins, including Chinese rupees and dollars, Tibetan *trangkas,* and copper *sho,* he did sums in his head, and then began to count out *trangkas* and *sho* to the value of a hundred Indian rupees or thereabouts; a work which took half an hour. When everything was completed, however, he noticed some Chinese characters on the note – for Indian notes always have their value inscribed in several languages – and refused to take it! The newer notes have omitted the Chinese script, and he, poor man, came to the conclusion that ours was obsolete, if not a forgery!

Leaving the town, we soon reached the river bank, where we saw the remains of a chain bridge, long since washed away, and now replaced by a ferry. The river bed here is about half a mile wide, but above Tsetang it expands to between 3-5km [2-3 miles]. Imagine, therefore, the long wide corridor of the Tsangpo, with the river mooning sluggishly along between harsh barren mountains at an altitude of 3400m [11,000ft.] and the wind roaring over the sandbanks, clogging the air with grit. As yet there is not the slightest hint of the enormous change which is to transform the river; it just flows placidly on in this wide shallow trough of the plateau, and might, as far as one can see, so continue for many hundreds of miles, even into China. All the more startling, therefore, is the abrupt change which takes place 240km [150 miles] east of Tsetang. For the first few miles the going was good, though rough. In the evening we reached Rongchakar, at the mouth of the Lhagyari River, which flows in from the south. There is a fine fortress here. At this point the main road leaves the Tsangpo, which breaks through a gorge, and follows up the stream to Lhagyari Dzong; then crossing a high pass, the Putrang La, it rejoins the Tsangpo again some 48km [30 miles] below Rongchakar. We, however, continued by the river-side as far as Trap, a village situated within the jaws of the gorge, in order to see whether at this season of low water we could get through all the way. At Trap we were told that there had once been a path on the right bank, but that it had been destroyed by an earthquake some years ago. On the left bank there was a difficult path high up on the cliffs, impassable for ponies. We were left, therefore, with two alternatives – a road from Trap to Lhagyari, and over the Putrang La, on the right bank; or a road via Oga Dzong and the Lung La on the left bank. The former was Bailey and Morshead's route of 1913, the latter was unexplored; we therefore decided to follow it, and crossed the river at Trap by coracle, an operation which took some time as the coracle will only carry four men in safety. Luckily we had a fleet of five coracles, complete with crews. Having crossed over to the left bank, we ascended a branch valley, crossed a spur, and dropped down into the valley of the Oga Chu, which enters the Tsangpo just above Trap. Meanwhile a change was coming over the vegetation. We had now left the plateau with its sub-arctic flora behind, and had entered on a dry-temperate region, in which shrub growth was a normal feature and even trees could exist. With the reappearance of woody plants, there is naturally a considerable increase in the herbaceous flora, though little was in flower.

In the Tsangpo Valley itself the first thing that caught my eye away up on a steep sandy slope was the amber glow of gorse, which turned out on closer inspection to be a species of Caragana, though it bore an extraordinary resemblance to gorse. In the villages were crab trees, walnut and peach, with hedges of Buddleia, and even clumps of bamboo. The rocky terraces were often covered with a thick scrub of *Potentilla fruticosa, Sophora davidii [viciifolia]*, Hippophae, Ceratostigma, Cotoneaster and Rose, with an occasional copse of birch, poplar and willow entangling ropes of a small flowered form of *Clematis montana (C. gracilifolia)*; and the ditches were filled with Sikkimensis Primula, which might have been *P. waltonii*. Characteristic plants of the rocky slope were an Incarvillea, growing 90cm [3ft.] high (*I. longiracemosa*), a robust Androsace and a thistle-like Morina, none of these being in flower; and in a bog I noticed *Primula tibetica*. Continuing up the Oga Chu we reached Oga Dzong on the 26th, and turned east again, up a wide level grazing valley, to the village of Pechen, where we halted for the night.

We usually marched from 10 till 4, with an hour's halt for lunch, which cost us fourpence, viz.: four eggs (casualties replaced), a penny; milk, a penny; firewood and unlimited assistance from a host of willing helpers, twopence. If it was fine we sat out in the open, beneath a tree; if wet, we sought shelter in a house. On the following day, however, we had to march about 40km [25 miles] and cross the Lung La, which is over 4880m [16,000ft.]; so we rose at 4.30 and got the slow-moving yak transport with the heavy baggage off at 5.30, we ourselves following an hour later.

It was a glorious morning, not a cloud in the sky, the sunshine sparkling on the frost. Immediately we entered a narrow glen, and for the first time saw Rhododendrons growing in Tibet, together with

Coracles on Yarlung Tsangpo.   FKW
A scene on the Yarlung Tsangpo River, below Tsetang, many miles above the Gorge. The expedition ferried across the river to the left bank and followed an unexplored route to the east. Coracles, much like these, are still occasionally used to ferry passengers, belongings, and animals across the quieter stretches of the river. They are made of yak hide stretched over a willow frame and rowed with oars.

many other shrubs. *Primula atrodentata,* which closely resembles the familiar mauve *P. denticulata,* was in flower on the turf. In the afternoon we halted at a herd's tent for tea before crossing the pass. The weather had changed and it was snowing hard. The ascent was easy, except for the last few hundred feet, where we sank knee-deep in the snow. The Lung La is a saddle between two high snow peaks. The valley head is filled with the remains of a glacier, the end of which had been truncated, and the face showed a regular alternation of blue ice with cream-coloured bands of dirty snow. Towards dusk we started down a steep boulder-strewn valley, and soon got out of the deep snow. There was quite a rich alpine flora here, with several species of Meconopsis and Primula, easily recognised by their dry fruits. Presently it began to snow again, and darkness coming on, we could not see where we were going. Being far ahead of the transport, there was nothing for it but to sit still on our ponies and leave them to find the way, which they did. Meanwhile, we had resigned ourselves to a night out, when suddenly we heard a shout, a wall loomed up ahead of us, and through the driving snow we perceived a man holding aloft a torch. Next minute we were being conducted inside the monastery of Chökorchye. Buttered tea by a charcoal fire soon restored the circulation, but the transport did not arrive for another hour. Chökorchye is a solitary monastery in a high alpine valley, many miles from the nearest village; not far away is a sacred lake in which the meritorious see visions.

Next day we descended the valley into wooded country, where the Rhododendron bushes were almost ready to flower. There were green lawns also, here strewn with the golden buttons of celandine, there flushed with rosy stars of *Primula pumilio* [*P. pygmœorum*], or violet and mauve with mats of *P. atrodentata*. In the afternoon we reached

Incarvillea longiracemosa **near Nang Dzong.**   **KNEC**
Recently described as a species in its own right, this spectacular plant, a
close relative of *I. lutea,* is found in the fairly dry valleys south of the Yarlung
Tsangpo. The flowers open yellow and as they start to age turn a rich red,
giving an unusual contrast. The plant takes several years to flower, after
which it dies. We managed to introduce this in 1998 but it is likely to prove
difficult to cultivate.

Morina coulteriana **at the Gyamda Chu/Yarlung Tsangpo
confluence.**   **KNEC**
The genus *Morina* is placed either in the Scabious family Dipsacaceae or in
its own family Morinaceae. The Tibetan forms have white rather than
yellow flowers but seem closer to *M. coulteriana* than the closely related *M.
longifolia.* This plant is quite common on the rocky banks and meadows on
both sides of the Yarlung Tsangpo from Miling to Gyala.

the wretched village of Tsegyu, where two hours were wasted effecting a change of transport. It was dark long before we reached Gyatsa Dzong, on the Tsangpo. Approaching the river through a narrow glen, darkness found us treading warily on a narrow ledge, high above the thundering torrent. It was rather nerve-racking, on the brink of the abyss in complete darkness, not knowing where the path went, and hoping that every turn of the glen would bring us to cultivation. But we went on and on, without coming to any sign of a village, though we passed groups of Tibetans sleeping in caves, with cheerful fires burning; however, luckily, it was quite warm compared with the previous evening. At last the glen opened out, and we reached Gyatsa at 10.30, though it was long after midnight when the transport stumbled in. By that time we were fast asleep on the floor, wrapped in our coats with our saddles for pillows, and so we remained till daylight. The maps show Chökorchye and Tsegyu on different streams, but there is only one stream rising from the Lung La on this side; it enters the Tsangpo at Gyatsa, some miles below the point where the main track on the right bank leaves the river to cross the Putrang La.

Primula atrodentata **on the Sirchem La.**   **AC**
A very common species in the Tsangpo Gorges region, this is essentially a
small version of the well-known drum-stick primula *P. denticulata.* Individual
plants are rather insignificant but a mass of them on a bank in the wild is
quite showy. In cultivation, but not a popular garden plant due to the rather
small flowers. This is a particularly fine example.

Sorbus rehderiana.   **KR**
Sorbus pose numerous taxonomic headaches. There are several taxa in
south-east Tibet which Keith Rushforth and Hugh McAllister consider are
best referable to *Sorbus rehderiana* complex. This picture was taken on the
Potrang La.

The summit of the Putrang La looking north-east. **KNEC**

The road from Tsetang east along the south bank of the Yarlung Tsangpo is forced to leave the river and to cross this pass. As Morshead and Bailey used this route in 1913, Kingdon Ward instead opted to row across the river by coracle and cross the Lung La, another pass further north. The Putrang La is approximately 4600m (15,000ft.) and boasts an array of alpine plants such as *Chionocharis hookeri* growing on the windswept summit.

Cupressus gigantea. **KNEC**

This striking tree is endemic to the Tsangpo valley, though curiously Ward does not comment on it in his book. It grows considerably larger than these specimens which look as if they have been planted in neat rows along the river bank, but are on a naturally occurring line marking the river's high water level. The tree was introduced by Ludlow, Sherriff and Elliot and there is a 10m+ (33ft.+) specimen at Kew, in London.

For the next three days we took things easily. The path was rough, and the valley barren, stark cliffs, seamed with gravel chutes, rising above a wilderness of sand-dunes; but the terraces were dotted with a thin, hungry ashen-grey thorn scrub, which manages to survive the fury of the wind and the long drought till the grudging summer rain comes. The river twists and turns sharply, but still moons along lazily between sandbanks down the echoing rock corridor.

But a change was already beginning like the long-drawn-out change of a late English spring. Villages embowered in trees become more frequent, little oases in the brazen desert; here and there a monastery hangs like a swallow's nest beneath the eaves of a cliff. Now a vague green flocculence is visible amongst the brown twigs of the trees, and along the village hedgerows a white foam of apple blossom tossed up by the wind is streaked with the gold of barberry. There are even a few flowers by the wayside, and everywhere are birds – rose-finches and larks, babblers under the bushes, red-legged choughs, hoopoes, and black and white magpies. Our transport mooned along too, with half a score of women and girls carrying boxes and bundles which could not be piled on the kicking ponies or the sleepy oxen. The women are short and sturdy, and are accustomed to smearing black varnish over their faces.

Along the Tsangpo to Tsela Dzong

On April 30th we reached a village called Trungsashö, which is the birthplace of the present Dalai Lama. The house in which he was born has been pulled down, and a temple built over the site. We were asked if we would like to see the Dalai Lama's sister, and met her taking the ponies to water! She was just a simple country wench, with a rather pronounced goitre, living on in the old village, completely unaffected by the knowledge that her brother was the ruler of all Tibet, and venerated as a god by millions outside the country. Had she lived in a democratic age, it is certain she would not have remained so reconciled to oblivion.

Next day we arrived opposite Nang Dzong, which caps a sugar-loaf peak of tilted schist on the right bank, and crossed the river, here less than 90m [a hundred yards] wide, for the second time. At this point it enters another gorge, whose cliffs are dotted with big Junipers. A slight detour is therefore necessary, and on the following day we crossed a ridge of limestone – the first limestone outcrop seen – behind Nang Dzong, returning to the river the second day.

From Nang Dzong we marched a few miles up a glen, where the stream was lined with bushes of Box, whose scarlet and orange leaves were very striking. Turning up the steep flank of the spur we presently entered a forest of poplar, willow and birch, and found our first Rhododendron in flower; it was *R. phaeochrysum*, already met with, bearing trusses of pale pink flowers. Higher up we came to larches, and crossing the Kongbo Nga La 4500m [14,750ft.] we found the alpine slopes covered with dwarf *Rhododendron nivale* and *R. primuliflorum*. It was snowing and we could not see far from the top, but we soon got down into forests of larch and fir above, with juniper and pine below, and halted at a solitary house. Some of the cattle transport failed to do the journey, but they turned up next day.

When we reached the Tsangpo again we seemed to be in a new world. A great transformation had taken place, for the valley was green with crops, trees and bushes. The houses had changed, the flat mud roofs of the plateau country being replaced by the wooden penthouse roof of the forest land. Dug-outs are used as ferry-boats, sure sign that there are big trees not far distant; and, indeed, below Nang Dzong forest frequently comes right down to the river's edge. But the river itself had not changed; it still flowed calmly on amidst a wilderness of dunes and sandbanks, and sometimes we voyaged from village to village by coracle.

Everywhere the people welcomed us, removing their hats and bowing as we approached, and sticking out their tongues at us as we passed. With outspread hands they brought gifts of eggs or milk or butter, and always a white scarf was presented, we

86

giving a similar one in exchange, according to the saying, 'sent with a scarf.' The weather was wet and gloomy, for it was an unusually bleak spring. Fierce draughts spun the sand aloft, rasping the cliffs; and under the pewter-coloured skies, the leaden water, dully gleaming, nosing its way amongst the wet dunes and snow-clad mountains, looked very forlorn. One wondered where all the sand came from, till one realised that in the summer the water is pounding the granite boulders together, and that from this mill an inexhaustible supply of sand is being ground, which the wind then piles up for future use. We passed numerous ruined villages, abandoned, I believe, because the cultivated terraces in the neighbourhood or the water supply had been overwhelmed by blown sand. A village once deserted is soon overgrown with thorn scrub.

To the south of us now lay the passes into Tsari and Pachakshiri, as the country at the sources of the Subansiri is called; but they were all blocked by snow, and would not be open for another two months. Indeed, we noticed as we travelled eastwards, that though trees and plants appeared in ever-increasing variety now, yet spring was more backward here than higher up the Tsangpo; this is evidently due to the immense accumulation of snow at the extreme eastern end of the Himalaya.

On May 4th we reached a village called Chake, smothered beneath a shimmering silver green veil of Aspen foliage. Up above grew forests of Picea and bamboo, and on the outskirts of the forest I found a heath of purple-flowered *Rhododendron bulu*. The very next day we found near the river bushes of a yellow-flowered rhododendron, the 'Mahogany Triflorum' as it came to be called afterwards, by reason of a big red-brown smudge at the base of the corolla. Except for that distinguishing mark, it closely resembles *R. triflorum* from Sikkim. The open cliffs were now covered with scrub oak instead of juniper, and in the numerous gullies which slashed the mountains into strange butts and pikes, one saw a variety of shrubs, such as Piptanthus, Oleaster, Euonymus, Buddleja and Spiræa.

Things were not very cheerful with us, however. Cawdor was unwell; Tom had been bitten in the hand by a savage dog; and not only did it rain every day, but the clouds came rolling up the valley like smoke, dripping steadily. There was always a wind which at this season blows up the valley, and it got more and more violent as we approached the great snow ranges; so that even when the weather was fine we were continually harassed and irritated by the sand blast. The one advantage of the rain was that it damped that down!

The transport too was exasperating, and as villages became more numerous, we had to change transport more frequently. Sometimes we had travelled barely a mile from one village, when we reached another, and, according to the custom of the country, had to change our transport again; if we changed less than four times a day we counted ourselves lucky. The ponies, which are never properly broken in, nearly always bolted, strewing wreckage along the track; packing-cases were stove in and valises ripped up; even our steel boxes did not escape in the general sabotage, but were either pierced by a rock, or had their locks wrenched off. The oxen, on the other hand, just lay down when tired, sometimes completely blocking the track; and no amount of hammering would make them get up again until they felt inclined to. Add to all this that our quarters were always filthy and generally draughty, and it will be seen that altogether we were in a bad way. However, there was a bright side to things also. Arrived at our destination, the kindly people always brought us hot buttered tea, and we could change our clothes by a fire. Moreover, we were now not so very far from Tsela Dzong, where we proposed to make our first halt.

On May 7th we reached Lilung, which stands on a considerable river of the same name. There is a path up the valley which leads to Tsari, though the country to the south of the Himalaya is said to be uninhabited. In the summer, however, many pilgrims go this way to the holy mountains of Tsari. The bridge over the Lilung River opposite the village had been washed away, and we were compelled to go a mile up the stream in order to cross by a new bridge. Near here we saw some Lopa (Abor) slaves, and learnt that about twenty-five years ago there was fighting amongst the tribes who inhabit the almost impenetrable hill jungle which lies south of the Assam Himalaya. As a result, some of the people crossed the mountains into the valley of the Tsangpo and were

Rhododendron triflorum **Mahogani Group, Doshong La.** **KNEC**
This rhododendron species is common in south-east Tibet and much of the Himalayan region. The Tibetan forms are hardier than those from further south and west, in Bhutan and Nepal, and lack the characteristic peeling bark. The majority of plants we have seen in Tibet have red staining and spotting in the throat (hence the name Mahogani), but cream and yellow forms are also common.

Rhododendron nivale **near the top of the Sirchem La.** **KNEC**
R. nivale can often be found in places too dry or too high for other rhododendron species. It has been reported to occur at 5800m (19,000ft.) in the Himalaya though this is probably an exaggeration. From a distance this species often looks like heather and colours the Tibetan hillsides a similar shade to the heather uplands of Britain in summer. Both members of the family Ericaceae, Calluna and Rhododendron enjoy a similar habitat on open windswept moors, growing on acidic, peaty soil, low in nutrients.

captured by the Tibetans. They seem quite happy under their taskmasters, who treat them well enough, otherwise they would presumably run away.

Now that we were back in the forest lands, we were infinitely better off than we were on the plateau; and though we found reason to grumble, especially at the wet cheerless weather, it was not nearly so cold as it had been, even at Tsetang, and there was unlimited firewood. Pine torches are used at night too. Food was plentiful, and we were able to buy fowls, eggs, flour, milk, butter, mutton and salt; also rice, curry and capsicum – these all being imported from Pemakö. We saw crops of peas and beans occasionally, and there were many fruit trees in the villages. But potatoes are very scarce, and when we came to the end of our supply, brought from Gyantse, three months elapsed before we were able to get any more. The valley here is about 4km [2 or 3 miles] wide, and one can see some

Spiraea sp. **probably** *S. arcuata* **above Pe.** **KNEC**
This fine Spiraea species grows in dry situations such as pine forest, oak scrub and at roadsides in much of south-east Tibet. It is often pink flowered, but near Pe most were pure white. This species occurs in Nepal, Tibet and south-west China.

Leptodermis microphyllus. **KNEC**
This stiff, spiny shrub grows in dry areas, in poor, stony soils, often close to the Yarlung Tsangpo. The combination of pink and white flowers is most attractive. Most species are not reliably hardy in most of Britain, requiring hot summers to ripen the wood. It may have potential as a garden plant in hot, dry climates.

The Yarlung Tsangpo west of Pe.   **KNEC**
Between the confluence with the Gyamda Chu and the gorge, the Yarlung Tsangpo flows through a wide valley with
extensive cultivation along the south side of the river. Crops include barley and vegetables. The snow-capped mountain
range in the distance forms part of the main Himalayan chain, along which part of the Tibet-India border runs.

distance in either direction. The river flows in a broad channel, broken by great sandbanks
between cultivated terraces which extend to the foot of the mountains. Much more rain
falls on the enclosing hills, especially those to the south, than in the valley itself;
consequently, they are covered with dense forest, which now comes down to the river.

We were almost directly beneath the Assam Himalaya which were still fathoms deep
under snow, and consequently the weather remained cold. Several large valleys come in
from the south hereabouts, and there are a number of passes at their heads, used by a
few Abors during the summer months; but practically all communication between
Pome and the Tsangpo is via the Doshong La. In fact, this part of the Tsangpo Valley is
particularly isolated; there is very little traffic up and down, Lhasa is a long way off, and
the people have little cause to travel, as they are well off with their flocks and herds and
cultivation, and receive exotic supplies from the Abors.

At a village called Tungdo we saw two prayer flagpoles each about 60m [200ft.] high;
and when, on May 11th, we crossed the Tsangpo for the third time, the canoes used were
12m [40ft.] long and 1.5m [5ft.] in diameter. Thus, there are some very big trees at no
great distance from the Tsangpo. Two dug-outs are lashed together by means of ropes rove
through holes in the gunwale. They are rowed with paddles, the rowlocks being made of
strips of raw hide. After crossing over to the left bank we had about 5km [3 miles] to walk
to Tsela Dzong, situated in the angle between the Gyamda River and the Tsangpo. At the
junction the Gyamda River is about 3km [2 miles] wide, and flows in four big streams,
with pastures and thickets between; but most of this land is submerged in the summer.

CHAPTER IV

A Botanical Reconnaissance

Around Tsela Dzong

Having made forty-five marches from Darjeeling it was a relief to settle down in a house again, and unpack our boxes feeling that we should not have to pack them again for two or three weeks at any rate. We could now set up our table, get out stores, and develop photographs. Cawdor was not very well, and Tom too was laid up; a rest all round was necessary before travel could be resumed, or the hard work of summer be begun.

Now came the excitement of the first botanical reconnaissance, and after a glance round at the scenery I decided on a route. There was indeed little choice. The *dzong* stands on a flat shoulder of a hill in the angle between the two rivers, and several hundred feet above them. The Gyamda Valley is nearly 3km [2 miles] wide at its mouth, and the Tsangpo itself is 1km [half a mile] wide. Thus we were hemmed in by two impassable obstacles, and could only go up the left bank of the Tsangpo, or up the right bank of the Gyamda River. But having got so far east, our main object now was to go upwards. There was nothing to prevent our climbing the slope behind the *dzong;* there was forest at no great altitude, and across the Tsangpo, on the slopes of the Himalaya, the forest came down to a still lower level. The mountains which flanked the river junction, though fairly high, were not high enough. They looked about 4300m [14,000ft.], but there was scarcely any snow on them. The Himalayan peaks, however, just across the Tsangpo, though not much higher, were still white with snow. Westwards, on both sides of the river, the mountains were lower.

There is no forest at the bottom of the valley, only thickets of thorn scrub; but sheltered glens, and even slopes which face inland are well wooded. A perpetual harassing blast blows up these wide valleys, and the dry rocky slopes are covered with scattered thorn scrub, consisting largely of *Sophora davidii* [*viciifolia*]*, Rosa sericea,* Caragana, Barberry, Ceratostigma, and higher up, oak. A large thistle-like Morina was coming up, and a small pale Iris (*Iris decora*) was in flower. But though there is no forest in the Tsangpo Valley till the mouth of the gorge is reached, there are trees in all the villages – apple trees, poplars, willows, elms, walnuts and others. There were two species of Poplar, both of them fine trees; *Populus alba,* the white poplar (or silver poplar as we called it), and another we called the golden poplar, whose young leaves are covered below with a skein of fine golden hairs which secrete a sticky polish. We never saw the former in flower or fruit, only the latter.

Looking down the wide valley of the Tsangpo at this season, to the bend at Temo, one saw a huge expanse of sand; but in the middle of the day it was a maze of dancing dust devils which gradually flowed together and formed a dense fog. However, that very first evening, being clear, we looked far down the valley and saw a rocky snow-bound peak and remarked on its height. Little did we reckon that we were even then gazing upon the loftiest peak in the Assam Himalaya, Namcha Barwa, which is plainly visible from Tsela Dzong. Water was supplied to the *dzong* through a flume 3km [2 miles] long, which brought it from a glen behind the hill. My favourite walk was along this flume, following the contour round the hill to the glen where the flume took off, and then down through the woods, past a hermit's cell clapped on to the cliff, to the main valley again. The hidden side of the hill was covered with a dense growth of small trees and Rhododendron bushes, and here *Rhododendron phaeochrysum* (K.W. 5656) was covered with domes of pink blossom. In the open it forms a stocky little bush, or shrub, but in the forest it is a stout tree 6m [20ft.] high. The buds are a rich rose pink, but the flowers are usually paler, with purple spots; some we saw in the forest, however, were covered with carmine-coloured flowers, and others in the open were almost white. It is a striking species, very free-flowering, and uncommonly hardy; I noticed young plants half a metre [a couple of feet]

Junction of Gyamda river with the Tsangpo at Tsela Dzong.   JC

high and not more than four or five years old, bearing great trusses of bloom. It is one of the most widely-spread species we met with, growing on both sides of the Tsangpo from the head of the gorge for nearly 320km [200 miles] westwards, with little variation. One thing we noticed, however. Round Tsela Dzong the under leaf surface, which is covered with a thick snow-white felt-like covering, was often disfigured by brilliant orange patches of fungus. Some trees were badly attacked, though they did not seem to suffer. As we went eastwards into wetter country, this pest disappeared.

Another Rhododendron which grew here to perfection was *R. triflorum* and its dark variety, which I called the 'Mahogany Triflorum' (K.W. 5687). In the valley it is a small compact scrubby plant with lemon-yellow flowers; but on these sheltered tree-clad slopes it formed a large bush 3.5m or 4.5m [12 or 15ft.] high with reddened flowers which were especially beautiful when the light shone through them. It is abundantly common in Kongbo, but does not extend so far west as *R. phaeochrysum*. The flowers vary from pale yellow – the typical *R. triflorum* colour – to salmon pink, mahogany, burnt sienna, and other tones. Moreover, the bushes were smothered in bloom and are as hardy as anything. One other Rhododendron grew on these wooded slopes – bright purple-flowered *R. bulu* which formed heathery tufts under the trees. Along the flume fragrant clumps of mauve *Primula atrodentata* flowered in April and seeded in May, and here also the mossy spires of a Cassiope shook their milk-white bells.

If one ascended the forested glen, where the flume took off, one found several small tree Rhododendrons, including *R. uvariifolium* (K.W. 5660), *R. phaeochrysum* ssp. *agglutinatum* (K.W. 5759), and finest of all, the glorious *R. hirtipes* (K.W. 5659). This last grew some 6m [20ft.] high and had large rounded leaves and loose trusses of three or four big bell-shaped flowers of the most delicate shell pink and ivory white, arranged in alternating broad bands. It was, I think, the most bewitching and exceptional Rhododendron species we saw. It was the earliest of the tree Rhododendrons to flower (neither *R. uvariifolium* nor *R. phaeochrysum* ssp. *agglutinatum* showing any signs as yet); its rose buds fade gradually as the pink and white flower expands. On rocks in the forests a straggling pink-flowered *R. primuliflorum* was just opening. It grows 2.5m [8ft.] high in the forest, but extends into the alpine region as a dwarf shrub.

Three times I climbed the mountain above Tsela Dzong called Pab Ri, 4350m

***Iris decora* and sandbanks by the Yarlung Tsangpo near Tsela Dzong.**   **KNEC**

This small lilac iris is very common in the dry meadows alongside the Yarlung Tsangpo and is found in similar habitats throughout the region. The flower stem can attain 30cm (1ft.) but in south-east Tibet the height is typically 20cm (8in.). The root can be used medicinally.

The Yarlung Tsangpo and Namcha Barwa from Temo.   KNEC

An unusually calm and clear day in June brings magnificent views of the Tsangpo Gorges massif from the north bank of the Tsangpo near Temo. Namcha Barwa is the sharp peak in the distance. This picture was taken from near Tsela Dzong, where Ward and Cawdor were based for a time.

[14,270ft.]. Above the thorn scrub, still on the open flank of the hill, came dense thickets of evergreen oak passing gradually into oak forest, where the trees were all draped with pale green lichen. Then after crossing meadows where the dead sticks of Primulas and Irises were conspicuous, one came out on to the open ridge, though forest still covered the sheltered slope, reaching to the crest of the ridge, but not overstepping it. Scattered bushes of smooth leathery-leaved *Rhododendron wardii* grew here, as well as the pink *R. primuliflorum*, and above that came a thick half-metre [two-foot] tangle of *R. phaeochrysum* ssp. *agglutinatum* scrub. Finally there was nothing left but tuffets and brooms of *R. nivale,* not yet in flower, mingled with a silken-leafed Cassiope.

On a fine day there was a splendid view from the summit of Pab Ri. Right below flowed the Tsangpo in a comparatively wide trough with its villages and white monasteries dotting the dun-coloured slopes. Immediately beyond rose the Himalaya, culminating to the north-east in the gigantic spire of Namcha

Right: *Arisaema flavum* **by the Yarlung Tsangpo.**   KNEC

A very common Arisaema in south-east Tibet, this dwarf species prefers much hotter, drier conditions than most of its relatives. It occurs in quantity along the Yarlung Tsangpo, but perhaps the most spectacular colony of all was found on the steep slopes up to the entrance door of the Potala palace, Lhasa.

93

Barwa. Westwards the dark jostling mountains edged with snow were lower; but away to the north glittered the snow peaks of the Salween divide. One day I boarded a skin boat below Tsela Dzong and floated down to the main river; the water of the Gyamda River was very clear, and I could see hundreds of fish, many of them of large size; but the Tsangpo was thick and muddy. Landing a mile below we continued down the right bank of the Tsangpo, past fields and villages, to Lusha, beyond the monasteries of Temo and Chamnar. There were hedges of Buddleia, Elæagnus, Euonymus and Hippophae, and a good deal of cultivation; for this part of the valley, just above the entrance to the gorge, is well populated. But all the cultivation in Kongbo did not yield much variety in the way of crops, fruit, or vegetables. Wheat and barley are the principal cereals; the only vegetables are turnips, potatoes, occasionally peas, and still more rarely, broad beans. As for fruit, crabs and peaches are plentiful, and there are also walnuts. Indeed, the country is better supplied with wild fruits than with tame ones, though the former are even more inedible than the latter. Cherries, gooseberries and currants we did not risk, even cooked; there were some excellent little strawberries, and several species of raspberry and blackberry were passable, besides blaeberries (dwarf vaccineums).

Primulas, rhododendrons and the *Dzongpön* of Chomo

At Lusha we saw the silver masts of birch trees sticking up out of a heather-purple sea of 'Lapponicum' Rhododendron (*R. nivale*), or awash in deeper mahogany seas of *R. triflorum*. But it was too early for alpine flowers yet. Returning to Tsela Dzong, we next crossed the Gyamda River and ascended the shoulder of the peak on the left bank. There was a solitary house up there, but to our surprise we found it untenanted. We were told that nobody lived there because the Pobas were in the habit of raiding it and stealing things while the owners were at work in the fields. Now the owners lived in the village below, but went up the mountain to till the fields. The weather was very unsettled with much rain, but one morning it suddenly cleared up, so we followed a path we had discovered which led to the top of the mountain, and after a stiff climb reached the summit. The peak is called Kongbo Peri, and though only 4560m [14,961ft.] high, it has a great local reputation as a sacred mountain; pious pilgrims come from afar to walk round it. On the way up we found several interesting plants in flower, amongst them the cherry-brandy coloured *Primula calderiana* [*P. roylei*] in the forest, and a species with tiny clots of pink flowers not much larger than a pin's head called *Primula glabra* ssp. *kongboensis* (K.W. 5703). This last was flowering in the snow all up the topmost ridge, whenever it was not smothered beneath hassocks of *Rhododendron nivale*.

The climb up the final ridge was hard work and we could see nothing of the scenery beyond, which was hidden by a nearer ridge. But at last we reached the top and then there burst upon us with stunning surprise an amazing panorama. To the south-east we could see the whole of the Assam Himalaya with Namcha Barwa 64km [40 miles] away, sticking up like a church steeple above cottage roofs; and north of that Gyala Peri crowned by a great snow dome. Northwards, the Salween divide filled the horizon from end to end, some of the peaks being over 7620m [25,000ft.] high. Such a barrier naturally is difficult to cross, and so we found it. The only river which rises behind, and cuts through, the range, is the Yigrong, a big tributary of the Po-Tsangpo. West of that come two passes, close together, the Pasum Rye La and the Tro La, the latter being on the China-Lhasa road. The Gyamda River and all its northern tributaries rise on the southern flank of the snow range, and nowhere cut through it. The trend of the Salween divide appears to be a little north of west, so that it cannot be a continuation of the Trans-Himalayan range, which, as we have seen, crosses the Tsangpo east of Tsetang. Returning to Tsela Dzong we made an interesting find on the dry oak-scrub clad banks, namely the Chinese *Primula pulchella* [*P. pulchelloides*]. It is a pretty mauve-flowered thing, but nothing to shout about; still I hardly expected to find it so far west as this.

At the end of May and beginning of June we had ten days of really fine weather, and the valley grew hot and close. Blossom burst from the bushes. A clump of butter-golden

Paeonia lutea var. *ludlowii,* flowered and so did the dainty Tamarisk. We walked through lanes of yellow dog-rose (*R. sericea*) into billowy blue seas of Sophora, whose previous year's seeds still lay scattered over the hard ground like a broken string of coral beads. *Clematis montana,* cool and virgin white in the sultry Jasmine-haunted air, trailed over every tree and bush. One afternoon we went for a walk up the Gyamda Valley as far as Pu-chu, about 8km [5 miles] distant. There is a small temple here, conspicuous for its golden roof, and noteworthy for its Chinese architecture, with curly corners. This roof was fitted with a system of bamboo drain pipes, the top of a long bamboo being split and opened out into a funnel to catch the rain-water, while the bottom opened on to a splash-board. The temple courtyard was almost deserted save for a few diseased beggars. One horrible leper, his hands replaced by stumps, sat on the steps in the hot sunshine working two prayer drums ceaselessly round and round by means of a rope. A large valley opens into the Gyamda Valley here and there are two more monasteries a few miles higher up. We were in a very religious part of Tibet. On the way back to Tsela we met the Chomo *Dzongpön* riding his pony, and surrounded by a knot of servants also mounted. We of course were on foot, and the *Dzongpön,* who knew not who we were, eyed us with ill-concealed disdain. 'Only beggars walk in Tibet' is a contemptuous and well-known phrase; and the *Dzongpön,* who was a stickler for etiquette, could scarcely believe his eyes when he saw us afoot. We returned his arrogant stare with interest, and after our man had answered one or two more or less impertinent questions, we cut the conversation short, and abruptly resumed our walk; we had taken quite a dislike to the *Dzongpön* of Chomo. At Tsela we occupied the official rest-house, a *dâk* bungalow kept up for distinguished visitors. The caretaker was a crazy woman, who lived with the cows in a shed. Though draughty the roof was water-tight, and the great advantage of the house was that we had it all to ourselves. Kongbo is a pastoral and agricultural country, and the people, though poor, are good-natured and cheerful.

Tibetan dress and customs

Just as in many parts of Tibet the universal garment is a sort of loose dressing-gown called a *chupa,* so in Kongbo the universal garment is a *gushuk.* Summer and winter day and night, by men and women, rich and poor, the *gushuk* is worn. Take a strip of thick woollen cloth about 2.5m [8ft.] long and 0.5m [18in.] wide; make a hole in the centre large enough to put your head through, and there you are, complete with *gushuk.* Sleeves? All you need do is to put your head through the hole, haul up 0.6m [2ft.] of slack fore and aft, fasten a belt round your waist, allowing the slack to bag over, and you have a model dress; the fashionable colour is a dull maroon red. Of course you wear more than one *gushuk,* at least in winter. When dirty, reverse and repeat. When cold, wear two *gushuks,* or three. When wet, wear a goatskin *gushuk* over the woollen one, hair inside; when fine, reverse the goatskin; when hot, wear one *gushuk,* pulling it well up above the knees. At night, undo the belt, and the surplus fold falls to the ground, making a long robe in which you roll yourself. It is a wonderful garment, the right thing at the right price. Men, women, and children enjoy it.

The fashion for men is a shorter skin *gushuk* and tight breeches of the same material, tucked inside long cloth boots. Hats are also worn in Kongbo; wide-brimmed, low-crowned circular hats like a parson's, made of white or black yak hair. The belt consists of a strip of leather with carved silver and brass buckles threaded on it. These belts are made in Lunang and are beautiful examples of the metal-worker's craft. Men wear their hair short, though it is often curly. Women have long hair, parted in the middle, glossy with butter, and pulled tightly back. Pill-box caps set jauntily on the side of the head are worn in fine weather, and hair hats in wet. A few days after our arrival at Tsela we paid a ceremonial visit to the *Dzongpön,* only to find that he had gone away, leaving his manager in charge. We exchanged presents with this gentleman, drank oily tea, and made arrangements about our mail, which was to be forwarded from the post office at Gyamda with the official mails, we paying half the cost of the messenger. Mounted couriers do the journey of 144km [90 miles] from Gyamda to Tsela in four days.

Rhododendron bulu **above Tsela Dzong.**   **KNEC**

'*Bulu medoc*' in Tibetan means any small-flowered or dwarf rhododendron so, rather comically, the name '*R. bulu*' means 'Rhododendron small rhododendron'. This species is found near the Yarlung Tsangpo in scrub oak at relatively low altitude and it should prove to be more drought and heat tolerant in gardens than most of its relatives in subsection Lapponica. No plants survived in cultivation from earlier expeditions and we introduced it for the first time in 1995 (Cox and Vergara 9503). *R. bulu* occurs in dry, low lying habitat, but there is very little morphologically to separate it from *R. nivale* which typically occurs at higher altitudes.

Rhododendron hirtipes, **north slopes of the Rong near Tumbatse.**   **KNEC**

Discovered by Kingdon Ward and endemic to south-eastern Tibet, this is a very attractive species characterised by its distinctive hairy stems and midrib. In cultivation it tends to open its flowers very early and is therefore vulnerable to spring frosts. It was re-introduced by Ludlow and Sherriff on both their expeditions to the area. This species is variable in colour, ranging from deep pink to pale pink and near white. On the steep slopes facing south near Tumbatse it forms the dominant rhododendron forest with *Picea* as the canopy.

There were two enormous Tibetan mastiffs chained to their kennels inside the courtyard of the *dzong;* and when anyone approached they set up a deep baying and tugged at their chains, making frantic efforts to get at the intruder. These brutes, though not naturally bad-tempered, are deliberately starved in order to keep them savage, and it would go hard with anyone who was set upon by a dog which stands nearly 1m [3ft.] high and weighs close on 90kg [200lb.]. They are kept only as watch-dogs. Besides the mastiff, there is one other well-bred dog in Tibet, and he is not common. I refer to the Tibetan poodle, a house dog sometimes seen in monasteries, or in baronial castles. He is something like a Pekingese but larger, not so dish-faced, and without the heavy mane. He has long hair and a curly tail carried over his back like a chow's; the few I have seen were black with a small patch of long white hair on the chest. In every Tibetan village, at least in the river gorge country, the usual loathsome pariahs abound; a surprising number of them are wall-eyed, a condition seen also in Tibetan ponies. But pets can hardly be said to exist in a country like Tibet, where life is hard and leisure unknown. Though not naturally cruel, even by our standards, people who have to struggle so hard to live at all as do the Tibetans, naturally expect animals to do their bit; they don't look after them and feed them for fun, and to do them justice the cruelties they inflict are such as they themselves would, and do, bear without flinching. Occasionally one sees a monkey chained to a pole in the central courtyard of the house; but tailed monkeys are hardly pets, and are kept more for amusement than love.

As to the cruelties Tibetans inflict on each other, these are no doubt severe when occasion arises. One hears much of the cruelty and callousness in countries where life is cheap; but no comparison with Western methods is fair (even if it will bear close scrutiny) because the standard is different. It is not that the Tibetan's senses are less acute than ours, but that his sensitiveness is. He is more callous about inflicting pain, but also more stoical about bearing it. The Tibetan suffering from horrible toothache, or badly wounded, cannot go to the nearest doctor and get an anaesthetic; he cannot even dull the ache with a morphia pill. He must just bear it. That he appreciates any effort to alleviate pain and cure disease we saw at Gyantse, where the medical officer is in great demand; while Cawdor's medicine chest made us many friends.

The Magistrate or Baron who persistently ill-treated his villeins would soon be put out of the way. No doubt crime is put down ruthlessly; and so it ought to be, in a country where a few stout ruffians can terrorise a whole district, and in the most effective manner possible. Criminals are sometimes beaten to death, or have their ears cut off, or are otherwise marked. But the only criminal we actually saw was a thief who had been beaten and condemned to wear leg irons for life, while being moved from *dzong* to *dzong* all over the country as a warning. He was clanking about the house quite happily at his work when we saw him. Less than a hundred years ago, in the reign of Queen Victoria the Good, convicts were sent in the hulks to Van Dieman's Land.

We had now been three weeks at Tsela Dzong, and had come to the conclusion that it was not really a suitable base. In the first place, it was too low down, the altitude being only 2900m [9,500ft.]; we wanted to find a village at an altitude of about 3400m [11,000ft.] above sea-level. In the second place, we were hemmed in on two sides by impassable rivers which prevented freedom of movement; there was only one mountain we could climb, without sleeping away from our base. In the third place, we were only just on the outskirts of the forest region, and too far away from the snow mountains which we hoped to visit. Mountains which rise far above the snow-line usually have a much richer flora than those which barely reach it.

There are three floras in Tibet: (1) The Plateau Flora covers the greater part of the country. There are practically no woody plants, and only a few hundred species of flowering plants, which, being of a sub-arctic type, are useless for horticultural purposes. (2) The Temperate Forest Flora of the upper gorge country. This includes evergreen Conifer forest at the higher elevations, and

Poba of Pome with felt hat and sword. **FKW**

This is typical attire from Kongbo. The Mönba hunters of the gorge wear a 'gushuk' made of takin skin rather than goatskin.

Paeonia lutea var. *ludlowii*.   **KNEC**
This spectacular Tibetan peony is a larger version of the yellow species *P. lutea* from Yunnan. It seems to occur in and around villages and as peonies have long been cultivated in China and Tibet, it may be of garden origin. South of the Zo La pass near Zayul we found dramatic displays of the species in hedgerows surrounding small fields. A fine and well-known garden plant, introduced by Ludlow and Sherriff in 1936.

Rosa sericea **forma.** *pteracantha* **between Pe and the Doshong La.**
                                                                  KNEC
According to W.J. Bean, the production of these large, red, wing-prickles is a random character found in the very common *Rosa sericea*. Examples have been recorded in Manipur, Yunnan and Sichuan, as well as in Tibet. The flowers are usually creamy white. An attractive if vicious plant: it is inadvisable to get caught in it!

A Tibetan mastiff near the Sur La. **AC**
These strong and fierce animals are used as guard dogs by Tibetan herdsmen. Typically they are tied up on a long chain outside the herders' tents, while they tend their yak at summer pasture. Colonel and Mrs. Bailey imported four Tibetan mastiffs to England, obtained while Colonel Bailey was Political Officer in Sikkim. In 1931 Mrs. Bailey formed the Tibetan Breeds Association in England and the first official standard for the breed was adopted by The Kennel Club.

deciduous forest at lower elevations. There are also alpine meadows full of flowers, and high alpine plants. About four-fifths of our horticultural novelties were drawn from this region. (3) The Rain Forest Flora of the lower gorge country. There is practically nothing but forest, the trees being in great variety; it is a sub-tropical Indo-Malayan flora and therefore useless for horticulture, unless the plants are grown under glass. Many of the most beautiful Rhododendrons are found here, as well as the finest trees. These Floras of course merge gradually into each other; at Tsela Dzong in fact we were in the transition region between (1) and (2), with forest on the most sheltered slopes and thorn scrub in the open; we wanted to get well within the Temperate Forest region, where we hoped to find extensive alpine meadows and pastures.

We therefore decided to cross the Temo La and make our permanent base at the village of Tumbatse in the upper valley of the Rong Chu, about two days' march east of Tsela Dzong. The advantages of the *rong* were obvious. We knew from Bailey's report that many beautiful flowers were to be found there; the immediate mountains were higher, and we should be nearer the entrance to the gorge, and to the snow-peaks. Tumbatse itself is 3550m [11,650ft.] above sea-level, so that we should be finding alpine meadow flowers on our doorstep, so to speak. Accordingly we packed our boxes once more, and on June 4th embarked in skin boats below Tsela Dzong. However, we had not voyaged far down the Tsangpo when we were put ashore at the village of Luding, where transport was awaiting us. We then proceeded more slowly over the burning sand-dunes, and down pleasant shaded lanes through cultivated fields; there seemed to be more tares (vetch) than wheat, but women were busy uprooting these. The midday wind came rushing up the valley, whirling the sand aloft, and we saw large numbers of yellow duck in the pastures.

In the afternoon we ascended the Temo Valley, and presently caught sight of the square fortress-like monastery perched on a high earth mound between two tearing streams. It is magnificently placed, and a most striking sight from below. In spite of having to change transport no less than five times – for the rule is you must change at every village, and these terraces are well cultivated – we reached Temo Gompa in the evening, and rode through the narrow street, lined with brooding lamas, to the guest-house. Here we were bidden to enter, and buttered tea was at once brought.

Rhododendron phaeochrysum on the Sirchem La.　　KNEC

The ubiquitous *R. phaeochrysum* covers huge areas of Yunnan, Sichuan and south-east Tibet, often to the exclusion of other species. Fifteen former 'species' have now been reduced in synonymy, and it is clear that *R. phaeochrysum* is the centre of a very variable cline. Though common in the wild, it is not particularly easy to cultivate, requiring cool roots and excellent drainage. The south-eastern Tibetan forms have thin indumentum which looks as if it has been painted on (agglutinated) and are therefore referable to var. *agglutinatum*. Some of the plants of this species on the Nyima La were affected by a fungal disease which caused darkened blotches in the indumentum on the leaf underside. Hopefully this disease will remain confined to the wild.

Primula glabra on the Bimbi La.
　　KNEC

Primula glabra is a variable and widespread species. These plants, photographed on the Bimbi La, north of Tsari, are quite showy but other forms are smaller and unspectacular. Material from Kingdon Ward's 1924 expedition was given the names *P. kongboensis* and *P. doshongensis* but taxonomists now consider them to be forms of *P. glabra*.

Lonicera setifera, in seed on the south side of the Nyima La.　　KNEC

Introduced by Kingdon Ward (KW 5688) in 1924, from Lusha in Tibet and not from the Assam Himalaya as some authorities claim. This is a fine species with pinkish, straw-coloured or white scented flowers appearing before the leaves (in February in Scotland). Ward describes the flower colour as 'straw yellow?' in his field notes but whether this is a guess, or from memory is not clear. The white forms are perhaps the most desirable. The stiff branches, hairy leaves and stems and the pairs of bright red fruits are all distinctive. This species was also introduced under SBEC 0656 from the Cangshan in 1981.

CHAPTER V

The Land of the Blue Poppy

Temo and the Temo La

Temo is an important monastery containing over 200 monks. It stands on a low hill in the midst of emerald green pastures, and commands the valley which leads, via the Temo La, to Pome. We found that ample supplies of rice, *tsamba* and flour were obtainable here, so we made it our rationing base for the season; it is only a day's journey from Temo to Tumbatse. Shortly after leaving Tsetang we had discovered, to our horror, that we had forgotten to bring any curry powder; and as curry is the staple dish on such a journey as this, solving compactly the problem of unskilled cooks and tough meat, without it we were at a loss. However we found that in Kongbo they understand the whole art of curry, obtaining supplies of the raw material from Pemakö, the province of mountain and jungle south of the Himalayan range. This *masala* comprised dried fruits, chips of bark, splinters of wood, and seeds; but the only ingredient I could recognise were the wheel-like capsules of star anise (*Illicium*). The whole was pounded in a stone mortar with a sausage-shaped stone from the river-bed, and made excellent flavouring.

There is a guest-house close to the *gompa,* standing in a pretty garden shaded by willow trees, and here we put up for the night. Having exchanged scarves, the *Depa* sent us a chunk of butter and three dozen doubtful eggs, to stimulate trade, and after tea we paid him a visit. We found him in a large airy room the walls of which were formidably hung with pistols and rifles like an arsenal. He was quite a young man, pleasant-mannered and good-looking, expensively dressed in Chinese silks and with an air of urbanity for which travelled Tibetans are noted. Eight years previously he had visited Darjeeling and Calcutta, and had there learnt to appreciate many of the material benefits of Western civilisation – firearms, for instance. He gave us Tibetan tea and Indian biscuits and we made a suitable presentation.

We left Temo Gompa on a beautiful summer's day, with larks singing overhead and butterflies playing underfoot, and marched first across boggy meadows inflamed with rosy patches of *Primula tibetica.* Above the meadows, the valley narrowed suddenly, and we found ourselves amidst thickets of Hippophae, *Rosa sericea* and Barberry, laced with white *Clematis montana,* all growing in a very coarse gravelly soil. In places the Clematis was a particularly gorgeous sight, hanging in frozen cascades from the tree-tops or wreathing itself round the bushes.

Wherever water oozed from the base of the hill, the thorn thicket was interrupted by bog gardens containing yellow 'Sikkimensis' Primulas, and clumps of the fine purple *Orchis latifolia,* which is frequently seen in English gardens; pinched bushes of *Rhododendron triflorum* also grew happily in these bogs, and flowered profusely. We soon reached Picea forest and for two hours climbed steadily by a good but steep and stony path. Along the edge of the wood grew drifts of *Primula chungensis,* its bright orange flowers impaled whorl by whorl on snow-white reeds; clumps of *Meconopsis betonicifolia* [*baileyi*] just opening its sky-blue flowers; and *Primula atrodentata.*

Before long Rhododendrons began to play a more active part, and presently we came upon a new species *R. faucium* which, though the flowers were over, was easily distinguished by its smooth tawny trunk, from which hung rags and tatters of papery bark. Eventually I found one tree bearing flowers of a delicate warm pink shade (K.W. 5732). Another species met with higher up, and just coming into flower, was a yellow *R. wardii* (K.W. 5736). The buds are often brick red, but the flush fades from them as they open, and the orange yellow clears gradually to a pure chrome. Camp was pitched early in the afternoon in a little meadow where two streams met; and after lunch I spent the rest of the day botanising. Not only were there many fine things in flower, there was also to the discerning eye, much coming on.

Next day (June 6th) we climbed to the pass called Temo La, 4270m [14,000ft.], and descending a few hundred feet down the far side, camped in the mouth of a small valley where the Picea-Rhododendron forest began again. Here we decided to remain for a few days while we explored the surrounding hills, which in places reached a height of over 4600m [15,000ft.], and were still under snow. We were now on the range which runs northwards to the Nambu La, forming the divide between the Gyamda River and its tributaries to the west, and the Rong Chu and its tributaries to the east; the latter flows to the Po-Tsangpo. Between the Temo La and the Nambu La, above Tongkyuk, there is no pass, or at least not one which is used. At the southern end of the range, where the Rong Chu rises, is a group of rocky peaks separating the *rong* from the Tsangpo. Northwards the range is of no great height until the Nambu La is reached, immediately south of which we noticed several snowpeaks. The highest peak in the neighbourhood of the Temo La is one opposite Tumbatse. I spent an uncomfortable night on this peak, which is 4900m [16,000ft.] high, in October, watching the snow congeal on the theodolite; when at last dawn came, it was so thick and heavy with cold mist that I could see nothing; and I made my way down the steep rock face, treacherous with its covering of snow, in some fear. It had been indeed a wretched and fruitless vigil, but before darkness set in the previous night, I had got a round of angles to the fixed peaks, and seen the evening sun glittering on the snow-bergs to the north, which are the great Salween divide.

Opposite this peak, just across the *rong,* is the conspicuous bottle-necked peak north of the Tang La which we called 'The Plug', from its resemblance to a volcanic plug; the tip of it is just visible from Tumbatse. We never climbed 'The Plug', because we were never on the Tang La or even at Tumbatse when the weather was fine. On the day we crossed the Temo La for the first time the weather was superb, every peak and pass visible. The snowy range from Gyala Peri in the north to Namcha Barwa in the south stood out as hard and clear as rock crystal against the delicate porcelain blue of the sky. Westwards we looked away up the flat valley of the Tsangpo, with its ribbon of water winding lazily between broad yellow sandbanks; six weeks later it had engulfed the dunes beneath a seething flood which filled the valley to the brim. Beyond the Tsangpo rose the snow-clad Himalayan range, faintly luminous against the blue.

At the summit of the pass the open moorland spread out league beyond league carpeted with dwarf Rhododendrons, which, with the exception of a bright purple *R. nivale* were not yet in flower. It was not till the end of June that the flowing tide of colour had crept up from the valley below to the alpine moorland. Then two species, startling in their delicate beauty, revealed themselves. The first to flower was an aromatic-leafed 'Anthopogon' (K.W. 5733), *R. laudandum* var. *temoense,* forming a dense brushwood 15-20cm [6 or 8in.] high. Its tight heads of flowers toss like white sea foam on a choppy ocean of dark green foliage. The other, *R. fragariflorum* (K.W. 5734), forms lowlier cushions and hassocks of gland-dotted basalt-green leaves awash in a surf of faintly fragrant flowers the colour of crushed strawberry. It has the flower characters of a 'Saluenense,' but not the foliage. The three were mixed up and woven together in endless patterns; one could throw oneself down on this soft springy carpet as one does on the heather-clad hills of Surrey, and gaze across the valley to the lofty white pillars which form the gateway to the Tsangpo gorge.

So far as dwarf alpine Rhododendrons are concerned we found two distinct associations in Eastern Tibet. There was this moorland association on the drier ranges to the north and west of the gorge, and there was the rock garden association on the Himalayan range itself. On the outskirts of the forest country the moorland association comprised only two species, the purple-flowered *R. nivale* and a pink-flowered 'Anthopogon,' *R. primuliflorum* as on the hills west of Tsela Dzong. A little nearer the snow range, but still sheltered behind the rain screen which stretches across the mouth of the gorge, this carpet becomes more varied, comprising several distinct species, one or two species of 'Lapponicum,' *R. laudandum* (var. *temoense*) with white flowers (the pink-flowered *R. primuliflorum* having

Clematis montana f. *grandiflora*. **PC**

The largest-flowered cultivated forms of *Clematis montana*, with flowers up to 7.5-10cm (3-4in.) in diameter are typically known as f. *grandiflora*. On several expeditions to China and Tibet we have located forms with much larger flowers. This was probably the largest of all, and having traced the flower into a notebook, I can confirm in true fisherman fashion that it was 15cm (6in.) in diameter. This form is now in cultivation but time will tell whether the plant is hardy and easy to cultivate and if the flowers are always so large.

Rhododendron faucium on the Doshong La. **KNEC**

Formerly considered a form of *R. hylaeum* but now described as a separate species, *R. faucium* is fairly common in the Tsangpo Gorges area. Out of flower it is readily distinguished by its smooth, peeling, pinkish bark and reddish-brown young leaves. The fine pink flowers open fairly early: typically March in cultivation and April-May in Tibet.

Rhododendron fragariflorum and *Cassiope selaginoides* on the Temo La, near the summit. **KNEC**

In the wild *R. fragariflorum* is a delightful species (the name means 'strawberry-flowered') with pink or purplish-pink flowers on a compact plant with tiny leaves. It usually grows out in the open in full exposure. Previous introductions have proved to be shy-flowering and tricky but new collections may make better garden plants. It is easily distinguished, even out of flower, by the mass of silvery scales on the upper and lower surface of the leaves. It is obviously very closely related to *R. setosum* from the Himalaya further west, and plants from east Bhutan are intermediate between the two species.

Hummocks of *Rhododendron fragariflorum* and *Cassiope selaginoides*.　　　KNEC
The moorland at the top of the windswept Temo La consists of hummocks of rhododendron species (*R. laudandum* var. *temoense, R. nivale, R. fragariflorum*), Cassiope, and Salix, interspersed with alpine plants such as Meconopsis, Primula and Lloydia. This is where we found the Ivory Poppy (the hybrid between *Meconopsis simplicifolia* and *M. pseudointegrifolia*).

meanwhile increased its stature and become more or less a wood-land plant), and the strawberry *R. fragariflorum*. The rock garden association of perpetual precipitation included a score of species, besides most of those already described. The climatic difference between the two regions is one of winter, not summer, conditions; the moorland species are of course the hardier, and certainly have to withstand much lower temperatures. Though poorer in Rhododendrons and shrubs generally, the dry winter alpine pastures are richer in herbaceous plants such as Primula, Gentian, Saxifrage, and Meconopsis.

Rhododendron laudandum var. temoense on the Nyima La.　　KNEC
This species was discovered and introduced under the collector's number Kingdon Ward 5848. The only two clones that have been grown under this name do not, however, match the herbarium specimens: the leaf underside is green rather than covered with very dark scales, and the flowers are lavender pink rather than white, suggesting that both clones are natural hybrids. In the wild this plant is very distinctive. It has tiny dark green leaves with a coating of what looks like chocolate powder sprinkled on the leaf underside. It has delightful pure white flowers (occasionally with a hint of pink) and usually occurs on very exposed moorland. Retaining the name var. *temoense* is not really justified. We could see no significant difference between the eastern plants in this area and the plants from further west in the Tsari area. What is more, the type specimen of var. *temoense* (meaning 'of the Temo La') was collected on the Doshong La. In cultivation the true *R. laudandum* has been a real challenge, growing 2-3cm (¾-1in.) in four years from seed. This may well explain why only a couple of natural hybrids (with added vigour) survived in cultivation, while the very slow-growing seedlings of the 'true' species did not.

An abundance of Meconopsis

By the second week of June three alpine poppies were in flower at the Temo La – the beautiful sky-blue *Meconopsis simplicifolia,* the very rare 'Ivory Poppy,' and a sulphur-yellow species *M. pseudointegrifolia. M. simplicifolia* (K.W. 5855) is usually found in small scattered colonies growing on loamy banks under the shelter of Rhododendron bushes, though not in deep shade. The stems grow 30cm [a foot] high, each ending in a single large nodding flower of a rich sky blue, with a sheaf of golden anthers in the centre. This is *M. simplicifolia* as originally understood, and as figured in the *Botanical Magazine* (tab. 8364). In recent years, however, a dingy violet-flowered plant, said to be perennial, has crept in under the same name. It was not until 1913, when Major F.M. Bailey sent to England seed of a form collected in the Eastern Himalaya, that the true biennial *M. simplicifolia* was restored to us under the name of Bailey's variety. This *M. simplicifolia* var. *baileyi* must not be confused with *M. baileyi* (now *M. betonicifolia*) which is quite a different thing and has never been in cultivation before. Our *M. simplicifolia* from Temo La, then, is a fragrant form of Bailey's variety. On the Doshong La we collected a variety with wine-purple flowers (K.W. 5855) and in Pemakö we collected seed of a plant growing on open alpine slopes which we took to be *M. simplicifolia,* though we did not see it in flower (K.W. 6245). This last may therefore be something different.

The sulphur poppy (*M. pseudointegrifolia*) (K.W. 5749) grows scattered over the Rhododendron moorland, and was just coming into flower. It grows 0.5 to 1m [2 to 3ft.] high, the main stem bearing a dozen axillary flower stalks which usually spring from a common level, each ending in a large bright yellow nodding flower. Tall and stately, these sulphur poppies are the most conspicuous objects on the moorland, looming above the other flowers like yellow moons. The 'Ivory Poppy' (*M. x harleana*) is referred to elsewhere, and on our first visit to the Temo La these three were the only species in flower. On the screes, however, I found the capsules of two more species which flowered before the end of the month. One was a prickly poppy, *M. horridula.* The main stem grows less than 30cm [a foot] high, and is composed of a number of separate 1-flowered scapes stuck together towards the base; there are usually several distinct basal scapes as well, each ending in a flower. Thus the plant is closely allied to the well-known prickly poppy of Kashmir (*M. aculeata*). The second is entirely different again. It throws up a jet of little gold and violet silken flowers, each borne on a wiry stem, to the number of twenty or more, which shake themselves out into a sort of Prince of Wales's Feathers. This is *M. impedita,* Morshead's variety; it also grows scattered on the cleanest windiest slopes, where it is extremely abundant (K.W. 5808).

There were two later flowering variants of alpine poppy. The first, *M. horridula* [*M. prainiana*], K.W. 5909, a tall 3-foot prickly plant, bears a simple raceme of pale watery blue unscented flowers, and grows on the highest boulder screes, in the topmost ice-worn valleys at 4600m [15,000ft.]. The last and loftiest (K.W. 5984), found nowhere below 4600m [15,000ft.] and up to 5200m [17,000ft.], is yellow-flowered, clothed with long silken champagne-coloured hair *M. pseudointegrifolia* [var. *brevistyla*]. Both flower in July. Nearly all these poppies, with the exception of the Ivory Poppy, might be called common; and we were sometimes able to see four and even five species in flower at the same time – a rare treat.

The wet-winter ranges, being thickly covered with Rhododendron, have little room for poppies. At the Doshong La we found only *M. simplicifolia.* Other species were not altogether lacking from the Himalayan range, for several of them occurred at the Nam La, where the climatic conditions were those of the dry-winter ranges, and the flora was consequently quite distinct from that of the Doshong La. It is a curious fact that, though the genus Meconopsis as a whole is noted for its lack of scent, and that blue flowers are generally scentless, the few species of Meconopsis which are scented have flowers of the clearest turquoise blue. *M. latifolia* from Kashmir, now a well-known garden plant, and the Chinese *M. speciosa* both have sweetly fragrant flowers. To these must now be added our Tibetan forms of *M. simplicifolia* and the dwarf 'Aculeate' poppy, *M. speciosa* [*M. Cawdoriana*] (K.W. 5751).

The mail arrives

We had barely left our camp for the daily excursion on June 8th when Tom came running after us, shouting that the Temo *Dzongpön* had arrived, bringing our mail. We therefore turned back, invited him into a tent, and gave him tea and biscuits while he produced a large packet of letters forwarded from Gyantse. I then showed him some of the plants we had collected, now drying in the press, in order to convince him that we really were the harmless lunatics we pretended to be. He had heard of course that we were visiting his country solely with the object of collecting plants; but it would not have surprised us if he had declined to believe in our midsummer madness without having seen alarming symptoms of it with his own eyes.

The *Dzongpön* who as usual was very spick and span in his purple gown with a jacket of imperial yellow silk and black plush boots and dish hat with scarlet mandarin tassel, had with him half a dozen splendid mules laden with supplies. He was bound for the *rong* to visit his yak herds, and would easily do the journey from Temo to Tumbatse in the day – seeing that it was now but 10 o'clock – against the two days we required. Indeed, on one occasion, Tom rode from Temo to Chunyima, a dozen miles below Tumbatse, in a day; the distance is about 55km [35 miles], with a high pass to cross and bad going down the boggy *rong*. But in Tibet a man well mounted will cover as much as 400km [250 miles] in a week. As for the post runners who travel day and night at a steady jog-trot, with frequent relays, they cover great distances at a surprising speed. Letters go from Lhasa to Gyantse, a distance of 192km [120 miles] with a wide unbridged river to cross, and a pass of over 4900m [16,000ft.], in forty-eight hours; and remote as Tumbatse is, on one occasion we received a mail from London inside forty days! At present postal communication in Tibet follows the two great highways – Lhasa to the Indian frontier, and Lhasa to the China frontier only; but it will gradually be extended.

This, our first home mail since we had settled down in Tibet, had been forwarded from Gyantse to Lhasa and had thence followed the China road eastwards as far as Gyamda, whence it had been brought on to Temo by private courier, with the official mails. It was a great temptation to cut our morning's work and read our letters comfortably in our tents, particularly as the day was wet. Eventually I compromised, and having read my home letters, left the others till tea-time; while Cawdor, always willing to make any sacrifice in the interests of the expedition, put his voluminous correspondence aside and came too.

We spent the day down in one of the deep steep-sided glens which run down to the Rong Chu, and found ourselves in a forest of small tree Rhododendrons, all bursting into flower. The lovely pink *R. hirtipes* and the yellow *R. wardii* were the commonest, with *R. dignabile* higher up. There were many others, some of which had *R. hirtipes* characters, but were not true *R. hirtipes*; others of which had *R. wardii* characters, but were not true *R. wardii*; and still others which had *R. dignabile* characters, but were not true *R. dignabile*. The most definite species was a tree with large flowers of pure ivory white; I chanced on one specimen here, and came across another in fruit in October (K.W. 6215: a natural hybrid of *R. hirtipes* wrongly attributed to *R. griffithianum*). Cawdor also spotted a distinct species of the *R. wardii* type, having cream flowers flushed almost salmon sometimes, with a crimson flash at the base of the corolla, and a speckled appearance on the upper lobe (K.W. 5757) (a natural hybrid, probably *R. wardii* x *R. phaeochrysum*).

The fine weather broke definitely on the night of the 7th, and though we remained in camp till the 13th it rained all the time. Nor were we luckier on future visits to the Temo La. In July we spent five days in pouring rain rounding the head of the Rong Chu from the Temo La to the Sang La – which is a pass for yak only. In September we crossed from Temo Gompa to Tumbatse once more, and it rained without ceasing; finally, we spent the first week of October at the Temo La and Sang La, and for one crowded hour had a vision of Namcha Barwa and Gyala Peri, which was worth six months' rain.

To return to our June reconnaissance. Rhododendrons were not the only shrubs met with and marked down for introduction. There was a Barberry (*Berberis*). Now Barberries in Britain, and particularly Asiatic Barberries, are legion, and though most

***Rhododendron campylocarpum* x *cerasinum* on the north side of the Doshong La.**   **KNEC**

This is a natural hybrid between the yellow *R. campylocarpum* and the red *R. cerasinum*. The taxonomy of rhododendrons is greatly complicated by the number of natural hybrids which occur in the wild and they appear in batches of seedlings from wild collected seed. Such 'rogue' plants were often described as 'new' species by taxonomists working in the early part of the 20th century. Until the 1970s, taxonomists working on the genus seemed reluctant to admit the evidence of this phenomenon but since 1980 extensive fieldwork in China, Tibet and the Himalaya has revealed how many so-called 'species' are merely natural hybrids. Where population of natural hybrids establish in the wild and start to breed, a process of speciation takes place over several generations. In this way a new 'species' can evolve over a relatively short period. This is particularly apparent after human intervention: along the side of a new road for example. In such conditions, natural hybrids often dominate.

***Meconopsis pseudointegrifolia* on the Nyima La.**   **KNEC**

This magnificent specimen was growing on the north-eastern side of the Dashing La, south of Pome. This species has become quite widely grown in cool climates, but recent experience has shown that cultivated plants and their offspring become gradually less fertile, requiring regular import of fresh seed from the wild. This species is one of the parents of the 'ivory poppy' *M. x harleyana.*

of them are as like as two peas, they have all been proclaimed Swans; the best way to avoid trouble was to avoid Barberries, Cotoneasters, Viburnums, and other collectors' geese altogether. Therefore, despite the fine glaucous foliage of this bush, I turned away unimpressed. But when the fruits reddened to coral beads dangling from the jet-black stems and the blue-green foliage was shot with scarlet and old gold in the fall, I could no longer refrain from collecting seed (*Berberis temolaica* K.W. 5773). A willow glowing with tall silver and red plumes was handsome, and amongst the dwarf Rhododendrons grew a small twiggy *Lonicera cyanocarpa* (K.W. 5918) with straw-yellow flowers which I passed by, until I saw the plummy blue-black berries with which it concealed its nakedness in the autumn.

Primula macrophylla var. *ninguida,* a rather blatant purple-flowered atrocity, grew on the open moorland, and was shamed to a husky whisper by the periwinkle blue of *P. sinopurpurea*, a close relative, very similar in appearance, but easily distinguished from it even in fruit. *P. sinopurpurea,* as usually understood, is a rather vulgar thing, but this was an aristocratic form, with the blue of the distant misty hills in its eyes (K.W. 5731).

***Meconopsis simplicifolia* on the Sirchem La.**   **KNEC**

A very variable species, in both colour and size of flower. The best forms are a magnificent blue while the poorest are a pinky-mauve, fit only for the bonfire. As Kingdon Ward points out, unfortunately the best forms seem seldom to adapt themselves to cultivation, and most cultivated forms do little justice to the magnificence of the best wild ones. It is easily distinguished from *M. betonicifolia* by the long, thick, coarsely hairy flower stalk with a single flower with five to eight petals. *M. betonicifolia* has several flowers (with usually four petals) and leaves on a thinner stem.

Rhododendron dignabile **on the north side of the Doshong La.   PC**
A white form of this showy species, quite common in wooded areas around
the Gorges area, but not introduced either by Kingdon Ward or Ludlow and
Sherriff as far as we can tell. Essentially this is a western version of *R.
beesianum* (which occurs itself in Pome), which differs in the absence of
indumentum on the leaf underside. In common with *R. beesianum, R.
dignabile* is likely to be tricky to cultivate and may be best grafted rather than
grown on its own roots. First introduced under Cox and Vergara 9569 and
Cox and Cox 7509.

Rhododendron dignabile **on the north side of the Doshong La.   PC**
A pale pink form of this species showing the fine rounded truss. Yellow
forms are almost certainly hybrids with *R. campylocarpum* or *R wardii*. We
found forms with creamy flowers in the Tsari area of south-east Tibet which
were intermediate taxonomically between *R. dignabile* and *R. wightii* of
Bhutan and Nepal.

Primula macrophylla **var.** *ninguida* **near the top of the Nyima La.   KNEC**
These magnificent clumps were in a meadow soggy from snow-melt just below the
summit of the Nyima La at around 4390m (14,400ft.). Richards considers this taxon to
be intermediate between two variable and widely distributed species, the Himalayan *P.
macrophylla* and the Chinese *P. chionantha* ssp. *sinopurpurea*. The type specimen (KW 5745)
was collected on the Temo La in 1924.

Berberis temolaica **above the Rong Chu on approach to
Temo La.   KNEC**
This fine species was discovered on the Temo La by Kingdon
Ward in 1924 and introduced by him. It was also introduced
by Ludlow and Sherriff from Tsari in 1938. Deciduous, with
pale yellow flowers, it is grown mainly for its wonderful
glaucous leaves. It would probably be more widely cultivated
were it not necessary to propagate it by grafting. *Berberis
calliantha* is the other important member of the genus
introduced on the 1924 expedition (KW 6308). A dwarf
species with large yellow flowers, it is characterised by its
holly-like leaves.

Introducing fine plants and describing flower colours and scents

Of all the plants mentioned in this chapter, which can we confidently pronounce first class? Just as growers at home require information which will enable them to grow the plants, so do they like to have the points of a plant summed up. They want to know what they are getting. It is therefore the duty of the plant collector to give a brief description of his finds, including habit (that is to say, growth form), colour of flower, and whether fragrant or not, foliage, fruit, autumn colouring, and so on. Such a description will give a good idea whether a plant is first or second class; but no amount of description will indicate whether it has quality or not – that indefinable air of good breeding which we find only in the élite. There are many otherwise first-class plants which just lack quality. But the describing of plants is not easy. Botanical description follows certain well-defined rules, which can be learnt; what we may call horticultural description, however, is another matter, and depends a good deal on our senses.

Now our senses are poor servants. Even colour sense, which is the most acute as it is the most important for our purpose, is weak. We have, it is true, definite names for many colours, but how many of us recognise them when we see them? But our colour names are few in comparison with the number of shades we wish to distinguish, and that is the measure of our vagueness. We are forced to fall back on a by no means standardised analogy. Thus we speak of sea green, navy blue, sulphur yellow, sage green, sky blue, and a host of other colours more or less recognisable, and that is as near as we can get to the required shade. That is to say, though most of us know what we mean by blue, green or yellow, when it comes to defining the kind of blue, green or yellow, we find ourselves groping after a sensation which continually eludes us. Thus we do not match flower colour, we merely indicate its quality; only haberdashers match colours.

The fact is, even a scientific classification of colour by wave-length is useless for our purpose, and for two reasons. In the first place, spectrum analysis deals with pure colours, whereas flower colours are generally mixed; and in the second place, we have to deal with reflected and not with transmitted light. Now the quality of reflected light depends on several factors besides the nature of the light itself, and particularly on the nature of the reflecting surface, which in flowers is infinitely varied. It also depends on the amount of light available for reflection, so that the same flower may take on different shades of colour according to the time of day or the state of the weather.

Smells are even more indefinite. Some are indistinguishable from tastes, or the two are so involved that it is difficult to say where one ends and the other begins. But there are only five primary tastes – sweet, bitter, saline, acid and pungent – not one of which can be confused with any smell; it is only when we come to deal with flavours that, again resorting to analogy, we get into difficulties. Thus we speak of peppermint or pear drops, hardly knowing whether we mean smell or taste; and which of us, unless he happens to be a chemist to whom amyls and ethyls are common objects of the breakfast-table, knows exactly what he means by the smell of pear drops? Only small boys invariably have peppermints and pear drops on their persons; to most of us they are nothing more than a hallowed memory. Thus, with every analogy we lose precision, and only plunge more deeply into misty abstractions. In fact, we can do little with smells except classify them as 'good' and 'bad' or 'aromatic' and 'foetid.'

It is this capital difficulty which prevents people from attempting to say much about scent in flowers and leaves. Even if we say that a flower has the scent of violets, or musk, or apple blossom, the information, probably inaccurate to start with, will be misunderstood by somebody else, since flowers smell differently to different people. All we can say safely is, that a flower is fragrant, or that foliage is aromatic. Scent in flowers and leaves is a curious and interesting problem. Some flowers exhale their fragrance only in the dewy morning, others only at dusk; many aromatic leaves only during the heat of the day. Fragrance is most commonly associated with white and yellow flowers, and least commonly with red and blue. Few Rhododendrons, with the exception of those in the Maddenia and Fortunea subsections [series], are scented, and the flower colour in those is nearly always white. Gentians, Forget-me-nots, Lithospermum, Anchusa, Cynoglossum and Campanula are nearly always blue, and not one of them is ever fragrant. I have already referred to the fragrance in Meconopsis. While on the subject of blue flowers, I might point out that there is a widespread belief that blue predominates at high altitudes. This is a popular fallacy, rarely borne out by facts. Blue is the most conspicuous colour in the alpine regions – a very different thing. It is also probably true that the greater proportion of blue flowers occur in the alpine belt; there are not many blue flowered trees or shrubs.

The daily and seasonal routine of the plant-hunter

The day's work in camp was as follows: we rose early, and I usually spent the hour before tea was ready writing descriptions of new plants discovered the previous day. Then came tea and biscuits, at which meal we discussed our plans, or, since it is not always safe to talk to an Englishman or a Scotsman before breakfast, read our books in stony silence. While the men were breakfasting round the fire, we dressed and went on with our

Frank Kingdon Ward's campsite in south-east Tibet.   FKW

work. Then we had breakfast, usually about 10 o'clock – porridge occasionally, curried chicken or scrambled eggs and *chappatties*. The only things that weren't severely rationed were flour, rice, *tsamba* and butter, all of which could be obtained locally, so that when we were hungry we demolished quantities of buttered *chappatties* – that is, thin baked cakes of flour and water. We had no bread, of course. After breakfast we went out on the day's excursion exploring, botanising or taking photographs, according to the weather, usually making some peak our objective. We returned to camp about 4, changed our wet clothes, had tea, and worked or read till supper-time. Supper – menu as at breakfast, with soup instead of porridge and a cup of cocoa to finish up with – was at 7. After that we talked and read by candle-light, recorded the events and observations of the day, and turned in at 10. How peaceful it all was! No train to catch in the morning, no unsatisfactory play to criticise, no income tax form to fill up, no income, no broadcasting, no hustle, bustle, and boost.

All the same, June is a strenuous month for the plant-hunter, and I often worked ten or twelve hours a day in order to keep abreast of the times. For in June all the flowers are coming out with a rush, and moreover one finds oneself fresh and eager for the task in an astonishingly new and beautiful world. Naturally, one tries to make the most of it. After the long journey by sea and land, it is immensely refreshing to settle down to a serious job. Of course, the pace does not – cannot – last. At the end of two months, altitude and weather – unceasing rain, begin to tell on the nerves. Reaction sets in; and you feel peevish. Then it is you know that the crisis is come, that if you are to get through the long season successfully, you must keep yourself well in hand, and keep a firm grip on things. August is the critical month. It is long and wet. The spring flowers are over, the autumn flowers are not yet out. If you can get through August with your flag still nailed to the mast, you are all right. Things begin to mend. The worst of the rain is over by September, and the weather is getting finer every day. Seeds are ripening, autumn flowers are blooming, and that shapeless shroud which for three months has muffled a dead world is being blown away to reveal the quick form reincarnated beneath.

Rhododendron kongboense on the approaches to the Tra La.   PC

This species is closely related to the more common *R. primuliflorum* but differs in its deep pinkish-red flowers. It tends to be a rather straggly bush with relatively small flowers when growing in woodland, but on open moorland it is much more compact. Not easy to please in cultivation, it needs perfect drainage and cool roots and tends not to be long-lived. The leaves have a pungent smell when brushed or rubbed. Smells are hard to describe: Peter Cox considered the smell 'strawberries' while his father Euan Cox described it as 'friar's balsam'.

Winter comes with its biting winds, its clear cold skies, its sunshine and snowstorms. By this time one is tired with a tiredness which knows no equal; not the tiredness which can be cured by a night's rest, or a week's rest. Every cell and fibre in one's body seems worn out, and it takes months of gradual rest and change of scene to renew one's strength. It is the effect of prolonged living at high altitude of course, not of late hours.

Temo La to Tumbatse

On June 13th we broke camp at the Temo La and started down, following a steep ridge between two streams. There was forest on our left – Abies-Rhododendron to begin with, Picea-Rhododendron lower down, and on the open valley side a heavy growth of mixed shrubs. It may be as well to give here some idea of the vertical sequence of Rhododendrons, in the 'dry zone,' that is to say, behind the first line of defence against the monsoon.

In the alpine region are the three dwarf species, growing together and opening in this order – 'Lapponicum' (*R. nivale*), 'Anthopogon' (*R. laudandum*), 'Saluenense.' (*R. fragariflorum*). Next, the small 'Lacteum' (*R. phaeochrysum*) forming a choppy sea of shrub by itself on exposed slopes, and the pink-flowered bush 'Anthopogon' (*R. primuliflorum*) on the edge of the forest, with a large-leafed 'Lacteum' (*R. dignabile*) growing inside the forest. Still lower down come the yellow and salmon *R. wardii* and *R. wardii* hybrids in the open, and the pink and ivory *R. hirtipes* in the forest. Here, too, are found large bushy Lapponicum (*R. nivale* or *R. bulu*) and *R. lepidotum*, both keeping to grassy banks on the margin of forest; the former sometimes extends upwards into the alpine region, the latter downwards into the lowest valleys. In the Picea forest belt there are also the small-leafed 'Grande' (*R. uvariifolium*) the pink *R. faucium* and the rose-purple *R. oreotrephes*, to be described presently. At the bottom level of Rhododendrons come the 'Taliense,' *R. principis* either as a tree in the forest or as a bush in the open; the mahogany *R. triflorum* and a purple 'Lapponicum' (*R. bulu*), probably different from the alpine forms, though not obviously so. These sixteen species were all we found above the 3000m [10,000ft.] contour in the dry winter region.

After descending 600m [2,000ft.] we reached the *rong*, a wide valley of open pasture and park-land enclosed by forested mountains, where hundreds of yak grazed. In the bottom of the valley were scattered juniper trees (*J. squamata/fargesii*), some of them nearly 60m [200ft.] high. The boggy pastures

Frank Kingdon Ward's tent in Tibet.   FKW

Rhododendron principis **above Trube (Tripe) on slopes of Namcha Barwa.** **KNEC**

This is one of the commonest species in south-east Tibet. Formerly known as *R. vellereum*, the name was later changed to *R. principis* to the annoyance of many. It is named after Prince Henri d'Orléans who discovered it in eastern Tibet in 1890. Very free flowering, its peak of bloom in Tibet is April-May, before most other species come into flower. It thrives in hotter drier conditions than any of its relatives and perhaps this drought tolerance could be exploited in cultivation. The species is characterised by the felted fawn-coloured indumentum on the lower leaf surface. This is clearly visible on the undersides of the young leaves which point upwards as they unfurl.

Rhododendron principis (**R.** *vellereum*) **flowering in the Tsangpo Valley. FKW**

were gay with flowers, and some of the wettest ground was occupied by tussocks of *Rhododendron nivale* which formed large colonies. Clumps of orange Primula (*P. chungensis*) and blue poppies peeped out from amongst the bushes which grew along the stream, and we noticed several cherry trees *(Prunus serrula)* in full bloom. After passing two or three houses and small villages and twice crossing the stream by good solid wooden bridges, we reached Tumbatse, a small village situated at an altitude of 3550m [11,650 ft.].

Rhododendron nivale **and** *Primula alpicola* **in the Rong.** **PC**

The most common dwarf rhododendron species in China are a large group of mainly purple-flowered species in subsection Lapponica. Kingdon Ward was well aware of how difficult the members of this series or subsection are to identify and few plant-hunters pay much attention to them. In south-east Tibet all Lapponica can be attributed to the species *R. nivale* or *R. bulu*. In the meadows of the Rong, near Lunang, the rhododendrons form patches in the grazing meadows and are left alone by the livestock due to their poisonous foliage.

CHAPTER VI

The Paradise of Primulas

Flowers of the Rong

The Rong Chu flows northwards from a group of high rocky peaks situated on the containing wall of the Tsangpo, immediately above the entrance to the gorge, and discharges into the Tongkyuk River. The upper part of the valley is a wide boggy pasture flanked by wooded slopes, with a swift stream hurrying through thorn thickets in the middle. Every mile or two there is a cluster of houses, dignified by the name of village, where a patch of drier ground is carefully fenced off from the grassland by a leaning palisade, secure behind which are grown barley, turnips and shallot; occasionally also cabbages. Herds of yak browse over the pastures. They belong, not to the villagers, but to the *Dzongpön* of Temo, whose jurisdiction extends over the upper *rong* as far as Lunang. Lunang itself, a village of thirty wooden houses, is built on a mound overlooking the lower valley, which immediately below narrows suddenly to a winding glen, where the stream fusses and frets over boulders, and trees grow down to the water's edge. The wide wet vale, gently sloping like a saucer, is ice-worn; the glen below is water-worn. Lunang stands on the terminal moraine of a vanished glacier. In the glacier valley, edging the stream and sheeting the bogs, are myriads of flowers.

In May the drier turf slopes of the moraines and banks are carpeted with the fragrant *Primula atrodentata* (K.W. 5664), whose snowy mauve mops borne aloft on powdered poles scent the air for yards. These are over by June, and are succeeded by many flowers, culminating in September with the resounding blue trumpets of a gentian very like *G. sino-ornata*. Then, in June, the wettest open bogs are rosy with little *Primula tibetica* (K.W. 5739), a sleek and glossy dwarf which sends up flowering stems as much as 10cm [4in.] high, bearing, maybe, three or four starry flowers of deepest rose pink with bright yellow eye. In September the thread-like capsules are ripe, full of gold-dust seeds; but, alas! scarcely one ripens now where two bloomed before, because the cattle browse this plant down. Still, it is not difficult to find, for it grows in bogs so wet and sour that little else will grow there except clumps of vivid orange lousewort (*Pedicularis*).

In the sunny meads, where the ground is marsh rather than bog, since treading here you do not break through the surface crust, grows the moonlight 'Sikkimensis' *Primula alpicola* var. *luna* [*P. microdonta*] (K.W. 5746), a beautiful flower, with a fragrance almost stupefying in its sweetness. The stem grows no more than 50cm [20in.] high, then spouts out on one side a fountain of rather large lolling pale sulphury flowers. It grows in sheets, in hundreds of thousands all up the wet valley, acres and acres of soft yellow radiance, distilling scent; but we saw it scarcely anywhere else. South of the Tsangpo it is replaced by 'Joseph's Sikkimensis.' There is an alpine form of the Moonlight Sikkimensis, flooding the high lawns with a more vivid yellow *P. sikkimensis* var. *pudibunda* (K.W. 5906). Along the grassy banks of the stream, forming sombre deeps amongst the light Primula shoals, are violet 'Sibirica' Irises (*I. chrysographes*, K.W. 5783), with a cobweb of golden threads woven over the falls. We found and marked one plant of this with yellow flowers, but unfortunately it set no seed at all.

When we returned to Tumbatse on July 3rd after our first trip to the Himalaya, the meadows were incandescent with the 'Moonlight' Primula; for July rather than June is the month of Primulas here, just as June rather than May is the month of Rhododendrons. The snow is not melted before June, and the Rhododendrons depend chiefly on snow-water for their early blooming; but the meadow flowers are children of the warm rain. True, *Primula atrodentata* flowers in April and May, revelling in the sunshine and gulping from the snow-water; the rosy *P. tibetica* has faded before the end

The Rong from the east side of the Sirchem La.   **KNEC**

From the west end of the Rong the paths to the Nyima La, Sang La and Temo La passes begin. The damp meadows are full of flowers, particularly primulas, and grazing animals. The hillside from where this picture was taken is a forest of *R. principis* and *R. hirtipes*.

Primula tibetica **in the meadows of the Rong Chu.**   **PC**

One of the commonest primula species in the Tibet-China border regions as well as the Himalaya, it is usually found in wet meadows and snow melt at high altitude. It has been recorded as high as 5200m (17,000ft.) or more near Everest Base Camp. It is successfully cultivated but is unlikely to match the carpets of bright pink flowers found in the wild.

Primula alpicola **and** *Iris chrysographes* **near Tumbatse.**   **KNEC**

The 'moonlight primula' *P. alpicola* var. *alpicola* (var. *luna*) is a popular garden plant in cool areas such as Scotland. In the Rong, the iris and the primula seldom grow next to one another, but the few that do give a stunning colour combination. Other colour forms seem to be relatively rare in the Namcha Barwa region, though Kingdon Ward reports colonies of var. *violacea* on some of the nearby passes.

113

Primula bellidifolia (ssp. *hyacinthina*) on the Nyima La.   **KNEC**
This beautiful member of Section Muscarioides (meaning 'like a grape hyacinth') has a sweet scent and is usually solitary rather than clump forming. These two examples were collected near the top of the Nyima La at approximately 4400m (14,450ft.). The flowers open with a strong flush of purple-blue and fade to pale lavender. John Richards gives subspecific status to *P. hyacinthina* while other authorities treat it as a synonym of *P. bellidifolia*.

Meconopsis x harleyana and *M. simplicifolia* on the Temo La.   **KNEC**
Kingdon Ward's 'ivory poppy' was identified by Sir George Taylor as a hybrid between *M. simplicifolia* and *M. pseudointegrifolia*. It is rare in the wild, and seemingly sterile. We were lucky to find two plants in flower in 1995 on the Temo La. A rogue in a batch of *M. pseudointegrifolia* seed collected on the Nyima La flowered at Glendoick and was a superb example of the hybrid. Kingdon Ward was frustrated that there was never any seed of his special poppy, but he was reluctant to believe it was a hybrid. In a footnote in *The Riddle of the Tsangpo Gorges* he writes: 'Since writing the above, I learn that an unknown Meconopsis, with no number, has been raised from our seed. This can only be the species collected in Pemakö in October, which we took to be a form of *M. simplicifolia*, not having seen it in flower. It differed from typical *M. simplicifolia* in its longer style and in having on the average twice as many flowering scapes – six to eight, against only three to four in *M. simplicifolia*. The number of this plant is K.W. 6245, and it was abundant in Pemakö. The question arises, is this the Ivory Poppy in its natural haunt, the half-dozen plants we found north of the Tsangpo being strays? We shall soon know when it flowers in 1926' . This was almost certainly another example of the hybrid.

Meconopsis pseudointegrifolia.   **FKW**

of June; and along the woodland glades which lead to the alpine pastures, 'Cherrybim' *Primula calderiana* [*P. Roylei*] (K.W. 5701) displays an umbel of sleek green cups, full of brown seeds, from the midst of a grass cabbage. But the versatile 'Sikkimensis' family are at home, the grape-hyacinth Primulas (*P. bellidifolia*) just in bloom, and those assorted freaks which thrive in the fens of Pemakö – Cherry Bell (*P. valentiniana*), the Daffodil Primula (*P. falcifolia*), the Golden Primula (*P. morsheadiana*) and others, are poking their heads through the snow.

Beautiful as were the meadows of the *rong*, a patchwork of colour exhaling fragrance, the finest flowers hid themselves modestly under the bushes, along the banks of the stream. Here amongst spiteful spiny thickets of Hippophae, Berberis and rose, grew that lovely poppy-wort, *Meconopsis betonicifolia* [*M. baileyi*], the woodland blue poppy (K.W. 5784). This fine plant grows in clumps, half a dozen leafy stems rising from the perennial rootstock to a height of 1.2m [4ft.]. The flowers flutter out from amongst the sea-green leaves like blue-and-gold butterflies; each is borne singly on a pedicel, the plant carrying half a dozen nodding, incredibly blue 4-petalled flowers, with a wad of golden anthers in the centre. The foliage is startling enough, the lower stalked leaves reaching a length of 60cm [2ft.], the upper ones sessile, their round-eared bases clasping the stem. Never have I seen a blue poppy which held out such high hopes of being hardy, and of easy cultivation in Britain. Being a woodland plant, it will suffer less from the tricks of our uncertain climate; coming from a moderate elevation, it is accustomed to that featureless average of weather which we know so well how to provide for it; and being perennial, it will not exasperate gardeners. If it comes easily from self-sown seed, as a few species do, it will be perfect. Unfortunately, like the majority of its kind, it has no scent.

Another good plant of the thorn thickets, flowering in June, is the bright orange-

Meconopsis betonicifolia. **FKW**

Ward collected the seed of the famous blue poppy, *Meconopsis betonicifolia*, previously discovered by F.M. Bailey on his expedition of 1913, below Lunang, in the *rong.*

Meconopsis betonicifolia **on the Temo La.** **KNEC**

Kingdon Ward knew that the blue poppy, the most famous garden plant from south-east Tibet, was a really significant plant, with enormous potential in the garden. This species was long known as *M. baileyi* (named in honour of the great explorer) and all cultivated plants seem to be of Tibetan origin. Sadly the name *M. betonicifolia* (named earlier from a Chinese specimen) takes precedence, so Bailey is unfortunately no longer commemorated by such a wonderful garden plant. The peak of flowering in Tibet appears to coincide with the summer rains in July. Widely grown in cooler climes such as Scotland, and a parent of the many forms of the hybrid *M. x sheldonii.*

flowered *Primula chungensis* (K.W. 5740), closely related to the fiery orange *P. cockburniana. Primula chungensis* is a distinctly taller plant than *P. cockburniana,* carrying five whorls of larger flowers on chalk-powdered stems. Unlike most of the Candelabra Primulas, which are meadow plants, this is a shade-loving species, a woodland plant, growing 90cm [3ft.] high amongst the rank herbage. By September it has been cast down and trampled on by the rain, so that at harvest time it is by no means easy to find. But the finest Primula of all is the Giant Cowslip Sikkimensis, *P. florindæ* (K.W. 5781).

Primula chungensis **near the foot of the Tra La.** **PC**

In woodland around the Namcha Barwa area, this is one of the most common primula species. It also occurs in Sichuan and Yunnan provinces of China. One of the candelabra primulas, it is an adaptable garden plant in Scotland and seeds itself at Glendoick. This spectacular colony of hundreds of plants was growing at the edge of yak meadows above the Rong Chu, near the foot of the Tra La.

Lilium nanum **on the Nyima La.** **KNEC**

Formerly *Nomocharis nana,* this dwarf lily species occurs over a wide area of the Himalayan region from Nepal east to Yunnan. It is fairly easy to cultivate in cooler climates in soil rich in organic matter and has been introduced several times, by Wilson, Kingdon Ward, Ludlow and Sherriff and several others. It is quite common in south-east Tibet occurring at high altitudes generally above the tree line on moorland and scree. The flower colour and markings are variable.

Where the Moonlight Sikkimensis grows the Giant Cowslip is not far distant, but always in the shade and always in running water. But it has a much wider distribution than the former, for it is found on both sides of the Tsangpo, from below Nang Dzong to well within the gates of the gorge. It was most happy in the woodland brooks, which in summer overflow and flood the thorn brake. Here it manned the banks in thousands and, wading out into the stream, held up the current. It choked up ditches and roofed the steepest mud slides with its great marsh-marigold leaves. Then in July came a forest of masts, which spilled out a shower of golden drops, till the tide of scent spread and filled the woodland and flowed into the meadow to mingle with that of the 'Moonlight' Primula. And all through August it kept on unfurling flowers and still more flowers, till the rains began to slacken and the brooks crept back to their beds, and the waters under the thorn brake subsided; but the seeds were not ripe till late October. It is the rampant growth, the massive size of the plant, its great stalked leaves and the rich colouring and fragrance of the flowers, which is so impressive. Sometimes you may see a colony growing on the bank of a shingly stream bed, from which the silt has been cut away, leaving the plants hoisted upon bundles of pink roots, as though supported by flying buttresses. But even without this aid, *Primula florindæ* (as I have named it, in honour of my wife) grows 1.2m [4ft.] high, bearing sometimes a hundred flowers in its mop!

The 'Moonlight' Primula, so abundant in the *rong*, is *Primula alpicola* [*P. microdonta*], now introduced for the first time. 'Joseph's Sikkimensis' appears to be the same thing, as it varies in colour – violet, claret, maroon, purple or white. In one form or another, therefore, *P. alpicola* has a fairly wide distribution, but the colour varieties and forms tend to segregate locally, and as already remarked, the 'Moonlight' Primula itself we did not see outside the *rong*. It is interesting to note that amongst the 'Sikkimensis' Primulas, though we find complex colour forms (as opposed to yellows), yet the dwarf forms, whether of the petiolate round-leafed group, or of the lanceolate-leafed group, are always yellow-flowered. The Candelabra and Sikkimensis Primulas are the garden flowers of the future. They both fall into two colour groups: (1) yellows, and (2) purples. Both are tall and stately, come readily from self-sown seed and, when massed, are very effective. The Candelabras cross easily, giving a fine range of hectic and soothing tones, which blend and contrast with wonderful results. The Sikkimensis Primulas have not yet been induced to cross, but there are signs that the time is not far distant when this will be accomplished, and we shall then have another series of rich colours in these exquisite forms to match with our Candelabras.

Life in the village of Tumbatse

Our house at Tumbatse in the *rong,* was one of those wooden-walled shingle-roofed peasant houses commonly met with in the wetter parts of Tibet, where timber is abundant. The inhabitants cleared out two water-tight rooms for us, themselves living in the large family kitchen which every Tibetan house boasts; and a third room, rather leaky as to the roof and draughty as to the walls, where stray travellers slept, was given to our staff. Here they cooked our meals, dried our clothes, and made themselves comfortable.

All the rooms were situated on the first – and only – floor, which was reached from the ground-floor stables by a flight of wooden stairs, or, since this was immersed in Stygian darkness, more conveniently from the court- yard by means of a notched tree-trunk. Our own quarters suffered likewise from darkness, a tiny window, closed by wooden doors like a cupboard, being the only source of light. One had to sit close up under the window, or remain in perpetual gloom. Even in summer darkness came early, and the dull weather increased the dinginess. However, though we had our headquarters at Tumbatse, from the middle of June to the middle of October, we were not there very often – a few days only in June, a week in July, a week in August, a week in September and a few days in October. On the whole we were pretty comfortable. The roof was water-tight, and though the wind blew through chinks in the wall and through the door and the window, as well as up through the floor-boards and down through a hole in the roof, which did duty for a chimney (bringing with it much soot), there wasn't much to complain of.

Our chief source of irritation was the farmyard, with whose fauna we waged a

Tumbatse, Ward's base camp for five months.   JC

perpetual guerrilla warfare, though neither side could claim much advantage when we finally withdrew our forces. This fauna included an indefinite number of unfed and fed-up dogs, which maintained a bitter hostility towards us till the last, numerous cocks, which crowed steadily from 2 am. till breakfast, and several miscreant pigs. On one side of the yard was situated the dairy, where great activity prevailed all the summer.

Operations are conducted as follows: The milk is poured into a big cylindrical wooden churn, which being as much as 1.2m [4ft.] high, must needs be sunk in a pit at one end of the room, to enable the operator to stand over his work. Armed with a curious weapon which may be described as a slotted wheel at the end of a broom-stick, he plunges it up and down in the churn. The milk froths and bubbles, and spouts up in jets through the slots, and the ultimate result is butter, which is made up into fids, and wrapped in leaves. This butter, when fresh, is rather tasteless, and when over-ripe, nauseating; but it is undeniably wholesome. Every wealthy family keeps a good

The village of Tumbatse.   KNEC
This house at Tumbatse is similar to the one Ward used as his base on the 1924 expedition, though it has stone rather than wooden walls. The shingles on the roof are weighted down with stones.

Prayer flags outside the village of Tumbatse.   **KNEC**

Kingdon Ward used this village as his base during his 1924 expedition. He reported being fairly comfortable, complaining only that 'the chief form of irritation was the farmyard'. The village seems to have changed little since 1924 (though it has apparently been destroyed by an earthquake and rebuilt). We were particularly charmed in 1996 by a spotted piglet, kept on a lead, who liked to have its tummy rubbed.

selection of these butter pistons, each with a different pattern of slots and perforations; for, of course, every county family makes its own butter, just as it roasts its own barley, grinds its own *tsamba,* and brews its own beer.

   The most interesting thing about our home was the front door. This door, a heavy wooden one, 2m [6ft.] high and as much across, led into the yard, whence you entered the stables and ascended to the living rooms; it was fastened by means of an ingenious wooden bolt, which deserves description. The bolt itself was hollow, square in section, with a curiously shaped slot cut in the top. It worked in a bolt-way in a wooden beam which was built into the stone wall, forming part of the lintel. Immediately above the bolt-way a wedge-shaped piece of wood had been cut out of the beam, leaving a groove, and the partition between this groove and the bolt-way beneath was bored through at two points diagonally opposite each other; the wedge had then been replaced. Two stout wooden pegs fitted loosely into these sockets, and projected half an inch into the bolt-way. When the door was fastened, these pegs dropped into the slots cut in the top of the bolt, thus holding it in position; no amount of tugging could now withdraw the bolt. To open the door a 30.5cm [12in.] key, with projecting teeth corresponding to the two slots in the bolt, had to be inserted down the inside of the bolt, from an arm-hole in the lintel, and the two pegs lifted, while at the same time the bolt was drawn back with the other hand. Of course, when the key was removed, the pegs dropped back of their own accord, and the apparatus, not being automatic, the same performance had to be gone through before the bolt could be shot home. Unless one had the knack, one sometimes fumbled a good deal before one could open the door.

More flowers of the *rong*

To return to the flowers in the *rong,* mention must be made of a fine Cyananthus which sprawled and flopped about over the ground at the edges of the cornfields without visible means of support. The stems at first make an effort to grow erect, but soon grow tired and lie down, forming a dense tangled carpet of green leaves, nestling amongst which, the big violet flowers play hide-and-seek. The plant is *C. lobatus,* but is an altogether bigger and more boisterous grower than the cultivated form from China, with larger flowers of a deeper and richer hue. In the *rong* it is a sheer weed of the cornfields, but it also ascends 600m [2,000ft.] into the alpine region, where it is a sturdier plant, growing erect, and scattered on the steep alpine grass slopes. Seed from both varieties was collected (K.W. 5949), and has germinated well. It is a late summer flower – in the *rong* it flowers through August and September, ripening its seeds very quickly, but in the alpine region, time being short, it was earlier. We gathered seed of the alpine variety as late as mid-October at the Doshong La, when snow lay deep on the slope and everything was in cold storage for eight months.

Round the home cornfields too, and in the hedges, grew a tall Adenophora, slender and dainty, whose tiny white or pallid blue pagoda bells, complete with long clapper, are as neat as can be. Still better was a 2m [6ft.] rue (*Thalictrum diffusiflorum,* K.W. 5899), sending up above the frothy maidenhair foliage, a great puff of mauve flowers, like an evening cumulus cloud. Sometimes one would see such a mauve cloud hanging 3m [10ft.] up in a bush, and on examination find that it belonged to a giant rue which had thrust its way up in darkness inside the branches and there burst into a shower of stars. This rue has what the hairbell Adenophora lacks – quality; which is an indefinable air of good breeding. It reminds one of *Thalictrum dipterocarpum,* but the perianth is larger, and usually 5-lobed and the leaves or rather leaflets are smaller.

Many other flowers there were along the margins of cultivation forming a rank tangle, from which one had to pick out winners; but I was not prepared to put my money on any of them, with the exception of a small white-flowered Morina, and that only because, like so many flowers in this country, it was sweetly fragrant. I have seen the same plant in Yunnan, but I cannot recall that it was fragrant there. As for shrubs, one found the same species of Rhododendron as at Tsela Dzong, and a few others; here they ventured out into the open, instead of always lurking in the hidden recesses of the mountains, for we were further inside the forest land.

A close heath of purple-flowered 'Lapponicum' covered large patches of oozing lawn,

Fine mature spruce trees. FKW
Spruce is the most widespread conifer in south-eastern Tibet. Some authorities recognize two or more species in the area: *P. balfouriana* var. *linzhiensis* is the most common while *P. brachytyla* occurs in the gorge around Gyala. The trees are a popular source of timber for building, and parts of the forest above the *rong* have been felled. There is a large timber depot near Lunang.

Cyananthus lobatus on the Pumo La in Bhutan. PC
This is a particularly fine form of this variable autumn-flowering plant. Interestingly there are white forms in the picture as well as the more common purple ones. White forms were introduced by Ludlow and Sherriff (L&S 872) from the Tibet/Bhutan border area and these may still be in cultivation. Ward found this species several times in the course of the 1924–25 expedition.

Rhododendron lepidotum on the Temo La. KNEC
The distribution of this species covers a vast area from Nepal and northern India across Tibet and Burma well into China. The Himalayan forms tend to be completely deciduous while those in south-east Tibet are generally evergreen. Kingdon Ward describes both yellow and purple forms, but so far we have located only purple ones in the Tsangpo Gorges area. One of the latest to flower of the dwarf species, few flowers open before the end of June in Tibet.

Thalictrum diffusiflorum in **hedgerows near Tumbatse.** **KNEC**
This species of rue, endemic to south-east Tibet, has much larger flowers than other species in the region. Similar to *T. chelidonii* which occurs further west and *T. dipterocarpum* which occurs further east. Listed by a few specialist nurseries, it deserves to become more popular.

where the ground flattened out at the foot of the steep forest; and just within the forest, lining a burn, we found one of our very best Rhododendrons, a bush form of *R. oreotrephes* hung all over with masses of rosy-purple flowers. The colouring was rich, and luckily we had found the plant in a good year, at its best; the glen was simply glowing with it (K.W. 5790). On dry sunny slopes, particularly on old moraines, amongst wizened bushes of the Mahogany Triflorum was an undergrowth of dusky crimson *Rhododendron lepidotum*, which bloomed in July. The precautions taken to ensure cross-pollination in this plant are significant. The flowers stand on edge, erect on their long pedicels, and slightly arched, so as to present only their mailed backs to the rain; a sensible enough provision in a flower which opens in the wettest month of the year. There are ten stamens of equal length, the filaments of the five upper ones being expanded at the base, while the upper edge of the corolla tube is slightly inturned to form a flange, where honey is secreted. On the upper lobes of the corolla are painted a number of darker spots and streaks, all pointing like fingers towards the honey bath, held up between the flange and the palisade of filaments. Insects want honey – or, in a few cases pollen, for food; they don't care two straws about pollinating flowers. But flowers want to be pollinated – and the aristocracy want to be *cross-pollinated;* a little honey costs them nothing, and they willingly pay that bounty to insects in return for a little solid cross-pollination work. An insect approaching this Rhododendron flower, reads the hieroglyphics on the corolla, and translating them, 'Step inside; this way, please,' reaches the honey without waste of time. While blindly probing for the concealed honey, it may entangle its legs with the pollen, which is in the form of elastic white threads, and carry some off to another flower. At any rate, these threads may often be seen festooning the lower stamens and trailing all over the flower, as though brought from elsewhere.

The average insect is doubtless a wiseacre; it aims at economy of effort, and goes straight to the point – in this case honey – without creating a disturbance elsewhere, or doing a stroke more work than is necessary to accomplish its purpose. But there is the usual village idiot to be considered – a clumsy oaf which always does everything upside down and inside out. The plant legislates for him, too – it is taking no risks. The device described insures that the clever insect shall concern itself only with the upper male part of the flower, without troubling itself about the female apparatus – which has nothing to offer. The clumsy insect would be sure to blunder into that, so the plant cleverly removes it out of the way by bending the style down till the stigma projects between the lower lobes of the corolla.

The most stupid insect, fuddled with honey and entangled with pollen threads, cannot now fall against the home stigma on his way out, and deliver the goods at the wrong door. The chances are it will carry them away and deliver them outside the 6km [4 mile] radius, where they will be entangled amongst foreign stamens and eventually blown on to a foreign stigma.

After Rhododendron there were perhaps more species of Lonicera than of any other shrubby genus, though it was not till much later that we found a twining one like our English honeysuckle. They were nearly all small trees, shrubs and undershrubs, remarkable for their flowers, or for their fruits, or both; and in one case for foliage. This last, *L. webbiana,* which was a small forest tree, produced such inconspicuous dull reddish flowers, that had it not been for the large varnished leaves, one would certainly have passed it by. But in the autumn it lured one with a different charm, displaying gifts of which none could have suspected it; for the fruits, dangling in pairs on 7.5cm [3in.] pedicels, looked more like wild cherries than anything else (K.W. 5822).

In the *rong* itself, the best honeysuckle was a small downy-leafed bush which grew in thorn thickets by the stream (K.W. 5776). It had large straw-yellow flowers, with papery wings,

A mass of *Rhododendron oreotrephes* below the Sirchem La.   PC

We were lucky to hit the peak of flowering of the *R. oreotrephes* in 1996 when the bright purple flowers gave a stunning show in the Picea forest. This is a variable and widely distributed species which can be white, pink, purple or bicolour. It is a popular garden plant in moderate climates for its freedom of flowering and fine, usually glaucous foliage.

Lonicera webbiana **on the approaches to the Nam La.**   KNEC

One of the most vigorous of the many Lonicera species in this region, *L. webbiana* can reach 6m (20ft.) in height. The flowers are rather small for the relatively large leaves, but are a striking bright red. Roy Lancaster describes the flowers poetically as 'poised beneath the leaf above like two miniature crows'. (He was describing *L. adenophora*, now considered synonymous with *L. webbiana*.)

Rosa wardii **on the Nyima La.**   KNEC

This rose species was discovered and collected by Kingdon Ward on the 1924 expedition (K.W. 6101) at Pasum Tso. Apparently seedlings raised from this number did not entirely match the wild material and were referred to as var. *culta*. *R. wardii* can be distinguished from other rose species in the area by the scented white flowers (*R. sericea* has cream flowers and *R. macrophylla* pink flowers) and the smooth, flask-shaped fruit. Introduced in 1995 under Cox and Vergara 9556 and has so far proved hardy and free-flowering at Glendoick.

succeeded by orange-scarlet berries. Abundant though it was, it set very little fruit, and I spent a lot of time hunting for berries. This was *L. hispida*. Not dissimilar in flower was a dwarf alpine species (*L. hispida* var. *setosa*– K.W. 5988), which formed prostrate mats on very steep gravelly slopes facing the sun (or where the sun ought to have been – and doubtless was, though always invisible). Very little else would grow here. This plant made a brave show in bloom and then collapsed. Not a fruit could I find the first day I searched (that was in November), and I was in despair; but on the second day I picked two seeds off a stone, where a bird had evidently been scraping its beak after making a meal off some berries, and continuing the search discovered a few squashed fruits and extracted the seeds. How I prized those half-dozen seeds no one will ever know, for it was never put to the ultimate test! At the third attempt, subjecting the whole area covered by the plant to intensive search, we were much more successful, securing numerous berries and not a few odd seeds left on the stones. But probably the best of the dozen Loniceras was an undershrub with lovely glaucous foliage and purple flowers, succeeded by big blue-black berries like sloes: *Lonicera cyanocarpa* var. *porphyrantha* (K.W. 5872). It is a very distinct new species, and it grew on a steep cliff in Pemakö, smothered amongst Rhododendrons and dwarf willow and many other shrubs. Two roses were abundant all over Kongbo. One was a large bush with deep rose-coloured flowers and bristly flask-shaped fruits like *R. moyesii* (K.W. 5834): *Rosa macrophylla*. The other, *R. wardii* with scented white flowers and smooth fruits, was less common (K.W. 6101).

The passes around the *rong*

There are several ways out of the *rong*, over the high ridge which separates it from the Tsangpo, though the only passes in general use are the Temo La and the Nyima La. There is no through traffic. Grain is brought over to the herds, and butter taken back – that is all. The other two passes are the Tang La, immediately above Tumbatse, with an easy ascent from the *rong*, but a most abominable descent to the Tsangpo; and the Pa La or Tra La above Lunang, almost equally difficult on both sides, and easily the worst of the four. The two latter are used exclusively by yak herds who visit the high pastures during the short summer; but owing to a serious epidemic amongst the yak during the previous year, we found both paths out of commission for the time being and the bothys deserted. Most of our collecting north of the Tsangpo was done on the Temo La and the Nyima La, which were within a few hours' march of us. Still closer was the Tang La, which we crossed once, and on which we camped several times. But the Tra La, which we crossed in July, on our way home from the Tsangpo, we desired never to see again, even in a bad dream.

P. calderiana on the **Podrang La.** PC
This is the commonest of the purple-flowered species in the Tsangpo Gorges region. It occurs over a huge altitudinal range and grows in woodland as well as on open moorland. Domestic animals trample it but don't eat it: they are probably put off by its notoriously unpleasant smell, described by some as 'bad fish'. Kingdon Ward refers to this species as *Primula roylei*.

Rheum nobile and **Fred Hunt on the Nyima La.**   **KNEC**
The giant rhubarb is one of the most spectacular plants of the high Himalaya. While other alpine plants tend to be low growing, *Rheum nobile* is gradually transformed from a small yellow circle of leaves to a 2m (6ft), almost luminous beacon which can be seen from great distances. The leaves perform the function of a greenhouse for the seeds ripening inside. Tibetans cut down the plant and eat the central stem, considering it a delicacy. On the Nyima La it was growing on boulder scree above the tree line.

The forests which clothe the slopes and fill the glens on either side of the *rong* are composed of Picea, and below with an undergrowth of Rhododendron, Lonicera, Euonymus, Rose and other shrubs. As one ascends the Rhododendron element increases, and Abies replaces Picea. There were hardly any flowers in the forest, except by the side of the path, or in clearings, where *Primula calderiana* [*P. roylei*] was always conspicuous. Though it has a vertical range of over 900m [3,000ft.], growing in the depth of the forest and on the open alpine moorland, this plant shows remarkably little variation except in stature. An interesting point is the effect which human interference has had on it. In the alpine region it occurs widely scattered over the moorland; but the small grassy alps on which stand the herds' bothys, and on which the yak are tethered at night, are red with it. These knolls must have been cleared by men in the first instance, otherwise they would be overgrown with dwarf Rhododendron, like the rest of the moorland.

On June 18th we made an excursion to the Tang La in order to see how the alpine flora was developing. Ascending by the moraine, we at once entered the silent depths of the forest, where long streamers of lichen fluttered from the trees and everywhere our feet sank into moss which upholstered the forest in yellow plush. One alp was white with drifts of Lloydia like a tiny Crocus, and higher up we found little fluffy patches of *Primula walshii*. with bright rose flowers (K.W. 5802). Crossing some screes, we reached a ridge between two ice-worn valleys, at the heads of which were cup-like depressions. We thought there might be lakes here, but they were silted up and covered with flowers. In the wet sand grew a white-flowered Cochlearia.

Rheum   nobile,   the   giant
rhubarb.   **FKW**

123

Spanish moss in trees on the Nyima La.   KNEC
Spectacular Spanish moss, *Usnea longissima* or *Lobaria pulmonaria*, is a feature of many of the forested areas of south-east Tibet, draping the Picea and Juniper trees in cobwebs of pale green.

Potentilla microphylla **var.** *microphylla* **on the Nyima La.**   KNEC
This beautiful, mat-forming species of the Cinquefoil with vibrant yellow flowers is typically found growing on mossy rocks from 3600-4800m (11,800-15,700ft.). This plant was formerly known as *P. microphylla* var *depressa*. Its very widely grown relative *Potentilla fruticosa* also occurs in Tibet.

Cassiope wardii **on the approaches to the Nam La.**   KNEC
This species of Cassiope was named after Kingdon Ward after he discovered it in 1924 on the Temo La. He was not successful in introducing it, however: this was achieved by Ludlow, Sherriff and Taylor in 1938. The relatively thick stems are edged with a mass of fine white hairs which separates this species from its relative *C. fastigiata*. The two species do hybridise in the wild. Rare in cultivation as it is difficult to propagate, though some hybrids raised from it, such as 'Muirhead', are easier to obtain.

Cassiope fastigiata **on the Sirchem La.**   KNEC
The 'middle-sized' of the three Tibetan Cassiope species, it was first introduced from the Himalaya in the 1850s. Quite large and vigorous, growing to 30cm (12in.), it can be very showy in flower. The Cassiopes belong to the family Ericaceae (which includes heather and rhododendrons) and enjoy similar acid soil conditions.

We were now at the precipitous foot of the 'Plug', whose summit was still covered with snow; and in the distance we caught sight of a remarkable vegetable. This was a giant sorrel (*Rheum nobile*, K.W. 5805), not yet full grown, but forming a luminous yellow pagoda, about 60cm [2ft.] high. It grows at a most astonishing rate, till it is about 2.2m [7ft.] high; but early in the year as it was, we could count these crazy vegetables across the valley half a mile away, yellow candle-flames against the dark background. A month later, when full-grown, they stood up out of the Rhododendron sea like lighthouses. Unlike the Chinese *R. alexandræ*, *R. nobile* does not form colonies, but springs up here and there on the steeper slopes. The Tibetans eat the young leaves, and we tried to make a cauliflower-au-gratin out of the heart of one; it was edible, but insipid.

Another interesting flower was the dwarf *Primula sinopurpurea* [*P. rigida*], found growing with another 'Nivalis,' *P. macrophylla* var. *ninguida,* on gravel patches amongst the *Rhododendron nivale*. It was not, however, till July that the flowers of the alpine region were fully out – except, of course, at the Doshong La, where the alpine Rhododendrons flower

Rhodiola himalayensis? **on the Nyima La.**   KNEC
The Genus *Rhodiola* was formerly considered part of the huge genus *Sedum*. This showy plant was growing on boulder scree near the top of the Nyima La. Other plants growing here included *Meconopsis speciosa* and *M. pseudointegrifolia*.

a month earlier. We spent July 5th-9th at the Temo La, marching round the head of the valley; and here we saw the dry winter region alpine flowers at their best. All the poppies were now flowering together, and though the heavy sky rained ramrods on them, they cared little. The big blue prickly poppy *Meconopsis horridula* [*M. prainiana*] (K.W. 5909) seems to epitomise the swift passing of summer in these alps. The long carrot-like root is as soft as a sponge, the stem hollow and watery; the first two or three flowers open and fade quickly, battered by wind and rain, to be succeeded by others, and again others. It is a flimsy jimcrack thing in spite of its beauty – here to-day and gone to-morrow.

Many brilliant louseworts were in bloom on the lawns, and drifts of yellow *Primula sikkimensis* var. *pudibunda,* and the beautiful blue cups of a gentian and crimson patches of *Primula dryadifolia* ssp. *philoresia* on the rocks. But by far the finest sight was the moorland, all frothy white with Cassiope and the 'Anthopogon' Rhododendron, and streaked with the purple foam of 'Lapponicum' and 'Saluenense', on which the sulphur poppies tossed and swayed like buoys. But the tree Rhododendrons were over.

Another conspicuous plant on the boulder screes was a species of Rhodiola (*Rhodiola himalayensis?*), which formed large compact clumps; in autumn the leaves turn scarlet. A feature of these alpine valleys of the *rong* is their semicircular or broadly oval shape at the head, constricting suddenly to a bottle-neck below. The upper valley is usually fairly level, with moraine dumps here and there, and screes all round; but the bottle-neck exit is always steep as well as narrow. Once in the alpine region, travel from valley head to valley head is easy, even over the very steep shattered ridges which divide one valley from another; nor is there ever any difficulty in crossing the range, from the head of one valley to the head of another. The yak herds wander freely all over these alps. The difficulty occurs when you want to pass from the alpine region to the *rong,* through the steep forests. There are only a few paths, and most of them avoid as far as possible the deep wooded glens, keeping to the crest of a ridge or a moraine. But in July we followed a bottle-neck valley from where the Rong Chu had its source and found the going bad.

CHAPTER VII

In the Rhododendron Fairyland

To the Nyima La

June is the month of Rhododendrons in Eastern Tibet. We decided that the snow would by now be melting on the Himalaya; and on the 20th we left Tumbatse on our first serious expedition. We had selected the Doshong La as our objective for several reasons. We knew nothing about it from the botanical point of view, but it was on the map, and it was close to the great snow-peaks; also it was near the Tsangpo, and therefore near Tumbatse, and being only 4100m [13,500ft.] high, might, we supposed, be an easy pass. Finally, it had been crossed from the south by Majors Trenchard and Pemberton of the Abor Survey Party in 1913 (and therefore existed in fact, as well as in theory). Unfortunately these modest explorers had published no account of their journey other than a few matter-of-fact statements in an official report. Thus our proposed trip was by way of being a Himalayan reconnaissance; the fact that it turned up trumps was due more to good luck than to foresight.

The day was moderately fine, with even a little dilute sunshine, and we crossed the high range which encloses the Rong Chu by the Nyima La, 4650m [15,240ft.], camping some hundreds of feet down the other side. There was no snow here, but we had a good view straight across the abyss in which flowed the Tsangpo to the Himalayan peaks, 32km [20 miles] distant; and the valleys there were so clogged with snow that it looked impossible to reach the Doshong La at all. The flora of the Nyima La resembles that of the Temo La, but of course we found a lot more plants in flower now. Amongst the sea of dwarf Rhododendron was a purple Nomocharis, the stem bearing a single nodding flower like that of *N. lophophorum* (now *Lilium lophophorum*). This is the little known *Lilium nanum* [*Nomocharis nana*] (K.W. 5809). The high grassy alps at 4900m [16,000ft.] were spangled with dwarf Primula, bearing large violet or mauve flowers with white eye and deliciously fragrant. This was *Primula chionantha* ssp. *brevicula* [*P. rigida*], one of the pretty 'Nivalis' type, with long slender sausage-shaped capsules. When we came to collect seed of it, not a capsule could we find where the grass had been carpeted with flowers; but we got some seed of it from a small patch found at the Tang La, just above Tumbatse (K.W. 5801).

It was at the Nyima La we first saw the 'Ivory Poppy' (Meconopsis sp. K.W. 5766), a beautiful member of the barbellate haired section. Whether it was a cream or ivory form of *Meconopsis simplicifolia*, which it closely resembles in habit, or a distinct species,

---

Above. **The top of the Nyima La.**   KNEC
The contrast between the volume of snow on the Doshong La to the south and the Nyima La is stark. This pass is significantly higher than the Doshong La at 4650m (15,240ft) but by June few patches of snow remain. Carried north by the prevailing winds, most of the precipitation falls on the main Himalayan range from Namcha Barwa west towards Bhutan, leaving the ranges further north in rain shadow.

I have been unable to decide. Certainly it closely resembles *M. simplicifolia* in all essential respects, and they occur in company. Against that must be set the circumstance that the Ivory Poppy tends to have cream and even sulphur-yellow flowers, rather than ivory white, which is contrary to all precedent. No Meconopsis is known – or has been known hitherto – in which the flowers are sometimes blue and sometimes yellow. Blues vary to violets, purples and reds; or the colouring matter may be entirely absent, so that a dead white results. Yellows also vary in shade, though to a less extent. But the yellow-flowered group and the blue-flowered group have always remained antagonistic.

Meconopsis speciosa **amongst boulder scree on the Nyima La.   KNEC**
One of the prickly stemmed species, it differs from *M. horridula* in its pinnatifid leaves (the leaf looks like a set of pinnate leaflets but is in fact a single leaf not divided as far as the midrib). This sometimes spectacular species is unfortunately virtually impossible to cultivate, despite numerous seed introductions. This specimen was growing on the Nyima La above 4240m (13,900ft.).

Another interesting fact about the Ivory Poppy was this: it was very rare – so rare that we counted only six plants of it, though these were widely scattered. I emphasise this point because it is an uncommon experience to come across a really rare plant. A plant may be common everywhere over a large area, or local – that is to say, found only in a few or even in only one locality, though common there; but it is very seldom really rare. Even when it appears to be so, it may be owing to the fact that one has reached only the outskirts of its distribution, where naturally it is rarer than towards the centre; further search towards that centre will generally reveal it in ever-increasing numbers. It is of course possible that we were only on the fringe of the Ivory Poppy's domain; but we covered a lot of ground, and it seems unlikely. When one considers what countless thousands of plants of almost any small species one sees in these mountains, it will be realised how startling is a rare plant. Some are more abundant than others; some more local; but generally speaking, the rarest plant is seen in thousands. The dwarf 'Nivalis' Primula referred to above was certainly local; we saw it in two places only on the one range, and close together, perhaps not more than a couple of thousand plants. But it occurs also in Western China, 500km [300 miles] farther east. The dwarf yellow Meconopsis is local, for we found it in only one locality, though it is abundant enough there. The 'Geranioides' Primula referred to below was rare at the Nyima La, but extremely common at the Pasum Lake. We saw hundreds of thousands of plants of the Giant Cowslip *Primula florindae*, of 'Joseph's Sikkimensis,' and of the Moonlight Sikkimensis (*P. alpicola*); and *Meconopsis impedita*, though scattered, occurred on every range we crossed, and over such a vast area that there must be literally millions of plants in Eastern Tibet alone. Even the big yellow Meconopsis (K.W. 5910) (*M. pseudointegrifolia*) which only grows above 4900m [16,000ft.], occurs on both sides of the Tsangpo and on mountain ranges 160km [100 miles]or more apart; so that it cannot be rare.

As for plants like some of the dwarf and scrub Rhododendrons, 'Sibirica' Irises, Pedicularis, Aster, and other sub-alpines, they are found in such staggering numbers that the brain fails at the thought of their abundance. To return, then, to the Ivory Poppy of uncertain relationship. We marked down our plants carefully, since the supply of seed was obviously so limited. Alas! when we came to collect it, hardly a capsule had set any seed at all! Such are the trials of the plant collector. There was still one chance, however. In fruit it was not possible to distinguish this plant from *M. simplicifolia*. Therefore by collecting seed of every *M. simplicifolia* one saw, one might be collecting seed of the Ivory Poppy too. Though I have no wish to arouse hopes which it is beyond my power to satisfy, those who have *M. simplicifolia* under the number K.W. 5737 may possibly harbour an angel unawares.

Another Meconopsis now seen in flower for the first-time proved to be a 'new' species of the Aculeate group – K.W. 5751, *M. speciosa* [*M. cawdoriana*]. It grows on grassy alpine slopes, attaining a height of 25 or 30cm [10 or 12in.], and boring as much as 1m [3ft.] into the ground with its long tap-root. The flowers are sky blue, with a shock of trembling golden anthers in the centre and deliciously fragrant. Amongst the Aculeate with sky-blue flowers this plant comes nearest to the Indian species.

Quercus semecarpifolia near Pe. **KNEC**

Evergreen scrub oaks cover much of the Sino-Himalayan region from Afghanistan east to W. China. Unsurprisingly, these have been described under numerous names and taxonomists have begun reducing their number. The classification is complex because of enormous variation in morphology due to the environment which affects leaf size, shape and plant stature. This fine specimen was growing in pine wood above Pe, on the approach to the Doshong La. In Sichuan trees of up to 30m (100ft.) have been recorded, but in Tibet it remains a low growing plant, typically 2-3m (6ft.6in.-10ft.).

The south side of the Nyima La

Descending the steep valley towards the Tsangpo we passed through forests of Rhododendron and so into mixed forest, where two interesting Primulas were discovered – both woodland species. The first was a tall plant carrying two or three whorls of dark chocolate red flowers (*Primula advena* var. *euprepes*); the leaves, which are brightly silvered below, have rather the consistency of wet wash leather. The discovery of this plant came as a surprise. Its nearest relatives – *P. maximowiczii* and *P. szechuanica* – are found 650km [400 miles] to the east, and it seemed hardly likely that they would turn up on the Himalaya. Yet here was one of them; and as though that were not enough, we found the other (*P. advena* var. *advena*) south of the Tsangpo! These two chocolate and yellow respectively like the north-west China plants (and moreover botanically almost identical with *P. maximowiczii* and *P. szechuanica*), differ from them in one important respect: they are both fragrant. As garden plants, however, they are not likely to be of much value. Experience shows that they resent our climate. Moreover, the flowers are small, and are made smaller by the way in which the corolla lobes are reflexed against the tube. Even their fragrance, therefore, will not save them; they are of botanical rather than of horticultural interest.

The second find was the 'Geranioides' Primula (*P. latisecta*, K.W. 5819), which formed small colonies under the trees in deep shade. The cut leaves and bright purple-pink flowers so closely resemble those of certain Geraniums that at first sight I could hardly believe the plant was a Primula. It is rare here, but abundant farther north, growing in loamy soil. Below this the forests became more mixed, with larch and fir, and many deciduous trees such as maple and birch. There was the fine *Lonicera webbiana* too, not much to look at in flower, but a beautiful sight in fruit; and some magnificent bushes of the rich purple *Rhododendron oreotrephes* overhung the stream. We saw this plant in only two glens, so conclude that it is local; but it was abundant in those localities, struggling for dominion with the bright yellow *R. wardii*. As we descended, the trees grew larger, reaching huge dimensions at an altitude of 3400-3700m [11,000-12,000 ft.]; but the forest as a whole was more open, on account of

Primula advena var. *euprepes* on the Nyima La. **KNEC**

In his book *Primula* John Richards reclassifies *P. euprepes* as a variety of the yellow *P. advena*, as the two are separated by little more than flower colour. (Halda retains the older name *P. maximowiczii* var. *euprepes*.) This species does not appear to be all that common in the wild, but Kingdon Ward found it in several locations. Like its yellow relative, this has a powerful scent and this factor, coupled with the small flower size, suggest that this species has an insect pollinator active at night.

Rhododendron oreotrephes on the Sirchem La, above the Rong. **PC**

Taxonomically, the south-east Tibetan forms of *R. oreotrephes* are intermediate between typical *R. oreotrephes* and *R. cinnabarinum* ssp. *xanthocodon* Purpurellum Group. Indeed some of the herbarium specimens from this area are attributed to one and some to the other. Further west, around Tsari, *R. cinnabarinum* Purpurellum occurs while typical *R. oreotrephes* occurs towards Yunnan to the east.

the heavy shade cast by the big trees. Here and there occur open meadows of tall flowers which are a sea of colours, chopping and changing as the wind blows.

Coming out of the forest on to the open hillside which was covered with scrub oak (*Quercus semecarpifolia*) and thickets of *Rhododendron principis*, where in the dry gravelly soil grew masses of *Primula pulchella* [*pulchelloides,*] we reached houses and cultivation. A steep descent brought us to the Tsangpo, and the ferry just below Pe, and we crossed over by canoe – two dug-outs lashed together, capable of carrying three ponies at a time. Close as we now were to the entrance to the great gorge, there was little change in the appearance of the valley from what we had seen several days' journey above Tsela Dzong. There were the same sand-dunes with their meagre growth of thorn scrub, the same steep gravel banks and rocky slopes thatched with bushes, the same absence of trees, except near cultivation. Just below Pe, where the ferry plies, the river broadens out into a great lake about half a kilometre [a third of a mile] wide. Its altitude at this point is 2960m [9,680ft.]. Immediately afterwards the valley contracts to a deep trench, cut through the glacial gravels, and the river, dropping swiftly, roars into the gorge.

Fritillaria cirrhosa on the Nyima La. **AC**

This species of Fritillaria is extremely variable in flower colour and size. In Tsari the flowers are yellow, while further east purple shades are more typical. Taxonomists consider it to be no more than a form of a single variable species. The epithet '*cirrhosa*' refers to the tendrils used to support the flower stems when growing through other plants.

The road leading from Pe to the treeline on the Doshong La.   KNEC

Just above Pe, at an altitude of approximately 3000m (9,900ft.) the forest is predominantly *Pinus armandii,* some of which appears to have been replanted. Pine forest is relatively dry and some of the plants which associate with it are evergreen oak, dwarf Cotoneaster, and Deutzia. Ascending in altitude are successive forest layers, though *Larix griffithii* and birch at around 3300m (10,800ft.) to Picea on drier slopes and Abies on wetter ones at 3400-3700m (11,200-12,100ft.) or more. The motorable road is long and winding while the more direct porters' path runs above it, though the forest. The road ends at the treeline, but it is often blocked well below this with fallen trees.

From Pe towards the Doshong La

After crossing the torrent which flows from the Doshong La, we reached Pe, where we spent the night; and on the following morning (June 23rd) we started up the glen towards the Doshong La. We had not gone far before we entered the forest, which here consisted of a large-coned pine *P. armandii,* and a small-coned species, *Larix griffithiana Picea likiangensis,* Poplar (*P. rotundifolia*), Birch (*Betula szechuanica*) and a great variety of shrubs, such as rose (two species), Deutzia, Pieris, and Lonicera, with clumps of Bamboo and several climbing plants, Smilax, Clematis, and others. The Rhododendrons were at first the usual species – *R. principis, R. wardii* and *R. triflorum,* but these were soon replaced by others, and in such bewildering variety, that it was evident we had struck a rich vein.

In the first stratum of forest, ground flowers, which grew along the side of the path, were the big mop-flowered Androsace and pretty *Pyrola forrestii.* This stratum was quickly replaced by another; and we found ourselves in Rhododendron forest, where the 'Barbatum,' pink 'Thomsoni' and small 'Grande' (*R. hirtipes, R. faucium* and *R. uvariifolium*) were respectable trees.

130

Abies forest at the road end on the Doshong La.   **KNEC**

Keith Rushforth has identified the Abies species belonging to the *A. forrestii* aggregate. The Abies in this area are intermediate between Himalayan and Chinese species, some closer to *A. chayluensis*. Spruce generally grow in moister conditions than fir and the two tree species are often associated with different rhododendron species. *R. wardii, R. cerasinum, R. viridescens* and *R. dignabile* grow beneath the Abies on the north side of the Doshong La.

Cypripedium tibeticum **on the Doshong La.**   **KNEC**

All too often, as with most orchid species, terrestrial orchids are ripped from the wild and sold in local markets or shipped off to collectors. Unlike in parts of Yunnan, such as the Cangshan with *Pleione forrestii,* this has thankfully not yet happened in south-east Tibet where this species is widespread. On the Temo La in 1995 we were lucky to see hundreds of plants in flower on the steep banks on the north side of the path. This form has unusually dark flowers.

131

Rhododendron cerasinum on the north side of the Doshong La.
KNEC

All the forms of this species in the Gorges area appear to be the 'Coals of Fire' type where the entire corolla is red. The Burmese forms, also discovered by Kingdon Ward, have two-toned flowers, red with white at the base, which he nicknamed 'Cherry Brandy'. In cultivation, this species has long-lasting flowers and it often opens some of them in autumn.

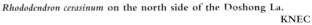

Rhododendron cerasinum on the north side of the Doshong La.
KNEC

Nicknamed 'Coals of Fire' by Kingdon Ward, this is one of the finest rhododendron species in the Tsangpo Gorges area. The dark red waxy flowers, with dark purple nectar pouches at the base of the corolla, are very distinctive. It occurs on both sides of the Doshong La and also in Burma.

Rhododendron aganniphum Doshongense Group on the Doshong La.
KNEC

Originally named *R. doshongense* but now considered to be a form of the variable and widespread *R. aganniphum*. Our observations revealed that the typical thin plastered indumentum is closer to that of *R. phaeochrysum*, and perhaps *R. doshongense* is best considered intermediate between these two species. This fine pink form was growing above the treeline amongst numerous other species of dwarf rhododendron at around 4000m (13,000ft.). Although tough enough to withstand very cold winters, this species, like most of its relatives, is very hard to please in areas with hot summers.

Rhododendron wardii blotched form on the Temo La. **PC**

The blotched forms of *R. wardii* collected by Ludlow and Sherriff in southeast Tibet in 1938 have proved to be some of the finest and hardiest forms in cultivation. Observations in south-east Tibet have revealed that in most areas blotched, spotted and pure yellow forms grow in mixed populations. The finest blotched forms have probably still not been introduced, but time will tell how good recently-collected seedlings are.

A mass of *Rhododendron wardii* by the bank of the Doshong Chu.   **KNEC**
R. wardii is one of the most spectacular plants of south-east Tibet and it is always in contention for the 'plant of the trip award' selected by participants at the end of expeditions to this area in spring. Where it forms the dominant species, the understorey of Picea forest can be turned into a blanket of differing shades of yellow. Rhododendrons bordering fast flowing mountain streams and rivers in China and the Himalaya have inspired woodland gardeners to create similar effects in Britain and elsewhere.

Presently came the first meadows, which in truth were bogs. The men said the ponies could not get through these, and wanted us to camp, then and there. It was they said, the only flat ground where we could camp. But as we were scarcely 300m [1,000ft.] above Pe, and obviously a long way from the pass, we refused to do so, disbelieving them on both counts. Persuasion of the men on our part, and of the ponies on theirs, had the desired effect; we surmounted the obstacle by unloading the ponies, and Tom was sent ahead to look for a camping-ground. Eventually we reached a meadow at the foot of the cliffs, and pitched our tents in a bog between two torrents. One torrent came from the Doshong La itself, the other from an equally steep valley which was blocked by an avalanche; the foot of the avalanche indeed was only a hundred yards from our encampment. The two valleys were separated by a high rocky ridge crowned by a truncated spire, which seen from below resembled the Potala at Lhasa. Both glens were heavily forested, and flanking the valley which led to the Doshong La was a lofty cliff.

No sooner were we settled in our watery camp, than the floral wealth of this old glacier valley began to dawn on us. The lower meadow was filled with Joseph's Sikkimensis Primula *P. alpicola* in five colours – violet, purple, maroon, sulphur, and cream, the last two forming an herbaceous border along the forest paths. The Giant Cowslip Sikkimensis (*P. florindae*) also grew here, on bog slides. But it was the Rhododendrons which provided the greatest surprise, and without stirring from camp we added three fine species to the collection. Lining the banks of the torrent, often hanging over into the frothing snow-fed water, was a brilliant-flowered 'Saluenense', *R.*

Foliage of *Rhododendron viridescens* in Pemakö.   KNEC

R. viridescens has rightly been recently reinstated as a species after the discovery of it in quantity on both sides of the Doshong La. Its relative *R. mekongense*, which grows nearby, is deciduous while *R. viridescens* is evergreen, with bluish leaves, and flowers around a month later. Flowers are usually cream or light yellow, sometimes with red spotting or flushing. The award form 'Doshong La' A.M. was raised from KW 5829. Kingdon Ward was not impressed with it, calling it 'an inferior species… with jaundiced flowers', but despite this it has proved to be a good plant in cultivation.

calostrotum ssp. *riparium*. It has the same twin flowers, large flattened pentagons of rich rosy purple, and the same dull rusty under-leaf surface; but in detail this Doshong La plant (K.W. 5828) differs considerably from the Burmese forms of *R. calostrotum* (K.W. 3390). In mass it is a wonderful sight, the clumps of glowing colour illuminating the dark roaring water over which it hung. In the bog were tufts of an inferior species (K.W. 5829), with hairy smelly twigs and leaves, and jaundiced flowers breaking into an unhealthy rash of greenish spots. This, however, did not flower till the end of June. It is evidently a variety of the Chinese *R. trichocladum* (later described as the type specimen of *R. viridescens)*.

The third species was a jewel of the first order. So far we had found no scarlet or crimson-flowered Rhododendron. But once well inside the great forest belt – which may be said to begin east of the 92nd meridian – we found several, none better than the one we now gazed upon for the first time. It grew in dense drenched thickets by the torrent, as a bush 2.5-3m

***Rhododendron calostrotum* ssp. *riparium* on the Doshong La.**   KNEC

A fine dwarf species which grows in the wetter mountains to the east and west of the Tsangpo Gorges. Amongst all the species on the Doshong La, this can be distinguished by its greyish leaves. The flowers are usually of a more purple shade than shown in this picture.

Acer caesium ssp. *giraldii* (syn. *Acer giraldii*). KNEC
This handsome Acer species is rare in cultivation. It is characterised by the bluish-white bloom on the young stems. In cultivation it forms a tree up to 12m (40ft.) or more. In the forest to the north of the Doshong La trees are up to 20m (66ft.). It has fine yellow autumn colour in Tibet.

Betula utilis bark. KNEC
Well known in cultivation, this species has a wide distribution from Pakistan in the west through the Himalaya into China. It is distinguished by its peeling bark and the hairs on the leaf underside. The wood is a useful building material and the bark can be used for paper-making and for water-proofing and roofing houses.

[8-10ft.] high; later we found it in the forest, a bigger bush, or small tree, 4.5-6m [15-20ft.] high. The flowers are large, fleshy, in loose drooping trusses of five, and of an intense burning scarlet; at the base of the corolla are five circular jet-black honey-glands, each about the size of a shirt button – hence the name Coals-of-Fire bestowed on *R. cerasinum* (K.W. 5830). It is one of the 'Thomsoni' series, and has the peculiarity of bending its flower-stalks almost into an 'S', the corollas hanging down, while the curved capsules stand erect.

A perpetual drizzle assailed the Doshong La. There is a low gap in the Himalayan range here between Namcha Barwa and the peaks to the south-west, the Doshong La itself being only 4100m [13,500ft.]; and as this is the narrowest part of the eastern Himalaya, the distance from the Tsangpo flowing north at Pe, to the Dihang (as the Tsangpo is called in the Abor Hills), flowing south at Forting, being less than 50km [30 miles], the rain-wind which rushes up the Dihang from Assam comes flying over this gap, flooding the pass and the valley below.

There is not room on the north flank of the range for much forest, but on the south flank there is ample room and the forest grows with a luxuriance only seen in regions constantly moist. Even on the north flank, however, the flora is extremely rich, different to anything we had seen on the other bank of the river. It was at first sight remarkable how different the flora was on the two sides of the range, considering the similarity of the climate in the upper regions. But this difference tended to disappear in the alpine region; and when we remember the contrast in conditions lower down it is not so surprising that the floras diverge more and more as we approach the Tsangpo on the one side, the Dihang on the other.

Clematis barbellata between Pe and Doshong La. KNEC
Identified as *C. barbellata*, although it does not appear to match the type description, this is an unusual looking species which we have found on several occasions in different locations, but which is not nearly as common in Tibet as *C. montana*. The deep red colouring on the inside of the sepals contrasts well with the paler, yellowish outside.

Bergenia purpurescens **on the Doshong La.**   **KNEC**
This familiar garden plant is very common in the Namcha Barwa area, where it is a companion plant of rhododendrons on the extensive moorlands, flowering at the same time. The leaves often colour well in autumn.

Iris chrysographes **at the campsite below Doshong La.**   **KNEC**
A relatively common plant in the Tsangpo Gorges region, this very showy Iris was a wonderful backdrop to several campsites, both on the Doshong La and in the Rong, near Tumbatse. The name means 'with golden markings' which occur to a greater or lesser extent on the falls of the flower. Growing to 40-50cm (16-20in.) this species was one of George Forrest's fine discoveries. In cultivation, this species crosses freely with its relatives such as *I. siberica*.

Rhododendron charitopes **ssp.** *tsangpoense.*   **KNEC**
This is a common species in the region with distinctive pink-purple flowers and aromatic leaves with pale undersides. Cullen reduced *R. tsangpoense* to a subspecies of *R. charitopes* which is found on the Burma-Yunnan border, while for some reason the more closely related *R. pruniflorum* remains a separate species. This species is not often cultivated due to its bud tenderness and unfashionable colour, but it can give a good display.

Rhododendron forrestii x R. aganniphum (R. chamaethomsonii) **on the Doshong La.**   **KNEC**
The widespread *R. forrestii* is a promiscuous species, crossing with many of its relatives and causing innumerable taxonomic headaches. On the Doshong La it crosses with *R. parmulatum*, *R. campylocarpum* and *R. aganniphum* (as in this example). Many specimens in herbaria and in gardens have been given the name *R. chamaethomsonii* or one of its varieties. The problem is that this specific name has been applied to natural hybrids with many different parent species. Kingdon Ward's 'Carmelita' almost certainly refers to some of the *R. forrestii* hybrids which are relatively common on the Doshong La.

In the alpine zone on the Doshong La

We spent a week at the Doshong La and climbed every day, but two days stand out vividly in my memory: June 24th, when we made our first ascent into the alpine region, and June 29th, when we crossed the pass and descended into Pemakö. But Pemakö deserves a chapter to itself, and I shall now confine my remarks to the flowers we discovered near our camp. The day after our arrival we set out from camp to ascend to the alpine region, selecting the avalanche as the best route. Thus instead of having to cut our way through the dense scrub which clothed the steep slope above the forest, we could walk on the snow, keeping to the open valley, where the torrent flowed beneath the avalanche. Nor had we climbed far when we began to find treasure. There were ruffled seas of 'Glaucum' Rhododendron (*R. charitopes* ssp. *tsangpoense*) K.W. 5844, with a pink foam of blossom frothing over it, and brilliant clots

Rhododendron *campylocarpum* on the Doshong La.   PC
Nicknamed 'Yellow Peril' by Kingdon Ward because it forms dense, impenetrable thickets. The Tsangpo Gorges
appear to be the eastern end of the distribution of this Himalayan species. The closely related Chinese *R. wardii*
also occurs here, and where the two species overlap, at or near the tree-line on the north side of the pass, many
intermediate forms occur. *R. campylocarpum* was introduced by Joseph Hooker from the Himalayas in the 1850s
and has been a popular garden plant ever since, though *R. wardii* has been more useful in hybridising.

of purple *R. calostrotum* ssp. *riparium*. Broad bands of sulphur and pink striped the sheltered
slope, where two scrub species, *R. campylocarpum* and *R. doshongense* (*R. aganniphum*), made
an impenetrable wire entanglement, 1m [3ft.] deep. The former became known as 'Yellow
Peril' by reason of its aggressive abundance. The slope was steep and difficult, so that we
halted often to regain our breath, and to collect specimens.

Once when gazing across the torrent to a steep grass slope, I pointed out to my
companion some brilliant scarlet leaves which formed a pattern on a rock; and he, taking
out his telescope, looked at them long and carefully. 'Why,' said he, at length, 'they aren't
leaves, they are flowers; it's a Rhododendron, I believe.' 'What!' I shouted, almost seizing
the glass from him in my eagerness; and gazing as he had done, I realised that he was
right. They were flowers, not leaves – flowers of vivid scarlet flaming on the rocks.
Straightway we tried to cross the torrent, but finding that impossible, continued up
stream to a dangerous-looking snow-bridge; this we might have risked crossing, so great
was our anxiety to reach the prize, but at that moment we observed another blaze at our
feet, and there was *R. forrestii* Repens gp. 'Scarlet Runner' as we called it, laced to the
rocks. For a minute we just stared at it, drunk with wonder. It lay absolutely flat on the
rocks, no part of the plant, not even the corolla, which is considerably larger than the
leaf, rising 5cm [2in.] above the surface; stems, leaves, and flowers cling as closely as
possible to the ground. Some of the mats were 0.5m [18in.] in diameter, with stems as
thick as a man's little finger, and must have been many years old. But the plant grows
slowly and keeps to the sunny side of the slope, sprawling over the barest gneiss rocks,

Rhododendron forrestii **Repens Group on the Doshong La.**   **KNEC**

The tiny creeping forms of this species (Scarlet Runner), found in full exposure, are what used to be referred to as *R. repens*. A short distance away in the lee of rock, out of of the fierce wind, are larger plants with larger leaves. Whether there is any genetic difference between the two or whether it is simply a matter of habitat remains to be seen. The very dwarf forms come into flower only a matter of days after the snow melts off them. They are likely to be under snow for seven to nine months of the year.

Rhododendron forrestii **Tumescens Group on the Doshong La.**   **KNEC**

This wonderful red species has caused a great deal of taxonomic confusion. Kingdon Ward reported finding three red entities on the Doshong La which he referred to as 'Scarlet Runner' (the lowest growing), 'Scarlet Pimpernel' – shown in this picture (a little taller) and 'Carmelita' (taller still). These were described as *R. repens*, *R. forrestii* var. *tumescens* and *R. chamaethomsonii*. It has since become apparent that all three are merely variations of a single species. All are therefore best referred to as *R. forrestii* or hybrids of it. This specimen has three or more flowers in the inflorescence and would have been referable to *R. chamaethomsonii* but, as typical *R. forrestii* grows nearby, flowers at the same time and seedlings raised from these plants produces offspring to match either 'species', it is impossible to justify maintaining two separate taxa.

Rhododendron forrestii **looking towards the Doshong La.**   **KNEC**
This picture, taken in mid-June, illustrates the shortness of the growing season on the Doshong La. As soon as the
snow melts off the higher ground, the alpine flowers are quick to start to flower. By late September or early
October the snow is returning and the plants disappear under a white blanket until the following spring.

where nothing else will grow. It is the first of its kind to flower and the first to ripen its
seed; for the winter sunshine melts the early falls of October snow, when the bushier
species of the lee slope are buried alive. Consequently it has to withstand much lower
temperatures than Carmelita (*R. chamaethomsonii*) and its allies; I have seen it lying out on
the bare rocks night after night in a temperature which approached zero. Scarlet Runner,
in fact, goes through the whole evolution of flower and seed production in the five
months, June to October!

A word as to the relationships and distribution of these creeping Rhododendrons, of
which *R. forrestii* [*R. repens*] may be taken as the type. They belong to a series of dwarf
undershrubs with blood-red flowers and are closely allied to the Chinese *R. neriiflorum,*
which gives its name to the series; they are entirely confined to the very wet ranges
separating the rivers which pour through the Himalayan gap. Thus they are alpine plants of
the temperate rain forest region, the region of winter snow and summer rain, and nowhere
else, from the extreme north-west corner of Yunnan, in China, across the headwaters of the
Irrawaddy in Burma, to the eastern end of the Himalaya in Tibet. The discovery of Scarlet
Runner (*R. forrestii*) on Namcha Barwa extends their known distribution 500km [300
miles] to the west, and forges an unexpected link between the eastern and western flanks
of the 'gap' flora; for hitherto the type was known only from the Mekong-Salween and
Salween-Irrawaddy divides, where it was discovered by Mr. George Forrest.

Continuing the ascent by a steep gully, we found ourselves ploughing through snow and an inextricable tangle of dwarf Rhododendron. There was nothing else but Rhododendron in fact – sulphur seas of Yellow Peril (*R. campylocarpum*) (K.W. 5853), lakes of pink *R. doshongense* (*R. aganniphum/R. phaeochrysum*) (K.W. 5863) and a vast confusion of 'Anthopogons' of all sizes and colours, which completely swamped the few poor little brooms of violet-flowered *R. nivale* (K.W. 5862). Above the Rhododendron turmoil there was only snow; we therefore made our way round the base of a cliff and over the spur which separated us from the next valley, descending towards the stream which flowed from the Doshong La. There we hoped to strike the path and return to camp. But it was not so easy as it looked. Below us was the valley under deep snow vaguely visible from time to time through rifts in the white cloud which came pouring over the pass; below us were cliffs, whose depths we could not plumb; and between the bottom of the valley and the path raged a torrent swollen with melting snow and half hidden by unmelted snow which concealed many a trap. We therefore advanced cautiously, in a rapture of joy at what we found. We were on a giant stairway of smooth rock, whose steps, ice-carved ledge by ledge, were filled with dwarf Rhododendron in astonishing variety.

At the top on the naked rock was Scarlet Runner in proud isolation. Sometimes it crawled over the flat, and reaching the edge of the step, shot out tongues of fire visible a mile away across the valley. It was already in full bloom, passing over lower down, and flowered so freely that mats and festoons were smothered beneath the blaze. The virgin snow dabbled with its hot scarlet, spread a bloody sheet over the tortured rock. A little lower down were the twiggy brooms of *R. campylogynum* [*R. damascenum*] or Plum Warner (K.W. 5842), its absurd little plummy mouths pouting discontentedly at us. Mixed with this, on the sheltered ledges, grew the more coarsely woven mats of Scarlet Pimpernel (*R. forrestii* Tumescens), another fiery 'Neriiflorum' (K.W. 5846). At first sight it looked like a darker edition of Scarlet Runner; but on closer inspection it was seen to be a bigger plant, with larger leaves and darker flowers, borne two or three in a truss instead of singly.

Just as Scarlet Runner was succeeded by Scarlet Pimpernel, so lower down on a lee slope, Scarlet Pimpernel was succeeded by Carmelita (K.W. 5847) (*R. forrestii* hybrids). This plant belongs to another branch of the family. It is bigger again, with still larger leaves, and flowers of luminous carmine, in threes. It grows socially, in 30cm- [1ft.-] deep tangles, and is not really a creeping plant at all, but prostrate with ascending stems; also, lest anyone should think that it is not sufficiently distinct from the other two, it may be remarked that it flowers and ripens its seed a fortnight later than Scarlet Runner. In October we dug it out of the snowdrifts in order to get seed; and the crimson conical capsules were found to be scarcely split at the apex, when those of Scarlet Runner, lying prone on the rocks, were wide open and empty. Next, amongst a chaos of fallen rocks, we found a thicket of Plum Glaucum (K.W. 5843) (*R. charitopes* ssp. *tsangpoense* Curvistylum gp.), one of the most striking species of all. The flowers are dark cerise, borne in pairs as in Plum Warner, but formed more after the pattern of Pink Glaucum, which the leaves with their white waxy under surface recall. In size it is intermediate between Plum Warner and Pink Glaucum, and it looks rather like a cross between the two; but it requires more shelter than Plum Warner.

Thinking that we should find this species abundantly lower down, and finding that we were at the moment in an awkward cul-de-sac, I omitted to mark this spot. We got out of the predicament, and – I never saw Plum Glaucum again! It was only by retracing my route laboriously up the cliff in October, when everything was hidden under a pall of snow, and every landmark wiped out, that at the third attempt I rediscovered the little hollow in which our only Plum Glaucum grew. How well I remember the occasion, for it was in the lilac dusk one frozen night when at last I came on it, excavated it, and triumphantly secured a little seed! As for Pink Glaucum (*R. charitopes* ssp. *tsangpoense*), whose silvered leaves and flat 5-flowered corymbs resemble those of *R. glaucophyllum* [*R. glaucum*], it grew everywhere in the bottom of the valley in billowy masses of pale pink and mauve tones. After crossing the torrent we found the path on the far side under the cliff, and descending through the forest reached camp. It had been a wonderful day.

Vaccinium sikkimense aff. with dwarf rhododendrons on the Doshong La.　　　　**KNEC**
Collected under KW 6227 and later identified as *Vaccinium sikkimense*. This species is rarely cultivated, though it grows well at Glendoick. On the Doshong La, it grows amongst the large number of rhododendron species such as *R. campylocarpum* and reaches 30-60cm (1-2ft.). The pink flowers are followed by black fruit which Ward describes as 'excellent eating'.

The 'anthopogon' rhododendrons and the Primulas of the Doshong La

The weather continued bad, though with fine intervals; cloud was always blowing over from the Pemakö side, and falling in a fine drizzle. During the next few days, however, we paid a visit to the pass, and explored the main valley, with excellent results. About 300m [1,000ft.] above our camp was a basin, now silted up and partly overgrown with scrub Rhododendron; once upon a time it had been a small lake, now it was a marsh, but in the winter it might, we thought, be a dry meadow. The torrent, after tumbling headlong 300m [1,000ft.] from the upper valley, flowed calmly, in a deep winding channel, gathering itself for the final rush and tumble down the valley to the Tsangpo. It was just the place for a camp, being on the fringe of the alpine region where all good things grow. From this glacier flat we climbed a steep cliff and immediately found ourselves in the upper valley with the giant's stairway on the right, and bold cliffs, striped with short rubble cones, on the left.

In October the upper valley was under deep snow, but by the end of June this had nearly all melted except for a permanent snow-bed at the top end; the head of the valley rose very steeply to the narrow pass, but we were able to ascend by the snowfield on a zigzag slant. The upper valley was also filled with moraine tips, which showed up darkly here and there out of a heaving sea of Rhododendron. The 'Anthopogon' Rhododendrons were many and various, and as these formed great bushy colonies alone by themselves, we must say something about them. On the steep broken slopes which lined the foot of the cliff, grew a bush species with brick-red flowers (*R. kongboense*) and long narrow leaves having a light chocolate-coloured indumentum. It was replaced in the hollows by a much smaller plant with sulphur-yellow flowers and large leaves with buff-coloured indumentum (K.W. 5849)

Primula falcifolia **on the south side of the Doshong La.**

PC

The 'daffodil primula' is one of the most distinctive and desirable Asiatic species. Unfortunately it has so far eluded any attempt to establish it in cultivation, though admittedly there have been a only a couple of attempts. Considered endemic to the Doshong La, it almost certainly spreads further east and west on neighbouring passes. In its native habitat, when not under snow, it receives almost constant rainfall, which is apparent in the rain drops on the lens in this photograph.

Diapensia purpurea **with** *Rhododendron forrestii*. **KNEC**
Diapensia purpurea is a most attractive and desirable alpine plant which has eluded most attempts to establish it in cultivation, though one or two alpine enthusiasts have managed to keep it going for a few years. It occurs in pink and yellow (and more rarely white) forms. The latter used to be known as *D. bulleyana* but the yellow (and white) forms are now considered to be simply colour variations of *D. purpurea*. On the very wet Doshong La, these burst into flower almost as soon as the snow melts from the patches of moorland where they grow.

(*R. cephalanthum* Nmaiense gp.). Other species or varieties had white or pink flowers, and leaves variously coated; it was really quite impossible to say which were species and which were not, but we found at least four very distinct 'Anthopogon' Rhododendrons, namely, the white-flowered chocolate-leafed species *R. laudandum* var. *temoense* (K.W. 5733), the pink-flowered woodland-shrub species (*R. primuliflorum*) (K.W. 5700), the red-flowered under-shrub species, *R. kongboense*, with long narrow leaves and light chocolate indumentum (K.W. 5850), and the cream-flowered undershrub (*R. cephalanthum* Nmaiense gp.) (K.W. 5849).

Two other Rhododendrons worthy of more than passing mention we found on the rubble cones which caught the midday sun – when there was any. At any rate, the snow melted here first in summer and did not come to stay till late in the fall, when everything else was already tucked up in bed and fast asleep. K.W. 5851 (*R. mekongense*) is a small compact bush with bright yellow flowers, flushed red on the reverse, opening before the leaves. It formed brilliant banana-coloured hassocks all up the slope, while in the thickets lower down the flowers were already over and the leaf-buds had erupted in a green haze. I thought it one of the best yellow-flowered species we met with. The other (*R. pumilum*) K.W. 5856, a very distinct species, was a wee thing which spread in tuffets over the ground, bristling with pinkish purple flowers. These are borne in pairs on long pedicels, and so long are the capsules besides, that they stick up through the snow like tiny fingers. The seed was not ripe till the middle of October, by which time the plants were buried under 30cm [a foot] of snow; but I could see the tips of the projecting capsules, and was able to excavate the plants.

It is impossible to do justice to the Rhododendrons at the Doshong La as we saw them in June; the valley, flanked by grey cliffs, roofed by grey skies, with the white snowfields above, spouting water which splashed and gurgled in a dozen babbling becks; and everywhere the rocks swamped under a tidal wave of tense colours which gleam and glow in leagues of breaking light. The colours leap at you as you climb the moraine: Scarlet Runner dripping in blood-red rivers from the ledges, Scarlet Pimpernel whose fiery curtains hang from every rock; Carmelita forming pools of incandescent lava, Yellow Peril heaving up against the foot of the cliff in choppy sulphur seas breaking from a long low

The swamp at the road end on the north side of the Doshong La.　　　**KNEC**
The flat boggy area of ground where the Doshong Chu reaches the treeline appears to be the campsite used by both Kingdon Ward and Ludlow and Sherriff on the night before they crossed and crossed back over the Doshong La in one day.

surf of pink (*R. doshongense*) whose bronzed leaves glimmer faintly like sea-tarnished metal.

Nor were the Rhododendrons, though the most showy and abundant plants of the high valley, the only ones. There were Primulas here which we saw nowhere else. On June 25th we climbed to the pass, and collected many species. The most interesting of these were the Golden Primula (*P. morsheadiana,* K.W. 5858), with nodding heads of rich golden-yellow flowers, and spherical capsules, filled with black seeds; the 'Daffodil' Primula (*P. falcifolia,* K.W. 5839), an extraordinary bog plant, with bright yellow fragrant flowers, borne singly or sometimes a pair on the scape; and Cherry Bell (K.W. 5859), which is *P. valentiniana,* a dwarf with one or two nodding flowers of dusky red, flowering amidst the melting snow.

In the high alpine region, above even the dwarf Rhododendron, were mats of pink and pale yellow Diapensia, glued to the rocks, and sheets of crimson 'Dryadifolia' Primula (*Primula dryadifolia* ssp. *philoresia);* and on the cliffs were dwarf Primulas such as the tiny *P. glabra* and the rosy eyes of *P. rhodochroa*. The snow was soft and deep, and it was a hard struggle up to the pass; on the other side we gazed down into a cauldron of whirling mist, through rents in which we could see only snow. It was hardly possible to move our camp over the pass yet, because the porters would not be able to carry our loads through such deep snow; but we noticed, stuck in a cairn at the top of the pass, something which fired us with the ambition to go down into Pemakö ourselves, even if we were unable to return the same day. It was a branch of a big-leafed Rhododendron, the first we had seen, one of the 'Falconeri' series. It was a fine leaf, bright cinnamon red beneath, olive green above; and certainly no such tree grew on our side of the pass. Obviously there was no great difficulty in crossing

Rhododendron cephalanthum Nmaiense Group on the Doshong La.
KNEC

Discovered by Kingdon Ward in Burma and again in south-east Tibet on the Doshong La in 1924 but seemingly never introduced, this form *of R. cephalanthum* can be pale pink, cream or yellow (as in this example). Successfully introduced for the first time under Cox and Vergara 9513, it has proved to be a neat plant. The yellow forms are likely to be the most desirable for collectors. The Nmaiense forms are distinct from typical *R. cephalanthum* and should perhaps have varietal status.

Rhododendron mekongense on the north side of the Doshong La.
KNEC

This deciduous rhododendron species and the indistinguishable *R. trichocladum* are found over a very wide area of Yunnan, Burma and Tibet. Kingdon Ward is disparaging about some of the paler forms, but the best deep yellow forms such as this are very showy. In some forms the flowers are pure yellow while others are cream with red markings on them (referred to var. *rubrolineatum*).

the pass ourselves, since we had reached the summit; besides, we met three men on their way over from Pemakö, carrying light loads. We therefore made a vow to go down into Pemakö until we came to this big tree Rhododendron. What we saw there may be left till the next chapter. On June 30th, following our trip to Pemakö, we broke camp at the Doshong La and returned to Pe, where we halted for lunch. Crossing the river by the ferry, we sought shelter in the first house we came to, as it was raining very heavily. Owing to our carelessness in sitting on a native rug to drink tea, we were silently surrounded by fleas; and no sooner were we safely in bed than they unmasked their batteries. A dreadful persecution followed, and we scarcely slept a wink all night. When daylight at last put an end to the torture, even the joy of killing some fifty intoxicated fleas, too fat to jump, was tempered by the reflection that several escaped, and it was two or three days before we were clear of them.

However, our morning tea had no sooner been brought in – and never did we need it more – than a native runner appeared with our mail, which put us in a better humour. It was barely two months since our last mail. After breakfast we started for the Nyima La, camping early in the forest so as to get a good night's sleep; and on July 2nd, in pouring rain, we recrossed the pass and descended through seas of scented Primulas to our home in the *rong*.

CHAPTER VIII

Pemakö: The Promised Land

The geography and peoples of Pemakö

Pemakö is one of the Tibetan provinces which lies on the south side of the Himalaya. It is situated chiefly within the great knee-bend of the Tsangpo, comprising what we have called the Assam Himalaya; but it also includes part of the upper Dihang Valley above the Chimdro confluence. Thus it is completely contained between the parallels of 29° and 30° and the meridians of 94°30' and 96°0', though it does not include the whole of that area and has no defined boundaries; on the flat it covers no more than about 65,000 sq km [25,000 square miles]. I give these details because Pemakö is an unknown and remote region. Not only is it extraordinarily difficult to reach from any direction; it is still more difficult to penetrate and explore when reached. Surrounded on three sides by the gorge of the Tsangpo, the fourth is blocked by mighty ranges of snow mountains, whose passes are only open for a few months in the year. Beyond these immediate barriers to east and west and south are dense trackless forests, inhabited by wild unfriendly tribes.

Pemakö consists entirely of ranges of lofty mountains separated by deep and narrow valleys. The Assam Himalaya, with its mighty peaks Namcha Barwa and Sanglung, forms as it were the solar plexus, and from this, great ranges radiate in every direction, throwing off in turn a confusion of spurs; and the whole, from the snow-line to the

---

Rhododendron keysii   **KNEC**
The very distinctive *Rhododendron keysii* was first introduced from Sikkim and Nepal in the 1850s and was reintroduced on several occasions from South-east Tibet, where it is common. It is useful for its late flowering.

The 'Rhododendron Fairyland' of the Doshong La. KNEC

The Doshong La is one of the finest places in the whole Sino-Himalayan region for dwarf rhododendrons and thoroughly deserves Kingdon Ward's nickname for it. In alpine rhododendron habitats, typically one, two or occasionally three species dominate. In contrast, the Doshong La boasts a large number of species growing together: within a small area on the north side of the pass we identified *R. forrestii*, *R. aganniphum*, *R. pumilum*, *R. campylogynum*, *R. kongboense*, *R. charitopes* ssp. *tsangpoense*, *R. nivale* and *R. laudandum* (var. *temoense*) and the three species in this picture *R. campylocarpum*, *R. cephalanthum* Nmaiense Group and *R. calostrotum* ssp. *riparium*. This may well be the world's best spot to see such a diversity of dwarf rhododendrons, provided you are there in late June and early July and don't mind getting cold and wet.

river gorge, is covered with dense forest. Add to this a scanty population confined to the main valleys; a climate which varies from sub-tropical to arctic, the only thing common to the whole region being perpetual rain; snakes and wild animals, giant stinging nettles and myriads of biting and blood-sucking ticks, hornets, flies and leeches, and you have some idea of what the traveller has to contend with.

The sub-tropical valleys of South-eastern Tibet are inhabited not by true Tibetans, but by various tribes of Tibetan stock, the so-called Tibeto-Burman family. Pemakö is occupied so far as we know by: (1) Abors, who are only one of several jungle tribes included under the Tibetan name Lopa. (2) Mönbas, a civilised people who emigrated from Eastern Bhutan a century ago, and are now found in the Tsangpo Valley in considerable numbers. (3) Kongbas or emigrants from Kongbo – a Tibetanised people. (4) Pobas, emigrants from Pome, the province which lies to the north of the Tsangpo bend; until recently Pome was independent of Lhasa, and the inhabitants are not true Tibetans, though they speak a more or less intelligible dialect of the Lhasa language. The Pobas have always been known as great robbers. (5) Kampas, emigrants from the great eastern province of Tibet called Kham. The Kampas are Tibetans in a comprehensive sense, though the more sophisticated Tibetans of Lhasa profess to regard them as country cousins; as a matter of fact they are a highly civilised, cultured, and progressive people. Their language resembles that of the Pobas.

Thus it will be seen that with the exception of the Abors, who were the original inhabitants, all the peoples of Pemakö are recent immigrants. The Pobas and the Mönbas between them drove back the Abor tribes towards the Assam frontier; and this movement is no doubt still going on, as more people settle in Pemakö. Why, it may be asked, this anxiety to settle in Pemakö? It is because this is the Promised Land of the Tibetan prophecy. This prophecy was to the effect that, when their religion was persecuted in Tibet, the people should go to Pemakö, a land flowing with milk and honey, where the crops grew of their own accord. Most races have their promised land,

Typical weather near the summit of the Doshong La.   **KNEC**

Kingdon Ward described his first crossing of the Doshong La: 'on the other side we gazed down into a cauldron of whirling mist, through rents in which we could see only snow'. The 1996 crossing of the pass was a hair-raising experience. It was snowing and we sank into soft fresh snow to just below the knees. The mist came down, making visibility very poor and it was difficult to keep to the right path, as inevitably everyone became strung out in a long line. As it turned out, the pass was not officially 'open' and we were amongst the first to cross it that spring.

and such legendary places must necessarily be somewhat inaccessible, hidden behind misty barriers where ordinary men do not go; otherwise people would quickly explore the land and explode the legend. Pemakö served the purpose admirably; and when twenty years ago the Chinese came to Eastern Tibet with fire and sword, the prophecy seemed about to be fulfilled. At any rate, many Kampas then emigrated to Pemakö.

But the Mönba migration had taken place long before that, and there have, doubtless, been other migrations. At this time, many Kampas were settling in Pemakö in order to escape the heavy taxation levied in Tibet; a reason which we could at any rate understand, though it would need more than five shillings in the pound to drive us there permanently!

The cairn at the top of the Doshong La.   **KNEC**

Although this pass is relatively low at 4100m (13,500ft.), due to the sheer volume of precipitation there are only a few months of the year when the top of the pass is not covered in snow. Tiny creeping forms of *R. forrestii* with bright red flowers grow amongst the rocks next to the cairn.

Pemakö is not directly under Lhasa, but pays taxes to the Raja of Pome, who claims the territory. The claim of Lhasa to Pemakö, therefore, depends firstly on the relations between Lhasa and Pome, and secondly on the relations between Pome and Pemakö. There can be little doubt that even Pemakö is becoming gradually more Tibetanised.

The province is of great use to Tibet as a source of rice – which is becoming popular amongst the well-to-do classes, supplementing the universally eaten *tsamba*. It also produces curry, dyes, and timber.

Crossing the Doshong La

We were up early on June 29th, and left camp at 8 o'clock. Two Tibetans accompanied us. No time was wasted in the home valley, and we reached the pass in two hours. So far the day had kept fine; but that was only because so far the mountains had hurled back the dirty stuff in Pemakö before it could cross the pass. We saw it heaving ominously down below, preparing for another onslaught; beyond that we saw nothing but endless snow, and two Mönba coolies toiling up. We went down as fast as we could, but the snow was soft and sticky. At the first glacier flat we came to a stream which was visible through holes where the snow had caved in, exposing beautifully stratified sections 3m [10ft.] thick.

We soon reached the lip of the next cliff, many hundred feet high, and too steep to hold much snow. Far below we could see a valley and trees. The descent was terrifying and the streaming water added to the danger; but before we were half-way down we came into marvellous thickets where every shrub seemed a desirable prize. There was a beautiful *Lonicera* with glaucous leaves and rich purple flowers (K.W. 5872), and a dwarf creeping willow, with erect spikes 5-8cm [2-3in.] high; but especially was there a tanglewood of Rhododendrons, stout bushy shrubs with ascending stems reaching a height of 1.5-1.8m [5-6ft.]. The most abundant was Pink Glaucum (*R. charitopes* ssp. *tsangpoense*), smothered in mauve or apple-pink blossom. Another species with azalea-like leaves and carmine flowers, having purple honey-glands at the base, or white flowers speckled purple, or even cream flowers, tipped with pink, were perhaps related to the 'Neriiflorums' (*R. parmulatum*). Their bell-shaped corollas, especially those with white flowers speckled purple, were crowded with hundreds of tiny flies.

I marked several distinct plants which were all jumbled up in the most awful confusion, and while doing so, caught sight of something a little distance away which astonished no less than it delighted me; it was a Rhododendron with bright orange flowers, that rarest of all colours. But it was no easy matter to reach the spot. It grew some way up the slope, in the midst of this tanglewood, which for long held me at bay. But in the end I reached the prize, to find a Rhododendron of the 'Cinnabarinum' type dangling orange tubes before my fascinated eyes. Most people know *R. cinnabarinum,* decked with its fleshy bright cinnabar red tubular flowers; with the sunlight streaming through it, it becomes enveloped in a wine-coloured aura and is one of the most lovely species. Substitute orange for cinnabar red and you have Orange Bill, the prince of orange Rhododendrons (*R. cinnabarinum* ssp. *xanthocodon* Concatenans gp.) K.W. 5874. The young foliage is verdigris coloured, and the bushes gleam shrilly against the snowy cliffs. But I had a really desperate time getting seed of it. It grew, as I say, well up the steep slope and often out of reach on the cliffs above. I went after it on October 22nd during a heavy snowstorm and got a few capsules. On October 26th I tried again; by this time the bushes were well snowed up, but I got some more seed, and it is a relief to think that the seeds are germinating, considering the awful strain on my temper while struggling in that accursed cold muddle.

At the foot of this wall the valley widened into a large amphitheatre shut in by high cliffs. Water splashed and gurgled down a hundred narrow slots in the cliffs, whence tons of snow had been vomited into the valley and lay there piled in an immense heap 14m [50ft.] thick. It looked as though it would remain there all the summer, dwindling slowly, till renewed by the first snowstorm. Yet there was evidently only one season's stratum there; and when we returned in October, almost the whole had disappeared save for a few crusts lying about in odd corners! Some idea of the destruction wrought by these chutes each spring was conveyed by boulders which lay scattered over the surface of the snowfield; most of them had no doubt been brought down by small avalanches.

The flowers were blooming bravely in this cold storage chamber. Water streamed down every slope, and every slope was quick with Primulas and baby Rhododendrons; it leaped in shrill cascades over every cliff, and every cliff was clogged with bushes. First we spied a gamboge sheet of *Primula chionota* (K.W. 5868), which grows on alpine turf or rock slopes with its feet in mud and water; and then a sheet of squat grey Primulas, and then a whole amazing alp of slender violet Primulas, and then a bogful of mixed yellow and white Primulas. Belike these last two were the same thing; and so it proved. But when we came to compare the squat grey and slender violet Primulas with the yellow and white, and found that they were all the same thing, only colour varieties, one marvelled more than ever at Nature's nursery. *P. dickieana,* for such is the plant's name, is no new thing. It is found on the wet alpine ranges of Upper Burma, Sikkim, and Tibet, though probably nowhere in such variety and abundance as here. It is not, I believe, in cultivation, though seed of it has been sent home several times (K.W. 3389). The fact is, these wet alpine Primulas, *P. dickieana, P. valentiniana* and others will not stand our climate. In October, when we came to collect seed of *P. dickieana,* scarcely a capsule could we find. Whole roods of it had left no trace. A few withered capsules were seen, and after long search a few containing seeds (K.W. 5869), but most of them came to naught. This was not surprising, for how were the flowers to be pollinated in this universal and everlasting deluge?

Crossing the avalanche, we descended a steep rocky path, where small trees and shrubs were mixed up with boulders, to a great flat marsh, where the forest began. And here we halted; for on the edge of the forest grew the big cinnamon-leafed Rhododendron which we were in search of. The flowers, now almost over, were white with a purple flash at the base of the corolla, in large fat bunches. Isolated trees on the edge of the forest grow as much as 7.5m [25ft.] high; but it also forms thickets by itself, and was very abundant from this point for several miles down the valley, in thin mixed forest. It belongs to the 'Falconeri' series, of which several species are known from China, Sikkim, and Burma; but the bright cinnamon-coloured under-leaf surface on this plant is quite distinctive (*R. arizelum* aff.). Ample seed was collected at the end of October (K.W. 5877). Amongst a mixed lot of shrubs and small trees I noticed the scarlet Coals-of-Fire (*R. cerasinum*), here forming a well-rounded tree; Birch, Maple, Larch, dwarf Cherry, Willow, Viburnum, *Rhododendron trichocladum,* Lonicera, Rubus, Rowan, Barberry, *Rosa sericea,* Ribes, Euonymus, and others I could not name. In the undergrowth were many interesting plants coming up, though few were in flower. The purple-flowered form of *Meconopsis simplicifolia* was common, and a big Arisæma (*A. elephas*) with chocolate-coloured spathe, the tip of which was drawn out into a whip-lash so long that it trailed on the ground.

We had now reached the edge of the snow, where the forest began; and the valley was just a swamp. We would have liked to explore further, but there was no time; and having rested a quarter of an hour to eat our rations, we started on the return journey soon after 1 o'clock. By this time the mist was pretty thick, and it was raining steadily, but through an occasional break we could see the snow-covered wall, 900m [3,000ft.] high, which separated us from our camp. It looked absolutely sheer; and in silence we took off our hats to Majors Trenchard and Pemberton, who first of all white men had crossed the Doshong La. Then we started on the job. Steady slogging through the snow brought us to the summit by 3.30, drenched and cold – we could not move quickly enough to keep warm when wet through, and the wind was very raw. This was decent going, however, considering that we had to halt frequently to mark Rhododendrons. We found one particularly charming dwarf species with small regular lilac-purple flowers, which spread itself over some of the moraines and gravel tips. It flowered again freely in October, though not on the same plants. Unfortunately it was one of the rarest species met with (K.W. 5876) (*R. uniflorum*). Once over the pass the weather improved and we even found the sun shining below, with light showers flying over our heads. We reached camp at 5 after a highly successful day.

***Rhododendron cinnabarinum* ssp. *xanthocodon* Concatenans Group in Pemakö.   KNEC**
'"Orange Bill, the prince of orange rhododendrons", I cried aloud, for I felt lyrical.' (F. Kingdon Ward, *The Romance of Gardening*). The story of the discovery and collection of the plant 'Orange Bill', described in *The Riddle of the Tsangpo Gorges* and several other books, has long been considered one of the greatest of all the plant collecting stories. In Pemakö, having followed Ward's instructions to climb up the steep, Berberis-clad slope to admire 'Orange Bill', we discovered that rather than the rare plant which Ward describes, there are in fact thousands of plants of it all over the hillsides on the south side of the Doshong La. But it did take eighty years to investigate the story! The long tongue-twisting name for this species is unfortunate as the plant deserves at least sub-specific status.

***Rhododendron parmulatum* in Pemakö: a selection of forms with some natural hybrids.   KNEC**
The distribution of this species appears to be confined to Pemakö. The flower colour varies from pure white to strong pink and occasionally red, though the latter are almost certainly natural hybrids. The pink-flowered clone in the bottom right of this picture appears to be *R. parmulatum* x *R. forrestii*.

***Rhododendron parmulatum* in Pemakö, a fine deep pink form. KNEC**
This is a very fine pink-flushed form of *R. parmulatum* with the typical deep spotting. In the base of each flower are dark nectaries which attract pollinators. This also attracts birds which peck through the flowers leaving a neat hole, and masses of small flies which look like extra spotting on the corolla until you peer inside and they fly away. Quite a good garden plant and easier to please than most of its relatives, but it often takes a good number of years before it flowers freely.

***Primula dickieana* on the south side of the Doshong La.   KNEC**
P. dickieana is quite common in the Sino-Himalayan region, on the wettest, monsoon-soaked slopes. It occurs in white, purple, magenta, yellow or pink forms. In some areas one colour dominates: in Pemakö two or three colours can be found, though yellow is the most common. It also occurs in Nepal and other part of the Himalaya. It has been introduced on several occasions, but as its wild habitat is so hard to reproduce in the garden, it seldom persists very long.

Looking south into Pemakö from the 'lip of the next cliff'.   **KNEC**

This picture was taken in early June, a few weeks later than Ian Baker's similar view on page 64. Kingdon Ward crossed on 29th June. 'The descent was terrifying' was Kingdon Ward's description of the climb down from what he called 'the lip of the next cliff'. We found it was safer to slide down on our backs using our feet as brakes and with skilled Nepali staff waiting at the bottom to catch anyone out of control.

The valley leading south from the foot of the Doshong La towards the Dihang river.   **KNEC**

Kingdon Ward described this wide, 'U'-shaped valley which descends very gradually towards the Brahmaputra (or Dihang). as 'a large amphitheatre'. As the valley descends, the flora gradually becomes more tropical. Steep slopes on both sides are covered with rhododendrons, primulas and other plants.

The Doshong La in Autumn

Looking back on the hill regions of Pemakö one is struck by two things: (1) the perpetual rain and saturated atmosphere; (2) the almost inconceivable wealth of flora. We superficially explored one alpine valley in Pemakö for a distance of perhaps 8km [5 miles], and in a few brief days collected about forty species of Rhododendron, half a dozen Primulas, and many other trees, shrubs and alpine plants. If we include the gorge of the Tsangpo in Pemakö, the number of Rhododendrons alone amounts to some sixty species. What, then, are the conditions which give rise to this extravagant flora? In the alpine region, a vegetative season lasting through five months of perpetual rain, and a resting season of seven months during which everything is buried under the snow. As we descend through the forest belt – Conifer forest, mixed forest, temperate forest – to the sub-tropical forest of the lower valley, the vegetative season grows longer, the resting season shorter, till at last there is nothing left but a slight check in the winter, and snow gradually disappears. But rain there is always, winter and summer. The inference seems to be that perpetual precipitation is the cause of this immense variation. Of course the rainfall at the Doshong La, even on the Pemakö side, is not by any means enormous; there are many places in India, for example, where the annual fall must be far greater. The point is that there is never any dry season; rain falls at all seasons of the year, and only in the alpine region is there a deliberate cessation of activity.

On October 21st we started on our second visit to the Doshong La, this time taking our camp with us. We intended to stay a few days in the valley on the far side of the range where we had halted for lunch in June, and if the weather showed any signs of being fair, we hoped to descend some distance into the forests. It was a gorgeous morning when we broke camp, and the marsh was glazed with ice. I started before the main body, as I had to leave the track to collect seeds, and it was half-past one before we reached the pass. By this time the wind was blowing up from Pemakö, and the sky was overcast. Presently the snow began to fly. The descent in the soft snow was worse than in June, and most of the plants were buried; but I resurrected seed of *Primula valentiniana, P. chionota*, Meconopsis, Lloydia, and other species. When we came to the cliff where the shrubs began, I soon found the purple-flowered *Lonicera* again, its stems now cloyed with luscious blue-black berries, and several of the rhododendrons. But Orange Bill, to my horror, I could not see! The fact is, it was the most abundant and conspicuous bush on the cliff above the track, its new leaves now of so startling a metallic blue-green against the dead-white background that the eye blinked and passed it over to alight on something more restful! Who would have thought that those massive verdigris-coloured bushes – so desperately out of reach too – were the same as the solitary shrub which we had seen swinging peals of orange-coloured bells in the thicket four months ago!

Below the amphitheatre, which was now almost clear of snow and carpeted with dwarf willows, were many flowers – violet Aconite, butter yellow Potentilla, Crawfurdia, Corydalis, and little heathery bunches of milk-white Cassiope (*C. selaginoides*), so frail and slender as to seem unreal in the October rawness. But these plants like it. Perpetual rain and snow have no terrors for them. The rasping wind which buffets and numbs on the passes is hardly felt where the flowers nestle close to mother earth. The saturated clinging atmosphere, the soft flying rain, the gentle wet kiss of the mist as it rolls on up the valley, they love. It is these caresses which soften the bleak attentions of a harsher climate; the dull kick of the frost, the hammer-blows of the naked sun, and the bite of the thin hungry alpine air. And so, three days later, on October 25th, after a ceaseless onslaught of snow-storms, we found many flowers exultant in the snow: fat flourishing clumps of Golden Primula and of the Daffodil Primula, aster, gentian, Pedicularis, *Rosa sericea, Rhododendron trichocladum* and others. Nor did the flowers look any more sorry for themselves than those which bloomed in June; indeed, the dwarf *Rhododendron uniflorum* (*R. imperator*) (K.W. 5876) was flowering much more freely now than it did then, and the winter flowers were more pink than purple. There were, however, two exceptions to the above statement. One of the best marked characters of the Daffodil Primula (*P. falcifolia*) was its fragrance; but the autumn-flowering plants were quite scentless. As for the Golden Primula (*P. morsheadiana*), its flowers were no longer so butter yellow, but looked anaemic, though otherwise happy.

This early winter snow plays a very important part in determining the vegetation and I must draw attention to a curious paradox, which may be stated thus: dwarf alpine Rhododendrons do not endure such low temperatures as many larger shrubby and bushy species. This is not perhaps obvious at first sight, but a little reflection will convince anyone that it is true.

By October 18th, all the alpine species found at the Doshong La were finally covered for seven months beneath the snow; and at this time the minimum temperature (sheltered) at the foot of the alpine slope rarely fell below -1°C [30°F]. Now it is clear that the shrub species such as Yellow Peril (*R. campylocarpum*) and Carmelita (*R. chamaethomsonii*), and the bushy undershrub species such as Pink Glaucum (*R. charitopes* ssp. *tsangpoense*), must entangle a layer of air beneath the snow-roof. They are not completely flattened by the weight of snow, and large cavities exist, as I found on exhuming them in order to collect seed. The result of the snow blanket is therefore to keep that air, and hence the plants, comparatively warm; warmer than the air outside, which is cooled by radiation and wind. Probably the temperature under the snow never falls much below freezing-point; at any rate, plants of Carmelita and Yellow Peril, buried under the snow, had not screwed up their leaves into tubes, and that is one of the first things a Rhododendron does in self-defence when low temperatures are experienced.

Now consider those alpine species which come from the drier ranges, *R. nivale* and *R. phaeochrysum*, for example; and the bush species from the valleys, the mahogany *R. triflorum*, *R. aganniphum* and others, what they suffer. In the first week of November at the Nam La, the temperature (sheltered) fell to -15°C [4°F]. in camp. The following Rhododendrons withstood this temperature: *R. lepidotum* [*R. elæagnoides*] (K.W. 5994), *R. fragariflorum* (K.W. 5734), *R. laudandum* (K.W. 5733), *R. phaeochrysum* (K.W. 5718), and *R. nivale*. Nor was this exceptional, since on four consecutive nights we had -7°C to -15°C [+21°F to +4°F]. Moreover, the temperature in the open fell even below this. Much lower down in the forest we recorded -4.5°C [+24°F], where grew many species of tree Rhododendron, including the pink *R. hirtipes,* yellow *R. wardii, R. lanatoides, R. uvariifolium* and *R. dignabile.*

Throughout January in the Gyamda River Valley the weather was fine, and the night temperatures were very low. On the 11th and 25th we recorded about -21°C [-5°F]; the 'Taliense,' 'Triflorum,' 'Lacteum,' 'Souliei,' and pink 'Anthopogon' Rhododendron were common here. Again, these were not exceptionally low temperatures, and near Gyamda in the same month, we experienced the following frosts ranging from -0.5°C to -12°C [+31°F to +10°F]. That is to say, the above-mentioned five Rhododendrons must be prepared to stand naked in severe frost almost any night for several months; for them there is no escape – they are not protected by snow. They grow, it is true, in communities, or in forest; but the temperature there can be little if at all above the readings of our sheltered thermometer. What is perhaps more important than the warm temperature at which these small snow-covered alpines spend the winter, is the fact that it is *constant*. Day and night, in calm and storm, the temperature beneath the snow blanket, once that is sufficiently deep – and a few feet is enough – does not alter.

In June, long before the snow is all melted, the Rhododendrons are flowering furiously. Jostling waves of colour chase each other up the valley. Rain falls almost continuously and the fast-melting snow supplies unlimited quantities of water; the ground is just a filter through which flows a constant stream. Above all, the atmosphere is saturated, and the sun, muffled by the flying scud, rarely breaks through. Quickly as the snow melts, however, there is such a vast accumulation of it that before the last drifts have disappeared October has come, and snow has begun to fall again. Thus these alpines are active for less than five months in the year; in that time they must flower, be pollinated, ripen their seed, and open their capsules. For the remaining seven months they sleep. Small wonder if we find them obstinate, and even sulky in Britain! Considering the treatment they get, the wonder is they are so amazingly adaptable, at least in some parts of the country. Obviously the districts most to their liking will be the west coast and the hill country. But in any case we are apt to work them to death, for in Britain the vegetative season lasts about nine months; and

Crossing a snow field in Pemakö.   KNEC
Walking over snow near the foot of the series of steep descents leading from the Doshong La to Pemakö. The roar of avalanches high up to the right on the slopes of Namcha Barwa can make this crossing hair-raising, especially when the mountain is obscured in clouds and mist.

Rhododendrons on the south side of the Doshong La.   KNEC
Picked branches from a group of rhododendron species which grow together on the steep slopes beside the path which leads from the Doshong La down into Pemakö towards the India border. The species are *R. cinnabarinum* ssp. *xanthocodon* Concatenans (orange), *R. charitopes* ssp. *tsangpoense* (purple) and *R. parmulatum* (white).

Rhododendron arizelum (affinity) in Pemakö.   KNEC
This species most closely matches *R. arizelum* but it differs in having a winged or flattened petiole rather than the typical rounded one. This feature is typical of species such as *R. basilicum*. The Pemakö plants seem to fall midway between these two species and have cream or pale pink flowers. The leaves have a handsome reddish brown indumentum on the underside. Like many large-leaved species, it does not flower freely every year: in 1995 there was plenty of flower, while in 1996 hardly any. Dr David Chamberlain is considering describing this taxon as a species or subspecies of *R. arizelum*. Introduced under Cox and Vergara 9527 in 1995.

Anemone obtusiloba with *Primula dickieana* in Pemakö.   PC
This species of Anemone has a wide distribution from Pakistan throughout the Himalaya as far as south-east Tibet and northern Burma. It occurs in blue, white or yellow forms, often in grazing meadows, in huge quantities, and over a wide altitudinal range. Tibetan forms are usually white.

Near the campsite on the south side of the Doshong La.   **PC**

The campsite used by Kingdon Ward and ourselves on the Pemakö side of the Doshong La is reached by this path from the summit of the pass. The path is under snow for most of the year but by June the snow has melted off at least some of it.

Arisaema nepenthoides **in Pemakö.**   **KNEC**

Arisaemas are one of the 'vogue' plants at the start of the new millennium. They fascinate and revolt people in equal measure with their extraordinary combination of the sinister and the suggestive. The distinctive head (known as the spathe), which looks like a striking snake, accounts for the common name of this plant as 'cobra plant' or 'cobra lily'. The Latin epithet means 'like a Nepenthes' or pitcher plant. This specimen was found on the south side of the Doshong La, in a forest of *Rhododendron sinograde. A. elephas* also occurs in this area.

Rhododendron fulvum ssp. *fulvoides* **in Pemakö.**   **KNEC**

Not recorded by Kingdon Ward on the south side of the Doshong La, probably because it occurs further into Pemakö than he reached, this species forms a rhododendron forest with *R. lanigerum* and *R. sinograde* at around 3000m (10,000ft.). It flowers relatively early, in April to May in the wild, and often as early as March in cultivation. It has a very wide distribution from Tsari and the Tibet-Bhutan border into Yunnan. The flowers are white or pink with dark spotting and/or a blotch in the throat.

they are exceptionally lucky if they can down tools for four. And then, when they have dropped off to sleep – we wake them up suddenly some bright sunny morning in February to tell them the obvious lie that Spring is come! How can we expect them to roll over and go to sleep again for another two or three months after that! Sometimes they do not hear the second call; they have gone home. Nor can we cover them up decently, as they are used to being covered; for snow in England is almost as rare as nuts in May, and our dwarf plants which sleep at a constant temperature for even months in Tibet, naturally suffer from insomnia, under the inconstant temperature their nakedness invites.

Alpine Rhododendrons, therefore, are bound to be awkward customers, and though far from despairing of them, I feel that the more we understand of the conditions under which they grow in nature, the more easily shall we succeed with them in Britain. In an abnormal year the mortality will certainly be frightful; but abnormal years are not unknown in other countries, and are equally fatal.

Autumn seed collecting

In the boulder moraine just above the marsh where our camp was situated the thickets were striped with brilliant colour, to which the lurid leaves of a Viburnum contributed patches of hot orange. It had very few fruits, however (K.W. 6246). Bunches of snow-white berries clustered on the bare boughs of the Rowan; long tassels of red fruit hung from the Currant; and the knobbly scarlet clubs of Arisaema thrust themselves into view beneath the bushes. It was late when I reached the swamp with the day's spoil. Cawdor and the vanguard of the transport had arrived, but there was no food, and we were famished as well as drenched. However, the last porters struggled in at 6 o'clock, just in time to get the tents up before darkness fell; we had some hot tea, changed, and sat down to supper at 9 o'clock. By that time we felt restored. The swamp was now even more of a swamp than it was in June, and continuous rain and snow during the next three days converted it into a lake; but as it was the only bit of flat ground we knew of, it had to suffice.

It was noticeably warmer on this side of the pass, despite the snow; after dark many moths came into the tent, and we heard an owl hooting. By 11 o'clock we were smothered in cloud once more, and it was raining heavily. On October 23rd I started up the valley with two Tibetans on an intensive seed-collecting campaign. It was raining at the swamp, but a little higher up a heavy snowstorm was raging, which made the work more difficult; nor did the conditions mend next day. However, we collected a lot of seeds of Rhododendron, Primula, Willow, and in fact almost everything we could lay our hands on, including several plants I had not seen before, such as the little rock Vaccinium with scarlet berries – K.W. 6249.

Every day large bodies of Mönbas, returning from Pe, crossed the pass, though there were not so many coming up now. From one of them Cawdor secured a bamboo bow, complete with arrows in case. The Mönba bow has a span of 1.2m [4ft.], and at the end where the string is fastened it is iron shod so that it can be used as a walking-stick. The arrows also, which are 60cm [2ft.] long, are tipped with iron and a notch is cut in the shaft behind the point so that it will break off and remain in the wound, leaving the deadly aconite with which it is smeared to do its work. Cawdor made the interesting discovery that the bowman wears on his left wrist a bracelet of woven bamboo about 8cm [3in.] wide.

The upper valley was now once more wreathed in snow, but its form was unmistakable. From the pass – a mere saddle in a high rocky ridge – to the swamp where our camp was situated, it descends in three enormous steps. The treads of these steps are snowfields for seven or eight months in the year and swamps the rest of the time; the risers are rocky cliffs, hundreds of feet high, over which the stream tumbles anyhow, cutting its way back until it is sunk in a groove. The glacial U-shape of the valley is very pronounced. The rock is everywhere a black and white banded gneiss, the narrow bands showing the most extraordinary zigzag contortions; they must have been subjected to terrific pressure after they were formed. Below our camp were larger boggy flats separated at longer and longer intervals by short descents until finally the valley became a V-shaped water groove. A big torrent comes in from the north and at the head of its valley is a snow-peak, evidently the one close to the Nam La called Temu Tse. To the south of our camp we occasionally caught sight of a lofty peak crowned by an ice cap, a true glacier it appeared; but the cliffs which flank the valley are so high and sheer that it is impossible to see over them. Vast accumulations of rubble, hurled down the cliffs into the valley, had been sorted and cleared, cut through and abandoned, by the ever-rushing torrents; these drifts have rather masked the old moraines, a process which the overwhelming vegetation has completed.

Usually the north-facing flank of a valley is well wooded, while the south face, being exposed to the sun, is covered with scrub only, or with a thick growth of herbaceous plants. But in the alpine valleys of the Doshong La this was reversed; it was the sheltered flank which was barren, the south face which was wooded. Nor was the reason far to seek. Here there is so much rain and so little sunshine that woody plants can quite well grow on the south face; while on the north face the conditions are so arctic and the snow lies so long that very little can grow there at all. Great gravel cones line the foot of the cliff, expanding fanwise into the valley. These are covered below with mats of dwarf Willow and Lonicera, or with thickets of *Rhododendron viridescens* [*R. trichocladum*]; and on their flanks, with a rank tangle of tall herbs – giant Umbelliferæ, Meconopsis, and other plants. Their tops, however, are quite bare, though the glens, being well sheltered, are filled with bushes.

Had the weather been fine we intended to have gone down the valley on a three days' trip, possibly as far as the Dihang, leaving our camp standing. But the rain continued and we learnt further that the porters were almost out of food; unless they returned to Pe for further supplies, October 24th was the latest date to which they could hold out, and on the 25th we should have to recross the pass. October 24th being moderately fine, however, we seized the opportunity to march down the valley as far as possible; and after breakfast we started.

Descending the next step, where a wilderness of shrubs and small trees flourished amidst a chaos of boulders, we crossed the torrent from Temu Tse and hugged the north-east flank of the valley, which was here about 550m [600 yards] wide. Crossing a marsh, we found ourselves in thickets of the 'Falconeri' Rhododendron, and another, *R. exasperatum*, whose bristly shoots recalled *R. strigillosum*. Thenceforward new Rhododendrons appeared in ever-increasing numbers. At first wide boggy pastures alternated with strips of forest, composed chiefly of Abies and Larch, with a bushy undergrowth of Rhododendrons; these were mostly the scarlet *R. cerasinum*, and a new species of the 'Grande' type (*R. lanigerum*). The path lay not far from the cliff, and we crossed several streams and gravel fans covered with a dense growth of shrubs, including Enkianthus, Rubus, a Lonicera with little polished black fruits like boot buttons, and an extraordinary Rhododendron with bunches of tiny fruits borne on the older wood (*R. keysii*: KW 6257). In places dense thickets of Bamboo made progress difficult, and the path was everywhere a black bog.

After continuing for several miles and descending over 300m [1,000ft.], we got into permanent forest which grew more and more varied as the steep descent continued; also the trees grew bigger and bigger. Here flourished strange Araliaceæ, a Podophyllum (*Sinopodophyllum aurantiocaule*), and other exotic-looking vegetables; but at least 50 per cent. of the rain forest was composed of *Rhododendron sinogrande* [*grande*], a tree 12m [40ft.] high, with leaves 60cm [2ft.] long and 22cm [8in.] across. But though we saw hundreds of trees we saw not a single one which had flowered this year. All the big trees – Abies, *Rhododendron sinogrande,* and others, were covered with a thick growth of moss, from which hung down the long straggling shoots of two epiphytic Rhododendrons. These were fairly common and I gathered seed of both – K.W. 6250 (*R. megeratum*) and K.W. 6251 (*R. micromeres*) –as well as of the other species. Moss is a sure sign of perpetual rain. Where there is heavy summer rain followed by a dry or cold season the trees are usually festooned with lichen. At 2.45 we halted under a cliff, where we saw a number of baboons playing; it was over four hours since we left camp, and we should barely get back by daylight. This was the nearest we got to the Dihang River.

As already noted, at the Doshong La the narrowest point of the loop is reached, the two limbs of the Tsangpo-Dihang, the one flowing north-east and the other south-west, being about 40km [25 miles] apart. Or, to put it in another way, the Himalayan range hereabouts

Rhododendron megeratum in the branches of Abies, Pemakö. **PC**

In 1995 we located this species growing on mossy logs, so we were most surprised in 1996 to find it growing in the clefts of conifer branches 5-10m (17-33ft.) up. These proved frustrating to photograph in the pouring rain, but was an excellent demonstration of one of the many rhododendron species which prefer to grow as epiphytes in wetter areas.

Rhododendron imperator in Pemakö, south of the Doshong La. **KNEC**

Kingdon Ward found a plant on the Doshong La which was named *R. uniflorum.* The type specimen of this is in such poor condition that not much can be deduced from it, but the cultivated plants under the name *R. uniflorum* appear to be natural hybrids of *R. imperator* (probably crossed with *R. tsangpoense).* *R. imperator* has been recorded from Burma and north-east India and occurs in Pemakö in quantity. The tiny pointed leaves with relatively large bright pinkish-purple flowers make this a highly desirable species for the rhododendron collector.

Rhododendron imperator in Pemakö, south of the Doshong La. **KNEC**

This species grows on soggy but steep cliffs and screes on the western facing slopes of the valley leading from the Doshong La down to Pemakö. In 1995 we located only a handful of specimens but in 1996 we saw a mass of plants in full flower, brightening up hillsides in the incessant rain.

Viburnum mullaha in Pemakö. **PC**

This Viburnum species is common on both sides of the Doshong La. It has showy white flowers and rugose leaves, variable in size, which are bronze when young. later turning dark green. This specimen was taken in the wide valley leading from the Doshong La south towards the Indian border.

Vaccinium nummularia aff. on a mossy rock in Pemakö. **PC**

In the extremely wet province of Pemakö, near the India border, rocks and fallen logs are usually covered with a thick layer of moss in which various rhododendron and vaccinium species grow. This species was first collected by Hooker from Sikkim in 1850. A fine plant for milder gardens, but badly damaged in severe winters at Glendoick. The pink flowers are followed by black fruit which are edible but insipid.

158

Foliage of *Rhododendron keysii* in Pemakö. KNEC

This species, closely related to 'Orange Bill', flowers very late, probably in July in Pemakö as there were no signs of buds opening in June. It has curious narrow tubular flowers in bunches, quite unlike those of any other species. The flowers are usually salmon-red and yellow on the lobes but Kingdon Ward's October 1924 collections (KW 6257) from Pemakö produced seedlings with pure red flowers. This form was subsequently named var. *unicolor*.

Rhododendron sinogrande **in Pemakö.** KNEC

This species has the largest leaves in the genus: up to 90cm (3ft.) in favourable circumstances. It tends to grow at an altitude of around 3000m (10,000ft.) and is found over a wide area of north-east Yunnan, Burma and south-east Tibet. It typically grows in dense forest where it flowers sporadically and lives to a great age, reaching up to 14m (45ft.). Kingdon Ward reported that he found it very hard to find seed of this species as it only flowered every second or third year. The huge trusses of creamy to pale yellow flowers open in March–May. This species is a feature of many west coast British gardens.

Cassiope selaginoides **on the Sirchem La.** KNEC

The Sirchem La pass, parallel to the Temo La, carries the Lhasa road from Bayi to Trulung and on to Chamdo and Yunnan/Sichuan. This is the smallest of the three Tibetan Cassiope species, with relatively large white flowers on narrow whipcord stems. An excellent rock garden plant for gardens in cool climates. The pink calyx in this example gives a particularly attractive effect.

Primula falcifolia **in Pemakö south of the Doshong La.** KNEC

The 'daffodil primula'. This was the best display of this species on our two explorations on the Pemakö side of the Doshong La. A resting bud collected by Ludlow and Sherriff in 1938 flowered twice in Edinburgh; that apart, there seems to have been no other successful introduction. Crossing the pass in autumn is fraught with risk as snow fall may make return impossible, so seed collecting remains tantalisingly difficult.

Podophyllum aurantiocaule **on the Doshong La south side.** KNEC

This fascinating plant was photographed by Kingdon Ward in 1924 but it was not successfully introduced. A close relative of the much more common *Podophyllum* or *Sinopodophyllum hexandrum*, it differs in that the white flowers hang down below the leaves. As this species only occurs in areas of high rainfall, the flowers are probably positioned in this way to protect the floral parts from the deluge. Found both in Pemakö and Pome and now in cultivation, though likely to remain rare for some time to come.

*Podophyllum
aurantiocaule.*   **FKW**

is 40km [25 miles] thick and 7600m [25,000ft.] high. But whereas at Pe the Tsangpo is
flowing at an altitude of about 2950m [9,700ft.], at Yortong the Dihang is flowing at an
altitude of about 800m [2,500ft.]. It is not surprising, therefore, that the watershed of the
Himalayan range should be unequally placed between the two limbs of the river; the
Doshong La is almost three times as far from the Dihang as it is from the Tsangpo. We,
being scarcely more than 13km [8 miles] south of the pass, were still 16km [10 miles] from
the Dihang River. There is a quaint prophecy amongst the Kongbo Tibetans that Namcha
Barwa will one day fall into the Tsangpo gorge and block the river, which will then turn
aside and flow over the Doshong La. This is recorded in a book by some fabulous person
whose image may be seen in the little *gompa* at Payi, in Pome.

It took me some time to ascend the valley, as there was much to collect; night had
fallen when I reached the torrent and it was raining hard. I made my way in the wet
misty darkness over the boulders and reached camp at 6.30, well pleased with the results
of the trip. Down below under trees and rocks we saw many Mönbas settling down by
their fires for the night; they were on their way back to the Dihang.

It was snowing fast when we got up at 6.30 next morning, and a miserable job it was, standing about in a swamp during a snowstorm, while we rolled up the frozen tents. At last we got
off and began the long climb to the pass. I added some seeds of the dwarf cherry (whose fruits
were almost black) to the collection and more Orange Bill; and on the way up the steepest
cliff I noticed, poking its long thin capsule up through the snow, a Meconopsis like the yellow
dwarf, *M. florindæ*; it could hardly be that plant, however, which grows in the forest – more
likely it was the allied *M. lyrata,* known from Sikkim and Burma – I saw only two plants, but
saved a little seed – K.W. 6259. Another plant of which I saved some seed was a lily, possibly
the purple-flowered Lily (*L. nanum*), described under K W. 5809. But it was a much taller
plant than that, and occasionally bore two flowers on the stem; besides, it flourished at about
3400m [11,000ft.], and the alpine flora of the Doshong La was on the whole very different
to that of the high and dry Nyima La. It was therefore difficult to believe that this was *Lilium*
[*Nomocharis*] *nanum* of the Nyima La (K.W. 6232). It must be remembered that when we
crossed the Doshong La on June 29th we did not see a tithe of the flowers which must colour
their slopes in July and August. The upper valley was then still under snow, as of course it was
now. Some plants we had since found in seed; but what dozens we must have missed! Still we
did what we could, and no doubt we skimmed the cream of the flora.

It was heavy going up to the pass, reached at 3 o'clock in the afternoon. But on the
other side the weather was brighter, and we soon got out of the snow and into sunshine.
One had to be careful to keep to the stamped trail, or one floundered in waist-deep, the
snow having drifted and filled up the hollows. We camped on the glacier flat as before;
it was a fine cold night with the usual frosty blustering wind tearing down the valley,
where the flowers slept peacefully in their snowy graves. But we must now leave
Pemakö, and returning to our base at Tumbatse, continue our summer travels.

CHAPTER IX

In the Assam Himalaya

Over the Tang La

The evening of July 4th showed a change in the weather. The rain ceased, the sky cleared like magic, and far down the *rong* to the north we could see the glitter of snow-peaks in mysterious Pome. A break in the rains! and immediately we made arrangements to go next day to the Temo La. Alas! we were deceived, for next day the rain came down harder than ever, and we reached camp dripping. I have, however, recorded our doings at the Temo La, and after five days and nights of ceaseless rain, we returned to Tumbatse.

On July 17th, still in pouring rain, we left Tumbatse on a second journey to the Himalaya, via the Tang La. Our route lay up the ridge of an ancient moraine one flank of which was covered with grass and flowers, while the other was clothed with a more or less dense growth of Rhododendron – the Mahogany *R triflorum*, *R. principis* and *R. lepidotum*. This moraine comes to an end in the village street. We soon entered the Picea-Rhododendron forest where the ascent becomes very steep, so that the pack animals had much ado to keep their feet in the mud. Above the forest we traversed over boulder screes, where blue poppies *M. horridula* [*M. prainiana*] flowered freely, to the head of the valley, and shortly afterwards stood on the Tang La, 4400m [14,885ft.]. Descending a quarter of a mile, we camped by an empty bothy, where the transport put up for the night.

The alpine turf here was yellow with a dwarf Primula (*P. pudibunda*), an alpine form

View from the top of the Temo La looking west. **PC**
On a clear day such as this, the view from the Temo La is spectacular, with the tops of Namcha Barwa and Gyala Peri visible in the distance to the east and the Tsangpo-Gyamda Chu confluence, seen here, to the south-west.

of *P. sikkimensis,* differing from it chiefly in size. On the drier ground were the three species of dwarf Rhododendron already described from the Temo La, all of them in flower. The strawberry 'Saluenense' (*R. fragariflorum*) was flowering best, the 'Snowball Anthopogon' (*R. laudandum*) and *R. nivale* making a rather poor show. There was also another form of *R. nivale* with olive and bronze leaves, which broke over the rocks in waves of purple. Next day we started down the valley towards the Tsangpo, the transport following a different path along the ridge. *Primula alpicola* var. *violacea* grew by the wayside, and was here mostly claret-coloured; it is curious how this plant, which occurs in at least five colours, tends to segregate the reds from the blues. Whether these colours will come true from seed or not is another question.

On leaving the moorland we came first into juniper forest, the gnarled trees wrapped in moss; then into bamboo and Rhododendron forest, chiefly *R. uvariifolium* and the pink-flowered *R. faucium* here a tree conspicuous for its smooth stem showing like lustre-ware beneath the tattered tissue-paper bark; and finally into oak forest, with lichen instead of moss for its dress material. Late in the afternoon we emerged from the forest on to an alp, where stood a single hut. We could now see the Tsangpo flowing towards us, and occasionally Namcha Barwa, indistinct behind the clouds; we also had a good view of the valley which led to the Nam La and observed several glaciers. After another stiff descent – and in this country it is more tiring to go down than up – we reached the village of Trube, and learnt that before we could cross the river we must either go down to Gyala, where there is a rope bridge, or up to Pe, where there is a ferry. For the river is here leaping into the great gorge, and is not to be trifled with. We decided to go down to Gyala.

The march down the left bank of the Tsangpo 13km [8 miles] to Shingche Chögye took us most of the day, and involved a good deal of climbing up and down. As we penetrated into the sheltered depths of the gorge, we found ourselves in Pine forest, where grew both the large-coned and small-coned pines; elsewhere the steep slopes were covered with bush growth, including species of Desmodium, Hypericum, Daphne, Barberry, Jasmine, Rose, Bamboo, Hydrangea, Ceratostigma and other plants, but nothing to fire the imagination of the plant collector; there were also many twining plants, such as *Codonopsis convolvulacea,* species of *Vitis, Schizandra, Cucurbita,* and *Clematis.* It was the flora of the glens coming down to the river-side. A couple of miles from Shingche Chögye we met a deputation sent by the *Depa* to prepare the way before us. They had brought with them, what was much more welcome, a bamboo ewer of beer. It was a good brew, and we quickly emptied that ewer and sent back for more. Arrived at Shingche Chögye, a collection of poor little temples clapped against the face of the cliff over which a glacier torrent leaps 60m [200ft.] into the Tsangpo, we were ushered into a leaky, rickety room, and kept busy till dawn putting up a stout counter-offensive against a night attack by fleas in force. We survived the ordeal, with wounded feelings.

July 20th brought another unpleasant experience – the crossing of the rope bridge. The river here is about 90m [100 yards] wide, with great swirls, but no rapids; it was now at flood mark, and whole trees were being swept along by the current. The bridge consists of two separate cables of twisted bamboo, 12.5cm [5in.] in diameter, tied to trees some 15m [50ft.] above the river on either bank. On these straddles a solid yoke-shaped wooden rider, with a span of 60cm [2ft.]; in each leg near the base, a notch is cut, which serves to hold the safety rope in position. First of all, creepers were cut in the jungle, from which a dozen rings were twisted and threaded over the two ropes; and through these rings was rove a life-line attached to the rider, by which the hauling was to be done. Then a man, tying himself on to the yoke, pulled himself across, carrying the end of the life-line; and the fun began.

It was arranged that we should cross first, as later in the day, with the constant traffic, the rope would begin to sag, and there was risk of a ducking. The ordinary person, after suspending himself from the rider, with his arms free for hauling, and his legs waving ungracefully, works his own passage; but royalty like ourselves were dealt with differently. We had two riders, one to support the body, the other to support the ankles; and never did man feel more helpless than I felt, bound hand and foot, suspended by two thin ropes over that great rushing river, and travelling by slow, cruel jerks, which rattled every tooth in my head, towards the distant cliff. However, the men hauled on the rope with a will, singing at their task, and in five minutes the torture was over.

The Depa of Gyala and a reconnaissance of the gorge

The *Depa* of Gyala himself came down to meet us, bringing refreshments, which were much appreciated after the ordeal; also two fine chestnut horses, on which we rode across cultivated terraces to Heath Robinson House, a comic barrack whose wooden walls were inclined at all angles. The whole place seemed to be shored up with sticks and tied together with string. Meanwhile we had observed a path following the right bank of the river close to the edge of the water; three jungly-looking men carrying loads were among the bushes. These men had disappeared by the time we reached the house, but we felt convinced they had just come up through the gorge. However, the *Depa,* whom we questioned on the subject, swore that there was no path, and that no one ever came up through the gorge: anyone coming from Pemakö, he said, crossed either by the Nam La or the Doshong La. We discovered later that this was more or less true, as the Tibetan authorities have strictly forbidden the tribesmen to enter Kongbo by this route.

The *Depa,* when pressed, admitted that there was a path to Pemaköchung, passable, he said, only when the river was low; but this was untrue, as the path is high up the cliff, though why he was so anxious to conceal from us the fact that a path through the gorge did exist we could not understand. We knew of course that Bailey and Morshead had gone down to Pemaköchung in 1913. Eventually he changed his tune, and showed us a note written by Major Bailey, guardedly extolling his virtues; he even volunteered to assist us! We made no secret of the fact that we proposed to return to Gyala in November and try to penetrate the gorge; since we had to depend on the *Depa* for food and transport. For the moment, however, we only wanted to go a couple of miles or so downstream to see a rapid which was throwing up great waves at the foot of a cliff where the river changed direction. So we started along the path we had discovered.

Before long we were paddling, the path being under water; and presently finding the bushes which edged the bank also submerged, we waded out round them till we were waist-deep, this being preferable to hacking our way through the thick growth higher up the slope. However, dusk approached before we reached our objective, so we felt compelled to return; and we reached Heath Robinson House after dark, just as a search party, armed with pine torches, set out to look for us. We did one useful thing – we marked the water-level on a tree-trunk. Ten days later we returned to Gyala, and made our way along this river-path with ease, not even having to wade; for the water-level had fallen 3.6m [12ft.]! On this occasion we reached the great rapid, only to find an unbridged torrent crossing our track. We searched for a way over without success, then selected a point where we might ford it. However, our two Tibetans flatly refused to accompany us, saying that we should be washed off our feet and swept into the river, where our fate would instantly be sealed. Cawdor and I therefore crossed by ourselves, holding hands, to the delight of the Tibetans, who cheered madly; on the return trip they waded into the water and assisted us.

Having crossed this obstacle, we were no better off, since further progress was almost immediately barred by the cliff above the great rapid. Here we obtained the first of twelve boiling-points taken at water-level in the gorge. Our objective being the Nam La, the most eastern pass over the Himalayan range, we had next to march some distance upstream. The river here is a wonderful sight, flanked by broad terraces one on top of the other, and broken by furious rapids. It twists violently from side to side, wrenching itself round the spurs, forcing its way by a series of jerks to the north, and at each bend glacier streams enter the river.

Near Trube, where we slept the night, three glacier streams from the snow range are crossed; the largest glacier – that from Namcha Barwa itself – descends to within 3km [2 miles] of the river, and its snout, buried under tons of gravel on which trees grow, is plainly visible up the glen. Formerly these glaciers must have crossed the valley, for their moraines are piled up on the left bank, and have been cut into terraces by the river. It is the glacial

Schisandra neglecta **near the Rong Chu.**   PC

This species of *Schisandra* appears to be rarely cultivated. It differs from the better known *S. grandiflora* in the smaller flowers which are pale yellow rather than cream. The family Schisandraceae is closely related to Magnolia and therefore shares a number of evolutionary primitive characters such as the indefinite number of spirally arranged floral parts. A woody climber with small, usually scented flowers. The edible red fruit are conspicuous in autumn.

Jasminum humile.   KNEC

The small bright yellow flowers of this species of Jasmine are unfortunately not scented. The well-known white-flowered, scented *Jasminum officinale* is also common in south-eastern Tibet. Both species are used medicinally and the scent from the latter is used to make perfume.

boulders which cause such a turmoil in the river-bed, where, at high-water, waves are thrown 6m [20ft.] into the air, and the river looks like an angry sea, racing madly down the steep slope into the gorge. The terraces are mostly cultivated and irrigated. Peach, Apple, and Walnut trees are common. The crops are protected by bird scares, consisting of a piece of birch bark, red on one side, silver on the other, kept flat by diagonal struts of bamboo, and suspended from a string; these move in the slightest breeze.

Rhododendron lanatoides, **below the Tra La, above the Rong.**   KNEC

This species was described in 1982, despite being discovered by Kingdon Ward (then identified as *R. coccinopeplum,* now *R. roxieanum*) on the slopes of Namcha Barwa in 1924. A handful of plants were found in Scottish and English gardens which were matched to KW 5871. This species is distinguished by its pointed leaves with thick fawn-brown indumentum and very early white flowers. We failed to locate it in 1995 but in 1996 we found first a single small plant and, a few days later, a forest of it. According to an Austrian who explored further down the valley, it was very common around the lower slopes of Gyala Peri. As the cultivated plants have proved to be very hard to propagate, the species has remained extremely rare and is therefore very desirable for collectors.

Lonicera hispida **var.** *bracteata* **on the Sirchem La.**   KNEC

This species is extremely variable, ranging from a tiny creeping alpine to rangy shrub to 3m (10ft.) or more and is perhaps the most common Lonicera species in the Tsangpo Gorges region. The attractive yellow flowers are surrounded by green bristly bracts. The typical *L. hispida* was first collected from Turkestan. The low growing var. *bracteata* was originally given specific status as *L. bracteata* when Ward introduced it in 1924.

Tibetan children at the campsite at Trube (Tripe). KNEC

The village of Trube (pronounced 'tree-pay') lies near the Yarlung Tsangpo between Pe and Gyala. From near here the trail to the Nam La begins. On rare days when the cloud clears, the peak of Namcha Barwa dominates the skyline high above the village. Trube lies below 3300m (10,000ft.) so the vertical face of the mountain rises an astonishing 4500m (15,000ft.) above the village.

Namcha Barwa from near Trube. KNEC

This photograph of the spectacular northern face of Namcha Barwa was taken on the moraine of a now retreated glacier, perhaps the one Ward describes as descending to within two miles (3km) of the river. We believe this moraine to be the location where Sir George Taylor discovered *Primula aliciae* (named after his wife.) With the retreat of the glacier comes the possibility that this primula is now extinct. Namcha Barwa at 7756m (24,440ft.) was for a time the highest unclimbed peak in the world. It was finally climbed by a Japanese party in 1992.

On the slopes below the Nam La

On July 22nd we started up the mountain from a village called Kyikar, and had a close-up view of Namcha Barwa, though the peak is not so impressive when thus foreshortened. We stood on a terrace, in fallow fields blue with a dwarf Erytrichium; and it was very difficult to believe that this mountain still towered 4300m [14,000ft.] above our heads! Entering a forest of larch and golden poplar, the latter discharging a perfect snowstorm of seed, we had to send the ponies back to Kyikar, while the loads were transferred to the backs of men and women. The track now slanted steeply up the flank of the mountain and soon disappeared amongst a wilderness of bushes and fallen trees; for the forest had been burnt here, and charred trunks lay in all directions. We had to make our own path, since no one had visited the pastures for a year or more. Finally we turned a shoulder and ascending through live forest and a field of purple lilies, came out into a beautiful meadow, full of violet primulas, where we camped.

Vast moraines covered with forests of Larch, Picea and Rhododendron, surrounded us. From the foot of one gushed a stream of sparkling water. In the meadow, besides violet Primulas (*P. alpicola*), were clumps of sky-blue poppy *M. betonicifolia* [*M. baileyi*]. Deep down in the glen, tree and bush Rhododendrons grew to the exclusion of everything else, the species being: the pink-flowered *R. hirtipes,* yellow-flowered *R. wardii, R. uvariifolium,*

R. dignabile, and another species not before met with, having yellow or
possibly orange flowers, and glaucous leaves. It was over, only one or two
fading blooms being noticed, but it appeared to be of the 'Cinnabarinum'
type. The Mahogany *R. triflorum* and *R. principis* were seen only on the drier
slopes above the glen. These two, abundant on both sides of the river, had
flowered and seeded well everywhere. *R. hirtipes* and *R. wardii* on the other
hand, also found on both sides of the river, and though they had flowered
freely (whence we infer that the previous season had been a favourable one),
had restricted the output of seed, and in this forest were particularly shy. *R.
uvariifolium* and *R. dignabile* had undoubtedly flowered badly, and seeded
worse. But the reasons for failure were not always the same, nor did they
necessarily depend on present circumstances.

In nature Rhododendrons rarely flower well for two consecutive years,
because a good flowering period, if followed by a heavy seed crop, uses up all
the plant's energy; there is none left over for building up next year's flower-
buds. If the plant flowers well this year, but for some reason does not set seed,
it may at the same time lay down resting-buds and flower well the following
year. In Tibet we noticed that many bushes flowered well, but seeded badly –
the capsules had aborted. This was probably due to lack of cross-pollination,
owing to a lack of insects; for the spring of 1924 was wet and cold, perhaps
unusually so. By the end of the year, however, these plants had on the stocks
a good crop of resting-buds which would bloom in 1925. Another common
cause of failure to produce flowers and seed seems to be due to a plant increasing so rapidly
that it oversteps its bounds before the conditions are ripe for it. Thus *R. sinogrande* first seen
in Pemakö in October, and again in the upper Tsangpo gorge, in December, though it
formed two-thirds of the forest, had not flowered at all here. We saw hundreds of healthy
trees without a vestige of flower. It was not till we got down to the lower part of the gorge
that we found fruiting specimens. This was probably due to some internal trouble due to
the plants spreading beyond its natural environment, because I observed exactly the same
thing with the giant Tsuga, referred to later. This tree I noticed as far west as Tsela Dzong,
and it was abundant in the upper part of the gorge; yet it was not till we were definitely on
the southern flank of the snow range that we found cones; and here they were plentiful.

It was the same with the 'Arboreum' Rhododendron (K.W. 6311) (*R. coryanum/R.
uvariifolium*). We passed through forests of this species in the upper part of the gorge, but it
was not till we reached the lower gorge that we found it ripening seeds. The inference is
that these species, though able to maintain life, are not able to breed under adverse climatic
conditions; the reproductive, though not the vegetative organs, are affected. The yellow *R.
wardii* on the other hand, had flowered well enough, but set no seed here because the
flowers had been attacked by a fungus which had reduced them to a black pulp.

Next day we continued to scramble over large moraines, covered with forest trees, or
with bushes of pink-flowered *Rhododendron primuliflorum*. Here I found not only the
chocolate-flowered *Primula advena* var. *euprepes* [*P. maximowiczii*], but a also yellow-
flowered species (*P. advena* var. *advena*), a fragrant Himalayan form of the Chinese *P.
szechuanica*. Both species grow about 1m [3ft.] high with as many as three whorls of
flowers, and are so similar in fruit that it is hard to distinguish them; var. *euprepes*,
however, can be recognised by its purple-tinted capsules.

Now came a very steep ascent through Rhododendron forest, *R. dignabile* and the *R.
uvariifolium* below, impenetrable thickets of the *R. phaeochrysum* var. *agglutinatum* above. We
also found a single clump of a Rhododendron not previously met with; the stiff narrow leaves
with their buff woolly coat, and the dead corollas still attached to the furry capsules, suggested
a close relationship with *R. roxieanum* (*R. lanatoides*). At last we emerged into the alpine
region and camped in a meadow at the foot of the cliffs, and some few hundred feet above
a glacier lake, the Nam La Tso. Opposite to our camp, across the lake, was a fine snow-peak
called Temu Tse, from which a glacier crawled half-way down the cliff, and there stopped, as

though sliced off with a knife. Further up towards the head of the valley were more snow-peaks, giving birth to four glaciers all of which discharged into one stream. This stream feeds the lake which empties itself down the valley we had ascended, the water flowing under the moraines and finally coming to the surface at their foot, where our lower camp was situated.

In the five days spent here we added considerably to the plant collection, and made the first ascent of the Nam La, though we did not cross the pass. We found a Caragana, bristling with spines (K.W. 6267), the dwarf *Lonicera hispida* var. *setosa* with straw-yellow flowers (K.W. 5988), two rock Primulas, and two mossy Saxifrages, with leafy stems and single nodding flowers. Others, of little use to horticulture, were, an erect Codonopsis, a Saussurea from the screes, several species of Cremanthodium (including the pink *C. palmatum*) Gentian, and Meconopsis; but we will confine our remarks to those plants which will shortly be seen in our gardens. A fine Potentilla (*P. arbuscula*: K.W. 5774), which I took to be a form of *P. fruticosa,* despite the very large size of its buttercup-golden flowers, formed low rounded bushes, massed in the broad gravelly delta of the stream at the lakehead. It was a brave sight, smothered with golden flowers, 2.5cm [an inch] in diameter. From its petals the local people make a feeble kind of tea. Near by at the foot of the cliff was a clump of Caragana bushes, their bare black snaky stems armed with clusters of pink spines, their leaves edged with long glistening silken hairs. The flowers are pink. On the gneiss cliffs, facing south, were small scraggy plants of a Rhododendron bearing pale yellow flowers, which would have been more striking if more abundant; the plants looked unhappy, as though they felt they had no business to be there, and formally protested against it by setting very little seed. It is a form of *R. lepidotum* (var. *elæagnoides*) from Sikkim.

With it grew the charming little violet-flowered *Primula baileyana,* a rock plant with a thick coating of snow-white meal so generously applied that it creates a small dust storm when you pluck it. This species is more abundant, however, north of the Tsangpo, and looked almost as unhappy here as did the yellow Rhododendron. It is a new species, which I have named in honour of my friend Major Bailey. Finally, in crevices of the highest cliffs at 5500m [18,000ft.], grew a closely allied and even more lovely Primula, for its larger mauve flowers are sweetly fragrant. These cliffs, which face south, are composed of a fine banded gneiss and are difficult to climb; a huge cone of rubble has, however, been shot down, and it was in a grassy hollow, between the foot of this cone and a moraine overlooking the lake, that our camp was situated. Streams have ploughed deep furrows in this scree towards the base, whence we obtained our water supply; and the path to the Nam La, after ascending the cliffs by this obvious opening, traverses awkwardly to the head of the valley.

The foot of the slope was packed with dwarf shrubs and flowers. Here grew the best of the creeping honeysuckles, with large tubular sulphur flowers projecting from paper skirts (*Lonicera hispida*); clumps of 'mossy' saxifrages, a few inches high, one species with purple, the other with golden flowers, borne singly on the leafy stems; the fragrant dwarf *Primula sikkimensis* var. *pudibunda,* the violet-flowered *Meconopsis impedita,* and other plants of botanical rather than of horticultural interest.

As one ascended the scree, however, this flora rapidly dwindled, first the undershrubs, then the herbaceous plants disappearing, to be replaced by certain rock plants – species of Saussurea, *Isopyrum grandiflorum,* various Umbelliferæ, Cruciferæ, Saxifrages, Gentians, and dwarf Primulas. The highest flowering plant of all was a mauve Primula, and though we did not see it in flower, we got seed of it later (K.W. 5973). It hung in tufts from the cliff crevices, and hence was usually out of reach. By climbing some of the chimneys at the apex of the scree, I secured a specimen, and subsequently a little seed; but the plant is not likely to be hardy with us. It is a rare but widespread species, discovered by Mr. St. George Littledale on his famous journey across Tibet in 1896, and named *P. littledalei* in his honour (K.W. 6003). Situated as we were about half-way between the Doshong La and the peak of Namcha Barwa, on the same range, I had naturally expected to find here a flora similar to that of the Doshong La; richer in species perhaps, since the pass was so much higher. It was, therefore, rather a shock to find that it was not only quite different, but much poorer, in woody species at any rate. We found three species of

Cremanthodium palmatum. **KR**
This photograph was taken in the autumn in a valley running from Macandro, twin peak to Gyala Peri, to the Rong Chu. Members of the giant family Compositae, Cremanthodiums are usually identifiable by their nodding flowers and usually yellow ray florets. This species is unusual in its pink flowers. Most alpine Cremanthodium species are a challenge to grow.

Mandragora caulescens **on the northern slopes of Namcha Barwa.**
KNEC
The European forms of mandrake have many folk tales associated with them, such as that the plant screams when you try to pull it up. This Chinese and Himalayan member of the potato family (Solanaceae) is a common plant with variable flower colour, from almost black to yellowish, and it surprises and delights those who see it for the first time.

Rhododendron at the Nam La not found at the Doshong La, as against fourteen species found at the Doshong La but not at the Nam La. The Doshong La claimed eight Primulas for its own, the Nam La six, and the same with other genera, each valley having species peculiar to itself. And yet the two valleys lay within 8km [5miles] of each other!

Up to the Nam La

On July 24th, the weather being fine, we decided to visit the Nam La, and ascending the scree by a zigzag path, we made our way up and down across the fluted face of the cliff, and thence across rock chutes to the moraines. Here the going was even worse. After ascending some distance, we crossed a small glacier, and found ourselves at the foot of a steep snow slope which led directly to the pass. It was now fairly late in the afternoon, and it seemed doubtful whether we should be able to reach the pass and get back to camp before dark, as the snow was quite soft; however, having come so far, we decided to risk it. Hugging the side of the cliff, as closely as possible – for we were on a glacier and did not know what the surface under the snow might be like – we struggled slowly along, sinking in up to our knees at every step, until finally we reached the summit at 4.15, where we rested for quarter of an hour.

We could see nothing on the other side, as the mist was flying up in our faces; and after taking observations for altitude, we prepared to descend. Throwing caution to the winds, we 'skied' down the steep snow slope, keeping more out on to the glacier, and descended in ten minutes what had taken us three-quarters of an hour to mount. Thence we recrossed the first glacier, which was about 70m [75 yards] wide, and scrambling over the moraines, soon reached camp. Several points were now clear. As reported by the Lama Serap Gyatso many years ago, the Nam La is under snow all the year round; in fact, the pass is actually occupied by a glacier, which on the other side is likely to be difficult. It had taken us rather over four hours to reach the pass; and though it was not 'officially' open, the going would be little, if any, improved at a later date. Therefore, since there was no camping-ground between our present one and the pass, it would be necessary to allow at least six hours to the pass for laden porters, and say two hours to get off the glacier on the other side and reach firewood. A night's bivouac in between, without firewood or water, would be merely uncomfortable in the summer, but it would be fatal in the winter. We could not risk it. As the pass is only

Primula baileyana **on cliffs west of the Sirchem La.**

An exquisite primula species in both flower and foliage. The flowers are a delicate shade of purple-blue and the leaves are covered with white meal. It grows on or under rocks and cliffs, facing south, and is a considerable challenge in cultivation, though a few experts have managed to keep it going. We found a small colony on the Temo La and a magnificent one on cliffs by the roadside on the Sirchem La, a pass on the Lhasa-Yunnan road parallel to the Temo La.

open for two months in the year, therefore, we must cross soon or not at all.

When we returned to the Nam La in November it was already too late; and though Cawdor did, after a great struggle, reach the pass again and even obtain a boiling-point reading at the top, his report of the conditions was such that we did not feel justified in risking our porters' lives by crossing. As a matter of fact the Nam La is very little used by the natives of Pemakö, and hardly ever by the Tibetans, though the headman of Kyikar village had been over, and knew all about it. He told us that two days' journey over the pass there is a monastery called Mandalting, where resides a holy hermit; pilgrims from Tibet occasionally visit him, to offer him food. Four days' journey from Mandalting, and close to the Tsangpo, is a Lopa village called Puparang.

One day we walked right round the lake, which is about 6km [4 miles] long and 1km [half a mile] wide. From the other side we had a splendid view of the whole snowy range from Namcha Barwa to Sengdam Pin, with the deep rent in the middle through which the Tsangpo has torn its way. Namcha Barwa, 7757m [25,445ft.] high, and Gyala Peri, 7238m [23,740ft.] high, are 22km [14 miles] apart. The fourth peak on the Namcha Barwa ridge which runs north-westwards is over 6000m [20,000ft.] and 13km [8 miles] due south of Gyala Peri. Through this 8-mile gap the Tsangpo tears its way at an altitude of about 2400m [8,000ft.], in a gorge which is, therefore, over 3000m [10,000ft.] deep. There is a notch in the ridge above the lake, and a path leads over into the next valley and so over another col into the Doshong La Valley.

The view to the north-west from the cliff above our camp was also extensive. South of Sengdam Pu are one or two lower snow-peaks with several shrivelled glaciers, forming part of the ridge between the Rong Chu and the Tsangpo; this ridge, as we have seen, is crossed by several passes, the Tang La being plainly visible. Fifty miles away to the north-west, beyond Tongkyuk, was the mighty snow-clad Salween divide, filling the horizon. On July 28th we broke camp and descending at a good pace, reached Kyikar in the afternoon. There is a hot spring near the top of the terrace, above Kyikar, where people go for a cure. On the following day we went downstream once more to Gyala. It was a bright sunny day, but hot and sticky in the gorge. At Gyala we had a treat, for we managed to buy a few new potatoes, the first potatoes we had seen for nearly three months; we also got some green peas.

On July 30th we recrossed the rope bridge, and after spending another flea-ridden night

The Nam La in November. FKW
The Nam La is a glacier-covered pass on a ridge that descends to the south from the summit of Namcha Barwa. At over 5180m (17,000ft.) the pass is rarely used and leads into the wild, uninhabited valleys to the east, in Pemakö. Frank KW and Lord Cawdor reached the crest of the pass on 24 July but did not descend into the clouds and mist rising from the moist, tropical valleys far below. They reached the pass late in the afternoon and 'Throwing caution to the winds, we "skied" down the steep snow slope…and descended in ten minutes what had taken us three-quarters of an hour to mount.' They returned to the area in November to collect seeds, when this photograph was taken.

in the Shingche Chögye tenement, started straight up the mountain side for the Tra La. This route also, which is very steep, and impossible for pack transport, had been out of commission for a season, owing to the yak epidemic, and the path was quite overgrown. The rain now began again, and we spent two joyless nights under canvas (having lost the way on the second day) before crossing the pass. We were, however, able to observe that this stream rises in some large glaciers on Sengdam Pu and the snow-peaks to the south.

On August 1st we crossed the pass 4875m [15,910ft.] and descended once more to the *rong,* reaching Lunang in the afternoon to find the sun smiling again. On the way down through the forest I found one of the most interesting plants met with throughout the expedition – a dwarf yellow-flowered Meconopsis, allied to the rare *M. lyrata,* which is a blue-flowered species of Sikkim and Yunnan. The latter, a high alpine, is not hardy in Britain, but there seems reasonable probability that this new species will be quite hardy since it comes from a moderate elevation, and is moreover a woodland species. Woodland plants are not subject to such extreme conditions of temperature and atmospheric dryness as those which have to be grown in the open; consequently, this yellow-flowered *M. florindæ* – a bright little species growing about 25cm [10in.] high, like the big blue-flowered polycarpic *M. betonicifolia* (*M. baileyi*), should prove a great acquisition. We spent the night at Lunang, and dried our clothes, continuing to Tumbatse the following day.

CHAPTER X

A Journey to the Lost Lake

Pome and the Pobas

On August 9th we left Tumbatse on a journey of exploration. Our intention was to travel northwards as far as possible, and in that direction we started down the *rong*. It was a fine summer's day, and as we splashed through the marshes, past acres of yellow primulas, we could hardly believe we were in Tibet at all. From the prosperous village of Lunang, with its thirty houses and small monastery perched on an ice-scored rock, we looked down the valley to where it suddenly narrowed; then the trees stepped down from the mountains and met on either side, and the overlapping spurs shut off the view. But looking back up the valley one saw the wide sweep of the pastures, walled by sombre forest, and in the centre the towering masts of scattered trees which tried to invade the bog-land. Below the foot of the Lunang moraine are ponds full of small water-lilies, and presently we crossed the Rong Chu by a wooden bridge and plunged into the forest.

We were now in Pome, the land of the Poba, over whom the central government of Tibet has, till recently, exercised little direct control. But since the present Raja married a noble Lhasa lady, daughter of Tsarong Shape, he has thrown in his lot with the central government, and keeps on good terms with the Dalai Lama. Perhaps his own authority over the wild and reckless Poba wears a little thin towards the confines of his country; but it must be remembered that the Poba have good reason to be suspicious of strangers and resentful of interference, since they were so badly beaten up by the Chinese in 1905; though they eventually exacted a bloody retribution for this wantonness.

It must inevitably happen in a country such as Tibet, just as it has happened in India, Burma and China, that the original inhabitants, or at any rate, the oldest inhabitants of whom we have record, are driven under cover by the newer conquering immigrants; this in the days before immigration laws were invented. As the new-comers advance, the weaker people are driven farther and farther back, seeking refuge in the mountains or the forests, where communications are more difficult than on the plains, and good hiding-places abound. No one would choose such unpromising country of his own free will, except as a last resort, to escape from his enemies, or nowadays to escape taxation. We are therefore justified in regarding the people of the deep and gloomy gorges of South-eastern Tibet as of aboriginal stock, which is where one would naturally search for them rather than on the wide plains which are open to all Asia. Much of the forested country, however, is quite unexplored, so at present we can do no more than indicate probabilities. But it is significant that this country is called Pome, and its inhabitants Poba; because the Tibetans call their country *Po*.

Since we can trace the Tibeto-Burman family from Tibet to Burma in an unbroken line, with the Tibetans in force on the plains at one end, and the Burmans in force on the plains at the other, it is a reasonable inference that they followed this route in their migrations. Indeed we can trace them along two routes, southwards from Tibet – via the headwaters of the Irrawaddy into Burma, and via the Brahmaputra and its tributaries into Assam. These two human streams must have diverged somewhere in the dim and misty regions of Pome or Poyul; and one might speculate endlessly on what actually happened. The result is fairly clear. The Irrawaddy column reached the plains of Burma, where they strove with other columns from the east, the Shans and the Talaings, and ultimately prevailed. Of course, some fell by the wayside, and after various marchings and counter-marchings, settled down and hardened into Kachins, Marus, Nungs, and other clans of the upper Irrawaddy jungles.

Thermopsis barbata **and** *Iris decora* **KNEC**
Two plants common in the drier valleys on the north side of the main Himalayan range.

Aster albescens **near Trulung (Pylung).**   **KNEC**
Also known as *Microglossa albescens,* this is a showy plant which is quite widely available in cultivation. It has a wide altitudinal range from 2100-3600m (6,900-11,800ft.) and occurs in purple and white forms. Here it was growing along the roadside from Lunang to Trulung in fairly dry conditions.

Clematis montana **'Burlinson's Blush' near Lunang.**   **PC**
Spotted growing next to the Rong Chu by David Burlinson while on a reconnaissance trip, this unusual form of *Clematis montana* has variable pink staining on the back of the flower. This form is now in cultivation but unfortunately the pink staining seems to be rather unstable and may not persist. *Clematis montana* and its close relative *C. gracilifolia* are extremely common in this part of Tibet and they can be found growing through and on rhododendrons, conifers, berberis and many other trees and shrubs. Almost all have white flowers. One of the most popular climbing plants for the garden, *Clematis montana* was first introduced from the Himalaya in 1831.

Did the Brahmaputra column ever reach the plains of Assam or not? We do not know. Assam was occupied about the first century B.C. (so it is believed) by the Kacharis, who are said to have come there from the foot-hills of Sikkim and Bhutan. Whether these people found the Assam plains occupied (and if so, by whom), or whether they were themselves of Tibetan stock, is not known It is at least equally likely that they were Hindus, and not of Mongolian origin at all. If Assam was at that time occupied, it is possible that it was occupied by people of Tibetan stock who had travelled south via the Dihang and Lohit valleys; on the other hand, it may be that the Pome people, having chosen the worst route, got bogged in the jungle and never reached the plains at all; or that they eventually emerged from the jungle only to find that they had been forestalled on the plains. At any rate, there is nothing now except the Mongolian element in Bengal to show that the Tibeto-Burman family ever reached Assam; though the Abors, Miris, Akas, Daphlas and other tribes remain behind in the Assam jungle to prove that they tried to. The difficulty in forming a true idea of the routes followed in these early migrations is that we look upon the country as it is today, instead of trying to picture it as it was then. But the features are always changing, they never are stationary; and in the 5,000 years history goes back, in a mountainous region of excessive rainfall, much may, and indeed does, happen.

A big swift river like the Tsangpo is ever scouring its bed. If it digs down only 7.5cm [3in.] a year, it will dig a bed 390m [1,250ft.]deep in 5,000 years. If a mountain range is being uplifted only 7.5cm [3in.] a year, it will rise 390m [1,250ft.] during the same period. If a glacier is retreating at the rate of 1 foot a year, it will go back nearly a mile, quite far enough to expose a pass, for example. At the same time vegetation and climate are shifting and changing; there is no stability, no finality. Therefore it is misleading to seize upon one factor and regard it alone as changing in an otherwise fixed world.

On the evening of August 9th, we reached Chunyima, the first village in Pome, where we were well-received by the inhabitants. There was another guest in the house – a servant of the Kanam Raja, or King of Pome. He was a tall, well-built man with a cheerful cherry-red face, and long wavy hair falling loosely over his shoulders like a King Charles' spaniel. His wife, though a Rongpa (that is, an in habitant of the *rong*),

The ruins of Nambu Gompa. KR

Ward stayed at Nambu Gompa on the journey to the lost lake. 'It was 7 o'clock before we reached the shelter of Nambu Gompa, a gaunt stone building, three stories high, occupied in summer by both laity and clergy, but deserted in the long cold winter – for it stands at an altitude of 4100m (13,503ft.). There were half a dozen lamas in residence, who looked after the spiritual welfare of the many yak herds scattered up and down the valleys'. Like most religious buildings, this one was probably destroyed by the Chinese during the Cultural Revolution.

was a pretty woman, but she declined to face the camera. Pome women, unlike Kongbo women, do not lacquer their faces, which is an advantage; for the Kongbo women look absolutely hideous when their faces are hidden beneath a shining black mask; perhaps the idea is, or was originally, to make themselves less attractive to men. But it is easy for a foreigner to get a prejudiced view of these customs, which are largely conventional; and a Tibetan girl with a varnished face may be as popular amongst her set as an English girl, chromatic with powder, rouge, and peroxide, is in hers. We declined the offer of a room in the house, on account of the excessive number of fleas to the square inch, and elected to sleep in a shed which, by unmistakable signs, proclaimed itself the dairy. Fleas seemed nearly as plentiful here as in the main building, though less brisk, possibly depressed by the odour from bacterial milk pails.

On the following day we continued the descent by flights of steps, and the weather being fine, it grew rapidly hotter. By the stream were all kinds of bushes and small trees,

Primula florindae **in the valley of the Rong Chu near Tumbatse.** AC

Discovered by Kingdon Ward near Tumbatse (very near where this picture was taken), and named after his first wife Florinda, it first flowered in cultivation in 1926 and has been a popular garden plant ever since. This is truly the giant of the genus *Primula*, and easily the tallest-growing species: stems have been recorded which exceed 1.5m (5ft.). It has fragrant yellow flowers in midsummer. It likes boggy conditions and has naturalised in streams in some Scottish gardens. Cultivated forms with pink flowers are hybrids with other species.

such as tree-of-heaven (Ailanthus), holly, and Weigelia, the first species of Enkianthus met with, and thickets of Gaultheria and Vaccinium; in the forest were a number of ground orchids, a species of Podophyllum, and the dainty twining *Leptocodon gracile*. But these proletarian plants, though interesting in their way, were soon put in the shade by two of the aristocracy, a small Rhododendron (K.W. 6069) (*R. virgatum*) and a lily (K.W. 6034) (*Lilium wardii*). The former was in fruit and grew in company with Vaccinium on the steep well-drained sunny pine and bracken-clad slope. Not very thrilling perhaps, and yet at the sight of it I whooped with joy. In May, two days before we reached Tsela Dzong, I had found the *Rhododendron virgatum* flowering in a bog – just one plant, with one large fragrant pink bloom. It was obviously in the first flight of Rhododendrons, and the next thing was to find it in bulk. For three months I searched everywhere without result, and had almost given it up in despair and tried to forget about it when lo! we had tumbled right on top of its pet preserve! The joy of discovery is, for the botanist, complete; but the plant collector derives more solid satisfaction from finding the goods in commercial quantity. Though we had never seen the plant in full flower, we received a hint of its qualities; it had bloomed profusely, and every branch was crowded with its rusty-golden capsules filled with straw-coloured seeds. It has the peculiarity of bearing solitary axillary flowers, all up the shoots. Later we found this plant on the rocks and cliffs of the Tsangpo gorge, and all the way up the Po-Tsangpo, one of the commonest Rhododendrons from Gyala to Tongkyuk. Its presence in a bog, where we first saw it, was accidental; it is essentially a plant of the pine forest.

The history of the 'martagon' lily was similar. We had seen a few plants in bud in the Tsangpo gorge near Gyala, in July. Here we found it in quantity, and in full bloom, an exquisite sight. Most of the country we had been through was too dry and possibly too cold for it; as soon as we got down into the pine forest region, below 3,000m [10,000ft.], it was common, growing on steep gravelly slopes amongst rocks nearly swamped by the bracken. But it does not grow erect unless support is at hand, for when the shining leafy stem has attained a height of about 1m [3 or 4ft.], bearing maybe a score of blooms, it lolls gracefully over, surrounded by a halo of fragrance. The flowers are a beautiful shade of pink, closely and evenly spotted with rosy purple. The large scaly bulb grows about 15cm [6in.] below the surface. In December, at the lower end of the Tsangpo gorge, and at an altitude of little more than 15,00m [5,000ft.], I found a lily in fruit on the steep grassy hills, which is perhaps the same thing; on the other hand, perhaps it isn't.

We now found ourselves on a well-kept and evidently much-used road, for it had been recently repaired at several points where landslides had partially demolished it. The valley grew rapidly deeper and narrower as the stream increased the grade of its bed, and to avoid falling into the bottom of the V, the path clung to the hillside, descending abruptly in flights of steps when opportunity offered. Hereabouts we met a pilgrim journeying to Lhasa. He carried his goods and chattels on his back, packed in a bamboo frame, and informed us that he came from Amdo, which is away up in the north-east corner of Tibet, by the blue lake, beyond the land of the Golak. Already he had been five months on the road, having dedicated himself to acquiring a large stock of merit by visiting the holy places. He was suffering from toothache, and was grateful for a little iodine and aspirin which Cawdor gave him. In the course of the afternoon we reached the Tongkyuk River, and turning westwards, crossed it half a mile above the junction by a good bridge.

From there we climbed up to Tongkyuk Dzong, which is perched on a knoll. It is a poor place, consisting only of the barrack-like *dzong* and a shabby monastery, which had been robbed of the few poor treasures it ever possessed by the Chinese. Nominally there were thirty monks attached, but they had dispersed to their homes for the rainy season, leaving only the sacristan in residence. We pitched our tents in the courtyard, which heavy rain soon after our arrival had converted into a lake; but we preferred death by drowning to death by dyspnœa in the squalid pens which surrounded the yard. The *Depa* was sick, but the inevitable 'manager' made arrangements for transport, and sold us food. Next day we descended to the junction of the Rong Chu with the

Tongkyuk River. The latter is considerably the bigger, and the grey tinge of the water suggested that it arose amongst glaciers, an observation we were later able to confirm. The altitude at the junction was 2,487m [8,157ft.]. The short break in the rains was now over, and when we started up the Tongkyuk River on August 12th, it was raining steadily. At the village of Temo, a mile up the valley, two carved wooden images of ogreish aspect guard the approach; they stand 2.75m [9ft.] high, but, being almost legless, are actually much larger. Another pair of these fetishes stood sentinel over the next village, but after that we saw no more.

Crossing the river twice we began to ascend more steeply, and late in the afternoon camped in a wet meadow where stood an empty herds' bothy. In the bed of the river were masses of giant cowslip Primula (*P. florindæ*); one I measured sent up a stalk 114cm [45in.] high, bearing a hundred-flowered umbel, 15cm [6in.] high and 13cm [5in.] through! Above this point the path keeps to the river-bed for a short distance, in order to avoid a cliff. To protect it, river training works have been installed. These comprise a stout wooden palisade backed by a low wall of boulders, behind which a wooden causeway carries the path along the bed of the stream; evidently this did not prove sufficiently strong, and the causeway was an afterthought. Anyway, it was under water now. But roads in Eastern Tibet go where they can, and no sooner had we negotiated these aqueous pitfalls in order to avoid a cliff, than we had to climb hundreds of feet up a cliff by rickety stone stairways in order to avoid a gorge.

On the rocks here we noticed both the purple and yellow-flowered *Rhododendron lepidotum* growing together, and within the splash of a cascade, on the almost bare granite slab, was a beautiful Cyananthus (*C. wardii*, K.W. 6082). From a large mat of pale green finely cut foliage enveloped in long silken hairs which cause it to glisten like spun glass, radiated the cobalt blue trumpet flowers, delicate as crêpe de Chine. Amongst this genus of Campanuleæ are some very beautiful plants, but they are not easy of cultivation in this country, probably because most of them come from too high an altitude. It must be remembered that plants from very high altitudes – say 4600m [15,000ft.] and upwards – enjoy a sub-arctic climate, and are hardly likely to flourish in Britain, at least in the south. We rightly reject plants which come from below 1800m [6,000ft.] in these low latitudes, holding that they need a sub-tropical climate. But the climate of Britain is no more sub-arctic than it is sub-tropical, so why a plant should be expected to thrive in Britain, simply because it comes from a very high altitude, passes the wit of man. But the Cyananthus referred to above is not a high alpine. It was collected at about 3400m [11,000ft.], which is a temperate altitude for the latitude; consequently it may thrive, though the long silken hairs are a danger signal. It was on December 30th when we passed this way a second time that I collected the seed, which has since germinated; there was no snow then, and the plant was shrivelled in the sunshine. Other plants seen on the cliff here were *Isopyrum grandiflorum* and *Primula pulchelloides*.

For two hours we marched through a wide, almost level boggy valley, which had long ago contained a glacier. North of us, and close by, was a great range of snow-clad peaks, of which we caught a glimpse in December. Patches of dwarf Rhododendron grew amongst the boulders of a moraine which dammed a small lake into a side valley. There were not many flowers here, except monkshoods in the woodland, and Primulas by the stream. It was 7 o'clock before we reached the shelter of Nambu Gompa, a gaunt stone building, three stories high, occupied in summer by both laity and clergy, but deserted in the long cold winter – for it stands at an altitude of 4100m [13,503ft.]. There were half a dozen lamas in residence, who looked after the spiritual welfare of the many yak herds scattered up and down the valleys. All this grazing land belongs to the Kanam Raja, whose Master-of-the-Horse was also domiciled under our roof in charge of the royal ponies, which were out at grass. We stayed a day at the *gompa,* and persuaded the cloth to pray for better weather, which they gladly did since we paid for these masses chanted for the soul of departed summer; but they failed to resurrect the dead and it continued to rain with unabated vigour.

Sorbus filipes **near Paku (now Bago).**   **KR**
Several introductions of this Sorbus species, related to *S. vilmorinii*, have recently been made from Tibet. It often
occurs as a shrub in exposed sites above the treeline, but in more sheltered spots can reach 4m (13ft.) or more. The
red-flowered Sorbus found above Showa is probably referable to this species.

The Nambu La and the Nam Tso Lake

On August 15th we resumed our march westwards, keeping along the base of the snowy
Salween divide, which lay to the north of us; and passing a glacier lake at the head of the
valley, reached the pass called Nambu La, 4560m [14,971ft.]. In the cold streams was
growing a 'Sikkimensis' Primula, (*P. waltonii*) with large glossy flowers of rich ruby red, or
port-wine colour, softened inside with white meal and wonderfully fragrant. In winter the
dry seeds of the 'Sikkimensis' Primulas are jerked out of the tubular parchment-like
capsule by the wind, and broadcasted; sometimes the culm itself is snapped off by the
weight of the snow. I considered we were lucky, therefore, to get good seed of the fine
ruby Sikkimensis species when we crossed the Nambu La after three days' snowstorm on
January 3rd, for the dead Primula stems, almost snowed under, were trembling in the
wind. Most of the capsules had long since shed their last seeds, but by collecting a large
bunch, sufficient dregs of seed were collected to germinate merrily three months later in
England (K.W. 6094). On the cliffs above the pass itself, facing north, and in winter buried
under an intolerable weight of snow, were several dwarf Rhododendrons, including Scarlet
Runner (*R. forrestii*), with a few lingering blooms, and Plum Warner (*R. campylogynum*)
bristling with its dusky plums six weeks after it was over and done with on the Doshong
La. It was the first time we had seen these pluvial Rhododendrons north of the Tsangpo.

The seed of the milk and sulphur 'Sikkimensis' *P. alpicola* (K.W. 6117) was not
collected till January 11th – also in the snow. The dwarf Rhododendrons, however,
were another story, and I spent an hour on the cliff above the pass, waist-deep in the
drifted snow, trying in vain to locate them, while Cawdor, lying in the snow, tried to
get a boiling-point reading on the pass itself; the reflection that I had collected seed of
both species on the Doshong La was cold comfort in circumstances which were already
cold enough. Descending 300m [1,000ft.], past a pretty glacier lake, where we noticed
several snow-peaks to the south of us, we camped in a meadow below the forest-line.

Next day a surprise awaited us, for we found that the mouth of this valley overhung a
much larger valley aligned at right angles to ours; at the head of the large valley was a
picturesque lake, the Nam Tso, surrounded by fir-trees, and into this lake flowed a glacier.
Descending the steep lip into the basin-shaped valley we entered upon a quagmire
disguised as a meadow, and sank over our ankles before we discovered it, while the ponies
had a miserable time. It was interesting to notice how the forest kept clear of this bog-land,
though fir-trees (*Abies* sp.) clustered thickly on the gravel mounds which held up the lake
at the valley head; another lateral glacier, now defunct, had pushed these across the main
valley. The meadow remained almost level, threaded by a sluggish meandering stream, and

Nambu La west side.

Ward describes this view: 'Descending 300m (1,000ft.), past a pretty glacier lake, where we noticed several snow-peaks to the south of us, we camped in a meadow below the forest-line. Next day a surprise awaited us, for we found that the mouth of this valley overhung a much larger valley aligned at right angles to ours; at the head of the large valley was a picturesque lake, the Nam Tso, surrounded by fir-trees, and into this lake flowed a glacier.' This picture was taken by Keith Rushforth who has retraced the journey taken by Ward and Cawdor from the Rong Chu to Pasum Tso.

ceased abruptly when the stream plunged suddenly downhill into the forest at the point where the glacier had ended. That was the odd feature of these glacier valleys north of the Tsangpo; they hardly ever showed any trace of the step structure so characteristic of the glacier valleys on the main Himalayan range – at the Doshong La and Nam La, for example – and in parts of North-west Yunnan. Nevertheless, the distinction between the ice-worn and water-worn portions of the valley was more sharply defined.

We were told that next day we should see a large lake; but no such lake was shown on our maps, though four or five days' journey away a lake called the Pasum Tso was marked. No white man had ever been through this country before. In the afternoon we reached a village called Lö or Lö-pa in a more arid region. The inhabitants showed a surprising lack of joy at our unexpected arrival, regarding us as so highly infectious that we were better isolated in the open under canvas than invited into a house. However, we inoculated them with rupees to such good purpose, that when we passed this way again five months later, they considered themselves out of danger, and swept and garnished the best room in the village to be placed at our disposal.

We could scarcely be surprised that once or twice we were coldly received by the villagers – the wonder was that we were so often warmly welcomed, before our curious mania for paying our way was discovered. After all, they have a wretched time under feudalism. Officials come and go demanding food and transport, which is supplied free gratis and for nothing. Being the custom of the country of course, nobody minds very much. But when strangers

who are practically guests of the Government come along expecting the same treatment, that is going a bit too far. Usually our reputation preceded us, and we did no more than we were expected to; but occasionally in some out-of-the-way corner like Lö, nobody had ever heard of us; and though they would not be rude to the guests of their country, they had no intention of putting themselves to great inconvenience on our behalf. Apparently it never entered their heads that we could be so simple as to pay for what we might have had for nothing. People don't. On the following day they were still indifferent, and the ponies having joined in the general boycott, it was close on noon before we started, despite the energetic action of Tom. However, we had only a short march, and having crossed a large glacier stream from the north, and noticed several snow-peaks and glaciers peeping up on either side of us, we ascended a ridge and saw below us the Pasum Tso. Descending the hillside and crossing a delta of gravel, we reached a village called Je, by the lake-side.

Pasum Tso

The Pasum Lake occupies a long narrow ice-worn valley between steep mountains. Towards the head are several snow-peaks, the most conspicuous of which is called Namla Karpo. The lake itself is about 16km [10 miles] long and 3km [2 miles[across, and stands at an altitude of 3700m [12,000ft.] above sea-level. We had hoped to find a way over the snowy range at the head of the lake, but though two big streams entered here, one from Namla Karpo and one from farther north, there is no pass at the head of either of them; probably the upper valleys are blocked by glaciers.

On the northern shore of the lake the mountains dip steeply into the water, and the path is carried at some height above the lake level. There is no shore, but there are two or three villages situated in hanging valleys. On the southern side the mountains are not so abrupt, and there is also the mile-wide delta of the Lö River (called the Shingso Chu) and its big tributary the Samtenling Chu, crossed below Lö. On this side the path keeps close to the water the whole way. Pilgrims gain merit by touring round the lake, and we thought we might as well do the same; unfortunately we cancelled our merit ration – if we did not positively lay up a stock of unrighteousness – by going round the wrong way.

Marching along the southern shore of the lake in the shade of the woods, where the Geranium-leafed Primula *P. latisecta* – now in fruit – was particularly abundant, we reached a village called Tsogo ('lake head') standing in a lagoon where a river flowed through wide water-logged pastures, and entered the lake. Just above the village, which was notable for its very tall flag-pole, visible from afar, the river divided, one branch flowing from Namla

A house in south-east Tibet.   **FKW**

Kingdon Ward writes: 'in forested parts of S.E. Tibet houses are built of timber: no metals, nails or screws are used. No glass: transparent paper is used instead.' This is probably one of the villages visited in August, perhaps Shoga Dzong, near Drukla Monastery. The houses in the Tsangpo Gorge rarely use this much stone in construction and most are elevated on wood pilings off the ground.

Mud watch towers or defence towers.   **FKW**

Sometimes known as Kongbo Towers. They are known locally as *dud khang* meaning 'demon houses' but were almost certainly built as places of refuge from marauding bandits. This tower is probably one of the ones Ward refers to near Pasum Tso.

Karpo, which we could plainly see up the valley, the other and larger stream coming from farther north. Between the two valleys stands another snow-peak called Chomodadzong. Namla Karpo is admittedly a very fine peak, visible from the lower end of the lake on a clear day, and from Je too, as a pyramid of snow and ice. The people are justly proud of it, and claim that it is visible from Gyantse, nearly 640km [400 miles] distant; but this we can hardly believe. On August 19th two mounted couriers arrived at Tsogo with a message of welcome to us from the *Dzongpön* of Shoga, an important village down the valley below the foot of the lake. We therefore set out with our escort – who were splendidly dressed in thick cloaks lined with blue, red trousering, long leather riding-boots, and grey Homburg hats – and crossing the river by a bridge, followed the northern shore of the lake. The wide meadow with the lagoon at the end, into which the river flowed from a steep rocky valley a few miles distant, afforded grazing for scores of cattle and ponies.

Close to the lower end of the lake, near the opposite shore, we noticed a small island, on which is built a monastery called Tsosang Gompa. It was noticeable that though both shores of the lake are wooded, it was mostly oak and pine wood along the north shore, Picea and birch forest along the south shore; the distinction was even more subtle than that, for here *Primula pulchella* replaced *P. latisecta* seen the previous day. A large and swift torrent has cut a channel through the moraine which blocks the lower end of the lake, and cascades into the valley below. There is a village at the foot of the moraine and a very rickety bridge over the river. Two more servants of the *Dzongpön* met us here, and presented scarves on behalf of their master; to which we made a suitable reply. Immediately below the valley broadened out into a flat grassy plain, where there was a little cultivation, but not much. Several villages, some in ruins, were seen, and after marching another 13km [8 miles] we halted for the night at Gyara. There were two interesting plants in the dry gravelly soil of this valley – a dwarf Erytrichium which formed little blue puff-balls, scattered over the fields, and amongst the thorn scrub a large coarse-leafed Onosma uncoiling its croziers of violet flowers. There is another and even better species of Onosma with pale blue Venetian glass bells occurring lower down the valley, where the soil is more sandy; and those, with the high-tension blue of *Cynoglossum amabile*, are the only nice-looking members of the Boraginaceæ we met with.

On August 20th, we covered the remaining few miles to Shoga Dzong in three hours, and found ourselves at a small village situated in the angle between two considerable streams, the Pasum Chu from the lake, and the Drukla Chu from the north-west. The *Dzongpön*, who had sent such pleasant greetings to us, was away on urgent business to meet the Commissioner from Gyamda, at Drukla Gompa, a short day's journey up the other branch of the river; and as we were told that we could cross the snowy range by following up this stream to its source, we decided to go on to Drukla Gompa next day.

All this country to the west of the Tsangpo bend is very dry, and we were rapidly approaching plateau conditions again. There was a certain amount of Coniferous forest up the glens, but not a tree in the valley, only bushes and thorn scrub; the further west we went, the drier it became, and of course as soon as we crossed the snowy range we were on the plateau, with not a stick of wood anywhere. Here and there, especially on the sites of ruined villages, are mud towers of curious shape, generally more or less battered, but sometimes in a good state of preservation and as much as 12-15m [40-50ft.] high, tapering slightly from the base. They are always in groups, three or four together for mutual support, and we counted several hundred in these rather arid valleys. From a distance they look not unlike factory chimneys, but they are as a matter of fact – or rather were once – watchtowers, hollow inside, and loopholed for defence. Staging was erected inside at various levels – you can still see the holes for the crossbeams, and the garrison could enfilade the attackers on any side.

One account says that these towers were erected by the original inhabitants of Kongbo, when the country was independent, and that they were captured and destroyed by the Tibetans when Kongbo passed under the control of Lhasa. Another account says that they were built by the Tibetans themselves some 200 years ago as a defence against the wild Pobas; though in that case – who pulled them down? Presumably the Pobas – unless of course they fell down. There is no doubt an element of truth in both versions, which are not difficult to reconcile; after all, the only point of real interest is, who built them? and that is the one thing we don't know. It may be remarked that such towers are common throughout the Tibetan Marches, from Kongbo to Szechuan. In the Mantzu Marches (Yunnan and Szechuan) they are usually octagonal in plan; in Kongbo they are polygonal.

Seeing so many villages in ruins, one supposes that they may date back only some fifteen years to the last Chinese invasion; for the Chinese troops passed through here, and crossed the Nambu La on their way to Pome. But though they did destroy some villages and a great many monasteries, most of the ruined villages date back to an earlier age, when the Tibetans were gradually expanding eastwards from the Lhasa region towards the gorge country; a movement which is still in progress.

Primula latisecta on the Nyima La.   **AC**
The members of Primula Section Cortusoides subsection Geranioides can be identified by their geranium-like (palmate) leaves. (A leaf can be seen in the lower right-hand side of this picture.) The distribution of *P. latisecta* appears to be confined to south-east Tibet. It has remained in cultivation since Kingdon Ward's 1924 introduction of it, though it is still rare. This specimen was found on the Nyima La close to where Kingdon Ward discovered it. It also occurs around Pasum Tso.

The island monastery at Pasum Tso.   **IB**

The small island monastery on Pasum Tso in Kongbo was first built in the 7th century by the Tibetan emperor Songtsengampo. Kingdon Ward and Lord Cawdor referred to Pasum Tso as 'The Lost Lake', visiting it in August of 1924 before their expedition through the Tsangpo gorge.

Onosma hookeri **near Layi.**   **PC**

This curious member of the Boraginaceae is quite common in south-east Tibet. The hairy leaves discourage grazing animals and can cause irritation to those with a sensitive skin. This specimen was found at a village on the approaches to the north side of the Bimbi La which crosses the mountain range between the Yarlung Tsangpo and Tsari.

CHAPTER XI

The Crisis at Drukla Monastery

Arriving at the monastery

Shoga Dzong comprises several houses placed in the angle between the two streams, at an altitude of 3230m [10,597ft.]. There is a fine wooden bridge over the Drukla branch, the road to the Gyamda Valley following the right bank of the combined river. On August 21st, after much delay owing to the absence of authority, we started up the Drukla stream with cattle for transport. Progress was painfully slow, and the valley being well populated, we were further delayed by frequent changes of transport. About midday we reached a meadow, and saw awaiting us at the other end, a smartly dressed deputation in long cloaks, big riding-boots, and grey Homburg hats; and as we approached, the *Dzongpön* of Shoga stepped forward. He had ridden out from Drukla to welcome us. We then sat down on the sward, and drank sour milk at his expense. After mutual expressions of goodwill, the *Dzongpön* and his bodyguard mounted their ponies and jingled off at a fast trot; while we mounted ours and followed at 3kph [2 miles an hour]. Presently we turned a corner, the river divided again, and crossing the lesser branch by a bridge we saw in front of us, at the foot of a lofty cliff, the monastery of Drukla.

Ascending the ramparts between rows of silent but curious monks who had collected to see the procession, we were conducted to comfortable rooms and prepared for the ceremony which we knew was coming. For not only was the *Dzongpön* of Shoga here, but no less a person than the Commissioner from Gyamda, a star of the first magnitude in this firmament. The Commissioner, the *Dzongpön* and the *Labrang Lama,* or high priest of Drukla, were in consultation over very weighty matters; but the arrival of two such distinguished guests sidetracked them for a moment, and they abandoned the council chamber in order to welcome us. When we had quenched our thirst with tea and changed our clothes, we requested the pleasure of our distinguished hosts, who came in force – the Commissioner, magnificent in Chinese silks, velvet boots, and scarlet tasselled mandarin's hat; the *Dzongpön,* scarcely less magnificent; the grand lama, a tall ascetic-looking monk, with a heavy jowl, a deeply-lined face, and shorn pate, in his dingy red gown; and a number of smirking minor canons and small bores of rakish not to say villainous aspect.

The presents were numerous and costly – for the recipients. The Commissioner brought a live sheep, a tin of Australian biscuits (I would never have suspected that biscuits were one of the products of Australia but for that happy chance) and two packets of stearin candles, rather moth-eaten. The *Dzongpön* brought eggs and flour; the good old abbot, eggs and flour, the clergy, eggs and flour; (five rupees); the villagers, eggs and flour; (five rupees). When we came to check the rations, we found we had 180 eggs, of which 179 exploded on contact; the one hundred and eightieth was a dud. To the Commissioner, the *Dzongpön,* and the good old abbot, we responded in kind; electric torches, pocket-knives, a looking-glass, two cakes of soap, and a bath towel found their way into the country houses of Kongbo. The clergy and the laity, having profiteered to some purpose, were paid in cash, and went off hugging their true-gotten gear. We now discovered what all the excitement was about. The minor ornaments of the church had long been indulging in the lusts of the flesh. It was the old story, wine and women. But the New Reformation is coming to Tibet; and suddenly, like a bolt from the blue, civil authority had struck.

'Immediate expulsion of sixty monks,' said the Commissioner briskly with that faculty the Oriental in power has for doing something really drastic, and damn the consequences. 'Theirs not to reason why.' Sixty monks were chosen, and pushed out into a cold hard world, to our great disgust; we only had to look at them to feel certain that the world would be safer for democracy if they remained safely shut up in a *gompa*. A more desperate-looking lot of gaol-birds we never had seen migrate.

Drukla Monastery in Tibet, north of Tsangpo.   FKW
Ward visited this monastery twice on the 1924-25 expedition. The curtains at the front are made from black horse hair.

Pony transport at a cavalry house in Tibet.   FKW
Kingdon Ward comments 'No frame is used, the boxes being roped into small, wooden saddles direct.' This picture was probably taken in the vicinity of Drukla Monastery.

At night we returned the visits of the potentates. As we went down the narrow cobbled lane, towards the Commissioner's room, we heard the blare of trumpets from behind the thick walls of the black-curtained temple, and the dull soulless rumble of drums. It was now dark, and a man carrying a blazing torch led the way; as we passed beneath the narrow windows of the temple, where service was being held, we could not help feeling sorry for the poor old man, whose children had erred so greatly. Now and then a barefooted monk, muffled in his robe, stole past us in the shadow of the wall, a sinister figure; dark thoughts were passing through their murky minds, no doubt. A cold wind blew from the snow-peaks and its icy touch seemed to warn us that trouble was brewing in this medieval monastery. But the Commissioner, young, handsome, debonair, outrode the threatened storm coolly. His bodyguard, fondly fingering their rifles, overawed the most truculent of the banished monks and kept the situation well in hand.

He received us in his well-furnished apartment with a charming smile, spoke of the difficulties of the road, hoped we were comfortable, and thanked us prettily for our presents. A strong silent man was our verdict. We drank sour milk. Next we visited the *Dzongpön,* who was much agitated at the sentence pronounced against the renegade monks. 'Formerly,' said he, 'Drukla was an important monastery, with 800 monks in residence. Owing to wars with the Pobas, which have continued down to the present day, and to the troubles with the Chinese a few years ago, the number has dwindled to 130, of whom 60 are about to be unfrocked.' Then we drank more sour milk. Our final visit was to the *Labrang Lama,* who lived in a dim torch-lit room up a steep wooden stairway. He, poor man, had his own troubles, but he welcomed us, and we commiserated with him in his hour of sorrow. Finally, having drunk yet more sour milk with him, we returned to our own rooms. It is only necessary to add that the sentence on the mocking monks was duly carried out; when we returned to Drukla in January, the great monastery was almost deserted.

Ata and Gyamda

On the two following days we continued up the Drukla stream, travelling now north-westwards, and passing through a number of villages. There were broad pastures here, but whenever the clouds lifted we could see snow-peaks peeping up behind the grey cliffs and it was evident we were at last getting into the heart of the Salween divide.

***Primula alpicola* var. *alpicola* (var. *luna*) near Tumbatse.**   **KNEC**
Kingdon Ward's 'moonlight primula' is one of the finest sights in the region. The Rong around Tumbatse is a carpet of flower in June with the sweet scent wafting up as you walk through the meadows. Other plants growing here include buttercup, *Geranium donianum* and *Primula tibetica.*

***Incarvillea younghusbandii* east of the Kongbo Pa La.**   **KNEC**
It is always a surprise to find incongruous bright pink *Incarvillea* species on barren windswept moorland, looking for all the world like litter thrown by passing cars (not that there are very many in Tibet). This very dwarf species was named after Sir Francis Younghusband who led the 1903-4 invasion of Tibet and who wrote the introduction to the original publication of *The Riddle of the Tsangpo Gorges.*

On the 23rd we reached the last village up this valley, called Pungkar; there is a monastery crowning a cliff, and the stream divides again. There is no bridge over the river, which in flood is not easy to ford; we had to go a mile above the village in order to cross, and nearly lost a baggage pony in the swift current. The people of Pungkar hardly knew what to make of us, and reserved judgement, but Cawdor turned the scales very definitely in our favour by healing the sick. When we returned in January, they flocked in force to meet us, and could not do enough for us.

The women in this valley not only blacken their foreheads but also rouge their cheeks, which gives them a slightly inebriated appearance. However, we saw one young lady at Pungkar who had not attempted to paint, and really might have won a prize in a beauty competition, leading to an engagement with the 'pictures'. Meanwhile we were coming to the end of the forest; every day in every way the country grew drier, and down by the stream there were only thorn bushes. Flowers were few, but amongst them I noticed *Primula alpicola*, with very fragrant milk-white or pale yellow flowers. This form differed from the usual in that it invariably bore flowers on two or three stories, and occasionally it ran to four. It grew in bogs under bushes in company with the Giant Cowslip Primula, but was rarely social; a plant here and a plant there with perhaps a small colony on a wooded slope.

One result of our leaving the forest country behind was that we were also leaving the rain behind; and for the next two days we had sunshine. Marching up the valley we noticed wild rhubarb which the men gathered and ate raw; it was rather sour and had marked effects, which caused considerable discomfort. All the upper part of the valley was glaciated, and we passed numerous hanging valleys, crossing the stream twice by wooden bridges. A branch valley leading over the Lachen La to the Yigrong River was pointed out to us. This pass, though about 4900m [16,000ft.] high, is open most of the year, and is said to be passable for transport animals.

After camping the first night above Pungkar with some herds who lived in black hair tents, we crossed the Salween divide next day by the Pasum Kye La, 5385m [17,230ft.], and had a fine view of the snows; though the glaciers have shrunk back so far on this range that one sees more rock than snow. From a hill 60m [200ft.] above the pass, I counted seven blunt-nosed glaciers flowing towards the valley which runs northwards, and three more flowing towards the valley which we had just ascended; and after descending from the pass, I caught sight of four more glaciers coming from another group of peaks. Barren screes and

Gentiana filistyla.   **KR**
One of several fine species of gentian in south-east Tibet, some of which have never been cultivated. *Gentiana filistyla* occurs in south-east Tibet and north-west Yunnan. It is closely related to *G. tubiflora*, differing mainly in the corolla shape.

moraines spread in all directions and the alpine flora which had gradually replaced the scrub in the upper valley, was now universal. Not a bush or an undershrub remained as far as the eye could reach; we were back in the 'bad lands' with yak dung for fuel, and turf, and flowers, but never a stick of wood. For two or three months in the summer there are plenty of flowers. A dwarf prickly poppy, bearing many blooms (*Meconopsis horridula*), was abundant on the moraines, and a violet Dracocephalum on the cliffs.

Having crossed the pass, we descended a couple of thousand feet to another yak camp, and halted for the night. Next day, after continuing a few miles, we joined the *Gyalam,* or main road to China, and presently reached a small lake, the Atsa Tso, at an altitude of 4554m [14,938ft.] We were now on comparatively familiar ground, several European travellers having passed this way, including the late General Pereira, only two years previously on his famous journey to Lhasa. Keeping to the south side of the lake, which is about 5km [3 miles] long and 1km [three-quarters of a mile] wide, we crossed the stream which flows out at the lower end and reached a miserable place called Atsa Gompa, where we halted. Across the valley to the south is a high rocky range, with several glaciers hidden away in the topmost glens; while to the north is a lower range, crossed by the Banda La, 5521m [18,110ft.], over which goes the road to Lharigo and Chamdo. Thus the river which rises from the Atsa Tso flows through a narrow valley between lofty ranges to the Lhari River, which is the source stream of the Yigrong; the Yigrong, in fact, rises north of the Salween divide, and cuts its way through the range. The Gyamda River, on the other hand, with its various tributaries, rises on the southern slopes of the Salween divide. Atsa is a bleak and dreary spot. The wind whistles up these bare valleys, and sudden storms swoop down from the heights. The pastures all down the valley were black with tents and yak now, but in a month or two the shadow of winter would fall on the plateau, and the herds would withdraw. Meanwhile we lived in the tiny temple, and were none too warm there with only an earthenware pot of smouldering yak dung. An excursion to the Banda La proved full of interest. It is a severe climb, but on a fine day the view is worth it. Far away to the north we saw three very high snow-peaks, Much nearer, in the east, was a fine pyramidal snow-peak, forming part of the southern ridge, the true Tsangpo-Salween divide, on which we counted six dying glaciers.

Considering that we were 4900-5500m [16,000-18,000ft.] above sea-level, the variety of flowers here was quite astonishing. One of the most curious was a gentian (*G. amœna*

Delphinium sp.   **KR**
Autumn in the Himalaya sees the flowering of numerous species of Delphinium and Aconitum. This fine species may be *D. potaninii*. Keith Rushforth reports that this species grows to approximately 2m (6ft.) in height and occurs in the Tsangpo valley including the section near the mouth of the gorge near Gyala.

or *G. urnula*) with tiny interlocking leaves, and white parchment cups etched with blue. Others we noticed were a crimson Arenaria with slate-purple anthers forming mats on the gravel; a dwarf Incarvillea (*I. younghusbandii*), a fat fleshy 'Nivalis' Primula in fruit, *Meconopsis horridula* and a yellow-flowered Meconopsis (*M. pseudointegrifolia*), brilliant louseworts, woolly Saussureas, dwarf Delphiniums with papery flowers which crackled and crinkled in the wind, rosette plants such as Lactuca which lie flat on the surface, anchored by an enormously deep tap-root, *Eriophyton wallichianum* with its purple flowers all tucked away beneath its umbrella leaves, Corydalis, chubby and blatant, glowing yellow Saxifrages, and bladder campion. Considering the extraordinary hardness of the soil everywhere, it seemed incredible that these plants could penetrate it to the great depths they did and must in search of water.

On August 29th we awoke to find it snowing heavily, the valley full of mist, and the hills all round white; but presently the sun came out, and the snow quickly melted. However, we remained at Atsa another day, while all the evening thunderstorms re-echoed from peak to peak, and the thunder rumbled up and down the glen. Next day we started south by the Lhasa road, having given up the idea of going as far as the Salween, since it was clear it would take us another ten days to get there. Passing round the south side of the lake again, we turned up a wide valley and travelled a few miles to a postal station called Kolep. Before we got there, however, we were struck in the flank by a blizzard, and hurled flat, drenched and breathless. The wind blew the rain through us like grape-shot. The animals could not move, and those which did not get under a neighbouring rock, simply fell down. It was very unpleasant for half an hour, but then the wind ceased and it just rained. We reached Kolep, shivering with cold, but some hot tea soon put us right. There were several tents and a few square cabins here. On the last day of August we continued up the valley, at the head of which are four small glaciers which feed the stream; this stream from the Tro La joins the one from the Pasum Kye La, and the combined stream flows into the Atsa lake. The stream which emerges from the lower end of the lake flows, as already noted, to the Yigrong River, which may therefore be said to have its source amongst the glaciers on the north flank of the Tsangpo-Salween divide. The Atsa Tso does not empty into the Pasum Tso, and has no connection with it.

The whole of this region has in the past been very heavily glaciated. Only remnants of the old glaciers survive; but their former extension is plainly indicated by moraines, trough lakes, held up by moraines, straight U-shaped valleys, and other unmistakable signs. After a stiff climb, we reached the summit of the Tro La, 5380m [17,650ft.], where we could see snow-peaks to east and south, and west, but it was too cloudy to observe very much. Following the usual steep stony path, we rapidly descended 457m [1,500ft.] into a wide grassy valley, running north and south. A stream, which had its source in a glacier not more than 8-13km [6-8 miles] away, flowed due south, and a herds' camp gave us an excuse to halt and have lunch; for the sun had come out. It seems curious even in August, to be able to lie on the grass at an altitude of 4,000m [16,000ft.] and picnic comfortably, but it must be remembered that at these great altitudes in summer, it is very hot in the sun. One must get out of the wind, of course; and a storm may burst almost without warning; otherwise it is delightful. But the winters are hard and long, desperately hard and very long, and the wind makes one gasp.

No sooner were we over the range and in the valley, than woody plants reappeared; and by the time we reached Tramdo – a 'one-house-power' village where the postal runners stay the night before crossing the pass – we were almost back in the forest lands. On September 1st we marched to Laru, after which villages became more frequent; and next day we covered 24km [15 miles] and reached Gyamda, during a violent thunder-storm. Gyamda is an important town on the road to Lhasa. So far we had travelled almost due south from Atsa. The Lhasa road here turns west again, but we had to follow the Gyamda River eastwards, in order to reach Tsela Dzong and Tumbatse.

Gyamda lies in the angle between the two rivers, one from the north, the other from the west, the former being crossed by a wooden bridge. However, we found that the bridge had been swept away by the floods, in consequence of the unprecedented rainfall of 1924. The stream was very swift, but we crossed safely in a coracle, and were quartered in a peculiarly dirty house. Cleanliness seems to be in inverse ratio to the size of the town. Gyamda and Tsetang are both sewage farms, but we stayed in many a lovely country house belonging to some wealthy commoner where everything was clean and wholesome. There is a post office in Gyamda, and there are also several shops, the best of which is kept by a Nepalese trader. Brick tea, candles, cigarettes, Homburg hats, fur caps, matches, and a few other things may be obtained.

Return to the Tsangpo along the Gyamda Chu.

We now turned eastwards down the wide valley, which is, for Kongbo, quite thickly populated. Our first halting-place was Napo Dzong. Though we did not arrive there till 9 o'clock at night, the *Dzongpön* had table d'hôte waiting for us, and we felt as though we were eating chop suey at the Chinese Restaurant in Limehouse. The room, too, was magnificent. It had glass window-panes, carefully protected with wire-netting outside, and with small curtains inside. The paved yard was a regular flower-show, gay with Hollyhocks, Asters, Sunflowers, Dahlias, Pansies, Geraniums, Roses, Poppies, Brompton Stocks, Tropæolums and other favourites. Clearly the *Dzongpön* was a man of taste, an advanced thinker, and a traveller. He had been to Calcutta and had brought back with him a tin of Sutton's Seeds; hence the Mammoth Show. Besides the garden there was an orchard full of peach and apple trees. The suite of rooms, placed at our disposal, were upholstered in the Chinese style, with chairs, tables, and a finely carved and curtained bedstead, fit for an Empress; there were also cabinets, and a painted prayer drum in a pagoda. Breakfast bore a close resemblance to dinner, the menu including roast yak, toadstool dumplings, sliced hard-boiled eggs, cold pork, and rice, the whole seasoned with vitriolic chili sauce, a drop of which inflamed the tongue to such a pitch that one had to stop eating for five minutes.

For the next two days the journey was uninteresting. We crossed the river to the right bank by a fine cantilever bridge and on the third evening slept at a place called Kangra. Just below, on the left bank of the river, was the little monastery of Namse, where the Shoga Dzong River comes in. Soon after that we crossed a big river from the south, and the valley widened out considerably. Everywhere we saw clusters of towers like those already described. Ever since leaving Atsa the weather had been dull and wet, with heavy storms from time to time; but though much rain falls here in the summer, the dry season is long and severe, with desiccating winds, and we were still on the extreme outskirts of the forested country. The bottom of the valley is almost treeless, though there is a good deal of thorn scrub by the river. The rocky flanks of the hills are covered with stunted shrubs, and it is only in the glens, and on north slopes well above the valley that one sees real Conifer forest. Already there were signs of autumn in the air, and we noticed some pretty combinations of colour, such as the scarlet berries of Cotoneaster against the grey flannelly foliage of Buddleja (*B. agathosma*), the silver shocks and ochre felt flowers of Clematis rippling over the fiery orange berries of Lonicera.

Amongst a few notable flowers were some fine clumps of pale violet Salvia and a magnificent blue gentian of which I shall speak later. In one village we noticed a clump of orange and black tiger lilies, almost certainly the far-eastern *L. tigrinum,* and probably introduced by the Chinese; at least we saw it nowhere else. It was no uncommon sight to see bunches of flowers placed in vases on private family shrines, and even in monasteries. September 7th was a beautiful day, and we marched through charming scenery, all craggy cliffs and pine forest, and the river smothered by bushes. The road, too, was unusually good. That night we slept in a baronial castle called Nyalu. In Kongbo a sort of feudal system prevails. The country is divided up into a number of territories belonging to the barons or land-owning class. Theoretically these barons are subject to the district magistrate or *Dzongpön,* but in practice they are almost as powerful and autocratic as he is, and are generally wealthier. Every *Dzongpön* spends as much of his time as possible in Lhasa; but the barons are more often to be found on their land. They are the great capitalists of the country, carrying on trade and agriculture, and financing local industries. The baron's fort usually stands by itself apart from a village, though there are usually one or two minor rich men in each village; and the contrast between the castle and the villein's house is great. The serfs live in the castle, and are fed and clothed by their lord.

At Nyalu, for instance, there was the great solid three-storied house built on a raised terrace with its stone-flagged courtyard surrounded by a high wall. Ladders led from one gallery to another, which could be closed by heavy wooden trap-doors, studded with iron nails. There were kitchens and store-rooms, the private chapel with its complement of two or three lamas always praying, sleeping apartments, gun-room, and wide galleries. Down below were the stables. Fierce dogs guard the doorways. The people work on the land, or in the house, weaving cloth, or sewing leather boots; caravans are sent out carrying the produce of the farm, and bringing back the produce of other regions.

On September 8th the valley began to sweep round from east to south, and in the evening we had a glimpse of the snow-clad Himalaya beyond the Tsangpo junction. A fairly long march brought us to Chomo Dzong, an important but rather neglected place, with a small monastery. In the gravel and sand of the valley floor we saw acres of the little glassy blue Onosma and of the larger hoary species, and I collected seed of both, supplemented by more later, as I was not certain whether it was quite ripe. Mixed with them were the more vivid china blue *Cynoglossum amabile* and the blue powder-puffs of the dwarf Erytrichium. Rhododendrons had reappeared after we crossed the Tro La. Indeed below Gyamda a bushy *R. nivale* was in full bloom. In these pine woods the *Rhododendron triflorum* replaces the *R. virgatum* of lower altitudes and *R. principis* is common in the thickets which cover the more sheltered slopes.

Below Chomo Dzong the valley widens out to more than a mile, and many villages, scattered houses, and small monasteries are seen. Some miles away, the white walls of Tsela Dzong, crowning the spur at the junction of the Gyamda River with the Tsangpo, are distinctly visible; we arrived there on the 10th and halted a day. Most of the flowers were over, but the sunny slopes were blue with Ceratostigma. The Tsangpo was now falling fast, and the sandbanks were emerging again, though the 3km [2 mile] wide mouth of the Gyamda River was still mainly water. We floated by coracle downstream to Temo, and retraced our steps over the Temo La, halting there for the third time; but again it rained without ceasing, and we were glad to return to Tumbatse,

Cotoneaster conspicuus. **KR**

This fine species of Cotoneaster was discovered and introduced by Kingdon Ward in 1924-25 from Gyala. In cultivation it is variable in habit, ranging from near prostrate to over 2m (6ft.). It was re-introduced by Ludlow and Sherriff from the same area. Its fine berries are not generally attractive to birds, so it makes a useful garden plant for autumn colour.

Androsace bisulca **var.** *bramaputrae.* **KNEC**

There are several species of Androsace in south-eastern Tibet. Two of the commonest are *A. graminifolia* and this species *Androsace bisulca* var. *bramaputrae*. We were lucky to come across carpets of this bright pink species in gravelly soils along the Gyamda Chu on our 1996 expedition.

Watch tower, Pasum Tso.
KR

Kingdon Ward described the watch towers around Pasum Tso: 'Here and there, especially on the sites of ruined villages, are mud towers of curious shape, generally more or less battered, but sometimes in a good state of preservation and as much as 12-15m (40-50ft. high), tapering slightly from the base. They are always in groups, three or four together for mutual support, and we counted several hundred in these rather arid valleys. From a distance they look not unlike factory chimneys, but they are as a matter of fact – or rather were once – watchtowers, hollow inside, and loopholed for defence. Staging was erected inside at various levels – you can still see the holes for the crossbeams, and the garrison could enfilade the attackers on any side.' Many of the watch towers (also known as Kongbo towers) are still much as Ward described them.

reached on September 15th, after an absence of just over five weeks.

The geographical results of this journey may be briefly summarised. In the first place we had crossed two important new passes, the Nambu La and the Pasum Kye La, and had discovered that unless one goes through the province of Pome, or up the Yigrong River, it is necessary to go a long way west before reaching another pass over the Salween divide. The route via the Pasum lake marked on the map we found to have no real existence, and as the lake itself is shown 50km [30 miles] out of position, this was not surprising. We had been able to place on the map the important Dzongs of Shoga, Napo, and Chomo; and to straighten out the course of the Gyamda River and its large northern tributaries, the Pasum and Drukla streams, all of which were in a sad muddle. Finally, we had discovered the monastery of Drukla. In the country which had been crossed by previous travellers, namely that from the Banda La to Gyamda, we had established the fact that the Atsa lake lies to the north of the Salween divide, and discharges into the Yigrong River through that great snowy range and not into the Pasum lake.

CHAPTER XII

Autumn Colours

Collecting seed in and above the rong

We remained three days at Tumbatse, and I secured the temporary services of an intelligent villager to help me collect seeds. *Primula chungensis, P. tibetica, P. florindæ, P. alpicola* [*microdonta*]*, Meconopsis betonicifolia* [*baileyi*]*, Cyananthus lobatus* and Iris were all collected, besides the orange berries of the best Lonicera. The weather was showery with intervals of sunshine; but we expected the fine weather to begin any day. We had two months in which to collect our seeds, and four passes to visit, two north of the Tsangpo and two south of the Tsangpo, on the Himalayan range; the latter could not be left till very late because it begins snowing heavily on Namcha Barwa in October, and everything would be buried by November. It would be better, we thought, to finish the Temo La by the first week in October, cross the Tsangpo and collect on the Doshong La for a fortnight in October, leaving the Nam La, which though more lofty, has much less snow, till the last. We could then start through the gorge, without having to return to Tumbatse. Generally speaking, unless plants are entirely buried under the snow, one can gather seed of them up to Christmas. The collector is apt to forget this, and think that he will lose his plants through not being able to get there till too late. The temptation is, therefore, to collect seed before it is ripe, rather than run the risk of losing it.

We worked out a programme which proved successful; but I had several frights before all the good things were harvested. On September 19th we moved into camp on the Tang La, and in the course of a week collected seed of *Meconopsis impedita, M. simplicifolia* and the two Aculeatæ; *Primula sinopurpurea, P. macrophylla* var. *ninguida, P. chionantha* [*P. rigida*]*, P. atrodentata, P. walshii, P. sikkimensis* var. *pudibunda,* and one of the many coloured forms of *P. microdonta* (*alpicola*) and the dwarf Lloydia.

The weather was terrible, with driving rain and hail, which had in it the sting of winter. Not once did we get a clear view of the snows, though the sugar-loaf cone of Namcha Barwa appeared floating on a cotton-wool sea one evening. So high is it that it not infrequently pierces the clouds. A few Saxifrages, Swertias, and Aconites were in flower, and in the upper forest were several untidy Compositæ. A mail arrived to relieve the tedium of isolation, and we derived much satisfaction from reading newspapers two and three months old; but most of them broke off at a crisis, and we were left with the tantalising legend 'to be continued in our next.' On the 25th we returned to Tumbatse, and next day I dashed on down the *rong* to Lunang and turning up the path which goes to the Tro La, reached the herds' bothy where the dwarf yellow woodland Meconopsis grew. The seeds were nicely ripe, and I collected several hundred plants on the wooded banks. We slept the night in the forest, and then returned to Lunang and Tumbatse, collecting seed of the cherry and two species of Lonicera *en route*. It poured with rain all the time, and the *rong* was such a bog it was difficult for the ponies to get along at all. The river was overflowing too.

On September 28th a message arrived from Lhasa requesting us to send to the Tibetan Government seeds of any flowers which they might be able to raise. The Dalai Lama is very fond of flowers, and at his private residence, called Norpu Lingka, or the Jewel Park, on the outskirts of Lhasa, grows a great many, which he tends with loving care. Naturally we were delighted to have this means of expressing in some degree our thanks to the Tibetan Government, and particularly to His Holiness, for permitting us to reside and travel in Tibet; and I dispatched to Lhasa seeds of nearly forty species of Primula, Meconopsis and other showy flowers which could be easily raised. In years to come it may be that Englishmen will see these rare plants growing in Lhasa gardens. During the next few days I had plenty of work to do packing seeds, and on September 30th we started for the Temo La; this was to be our last trip north of the Tsangpo, before starting for the gorge.

190

As luck would have it the day was fine and the forest was lit by the lurid glow of scarlet, orange and champagne-yellow leaves. Sending the transport round by the main route, we followed a yak trail straight up the mountain, and when we reached the alpine moorland, traversed over hill and dale to the pass. But it was farther than it looked, and towards evening a very cold wind blew over the bleak mountains. Mist and rain rolled up the valleys, and it was dark when we stood on the last col, drenched and chilled. However, we could just make out the glow of a fire far down the valley, and we arrived in camp at half-past six, going dead slow over the rough on account of an almost impenetrable mist, to drink cup after cup of scalding tea. In the night the rain turned to snow, but this soon melted again.

So far we had collected no Rhododendron seeds, and the position was a little delicate. Most of the Rhododendrons found on the north bank of the Tsangpo are found also on the south bank, but neither so abundantly nor in such fine feather. It would be much better to collect the dry winter species on the north bank, than the moist winter species on the south bank; especially as we could not count on finding every species again, once we had crossed the river. Two or three species certainly were to be found – so far as our experience went at any rate – *only* on the north bank; for example, the rose purple *R. oreotrephes*. But it is a waste of time to collect Rhododendron seeds before October, and it is safer to leave them till the middle of the month, and give them the chance of a little autumn sunshine. On the other hand, while one can if necessary leave Primula and Meconopsis till Christmas, and still be sure of saving seed, so long as the plants themselves are fairly common, no such liberty can be taken with Rhododendron. A fortnight of fine dry weather in November, and they open wide their wooden capsules; a breath of wind and poof! away go the seeds like dust. The danger of snow on the moist-winter ranges has already been referred to, and we were soon to have a lively experience of its ravages.

Our programme, which in view of the bad weather we dared not modify – for rain here meant snow on the Doshong La – included the evacuation of Tumbatse not later than October 11th, and camp on the Doshong La not later than the 15th. It will be seen, therefore, that the Rhododendron problem was urgent. From the Temo La we marched round the head of the valley to our old camp at the Sung La, where we spent the next three days. The weather was what the newspapers called unsettled; that is to say, when it wasn't raining it was snowing. We collected seed of the two large yellow poppies, *Primula* (*dryadifolia* ssp.) *philoresia,* a Lloydia, and two dwarf gentians, besides adding to our holdings in other alpines. A twiggy honeysuckle *L. cyanocarpa* K.W. 5918 which was woven into the dwarf Rhododendron carpet and whose stock in flower was below par, now showed a surprising recovery; for its bare twigs were studded all over with blue-blackberries like large sloes.

On October 4th we returned to the Temo La, and that evening, following a heavy hailstorm, the great snow range, stripped of every shred of cloud, stood out as bold as sugar-candy. Try and picture the scene! We stood on a range of mountains 4600m [15,000ft.] above sea-level, looking eastwards across the narrow wooded valley of the Rong Chu; immediately beyond that a rocky range, 4600-5200m [15,000–17,000ft.] high, notched by the Nyima La, stretched across our horizon. Above that again, and only 40km [25 miles] from where we stood, rose the great snow barrier, broadside on. Its southern sentinel peak, Namcha Barwa is over 7575m [25,000ft.] high; its northern sentinel peak, Gyala Peri, over 6970m [23,000ft.] high. Between the two are four other peaks over 6060m [20,000ft.] high, and the whole fills 24km [15 miles] of horizon, with the rock range lying crouched at its feet.

Anyone coming from the north, knowing nothing about the Tsangpo, and descending eastwards to find it flowing northwards, would be bound to think that it skirted along the edge of that mighty barrier, flowing northwards indefinitely. Or, if he descended to the south and came upon the river flowing east, he would say that it must turn south before it reached Namcha Barwa. And yet both would be wrong. The river, as we have seen, does turn northwards by Namcha Barwa, seeking a way of escape; but finding none, after flowing for two-thirds the length of the snow range, it turns on it and rends a passage through. From where we stood it was impossible to believe that the snowy range was not solidly continuous; and yet we knew that the river pierced its heart, breaking through within 8km [5 miles] of Gyala Peri, and within 16km [10 miles] of Namcha Barwa. There is indeed a gap here, and far away a distant snow-peak showed up like a sabre tooth. That night it froze sharply under a clear sky and the snowy range gleamed hard and cruel in the cold moonlight. It was a marvellous dawn, but no sooner was the sun up than clouds began to threaten, and before 10 o'clock the panorama was ruined. However, I fondly imagined that the sky would clear again towards evening, and went off to climb a mountain whence I could get a more extensive view. Here I spent a cold night, without much result, as recorded in Chapter V.

Back in camp on October 6th, we only stayed long enough to have breakfast and pack; in the afternoon we started down, presently camping again in a meadow, where we collected seed of *Primula pseudocapitata* [*P. capitata* ssp. *sphaerocephala*] the best Barberry, a willow, and several Rhododendrons. On the following day we continued the descent to the *rong* and rode as quickly as possible down the valley to Tumbatse. There was no time to waste, as we intended to leave in three days. Stores for the return journey and our plant collections were packed and left at Tumbatse, to be picked up by Dick and Sunny Jim later. The rain still kept on, but not so continuously as in the summer. Every day I went out after seeds, assisted by two small boys who showed symptoms of intelligence. In one glen I found the prize honeysuckle (*L. hispida* K.W. 5776) fairly abundant and fruiting well; it requires shade and ample moisture to ripen its fruits. As usual, many plants were verminous. We picked scores of desiccated grubs from amongst the seeds of *Meconopsis impedita,* both seeds and grubs dropping out as the capsules dried; of course it would not do to pack up the grubs with the seeds, so they had to be picked out by hand first. The two alpine Aculeate poppies were also bugulous. Despite this destruction of potential plants, *M. impedita* is by far the most abundant and widespread of the alpine poppies in Kongbo – indeed the species is found nearly 650km [400 miles] to the east, in Western China. What part then do the grubs play? True, the insects which produce the grubs must keep in contact with the plants at whose expense their offspring will thrive; and in order to make certain that there shall be food – seeds – for those offspring, they may, deliberately or unconsciously, pollinate the flowers. But the two Aculeate poppies set plenty of good seed, though they are not nearly so common. Neither are *M. simplicifolia,* nor the big yellow poppy, though both set abundant seed, and therefore are pollinated; but they do not feed a private staff to do the work. Thus it is difficult to connect the abundance of *M. impedita* with the grubs in the capsules.

The seed collector, however, soon finds that nearly all seeds are fair game for army corps of spongers, which may or may not make some return to the plant. This is particularly true of the tropical forest, where the struggle for existence is most bitter; but it is also true of the chill alpine regions, where the struggle with conditions increases in proportion as internecine warfare decreases. Thus the collector has much to cope with, besides distances and climate. His plants may fail to set seed at all, or the bulk of the seed may be destroyed or scattered before he comes on the scene. Then the seed has to pass through the tropics and make a sea voyage, and it may be anything from three to five months before it can be sown in England.

We sent home seed of about 250 species, the earliest collected in September, 1924, the latest in February, 1925. Most of them were gathered in the snow, and faced over [-18°C] 40°F of frost on the Tibetan Plateau during the return journey. They then passed through India, facing a temperature of over 90° F [32°C]. It is not to be supposed that the seeds actually withstood a range of temperature which exceeded [50°C] 130° F. Indeed, it was my business to see that they were not subjected to this intolerable strain. The bulk of them were placed in envelopes and packed with plenty of paper in tins which were then soldered down. Arrived in India, these tins were put in cold storage on board the ship and travelled home so. A great many seeds were also brought home in thermos flasks – sample packets of all the best species were carried in this way; and though I do not pretend that these were maintained at a constant temperature throughout, the change must have been a gradual one, nor would the heat be so hot, nor the cold so cold, under these conditions.

Norbu Linka, the summer palace of the Dalai Lama.   **AC**
During his 1924 expedition, Kingdon Ward was asked to send seeds to Lhasa for the Dalai Lama to grow at his
summer palace, the Norbu Linka. History does not relate whether these seeds survived and flowered. One of the
Ludlow and Sherriff discoveries from Tsari was named *Rhododendron lopsangianum* in honour of the 13th Dalai
Lama Lopsang Den Gyatso who died in 1933.

The first lot of seeds reached England on March 20th, and were distributed and
planted immediately. The last lot arrived on April 20th, and before the end of the
month all the seeds had been planted at Kew, at Edinburgh, at Wisley, and in a hundred
other gardens in Britain. Seeds were also promptly dispatched to New Zealand, South
and East Africa, South and North America and elsewhere. At the time of writing, out
of over 250 species, about 2 per cent. have failed to germinate; but there is every reason
to suppose that some of these will germinate next year.

Seed collecting on the Nyima La and Doshong La

Summer was now over and with scarcely a halt winter was surging down on us. On
October 11th we started for the Tsangpo, crossing the Nyima La and camping on the
other side of the pass. Next day, the snow-peaks still being invisible, I started to collect
Rhododendron seed. Purple 'Lapponicum,' (*R. nivale*) strawberry 'Saluenense' (*R.
fragariflorum*) and snow-white 'Anthopogon' (*R. laudandum* var. *temoense*) were gathered,
also the purple [*Nomocharis*] *Lilium nanum, Primula bellidifolia* [*P. atricapilla*] and *P.
cawdoriana,* and two beautiful little Saxifrages. Quite 75 per cent. of the capsules of the
R. fragariflorum which had flowered so freely, were bad, destroyed by a fungus. A worse
blow followed; for of three Ivory Poppies marked down here, not one had set seed!

We went down the glen next day, collecting Rhododendron and other seeds *en route*.
We could find only two plants of the big chocolate-flowered *P. advena* var. *euprepes* [*P.
maximowiczii*], the Geranium Primula (*P. latisecta*) had sulked and set no seed, and the

best Rhododendron, the rosy-purple *R. oreotrephes*, was not ripe. I sent Dick back for seed of the last-named three weeks later, with satisfactory results, and the Geranium Primula was collected by the Pasum Lake in January, though the available supply of seed was, by that time, scanty.

We halted for the night at the first house, on the scrub-clad slope, just below the forest. The capsules of *Rhododendron principis* and *R. triflorum* were fully ripe here, and the small leaves of the *R. lepidotum* turning brave colours. On the dry bank under the oak scrub, *Primula pulchelloides* and the large Androsace were seeding, and here too grew masses of a magnificent Gentian, G. *waltonii*, which recalls G. *asclepiadæa*, though its flowers are more numerous and of a more incisive blue. There was a great sprawling rosette of dark green shining leaves from the centre of which sprang several leafy columns bearing so great a burden of upright blue cups that they bent under the weight and flopped over. Nests of amazing blueness lay gleaming icily there on the dry sun-baked gravel, soaking up heat and light; and three weeks later Dick collected seed of this, the finest gentian known to me (K.W. 6221).

We crossed the Tsangpo by canoe, and rode to Pe, where we found great activity. The tribesmen were coming over the Doshong La from Pemakö for salt, bringing in exchange rice, maize, canes, and curry; the canes are cut up and used for whip-stocks. A Government official was at the receipt of custom, taking over the produce and giving out salt in exchange. Besides trading, the people were paying their annual tax. Every family pays a tax in kind, according to its wealth; the poorest pay 14 *seer* of rice. The produce goes half to Tsela Dzong and half to Tongkyuk, both Kongbo and Pome claiming rights in Pemakö. But the tax is levied only by the Kanam Raja, or King of Pome, whose representative was also at Pe. Pome, however, now owes allegiance to Lhasa, and since taxation has gone up in Tibet, much to the disgust of the Mönbas, there has been a good deal of dissatisfaction in jungle circles. The salt which these people take back with them has already travelled far, having come from Central or Western Tibet. But many of the people themselves have come long journeys, carrying loads which weigh 32-36kg [70-80lb.]. Even small children carry 9-14kg [20-30lb.] loads. Most of the people we saw in Pe were Mönbas, a few Kampas. But most interesting of all were three Lopas, as the Tibetans call the most surly, savage and benighted of the Assam tribes. These dwarfs (they stood less than 1.5m [5ft.] high) had come twenty-five marches to buy salt, and were evidently the folk we call Abors.

It was surprising enough that such small, ill-nourished men should carry loads weighing 36kg [80lb.] over tracks that would break a white man's heart; but to have crossed the Doshong La in deep snow, almost naked, was even more astonishing! For the only garment they wore was a coarse red-dyed shirt of hand-woven cloth, not reaching to the knees, with a small flap beneath for decency's sake! Just imagine it! Bare legs, bare feet, bare hands, bare heads, in that bitter wind! A second garment, like a Tibetan *gushuk*, is worn at night. With such heavy loads they can only travel very slowly. Indeed, while we ourselves were in camp on the Doshong La, they tried to cross the pass, but were driven back by a fresh fall of snow; the wonder is they did not perish outright. Instead, they hid in the forest for a day, and then, when the storm was over, crossed safely!

These Abors knew no word of Tibetan, and all the resources of the local interpreter were strained to hold a brief conversation with them. They were suspicious of us and surly, scowling at our advances. For ornament, these Lopas wear bead and chain necklaces and large hollow silver ear-rings, like a back collar stud the size of a half-crown and an inch through. A short chopping knife is carried in a basket sheath round the waist, and a bamboo bow with bamboo string and poisoned arrows. We bought an ear-ring for two rupees, but it was evident that they did not want the money; they did not know what it was or what to do with it; an empty sardine tin was more coveted! The Mönbas and Kampas were very different; and though obviously uncertain of our intentions, they made friendly advances and were glad to sell us their wares — neat little baskets of woven bamboo, beer jugs covered with coloured matting, garters, and other hand-made articles,

Porters with dogs and baskets. FKW

This photograph is probably not from the Tsangpo Gorge itself, but probably along the upper portions of the Yigrong or possibly to the east of the gorge. The woven, split-bamboo baskets are still used throughout the gorge. Ken Storm writes: 'On our journey retracing Kingdon Ward's route to the "Falls of the Brahmaputra" in 1996 the porters harvested bamboo from Netang, a small, marshy valley below Gyala Peri and made new baskets there during the journey. Where the terrain permits, dogs often accompany hunters and share the bounty of a successful hunt. Our guide, Dungle Phuntsok, said that his grandfather was greatly impressed by a small dog trained to fetch objects from Kingdon Ward and Cawdor's pack, at camp beyond Sengchen.'

they brought over with their jungle produce. Cawdor, who was very keen on all these tribes, their manners, customs, arts, and crafts, made quite a good collection of native articles; he also wrote exhaustive notes on everything concerning them. This was particularly interesting to me because his knowledge and keen eye for detail enabled him to draw my attention to lots of things about them which I should otherwise have missed.

The village being full, we camped in a grove of trees hard by and next morning started up the valley for the Doshong La. Masses of coloured leaves – Viburnum, Rowan, and Birch – illuminated the dark forest like the burning bush, and we collected many seeds. Arrived at our old camping-ground, now more swamped than ever, we had a quick lunch, and while the men were pitching the tents, climbed up to the glacier flat to reconnoitre. The place was a marsh, but we selected a knoll in the centre for a camp. Where massed Rhododendrons did not crowd every square foot of ground, grew two species of Vaccinium, whose blue-black berries were good eating. I also found in fruit here a Rhododendron not seen in flower (K.W. 5861) (*R. forrestii/R. doshongense* x *R. campylocarpum*), and on the sheltered cliff in dense thickets of *R. dignabile* and *R. campylocarpum* (K.W. 6229).

This was all very well, but I got a nasty jolt none the less. Just here we met the wind rushing over the pass, driving a heavy spray before it; 300m [1,000ft.] higher up where our gem Rhododendrons cowered, snow was falling fast. As though to reassure us that the job was really going to be a difficult one, I found that nearly all the seeds from the one known clump of Golden Primula (*P. morsheadiana*) had been sluiced out of the open capsules, while the solitary clump of Daffodil Primula (*P. falcifolia*) yielded no seed at all! I spent an hour searching the bog for more Golden Primula, and found several unsuspected plants under the bushes; but they had all lost their heads! It was now raining harder than ever, besides being very cold, and as it was getting late, we decided to return to camp. All that evening scuds continued to sweep down the valley, washing out the stars, which twenty minutes later would be shining brilliantly again; but I spent a sleepless night.

We had intended to move our camp to the glacier flat next day (October 16th), but the porters, who evidently did not want to go, strolled in late, and blandly informed us that they had finished their food. We made the best of a bad job, sent half of them down to Pe with instructions to bring back rations for a fortnight, kept a firm eye on the

Pe and the Yarlung Tsangpo.   KNEC
The village of Pe provides a number of professional porters who carry loads back and forth across the Doshong
La into Pemakö. Although there is now a road from Pome to Pemakö, it is often impassable due to landslides. As
well as general transport of goods in and out of Pemakö, the porters are employed by the Chinese military to carry
food, equipment and ammunition to the army garrison located near the Dihang (Tsangpo) where they guard the
disputed frontier with India.

other half, and sat tight. After all, it was terrible weather – bitter wind with driving rain
– and if there was one thing we needed for the alps it was fine weather. We had yet to
learn that it never is dry at the Doshong La. I went out seed collecting and was lucky
enough to find in fruit a *Rhododendron hirtipes* of unusual habit, forming a close-set
twisted scrub on the gneissic cliff (K.W. 6223). Growing beneath it *Diapensia purpurea*
was in fruit, bristling with long quills each of which ended in a red beak; these red
beaks turned black before they split (K.W. 6226).

It was now high time to start collecting Rhododendron seed and half a dozen species
were gathered, including the purple *R. calostrotum* ssp. *riparium*. Now that autumn had
picked out the broad-leafed trees, the dark wall of fir forest was smudged with the hot
stain of death – gamboge and vermilion and old gold; but the undergrowth was already
rotten and downtrodden. On October 17th the porters came early, so we broke camp
and climbed to the glacier flat, where we camped on our knoll; but I went on up the
300m [1,000ft.] foot step to the alpine valley, anxious to know the worst. On the way
up I found a lot of Golden Primula capsules full of seed, which put me in good heart,
and also collected some Barberry and Lonicera berries; but it was Rhododendrons I
wanted chiefly. Deep snow covered the valley, and save for the howling wind an awful
silence brooded over a desolate world. Almost in despair I set to work madly digging
in the snow, and in two hours had excavated some capsules of Scarlet Pimpernel (*R.
forrestii*), *R. charitopes* var. *tsangpoense*, *R. cephalanthum* Nmaiense and *R. pumilum*.

That night the wind hummed over the pass, threatening to uproot the tents, and filling

The outskirts of the village of Gyala, gateway to the Tsangpo gorges. **IB**

The village of Gyala was the scene of some complex negotiations to ensure that Ward and Cawdor were allowed to continue into the Gorge:'When we reached Gyala, itching to be off, a difficulty arose. The local Baron, who lived in Heath Robinson House, had indeed promised us every assistance; he now informed us that he could not supply the transport, but said that he was getting it from a village up the river. Would we wait two days?...' In April 1993 our expedition enters pastureland on the outskirts of Gyala. The peak of Gyala Peri towers above on the left bank of the river.

the air with fine snow dust. All the next day it continued to blow a regular blizzard, with driving snow; but early in the afternoon the snow ceased, the sun came out and I raced up the valley to collect seeds. Luckily I managed to locate much lost treasure, and on the following day we made a good haul of the best stuff. Scarlet Runner proved an exception; it was not snowed under, but it had opened its capsules and scattered a lot of its seed. The Primulas gave no trouble, nor did the lilies. Digging Rhododendrons out of three feet of snow in that bitter wind was an extraordinarily unpleasant job; but it was an immense relief to be able to do it. The expected fine weather still delayed, and we were compelled to spend three days at this camp, partly to ensure a good supply of seed, which accumulated slowly, partly because we wanted fine weather for the trip to Pemakö. Wind and snow continually hindered us, but the work went gaily on, and not only did we get seed of every plant we had found in flower, but also of several we had never seen before.

Every day large bodies of Mönbas crossed the pass, which in another month would be blocked. Though better clad than the Lopas, they usually wore only one garment apiece, consisting of a long, loose *chupa,* or dressing-gown of grey cloth, tied up above the knees by day and let down at night. Most of them went barefooted, a few wearing long Tibetan boots with hide soles and cloth uppers or even binding strips of cloth round their feet. Those who did this also tied strips of bamboo over the instep lest they skid on the snow slopes. On October 18th Cawdor went up to the pass, and reported it easy, despite the fast-rising snow; and on the 21st we moved over into Pemakö, as described in Chapter III.

On the 25th we were back at the glacier flat, and I spent the 26th on a last seed hunt.

It was a glorious morning after a sharp frost, and I thoroughly enjoyed the six hours I spent in the snow; also I discovered a cache of Scarlet Runner, and Plum Glaucum. One of the most lovely sights on the mountain now was Yellow Peril (*Rhododendron campylocarpum*) which outrode the snow in billows of bluish green. The 'silver Lacteum' (*R. aganniphum* Doshongense Gp.), too, was not yet engulfed. During the descent to the lower meadow on October 27th I collected seed of the tree Rhododendrons, all of which were now ripe – the small 'Grande' (*R. uvariifolium*), 'Coals-of-Fire' (*R. cerasinum*), the pink 'Thomsoni' (*R. faucium*) and the big 'Lacteum' (*R. dignabile*). The weather broke again and a snowstorm came whirling over the pass, tearing the trees inside out.

Pe to Gyala

Next day we returned to Pe with the booty, collecting till the last minute. This time we were given quarters in a house, which was absolutely necessary now that we had nearly a hundred newspapers of seed-vessels to spread out on the floor. Crowds of Mönbas were still coming and going, and a regular market was being held. Besides salt, they were taking back with them live sheep and goats, and even dogs. Next day the official invited us to lunch – or rather cooked an elaborate lunch for us. First of all cups of raw spirit and buttered tea were placed on the table, and these were followed up by (a) saucers containing strips of raw turnip, (b) saucers containing chopped meat and sliced chillies, and (c) a large bowl full of macaroni and meat, floating corpse-like in anaemic soup. We ate these, sweating from every pore, and they were removed, and full dishes substituted; we ate those breathing hard, and the third course, which was like the first and second, followed; but when we had finished that we had to surrender. Apparently our host was prepared to supply as many courses as we felt we could manage; but though climbing in wind and snow makes one hungry, unless one is accustomed to full meals the breaking-point is soon reached. That night was the last of the fun fair so to speak, and the *Depa* gave a dinner and dance in our house. We rather felt we were paying the piper, as we had just handed over a substantial cash balance for our transport.

The *Depa* sat cross-legged on his cushion, with a fur cap as big as a busby on his head, and fifteen others crowded into a room which would barely hold six comfortably. Illumination was supplied by the fitful blaze of pine-wood chips, which smoked and spluttered on the hob. There were dances – Tibetan dances, Mönba dances, Kampa dances, even Poba dances. The company, which was mixed, took it in turns to amuse the *Depa*, who joined uproariously in the songs. The thirst provoked by all this melody was attended to by a woman who went from guest to guest with an inexhaustible stoup of beer. Music for the dancers was provided by the audience, who sang. The Tibetan dancers stamped a good deal, but the timing was bad and it was impossible to distinguish any rhythm in the caterwauling that went on. The idea is to hold on to the last note as long as possible, which gives every one a chance of coming in and getting at least one note right.

After the Tibetan national clog dance, a tall, nice-looking Mönba with shingled hair took the floor. He sang a slower, sadder song as befitted one from the jungles, and waved his arms about. It reminded me of a Burmese *pwe*. Then came the turn of the long-haired Pobas, who were very drunk. A goitrous old man, his face creased as though some one had pleated it while he was still a baby, and forgotten to iron it out afterwards, danced and stamped and sang, with great energy, to the delight of the audience. He was very active when others were performing, and 'gagged' during the songs; to judge by the girlish giggles and hoots of mannish laughter with which these gags were received, he must have got home with many a bucolic *riposte*. And so the entertainment dragged on and petered out with the pine chips, while the *Depa* continued to the last to beat time with his hands and join in the chorus. At midnight the meeting broke up, everybody being more or less intoxicated.

The last three days of October were brilliantly fine; the rains were over. From

Women coolies of Gyala who accompanied Cawdor and Kingdon Ward through the Gorge.   FKW

People of Kongbo Province. Felt hats made out of yak hair. 'The fleas have a grand time'.   FKW
This photograph appeared in the original edition of the book with the caption: 'Men coolies of Gyala who accompanied us through the gorge.' Ken Storm writes: 'On our visit to Gyala in 1993 we showed the photograph to the villagers who recognized their relatives. Western style clothing is more common in the area today although some continue to wear the sheep or takin-skin tunics shown here. All the men still carry the long knife sheathed in a wood scabbard worn at their waist. The traditional felt hat has apparently fallen out of fashion. We did not notice any during our travels into the gorge.'

the slope above Pe we had a startling view of the snow-wall from Namcha Barwa, whose conic tip showed above the near ridge along the sloping shoulder, to the river gap, and so up again to the rounded hump of Gyala Peri. We left Pe on the 31st and marched by a high path to the cultivated terrace on which stands Kyikar. The river had fallen 6.25m [20ft.] and was fretting shrilly over the skeleton moraines, as it galloped into the gorge. Our friend the headman provided us with the best butter and bannocks we had tasted for a long time, as well as with his own excellent brew of beer. Next day we reached our first camp below the Nam La, and ascended to the upper camp at 4,300m [14,000ft.] on November 2nd. What an odd contrast to the Doshong La, only 8km [5 miles] to the south! All the streams had dried up, and there was only just enough snow near our camp to provide us with water! On the other hand, the cold was intense, the sheltered thermometer showing -15°C [+4°F] on the night of November 5th.

In the course of a week, I collected seed of *Primula baileyana, P. littledalei, P. advena* var. *advena* [*P. szechuanica*]*, and other species; several Rhododendrons, including the yellow-flowered *R. lepidotum* [*R. elæagnoides*]; and some good Saxifrages. We also mapped the valley, fixing the positions of the Nam La, and of the snow-peak we had discovered called Temu Tse. We had intended to cross the pass, but Cawdor, who after a hard struggle reached the summit on November 6th and succeeded in getting a boiling-point reading, was of opinion that the porters would never do it. So we gave up the idea; and felt justified when the weather broke again on the 7th and it snowed for three days. Had we crossed over into Pemakö we should certainly have been caught on the wrong side of the pass, unable to get back; and that would have upset the trip through the gorge, which was more important.

On November 7th we descended to the lower camp; we could indeed easily have reached Kyikar, but there was still a lot of seed to collect, so we took our time. Back in Kyikar, seed collecting was virtually over. It only remained to pack the specimens before starting out to explore the gorge. Four days were spent in clearing up this work, and making final preparations for the plunge into the unknown; and on November 12th we moved a few miles down the river to Lungpe, reaching Gyala on the 13th. The last snowstorm had blown itself out, and the weather was brilliantly fine in the gorge, with sharp frosts at night; but it was evident that we must expect storms at frequent intervals. When we reached Gyala, itching to be off, a difficulty arose. The local Baron, who lived in Heath Robinson House, had indeed promised us every assistance; he now informed us that he could not supply the transport, but said that he was getting it from a village up the river. Would we wait two days? We had indented for twenty stout male coolies, and these he had not in stock; also for rations for all, ropes, and axes. The second part of the indent he was able to fill from the quartermaster's stores, which every Tibetan Baron has at his command. But the stuff was useless without men to carry it. It appeared that there had recently been an epidemic in this district, resulting in the death of six men, including two stout warriors formerly employed by us, and known as Henry the Eighth and the Duke of Monmouth, and a woman, Anne Boleyn.

This was awkward; nor did I like the alleged S.O.S. call for assistance which he sent out, knowing full well that he had no power to levy transport outside his own district and that such messages as he did send out must have an entirely different purport. And so it proved. To-day's bright thought had suddenly struck the rascal. Suppose we were exceeding our brief in trying to pass through the gorge where no track was, and no one ever went? Would he not get into trouble for failing to stop us? Besides, here was a way out of the dilemma; he had promised us coolies, and behold through no fault of his own he could not conveniently supply them. Why not get an official veto put on the project? Accordingly our friend sent a secret letter to his superior up the river asking whether the journey was in order! Now it so happened that our friend the Commissioner of Gyamda, continuing his whirlwind campaign against the renegade monasteries of Kongbo, was just now at Temo, and had called the ecclesiastical authorities to a conference there. Even Pemaköchung, 50km [30 miles] down the gorge, had heard that clarion call and obeyed. Gyala's letter then came to the Gyamda Commissioner. The answer must have surprised him. It conveyed not only immediate orders that we were to be supplied with porters at all costs, but also that the bearer of the letter, a lama from Pemaköchung, who some years previously had been on a pilgrimage to the Holy Rock, must guide us through the gorge! Now you might search the whole of Kongbo and not find five men who had ever been through the Tsangpo gorge; so we were exceptionally lucky.

The Baron now had his orders, and henceforth he was helpful. Every household in his poor little district was subpoenaed and by means of a levy on his own domestics, he at last scraped together twenty-three coolies – ten men and thirteen women. It must be clearly understood, of course, that for this enterprise we could take no transport animals of any description, no ponies, or mules, or even yak. The gorge is filled with cliffs and boulders and dense trackless forest, through which the howling river rushes with a resounding roar. Therefore, everything had to be carried by coolies, most of whom must carry rations. All our heavy baggage – boxes, tents, camp equipment and so on – had to be left behind at Gyala, in charge of Sunny Jim, and six weeks elapsed before we rejoined the main body. Tom was to accompany us the whole way, and Dick was in support as far as Pemaköchung, whence he would rejoin Sunny Jim at Gyala, and so to Tumbatse, where the remainder of our kit had been left. Tumbatse is only two marches from Tongkyuk, where we arranged to reassemble for the journey home.

CHAPTER XIII

The Gorge of the Tsangpo

Into the gorge

November 16th dawned brightly, after 5.5°C [10°F] of frost. Final preparations were soon made, and at 10.30 we started on the journey, our party including Tom, Dick, the Walrus, twenty-three porters, a sheep, and two dogs. Just outside the village some one had set light to a heap of juniper branches, and the coolies now stood round, passionately repeating long prayers to the spirits, that they might guard them from the dangers of the gorge; then each cast into the flames a pinch of *tsamba*, to seal his vow. Immediately afterwards we began to climb the steep pine-clad flank of the cliff. The torrent which had caused us so much difficulty in July was crossed high above the river, and ascending higher still we finally halted for the night near the summit of the great cliff called Musi La, that is 'sulphur peak'; a cold sulphur spring rises here, and has coated the rock with a gummy deposit. That night the weather changed, and the temperature fell only to freezing-point – a bad sign. About noon next day the sky clouded over and it began to snow.

Meanwhile we continued to climb till we were 600-900m [2,000-3,000ft.] above the river. As we passed from a more sheltered to a more exposed face, or descended into a deep glen, or climbed up or down, the vegetation changed completely. At one moment we were in pine forest, then in bamboo forest, again in mixed forest, where maple and birch trees, large as they were, looked dwarf beside the gigantic Picea trees. We could not measure these last, but estimated them to be 60m [200ft.] high and 2.5m [8ft.] in diameter near the base. The massive trunk rose unbranched for 30m [100ft.]. After

Above. *Rhododendron glischrum* ssp. *rude* in Pemakö.　　　　　　　　　　**KNEC**
This subspecies of *R. glischrum* was first introduced by George Forrest in 1924. The chief distinction between it and the more easterly distributed ssp. *glischrum* is supposed to be the presence of hairs on the upper surface of the leaf, but this distinction is not very consistent. We have noticed that ssp. *rude* tends to have paler, typically smaller leaves, and pinker or paler flowers than ssp. *glischrum*. All the Pemakö plants we have seen are closer to ssp. *rude* than to ssp. *glischrum*. It crosses with *R. campylocarpum* in Pemakö giving rise to hybrids wrongly attributed to *R. selense* by taxonomists. A fine garden plant for moderate climates.

Right. *Rhododendron uvariifolium* in forest below Doshong La, north side.　　　　**KNEC**
This rhododendron species is one of the commonest in the China/Tibet border region. It forms the dominant forest in much of this area around 3400m (11,000ft.). The Tibetan plants were described as var. *griseum* and indeed cultivated plants under this name are usually distinctive. Observation in the field in Tibet reveals that the typical plant is more or less indistinguishable from Yunnan plants, so there seems little justification for retaining the varietal name. Early flowering (in April-May). On the Doshong La it grows in Picea forest with many other rhododendron species such as *R. wardii, R. faucium, R. hirtipes* and *R. cerasinum*.

climbing a cliff we turned a shoulder and found ourselves in dense Rhododendron forest, which was already covered with snow. The species were: *R. hirtipes, R. faucium, R. uvariifolium, R. cinnabarinum* or *R. oreotrephes* and the sticky 'Strigillosum' (*R. glischrum* ssp. *rude*). Then, descending 300m [1,000ft.], the composite Rhododendron forest gave place first to *R. uvariifolium* forest, some of the trees being 12.5m [40ft.] high and 1.2m [4ft.] in girth near the ground, and still lower to bamboo forest. Here we made our second bivouac on a slope so steep that the men had to build platforms to sleep on.

Next day we descended to the river bank, marching through forest as usual, and camping under a rock at the foot of a cliff. It was a fine place for a shelter, and we slept comfortably, though our roof was quite wasted, as no rain fell. The river here is a tossing sea of waves, the bed being choked with boulders. A little lower down a glacier enters the river at an altitude of 2645m [8,730ft.]. Five glacier streams from Sengdam Pu and Gyala Peri flow into a large basin-shaped valley, from which one stream emerges, and flowing on down a steep narrow gully, reaches the river. At this point the vegetation changes again, and whole new tribes of Rhododendron appear. Foremost amongst these are species of the 'Maddeni' series, including a form of *R. maddeni* itself. It makes stout bushes on the rocks, in company with two species of the 'Virgatum' series. Epiphytic Rhododendrons also appear, chiefly the little box-leafed *R. vaccinioides*, with dangling apple-cheeked capsules, 2.5cm [1in.] long and no thicker than a bodkin. Bunches of scarlet berries hung from the long twining stems of a Solanum, or deadly nightshade.

We had a long march in prospect next day, so the ration coolies set out at 8 o'clock, while the higher command were breakfasting and packing up the bedding. Eventually we got off at 9 and climbed a cliff which brought us on to a narrow forested shelf. From a bluff we presently obtained a good view of the valley ahead, and the galloping river, all foam and fury. Climbing up and down over wooded spurs we halted for the third night under a high cliff. Now the rocks right down to the river were covered with Rhododendrons which, in fact, formed the bulk of the forest. The species familiar to us in Kongbo had almost entirely disappeared, only the pink *R. faucium* remaining; they had been replaced by Indo-Malayan types – species of the temperate rain forest.

One of the most interesting of these was a 'Maddeni' with oval rugose leaves and peculiar venation, the sunk channelled veins of the upper surface standing out prominently on the lower (K.W. 6286). It was *R. megacalyx,* a species I discovered in the Burmese jungle many years ago. The almost spherical capsule completely enclosed in the leafy calyx is like no other 'Maddeni.' It grows on the sheerest cliffs, and in addition to being uncommon, is often inaccessible. Another fine species was the big-leafed *R. sinogrande/R. montroseanum* (K.W. 6261), already described. We noticed many young plants and seedlings here, and a few days later, on a moraine in the forest, I found a young tree, only about 2.5m [8ft.] high, with several trusses of fruit. In swampy places there grew a spreading untidy shrub with more or less ascending branches – one of the 'Irroratum' series with blood-red flowers (*R. venator,* K.W. 6285). This plant we saw henceforth almost daily, and it was especially abundant in the swamps round Pemaköchung, where it took on almost the appearance of mangrove.

The bulk of the forest, so far as Rhododendrons were concerned, was composed of a leathery-leafed tree with blood-red flowers – *R. ramsdenianum* and a purple-flowered 'Arboreum.' (*R. coryanum* aff). The former (K.W. 6284) had bloomed at high pressure, and was everywhere crowded with large trusses of good fruit. Not so the latter; and, common though it was, many days passed before I found a fruiting specimen far down the gorge (K.W. 6280, 6311). I have mentioned the colour of the flowers in several instances, but it must be remembered that these were only stray blooms which had opened out of season. Early spring is probably the flowering season. The forest then, tier on tier from the dripping snow to the rocking river, must be one incandescent lava stream of Rhododendron blossom. Altogether I counted no less than twelve good species and true this day. Not only were they even out of flower, the most conspicuous feature of the vegetation, but some species formed forests almost entirely by themselves.

This was particularly noticeable with *R. sinogrande, R. ramsdenianum*, the 'Arboreum' and *R. venator*. Many species were epiphytic on various big trees, and the cliffs supported masses of *R. maddeni* and *R. virgatum*.

Presently we descended into the river-bed for the first time, but the going was not easy; at the base of the forest was a stone breakwater made of smooth blocks as big as houses, and jammed amongst these like broken matches were huge tree-trunks bristling with splinters. After climbing up and down over these obstacles for some time, our ears filled with the roar of the river, we camped under a rock in the forest; we had been marching seven hours, but had only done about 16km [10 miles]. The procedure in camp is as follows: A site was selected for our bedding under a rock or a big tree if possible, and bamboos were cut and piled so as to form a mattress. Fires were then lit, and we all had tea and something to eat. While the porters were collecting firewood, Cawdor and I botanised, or took photographs, or observations for altitude, and about 7 o'clock we had supper, which consisted of soup and curry. Then, sitting round the fire, we wrote up our diaries, talked till we were sleepy, and turned in about 9 p.m. Often we could not sleep, either because we were too cramped, or because the ground was too hard, or because it was raining and we had no cover, or simply because we were too excited or not sufficiently tired. About 6 o'clock we awoke, and breakfast was ready by 7. There was little delay over starting, since we slept for the most part in our clothes, and our blankets were soon rolled up. By half-past eight we were off, and the length of the day's march depended on the time it took to reach a good camping-ground. So long as we were close to the river, we could bivouac almost anywhere; but up on the cliffs water was scarce, and it usually fell out that we must halt either very early or very late.

Pemaköchung and the legend of the great falls

On November 20th, after a fine night, followed by a heavy dew in the early morning which drenched the forest, we scrambled down the cliff and got our third boiling-point reading in the river-bed since leaving Gyala. The altitude was 2580m [8,506ft.]. Our day's march lay partly in the river-bed, partly in the forest. Early in the afternoon the river suddenly swung due south, and through a window in the jungle we looked out and saw the northern glaciers of Namcha Barwa, coldly menacing, relentlessly pushing on as though to engulf the forest; but as a matter of fact they are withdrawing their forces. Next minute we came out on to cultivation. Nothing could have come as a greater surprise. The great river was plunging down, down, boring ever more deeply into the bowels of the earth. The snow-peaks enclosed us in a ring of ice. Dense jungle surged over the cliffs, filled the glens, and marched boldly up to battle with the snow. And in the midst of all this strife, in a quiet bay in the mountains, round which the maelstrom of river, forest, and ice fought dumbly for dominion, was one poor little badly cultivated field! Ascending by a path to a terrace, we saw perched on a knoll, in the midst of a great swamp, the little wooden monastery of Pemaköchung; and here the Walrus invited us to stay in the temple. The famous lama Kintup visited Pemaköchung in 1881, when trying to trace the course of the Tsangpo, but was unable to proceed farther. He reported the Tsangpo to be 40m [2 chains] distant from the monastery, and said that about 3km [2 miles] off it falls over a cliff called Sinji-Chogyal from a height of about 45m [150ft.], and that there is a big lake at the foot of the falls where rainbows are always seen.

From the explorations of Bailey and Morshead in 1913, it became clear either that Kintup had got mixed – for the account of his three years' wanderings were dictated from memory, or that a mistake was made in translating or recording his story. 'Sinji-Chogyal' is evidently Shingche-Chögye opposite Gyala, where a stream falls 45m [150ft.] over a cliff into the river, and there is only a small fall on the main river at Pemaköchung. Bailey saw this when the river was in flood, and described it as about 9m [30ft.] high, and Cawdor saw it at low-water, and described it as more of a rapid than a waterfall. At any rate, it is not the impressive sight geographers had been led to expect. Bailey and Morshead, after overcoming tremendous difficulties, had followed

***Rhododendron sinogrande, R. lanigerum* and a hybrid between them, Pemakö.**   **KNEC**

In search of *R. montroseanum* in 1995 on the south side of the Doshong La we found a forest of *R. sinogrande*. The obvious natural hybrid between the large-leaved *R. sinogrande* (cream flowers) and the small leaved *R. lanigerum* (red flowers) would almost certainly have pink flowers and it appears to be very close to what is cultivated as *R. montroseanum*. It is very likely that KW 6261 contained seed of this natural hybrid. Kingdon Ward was convinced that he had simply found *R. sinogrande* (which indeed he had) and there are no wild origin herbarium specimens of *R. montroseanum*. Ludlow and Sherriff reported finding *R. montroseanum* in the gorge, but the flower description sounds more like *R. uvariifolium*. There do not appear to be any cultivated plants from the Ludlow and Sherriff expedition.

***Rhododendron montroseanum* at the R B.G. Edinburgh.**   **KNEC**

This large-leaved rhododendron species has a curious history. Kingdon Ward never found this species as such in the wild: he found and collected *R. sinogrande*. A mixed seed number KW 6261 from the gorge (which also included *R. exasperatum*) produced a large number of fairly uniform large-leaved seedlings. These plants were given the name *R. mollyanum* after Molly, Duchess of Montrose, who raised the seedling which became the type specimen. The name 'mollyanum' was found to be illegal, so was later changed to *R. montroseanum*. It has smaller leaves than typical *R. sinogrande* and the flowers are pink rather than pale yellow-cream. This fine specimen was grown from the original Kingdon Ward seed and is at the Royal Botanic Garden, Edinburgh. This species can be identified by its large, dark green, rugulose leaves, with a pale plastered indumentum on the lower surface, and by its pink or white flowers.

***Rhododendron venator,* a cultivated plant from Ludlow and Sherriff seed.**   **KNEC**

Collected by Kingdon Ward, this species was seen in flower by Ludlow and Sherriff in 1947 in the gorge where they described it as 'loose straggling tangled thickets'. It has been recorded only from the Tsangpo Gorge. In cultivation it is free-flowering with loose trusses of fine red flowers (the epithet 'hunter' refers to the scarlet hunting coat) and makes a good medium-sized plant for moderate climates: eastern Scotland is perhaps the limit in terms of hardiness.

***Rhododendron megacalyx,* a cultivated plant at Glendoick.**   **KNEC**

This species was discovered in Burma by Kingdon Ward and was described in 1916. Ward found it again in the Tsangpo Gorge (KW 6286). One of the most distinctive members of the large Maddenia subsection (most of whose members have pale pink or white, often scented flowers), this species is characterised by the deeply veined leaves and the extended lower lobe of the corolla which is reminiscent of a pelican's pouch. It is also characterised by the large calyx (hence the name); the pink calyx (surrounding the white corolla) can be clearly seen in this picture. A fine species with a sweet scent which can be grown outdoors only in mild climates. A good plant for a large greenhouse or conservatory.

The world's deepest river gorge, Tsangpo, south-east Tibet.   **KSJ**
A snow-corniced peak crowns the Namcha Barwa massif above the Tsangpo River just above Pemaköchung. The gorge here is over 4880m (16,000ft.) deep. In places avalanches thunder down the steep flanks of the mountain all the way to the river. The view is from a saddle on a spur thrown off Gyala Peri, looking upstream.

the river for another 16km [10 miles], and still there were no falls. But there remained a gap of 80km [50 miles] more or less, about which absolutely nothing was known; indeed, for half that distance there was said to be no track of any sort near the river, which was hemmed in by bare rock walls several thousand feet high. Was it possible that hidden away in the depths of this unknown gorge there was a great waterfall? Such a thing was quite possible, and it was this question that we were resolved to answer. We would, if possible, go right through the gorge, and tear this last secret from its heart.

The Falls of the Brahmaputra have for fifty years been the great romance of geography. Everything, even tradition in Tibet itself, pointed to their existence. The Tsangpo near Lhasa flows at an altitude of 3700m [12,000ft.] above sea-level: the Dihang issues from the Abor Hills at an altitude of 300m [1,000ft.] more or less. 240km [150 miles] east of Lhasa the Tsangpo, still a big calm river, disappears into the mountains, and after following a course which could only be guessed, reappears in Assam. It has bored its way clean through the mightiest mountain range in the world, and in doing so has descended the enormous height of 3400m [11,000ft.]! What more natural than to suppose that somewhere in the depths of that unknown gorge was hidden a great waterfall! The belief in the falls persisted long after the identity of the Tsangpo with the Dihang had been established beyond reasonable doubt; indeed, it grew up *after*, and largely in consequence of, that discovery. For if the Tsangpo were, as was formerly believed, either the Irrawaddy or the Salween, its course would be so long that there would be no necessity to postulate a waterfall in order to bring it down to the plains at the right point. Moreover, it was largely owing to Kintup's exploration, combined with that of another famous *pandit*, Kishen Singh, that the final identity of the Tsangpo with the Dihang was established; and Kintup, as we have seen, reported a waterfall 45m [150ft.] high.

Even after Bailey and Morshead had shown that Kintup was wrong, the question was not finally settled; for there still remained this 80km [50 miles] of gorge unexplored. It is true that there had always been a school of sceptics – hard-headed matter-of-fact geographers – who, arguing from analogy, coolly pointed out that since no other river which rose behind the Himalaya boasted a waterfall, it was therefore very unlikely that the Tsangpo would prove an exception. But for that matter there was a school who right up to the time of Bailey and Morshead's journey stoutly maintained that the Dihang was not the Tsangpo. The retort to these unbelievers was, indeed, crushing: if the Dihang, as you maintain, rises in the Abor Hills south of the Himalaya, how do you propose to get rid of the Tsangpo? Unless you are prepared to make it sink into the earth, it must be the Dihang! The answer to the mathematicians, whose case was a good one though by no means overwhelming, still left the matter open. Waterfalls depend as much on geological structure as on geography. If there should happen to be a band of soft rock crossing the lower part of the gorge, with harder rock above, the formation of a waterfall would be by no means impossible. And there we were left. We approached the matter with open minds and were prepared for almost anything, except the possibility of failure to solve the problem.

We remained at Pemaköchung on November 21st, in order to rest the porters. Cawdor descended to the river to see Kintup's fall and get a boiling-point, while I went up the mountain on a botanical excursion. After picking my way across a bog, making from one nodal thicket to another in no little alarm lest I should disappear in the morass, I reached a dismal swamp, fenced with a network of Rhododendron and other trees. Thence I ascended the steep rocky bed of a torrent, above which, on the grassy slope, grew a dwarf Iris, with a long narrow, almost cylindrical capsule – possibly one of the 'Ensata' group. I collected seed of this (K.W. 6289). Mounting the earth ridge I soon began to meet with Rhododendrons in great variety, nearly all of which yielded seed. However, I soon found I had chosen an impossible route. The face became almost sheer, and had it been bare of vegetation, it would have been inaccessible. But it was not bare. It was clothed with a tangle of Rhododendrons, so hard-stemmed and growing so thickly that it was possible to haul oneself up, practically walking on top of them. But it is hardly necessary to add that this was a most exhausting mode of progression, and by the time I had pulled myself 30m

[100ft.] up the cliff, waist-deep in the scrub, through which, however, I frequently put my foot with such violence that I was in danger of either twisting my ankle or being wrenched from my hold, I had to give it up. Meanwhile, I had found several new species which promised to be of interest. Perhaps the oddest-looking was a 'Barbatum' (*R. exasperatum*) with very large leaves and persistent bud scales which bristled all up the wooden stems in a rather untidy manner; but of this, to my chagrin, not a single capsule could I find. A second species was one of the 'Brachyanthum' type, but growing taller and lankier than Pink Glaucum, and with quite different foliage (*R. tephropeplum* K.W. 6303). *R. edgeworthii* was a third species, the 'Virgatum' (*R. auritum* K.W. 6278) made a fourth, and there were several others. On bare ledges, away from this awful tangle, a bushy dwarf species formed tussocks and brooms on the mossy floor by itself. I should have taken it for *R. campylogynum* but for its solitary flowers and short stalks (K.W. 6301: *R. pemakoense*). This was on the sheltered side. On the other face grew *R. sinogrande,* and several more tree species.

Returning to the monastery after a hard day's exploration and by no means dissatisfied with the result, I packed my seeds, and we made preparations for continuing the journey. Our forces had now to be reorganised. Dick was to remain here a week to collect Rhododendron seed. With him would remain the most querulous of the old ladies, and two more would be detached and sent back to Pemaköchung after three days. The four of them were then to return as quickly as possible to Gyala. There Dick would rejoin Sunny Jim, and they had instructions to take all the heavy kit back to Tumbatse, and to proceed thence down the *rong* to Tongkyuk, there to await our arrival. Meanwhile we, with Tom and the Walrus and twenty porters, fourteen of whom carried only rations, would push on through the gorge, and leaving it by the Po-Tsangpo, reach Tongkyuk from the south. The Walrus collected a lay follower of his own here to carry his basket; he proved one of the stalwarts and a droll fellow.

Meanwhile, a great change had come over the Walrus himself. For the first two or three days he had walked solemnly along, his hands clasped behind him, his eyes cast on the ground, as though he were going to the stake in holy meditation. But now he became quite sprightly, cracked jokes, told stories, cackled with laughter and, above all, became a very efficient butler and aide to Tom. We found him so invaluable, indeed, that when we reached Payi [Payu, Payul, Bayi, Bayu, or Bayul], instead of sending him back through the gorge to Pemaköchung, we took him with us to Tongkyuk, and from there sent him on to Clay, and so to his little wooden hut by the best road. We now took stock of our party, which comprised, besides ourselves, Tom, Shock-headed Peter, the Lay Reader, the Glowing, Curly, Pemaköchung, the Walrus, seven other male porters, and eight women, headed by the Bakeress, and Lydia and Mary Bennett.

Below Pemaköchung

Before we started on November 22nd the usual ceremony to ensure good luck was performed. A smoke screen rose from the altar, the coolies gathered round and sang a mournful song, and at the same time cast some grain into the furnace. Then every one marched once round the temple, gave a final vigorous jerk to the rickety prayer drum, which squeaked dismally in its sockets, and turned towards the river. We were off. For several miles we marched through swamps and dense forest where the undergrowth grew 1.8m [6ft.] high: crossed the Tailing glacier torrent by an awkward tree-trunk, and the Sanglung glacier torrent by a dangerous-looking log, and after little more than four hours' march, camped under a boulder in the river-bed, at the foot of an enormous spur.

The course of the river is very tortuous here. Below Kintup's fall it makes a U-bend to the south round a sugar-loaf peak, which caps the end of a spur from the north; it then skids round the Sanglung cliff and plunges away towards the north-east, interrupted by occasional violent jerks to north and south. The cove in which we bivouacked was cluttered with stones and driftwood, and a breakwater of vertically tilted gneiss runs out into the wild river, which crashes down a 3m [10ft.] drop and swings to the north. Spinning stones have drilled holes in the hard rock, some of these

Pleione scopulorum in Pemakö. **KSJ**

This tiny orchid grows on cliffs and rocks in the wet climate of Pemakö, both south of the Doshong La and in the Tsangpo Gorge itself. This specimen was taken above Pemaköchung, in the heart of the gorge, at around 3000m (10,000ft.). *P. scopulorum* is very variable in flower colour, having been found in white, yellow, magenta and scarlet-rose forms.

Rhododendron exasperatum in Pemakö, south of the Doshong La.
KNEC

This species is the most easterly occurring member of Subsection Barbata, a subsection characterised by red-flowered species with bristly foliage. The name does not refer to the hardship endured by Kingdon Ward in discovering it, but instead refers to the roughness of the hairs on the leaves and branchlets. It seems to be rare in the wild, tending only to grow on mossy rock in areas of high rainfall such as Pemakö and the Tsangpo Gorge. There is probably only one red-flowered clone of the species in cultivation under KW 8250. The pictured specimen has paler, pinkish-red flowers. *R. exasperatum* is characterised by its purplish brown new growth and its persistent bud scales which can be seen here hanging down beneath the whorls of leaves.

mills being very deep. There are also some cold sulphur springs under a ledge, but these are submerged at high-water. In the river-bed we took a boiling-point observation, which gave an altitude of 2450m [8,090ft.].

We found it difficult to sleep here; the thunder of the river was almost deafening, and the whole earth seemed to vibrate with the loud impact of loaded water. After a minimum temperature of 8°C [45°F] in the night, we got away early on the 23rd. There was fresh snow on the trees not very high up, but the day kept fairly fine, with glimpses of sunshine; the clouds, which clung obstinately to the snow-peaks, however, warned us that a storm was brewing. Almost immediately we were in difficulties, with an awkward cliff to climb, followed by a nasty traverse round the face, along a narrow ledge which overhung the reeling river. The pioneer party went first, and we hauled the women up, the men posting themselves at intervals along the ledge and handing them along. After that, we made our way through the forest for an hour without further adventure, until the way was blocked by an overhanging cliff. Here the main body sat down, thinking that the end had come. A more formidable obstacle at first sight it would be difficult to imagine. It was over the cliff, or back; there was no way round, with the river battering at its foot. Fortunately, there was a chimney or narrow cleft about 9m [30ft.] high between the main wall and a detached stack. If we could climb that, the thing was done. At this crisis Curly, the Lay Reader and Shock-headed Peter performed one of the most remarkable feats of rock-climbing I have ever seen; they went straight up the almost vertical outer buttress like cats! Next they felled two small trees, cut steps in them, and lowered them into position in the chimney which was too wide and too smooth to climb otherwise, and made fast; two ladders had to be used because there was a block half-way up the chimney, the upper ladder standing precariously on a sloping ledge.

The porters now went up hand over hand. Some of the stoutest even went up with their loads, and Cawdor carried his rucksack up without turning a hair, and descending again, helped the others. But I liked not the look of it, and shed my rucksack at the top of the first ladder, breathing a sigh of relief when I reached the ledge, and safety, above. Tom then tactlessly suggested that as it was getting late, and the pioneer party who had

Rhododendron headfortianum (R. taggianum) **KW 6310 at Windsor, England.** **KNEC**
This plant was discovered by Kingdon Ward in 1924 deep in the Gorge, near Pemaköchung. This species has been placed by Cullen in synonymy with *R. taggianum*, but it deserves to retain some botanical status as it is very different from typical *R. taggianum* and has an isolated distribution. The foliage of the pictured plant is very distinctive, but it does not entirely match the specimen found in the Gorge. The species was described from a cultivated specimen raised from seed of KW 6310, raised by Lord Headfort in Ireland.

Rhododendron leucaspis **on a rock in Pemakö.** **KNEC**
This species was discovered and collected out of flower by Kingdon Ward under KW 6273 in the Gorge, but was described from a cultivated specimen grown from the seed. The story of its discovery is told in Kingdon Ward's posthumously published book *Pilgrimage for Plants*. In 1995 we were delighted to find it on the south side of the Doshong La, perched on the rocks surrounding the campsite used by Kingdon Ward when he explored Pemakö. It is very closely related to *R. megeratum* which also grows nearby. This species needs perfect drainage in cultivation and likes to grow on mossy logs or in old tree stumps. The pure white flowers have attracted breeders to raise several successful hybrids from it including 'Snow Lady' and 'Ptarmigan'.

explored for another half-mile had not come on a camping-ground, we should descend the chimney again, camp at the foot and start fresh on the morrow. I flatly refused. I had got safely up the beastly thing, and nothing on earth would reconcile me to chimney-climbing as a habit. Once at the top, there I intended to stay; and to clinch matters I scouted ahead as fast as I could go. Eventually we bivouacked in the forest just above the river, having made some 6km [4 miles'] progress in seven hours.

As a result of the hold-up at the chimney, I was able to botanise for an hour, and thereby added seed of two interesting plants to the collection. One was a baby 'Maddeni' Rhododendron with an enormous capsule (K.W. 6310 *R. headfortianum*). It flowers when about three years old and no more than 22.5cm [9in.] high, though it eventually grows bigger than this. Like many of its class, it is generally found growing high up on trees, but sometimes it will content itself with a boulder in the river-bed. Nowhere common, it is distributed through the lower part of the gorge in the Rhododendron-Conifer forest, that is to say, at an average altitude of about 2400m [8,000ft.]. It also appears to flourish in Eastern Bhutan, where I found a plant (K.W. 6415 *R. dalhousiae* var. *rhabdotum*) which in fruit at any rate is indistinguishable from it. *R. lindleyi* of the Sikkim-Bhutan Himalaya is its nearest ally; indeed, our species may be that, but as we did not see it in flower, it is impossible to say for certain. The second plant of which I secured seed was a big climbing rose, which raised itself 12m [40ft.] into the air before smothering a small tree in its prickly toils (K.W. 6309). It bears large erect bunches of spherical bright apple-yellow hips. The seeds have germinated with remarkable haste, instead of lying in the soil for a year as rose seeds usually do; so it is probably a quick grower. This day we saw for the first

Rhododendron pemakoense **above Pemaköchung.** **KSJ**
This species is endemic to south-east Tibet and was discovered by Kingdon Ward near Pemaköchung in the heart of the gorge. This picture was taken by Ken Storm very near where it was first discovered. Kenneth Cox also found *R. pemakoense* in 1996 (CC 7561) on the east side of the Dokar La which connects the Tsangpo Gorge to Pome. A delightful compact species which is extremely free-flowering. Its only drawback is that its swelling buds are very easily frosted. A parent of several dwarf hybrids including two of the Glendoick 'bird' series, 'Phalarope' and 'Snipe'.

time the beautiful silver-green weeping pine (K.W. 6315, *P. bhutanica*).

On the following morning we got another boiling-point in the river-bed, altitude 2350m [7,655ft.], and then proceeded on our way, cutting a path through the forest. We could see from an occasional blazed tree-trunk, its wound long since healed over, or from a stump which had sent up suckers, that men had once passed this way. A party of Mönbas, it is alleged, arrived at Gyala a few years ago, but were sent back by the *Depa,* and told to go round by the Doshong La. Such a policy is intelligible enough. In the first place, the country as far west as Temo has long been subject to raids by the tribesmen below, and the Tibetan authorities would be only too anxious to close every avenue of approach. In the second place, it would be difficult, if not impossible, to collect taxes from people using the gorge as a means of entry into Kongbo; whereas it is a simple matter if communication is restricted to the Doshong La. Difficult as it was to cut our way through the forest, however, we realised that without the forest we would not be able to get along at all. On either side of the river the cliffs are either sheer, or very steeply sloping, and then worn smooth. There is rarely a cove to which one can descend, except where a stream breaks through; and the litter of huge boulders in the river-bed makes progress there well nigh impossible.

At one time we found ourselves on a narrow rock-ledge just above the river; bunches and festoons of *Rhododendron virgatum, R. vaccinioides,* and other species, hung above our heads, and billowing masses of *R. maddeni* lined the edge of the cliff below. We were smothered in Rhododendrons. As for the trees, there were oaks, and holly, Tsuga, juniper and weeping pine, tree-of-heaven, and a great many others. After a short march we came to a cliff and had to descend to the river-bed. It looked awkward. To make matters worse, several of the women sat down and began to cry. The pioneer party, or public works department as we called them, made light of the difficulty, of course, and soon found a way down; Cawdor, Tom and I, having taken off our boots, followed, and the frightened women were pushed and pulled along by willing helpers who carried their loads down for them. We found ourselves in a small cove, hemmed in by river and cliffs. About a quarter of a mile ahead a big stream – the Churung Chu – enters the Tsangpo, and the river slews round again, flowing north. Thus we had no sooner descended to this cove than we had to climb out of it again; but the pioneer party, having sent back word that they would have to make more ladders to scale the next cliff, we decided to halt in the cove for the night. Log platforms were made for our bedding amongst the boulders, but it was both hard and cold. The altitude was 2330m [7,600ft.].

Next day, November 25th, we sent two of the women porters back to Pemaköchung, a journey which, unburdened as they were, they would easily accomplish in two days, possibly in one. Cutting our way steadily through the forest, we descended into the deep bed of the Churung, crossed it without difficulty, and found ourselves on a distinct path. There was a drinking pool here, with fresh tracks of 'takin,' that strange heraldic bovine of the bamboo forests, from Bhutan to China. It was takin, too, which, in their annual migrations up and down the gorge, had made the track on which we now found ourselves. Ascending about 300m [1,000ft.] above the river, we presently came to a cliff, which we descended with the aid of the rope. It was probably at this very cliff that Bailey, having with him only one coolie, was held up and forced to return in 1913; but we could not identify the place with any certainty, for ten years is sufficient to change the scenery a good deal. About the middle of the afternoon we halted under a cliff, having come about 5km [3 miles.]. During the next four days we made very slow progress, averaging no more than 5km [3 miles] a day. The difficulties were immense. Each morning the pioneer party started off early, cutting a path for a mile ahead, the coolies following. When the main body came up to the head of the path four of them dumped their loads and returned for those of the pioneers, which they then carried to the end of the made track, while others carried their own. In this way the loads were relayed to the path head.

The river continued to advance by jerks in a general north-east direction, with fierce rapids which ate hungrily into the core of the mountains. Already we seemed to be far below the level of the ground, going down, down, into the interior of the earth; and as though to emphasise the fact, the temperature grew steadily warmer. And the gorge was growing ever narrower, the gradient steeper, till the power behind the maddened river was terrific. Its blows fell on rock and cliff with frightful force; and at every turn a huge cavernous mouth seemed to open, and gulp it down faster and faster.

On the 26th we reached another glacier torrent, the Shegar Chu, derived from the mighty Sanglung peak, now due south of us, and so close that its icy breath sometimes chilled us to the bone. We camped under bushes in the stream-bed, and could plainly see the ice-wall at the foot of the glacier, a couple of miles up the valley. On the following day we discovered that part of the plane table tripod had been lost, and while men went back to look for it, I attempted to reach the foot of the glacier by following up the Shegar Chu; but after an exasperating scramble over the abandoned moraines, I found that the glacier was inaccessible by this route. The moraine extends some 5km [3 miles] down the glen below the glacier foot; the burn is now cutting terraces in it, the uppermost being already covered with forest. Here I found a small bush of *Rhododendron sinogrande* bearing ripe capsules – the first I had come across.

Arriving back at our camp after two hours' struggling in the earthen glen, I found the party had only advanced a quarter of a mile, owing to the difficulty of crossing the burn. Also the coolies who had gone back to look for the lost plane table gadget had returned empty-handed; so Tom started off to seek it by the wayside. After further delay we effected a crossing of the burn, and then climbed a steep cliff in thick undergrowth, which drenched us, for it had been drizzling steadily now for some hours. Finally, we reached a flat-topped cliff covered with weeping pines and juniper trees. Parting the bushes on the edge of the cliff we peered over and saw the river 300m [1000ft.] below; we could have dropped a stone straight into it!

There was a whole grove of weeping pines here. It is a grand tree 45m [150ft. high], with long slender needles in sevens, and big pendent cones; the shimmering bluish-green foliage is beautiful. There was also a giant oak tree, with flaking bark which recalled the Plane. One I measured was 5.45m [18ft.] in girth 1.8m [6ft.] from the ground. Evidently we were approaching another stratum of vegetation, for there now appeared for the first time a large deciduous Magnolia (*Magnolia rostrata*) with leaves 50cm [20in.] long by 25cm [10in.] wide, and cones 12.5cm [5in.] long. It must be a magnificent sight in leaf and flower – it stands 9-12m [30-40ft.] high, and is not uncommon in the upper rain forest, around 2100-2400m [7,000-8,000ft.]. Then there were Castanopsis, and masses of the climbing sausage-fruited Akebia, and more 'Maddeni' Rhododendrons with thick leathery leaves, squat capsules, and pink flowers, besides vines and creepers of various kinds; *Rubus lineatus,* a species of Agapetes (in flower), Deutzia, and the charming dwarf *Berberis calliantha* K.W. 6308 with large pendent berries, bright scarlet in colour. In the course of a march such as ours, one can get quite a good general idea of the flora, but only a very poor idea of its infinite variety; for the flora of the Tsangpo gorge covers the whole gamut, from the tropics to the Arctic.

Gorge of the Tsangpo, below Pemaköchung.   FKW

211

CHAPTER XIV

In the Heart of the Himalaya

Leaving the Upper Gorge and hunting takin

November 28th was fine again and we made fair progress, though the descent from the 300m [1,000 ft.] cliff gave some anxiety. There was a forest of alders below that, and then a great sandbank, on which we noticed the tracks of several wild animals. A tropical note was added by a troop of noisy quarrelling monkeys, which made the forest ring with their cries, and Cawdor saw a herd of takin on the other side of the river. We were still following their tracks on the right bank. The men collected bushels of toadstools for supper; and glued to the cliffs we saw a huge fungus, like a flattened bath sponge or a double-decked cake, the lower half white, the upper half honey-coloured. We were told it was good to eat, but though we saw several more, they were all inaccessible. Camping again in the river-bed, we got another boiling-point 2180m [7,153ft.]. Two streams from Sanglung enter the river at this point, close together.

November 29th was our last day in the upper gorge, for by evening we had come up against a cliff beyond which it was impossible to advance. We were by no means certain when we started that we could reach the foot of this cliff where the river doubled back on itself, flowing towards the west, for an immense landslide had spoilt the scenery, and we had some difficulty in crossing an arm of the river, and even in getting along at all. Eventually we surmounted all obstacles and hacking our way through dense scrub which presented an impregnable front on the steep slope, camped in the river-bed again, having covered 3.2k [2 miles] in six hours. The altitude was 2150m [7,098ft.].

The scrub just mentioned through which we had to force our way was an extraordinary assortment, consisting of *Rhododendron virgatum* and other species,

A takin photographed at a reserve near Thimphu, Bhutan.   **IB**
Takin are hunted and revered as sacred animals much as the buffalo was worshipped by native Americans. Their horns as well as their flesh are considered to be potent medicine against infertility.

Mönba hunters and an old, bull takin.   **KSJ**
The age of the animal, about twenty years, was determined by examining the teeth and tasting the marrow. All parts of the takin are utilized and the hunting is restricted by the amount of dried meat the hunters can consume on the spot and that can be carried out on their backs. The takin is considered a sacred animal. One name for the animal translates as 'sacred food of the gods.'

Hunters prepare takin skins along the banks of the Tsangpo. **IB**
This picture was taken in 1993 a short distance downstream from the ruined monastery of Pemaköchung. The
northern walls of Namcha Barwa tower above. Although devout Buddhists (normally vegetarian), the hunters
consider takin a sacred animal to hunt which, after death, will transmigrate to the Elysian paradise hidden in
Pemakö's innermost depths.

Gaultheria, Berberis, Buddleia, Cotoneaster, Elæagnus, Deutzia, Hydrangea, Birch,
Alder, Pinus and Tsuga. It clothed a smooth rock slope facing the sun, the shrubs
compact and wiry, the trees stunted and twiggy; we had not seen such a close formation
before. Arrived in camp, one of the porters collapsed. Our men, as I have said before,
were excellent, and they did yeomen service. But, after all, they were used to it, and
though we could not but admire their strength and stamina, we had to confess that they
had no do-or-die tradition to fall back on, no reserve moral force – in short, no guts.
If anything went wrong they caved in. The deeds which seemed to us – rightly, I think
– fine, were everyday work to them. It was in adapting themselves to the unusual, the
unexpected, that they failed completely, like children. So long as they were in their
element, they might lead, and we were content to follow; but as soon as unusual things
began to happen, it was for us to lead, and for them to follow. It was here that Cawdor,
who was daunted by nothing, rendered invaluable service.

As I have said, one of the porters, feeling sick, collapsed and cried like a child. His
friends rallied round, and revived him by black magic as it appeared to us. The Lay
Reader took from a leather wallet he wore suspended round his neck some charms
carefully wrapped in little pieces of paper; one contained seeds, another bits of rag, a
third written prayers. Some one produced a pan of hot charcoal, the charms were
thrown in, and a thin curl of blue smoke tickled the patient's nostrils. He coughed and
spluttered feebly, and gave himself up to a painless death. Then appeared the Walrus. He
sat down by the sufferer, muttered long prayers, and with his rosary beat the victim over

the head. Clearly they were determined to get something into his head by hook or, if necessary, by crook. The upshot of it all was that by the morrow he was sufficiently recovered to come on with us. He had, indeed, implored us to rest there a day; but all we could promise was that if he was too ill to move next day, we would detach one of the women to stay with him, leave them sufficient food, and send back help as soon as possible. Obviously, we could not risk starvation for the whole party. The Walrus reckoned that we were still three days' march from the nearest village, and already some of the more improvident of the porters were cutting down their rations. We ourselves were within the margin of safety, but we could not have fed the company for a day.

However, nostrums, prayers and blows effected what we could not have effected ourselves, since we were unable to diagnose the malady; the man was relieved of his load; and rather than remain behind in that stormy crack – as he frankly admitted – he tottered after us. Two days later he was quite well again. We camped amongst the boulders, as I have said, close beside the thundering river. A quarter of a mile ahead a blank cliff, striped by two silver threads of water, towered 300m [1,000ft.] into the air. The river came up against this cliff with terrific force, turned sharp to the left, and was lost to view. We scrambled over the boulders, crossed a belt of trees and a torrent, and made for the foot of the cliff in order to see what became of the river; but even before we got there our ears were filled with a loud roaring noise. As we turned the corner, and before we could see straight down the river again, we caught sight of a great cloud of spray which hung over the rocks within half a mile of where we stood. 'The falls at last,' I thought! But it wasn't – not *the* falls. A fall, certainly, perhaps 12m [40ft.] high, and a fine sight with rainbows coming and going in the spray cloud. But a 9-12m [30-40ft.] fall, even on the Tsangpo, cannot be called the falls, meaning the falls of romance, those 'Falls of the Brahmaputra' which have been the goal of so many explorers.

Nevertheless, we stood spellbound, as well we might. The river here swung round to the west, boring its way between two mighty spurs which jutted out, one from Gyala Peri, the other from Sanglung. Cliffs towered up on both sides, so close together that it seemed one could almost leap from crag to crag; and the cliffs were smooth as well as sheer. Only high up against the skyline did a few trees cling like fur to the worn rock surface. Obviously we could get no further down the gorge; to scale the cliff seemed equally impossible. But above our camp the cliffs were to some extent covered with shrub growth; and up these lay our route, as I was to learn on the morrow. It rained in the night, and having no cover we got soaked and slept badly. Nor did things look any better on the following day, November 30th. However, we had to go on, and we faced the cliff early, cutting a path through the belt of forest to the rock foot. Then the fun began. Of that climb I have only an indistinct recollection, beyond the memory that it was a nightmare. The cliff was all but vertical. Here and there it was rent by cracks and joints, out of which grew bushes; and these we followed sometimes on a slant, sometimes hauling ourselves vertically up the face by means of the bushes. A false step meant disaster. At one place we had to stride across the cascade which splashed and slithered coldly down the slab face. It was an awful moment, but every one got safely across. At last we reached the second cascade, right on the corner where the river turned; here we had to use the rope to climb a short cliff, and above that we found forest and security. Here I noticed an ash tree and a curious bush which I had previously taken to be a Rhododendron, though it was not. But perhaps the most astonishing fact of this climb is that takin had been up the cliff before us! We followed their track, basing our route on theirs. Indeed, at the summit, in a glen from which the second cascade originated, we found a dead takin. It had been caught in a rope noose, set by some Mönba hunters, and in trying to free itself, had fallen over the cliff and broken its neck. As a full-grown takin may easily weigh between 272-318kg [600-700 lb.], and stand 60cm [2ft.] high at the shoulder, it is no small feat for it to climb such a cliff as the one we had just climbed. But the fact is the takin must needs be a powerful beast to force its way through the dense bamboo growth on whose foliage it feeds. The traps set by the Mönbas are of the simplest description, and the migratory habits of the takin are its undoing. All the hunter does is to build a stout fence across a well-worn track, leaving only one gap; if possible a track is chosen from which the animal cannot make a detour, the fence at one side resting on the cliff. A noose of bamboo rope is suspended in the gap in such a position that the animal must insert his head, whereupon it is drawn tight when he tries to force his way 'through; eventually he strangles himself.

Having reached the deep stony glen above, on the Sanglung spur, 480m [1,852ft.] above the river, we cast about for a place in which to spend the night. The flanks were very steep, and though there was forest above, it looked remote, and almost as inhospitable as the glen. Our party split up, and six of us selected an eligible site on the face, while others, more fortunate, went up into the forest and slept snugly in a hunter's lair which they discovered. At dusk it began to rain, a bitter wind sweeping down the glen off the snowfields. The fire smoked evilly. We huddled together, drenched and shivering; but as there was not room for all of us round the fire, which gave out a minimum of warmth with a maximum of smoke, I retired after supper, and crept into my fleabag, where I slept soundly in a puddle. Cawdor sat up all night by the fire, dozing occasionally; while Tom, the Walrus and the Bakeress kept him company. Funniest of all was Pemaköchung, the Walrus's servant, who kept one bare foot warm all night by nursing it, and the other by thrusting it into the pit of the Bakeress's stomach. He was a cheerful youth, and was thoroughly enjoying himself, affording us much comic relief.

We woke very early on December 1st, but after the discomforts of the night it was late before we got off; the porters were on the verge of mutiny and required a little tactful handling. We followed a hunter's trail now, ascending through forests of giant Tsuga, Rhododendron and other trees. Through a gap we caught sight of the snows, still wreathed in cloud, but occasionally appearing; behind us, due south, the saddle between Sanglung and Namcha Barwa; on our left front, the hooded peak of Gyala Peri, continuous with which was a whole range of snow-peaks stretching away eastwards towards the Sü La. Somewhere thereabouts the Po-Tsangpo joined the Kongbo Tsangpo. We now found ourselves on a very steep path on the edge of the forest with a steep drop into the bare glen on our right. The trees increased in size, and there were many small epiphytic Rhododendrons on the moss-clad trunks. In the upper forest snow lay on the ground.

At last we reached the crest of the long Sanglung spur, and could look over into the gorge of the river on either hand. Far away a patch of emerald green looking no bigger than a pocket-handkerchief spread out to dry shone on a chequered slope; it was a cultivated field. We marched north-westwards along the crest of the spur for a mile, through forests of giant Abies and tree Rhododendrons, whose leaves hung stiffly down in the snow. We were now 1125m [3,714ft.] above the river, or 3276m [10,812ft.] above sea-level; crossing the ridge, called the Shengchen La, we began to descend steeply. Soon we reached a pool in the forest and halted for the night. Great fires were lit, shelters were built, our blankets dried, and that night we lay down on soft couches of silver fir branches and slept soundly.

Towards morning, after a fine night, it grew so cold that we had to get up; but the temperature only fell to -1°C [30°F] under the trees. However, the two 'Grande' Rhododendrons (*R. sinograndе/montroseanum* and *R. lanigerum*), the 'Falconeri' (*R. arizelum*) and the sticky-haired 'Barbatum' (*R. glischrum* ssp. *rude*) (K.W. 6255, 6261, 5877, 6256), all have to withstand snow and temperatures below freezing-point; nor had they yet encountered the most severe weather of the season. I collected seed of the silver fir here from the many big cones which were lying about (K.W. 6332).

Hunter with takin.   **FKW**

Lissu hunter with takin he has just killed with a crossbow. Takin had come out of forest to a salt lick. This photograph was taken on a later journey, east of the Tsangpo Gorge. When Kingdon Ward travelled with the hunters of Sengchen they shot a takin with a 'gas-pipe matchlock' just above the 'Falls', along the lower portion of the stream that descends from Netang. Crossbows were probably never used in the upper portion of the gorge although snares are still frequently set along well-used takin trails here. Today's hunter uses a small-bore rifle. All parts of the animal are utilized – the meat is dried over a fire and the skins stretched and dried for clothing or used for floor-coverings in the homes.

Elaeagnus umbellata var. *parvifolia* between Lunang and Trulung (Pylung). **KNEC**

This deciduous, thorny shrub has showy fragrant white flowers in spring and very distinctive silvery leaves. The upper surface of the leaf gradually becomes glabrous but the underside remains silver. Quite rare in cultivation, but deserves to be more widely grown.

Rhododendron lanigerum in Pemakö. **KNEC**

In cultivation this species opens its flowers as early as February, but on the south side of the Doshong La it was in full flower in mid-June. Characterised by large rounded flower buds and tightly packed rounded trusses of twenty to thirty flowers, *R. lanigerum* is closely related to the Himalayan *R. arboreum* and the Chinese *R. arboreum* ssp. *delavayi*. The Tibetan forms were once described as *R. silvaticum* but, apart from flower colour, there is no significant difference between this and *R. lanigerum* previously described from north India.

Payi to the rope bridge

The descent down the east flank of the Sanglung spur, at first northwards along the face, and finally north-eastwards along the crest of a minor spur, took us nearly five hours; but there was a track all the way. Passing through Conifer forest into Oak forest, we soon got down into jungle, and a wealth of new trees; *Rhododendron maddeni* was in fruit and a new species with tiny capsules in threes, which I did not recognise (K.W. 6335 *R. scopulorum*). There were big bamboos, giant Araliaceæ with huge palm-like leaves, queer orchids, such as *Cirrhopetalum emarginatum,* in flower on the moss-clad tree-trunks, and many other things. And then suddenly the abrupt descent ceased and we came gently down into cultivated fields, and saw clusters of wooden huts in the distance. We had descended about 1500m [5,000ft.] from the top of the spur, though we were still a good 300m [2,000ft.] above the river.

Now we were in a new world. How surprising it was to see fields and houses. Nay, the surprising thing was that we were in the world at all! While we had been following the river as it gnawed its way through the Himalaya, wedged between those magnificent snow mountains, nothing seemed more unlikely than that we should ever reach civilisation again. Every day the scene grew more savage; the mountains higher and steeper; the river more fast and furious. Had we finally emerged on to a raw lunar landscape, it would scarcely have surprised us, but for one thing. As the river, rushing like a lost soul between the hot hell in the heart of the Himalaya and the cold hell on the wind-swept peaks which guard the gorge, grew more dynamic, as the scenery grew harsher, and the thunder of the water more minatory, the touch of Nature came marvellously to the rescue. Everywhere, by cliff and rock and scree, by torn scar and ragged rent, wherever vegetation could get and keep a grip, trees grew; and so, from the grinding boulders in the river-bed to the grating glaciers above, the gorge was filled with forest to the very brim. 3000m [10,000ft.] of forest coloured those cold grey rocks of tortured gneiss; and when the summer rain weeps softly over the scene of riot a million trees will flame into flower and strew their beauty over the ruin.

And so on a sunny afternoon we marched into Payi, or Payul, amidst gardens of Cosmos and tobacco. We felt triumphant, though there was more to do yet – indeed, the hardest part of the job still remained to be done; but first we wanted to sleep, and sleep and sleep. The river at Payi looks no bigger than it did where we last saw it, in spite of the extra volume of water derived from the Po-Tsangpo; but we were at least 300m [1,000ft.] above it. Immediately below Payi is a rope bridge, connecting with the path on the opposite side

Rainbow falls. IB

Rainbow Falls, which Kingdon Ward saw only from upstream and estimated to be 6-12m (20–40ft.) high, is actually more than 21m (70ft.). Cataracts lace the surrounding cliffs and spill into the Tsangpo. It was up this rock wall that Kingdon Ward and Lord Cawdor climbed out from the gorge.

of the river, which leads to the Sü La, or Zu La as it is pronounced here. There is no path down the right bank, and the cultivated slopes end in a high cliff, which extends downstream for some distance; two fine cascades are visible below. The river flows east for 3-5km [2 or 3 miles], then bends northwards round a spur before resuming its course.

   Across the river is a range of snow-peaks, and above Payi is the great bulk of Sanglung, 7018m [23,018ft.], with a terrific snow cliff facing eastwards; east of that again are several smaller snow-peaks, and then the range, which just west of Sanglung had attained the dazzling height of 7758m [25,445ft.] in Namcha Barwa, sinks down and melts into the low rounded jungle-covered hills of the Abor country. A much greater variety of crops is grown here than in Kongbo. Chief of these are: in spring, barley; in summer, maize; and in autumn, buckwheat and millet. We noticed also castor-oil, hemp, chillies, limes – rather hard and tart, but refreshing – small apples – also rather hard, but sweet – and bananas. The change of diet with dessert did us good. Quarters were provided for us in the local temple. We found that every village, however small, has a temple; for the people make a great outward show of Buddhism. But when they pray, they pray in secret, closing the temple door, and sacrificing fowls, whose blood and feathers are smeared on an altar in the jungle.

The high priest, a pleasant-looking man, promised us transport for the following day, our objective being Gompo Ne, at the confluence of the Po-Tsangpo with the Kongbo Tsangpo; and everything was settled in the most satisfactory manner possible. We had arrived quite unexpectedly. Nobody knew who we were, why we had come, or whither we were going; and before the people could recover from their astonishment, we were gone again. That was the plan; and it worked. Meanwhile Tom, who was in great spirits at the success of the journey, decided to give the coolies a Sunday School treat, and preparations were soon made. A fire was lit in the courtyard, an iron vat of water placed on it, and a great tub of germinating grain–barley and bird-seed–purchased. While we were finishing our supper by candle-light in the shadow-haunted temple we heard the Bacchanalian revels, and went out into the soft moonlight which silvered the valley. Everybody was squatting cross-legged round the fire, and girls were busy pouring out the warm hissing liquor from bamboo bottles. Snatches of song and laughter floated up to the bright stars, and the muffled roar of the river sounded like distant city traffic.

The liquor was produced by the simple process of pouring warm water on to the bird-seed at the top of the tub, and drawing it off at the bottom by removing a bung. The first edition was fairly strong, since it had been standing; but as more and more was called for it rapidly lost strength, until finally we were drinking nothing more intoxicating than water. The proof of the spirit is in the drinking, but I doubt if the alcoholic content of this bird-seed brew ever exceeded 3 per cent. The weak point about all these country brews – apart from their lack of specific gravity – is their inconstancy. No two brews are ever alike. Occasionally you taste a vintage which is just frolicking foam. One sip, and the world is trans-formed; it would make the first Sunday in Lent at the parish church look as jolly as a revue. You feel as though you could address a Temperance League meeting at the Trocadero on Boat Race night, or shout down an undertaker's mute at an Irish race meeting. But after that fleeting glimpse of the golden age, the next brew washes it off the slate: it is just soap-suds.

It may be remarked that all the peoples and hill-tribes of South-east Asia, civilised or uncivilised, distil liquor. The staple grain of the country is used in their manufacture – barley in Tibet, rice in China, maize or millet in the hill jungle. There are usually two kinds – the crude liquor, weak, variable, thick and musty; and a more refined spirit, also of uncertain but greater strength, and without the foreign bodies which are so freely suspended in the former. This spirit, which has the appearance of gin, is kept in small stone bottles and produced only on ceremonial occasions or for honoured guests. In the hill jungle everybody drinks – men, women and children. Certain functions – a wake, or a wedding, or a holiday – are great occasions for drinking, but except at these bibulous festivals you very rarely see a man drunk, and then only because his alcohol is more methylated than absolute. Subjected to a process of fractional distillation, how many alcohols, aldehydes, ketones and other complex carbon compounds would this liquor give birth to! That is why these country cocktails are so dynamic.

We had made arrangements for the pick of the porters to come on with us, while the remainder returned to Gyala. Accordingly, the Walrus, Shock-headed Peter, the Lay Reader and the Bakeress stayed. We gave the returning party a handsome present, in addition to their pay (which apparently all went to the *Depa*), and took the others on at an increase of wages, which was to be their very own. Richly had they deserved it. Owing to the festivities of the previous evening everybody was very sluggish next day, and it was nearly noon before we got off. Quite early, however, we sent off an 'arrow letter,' which the village scribe wrote at Tom's dictation, to the up-river villages, warning them of our approach and requesting such transport and supplies as we might require.

This letter, written on very coarse unsized paper with a bamboo point dipped in indian ink, was wrapped round 60cm [2ft.] of bamboo with two white feathers stuck in the end, indicating express, and entrusted to the village long-distance runner; it went off hours before we did, and we met the man coming leisurely back soon after we started. A very jungly-looking lot of coolies were told off to carry our loads, which were crammed into bamboo baskets, supported by a head-band. The men, though sturdy, were dwarf in stature and had almost simian faces; nor was their intelligence much ahead of their looks. Arrived at our destination, which, owing to the late start, was the summit of the next spur, they put down their loads and proceeded to do nothing. Even when Tom galvanised them to feeble action, they were almost useless, and it fell to the permanent staff to cut branches for our beds and collect firewood. It then turned out that there was no water, and two men were sent back to the village to fetch some, under pain of death. They came back a couple of hours later bearing a basket full of bamboo tubes containing sufficient for drinking purposes; but we had to postpone washing.

Our coolies called themselves Mönbas, but they were really nothing of the sort, though they wore one Tibetan garment apiece, a sort of dressing-gown or *chupa*. They were barefooted, and had shingled black hair, forming a mop which hung straight down all round. It was fairly evident that they were either Pobas, or more probably Lopas. Of course, sophisticated persons never admit to being Lopas, who are looked down upon by the urban population as savages; they call themselves Mönbas. We were now in an entirely different atmosphere, and the stratum of vegetation which we had reached showed that we were at a much lower elevation. The south-facing slopes were not thickly forested, but covered instead with bracken, long grass and scrub, with scattered pine, alder and oak trees. A slender twining Crawfurdia hung out dozens of purple bell-flowers; a Strobilanthes was in flower; and so too was the beautiful pink *Luculia gratissima*. If only one could grow that shrub in England, what a revelation it would be! On the rocks – which were composed chiefly of mica-schist and fine-grained gneiss, and on alder trees especially, were masses of orchids, though few of these were in flower.

Next day (December 4th) we marched through thick forest, climbing gradually, till we reached the summit of a long ridge which runs out from the great cliff facing the Po-Tsangpo confluence; thence we descended steeply to a solitary house, and presently reached a village of three houses, with the inevitable temple, not much bigger than a hen-coop. A five-day mass was being held to cast out the devil from a sick man, and the din was fearful. Drums, cymbals, whistles and catcalls vied with each other; and though our arrival caused a temporary stoppage while the band took a look at us, they soon fell to it again more violently than before. However, we were warmly welcomed by the High Priest, and the all-solvent beer was produced; meanwhile we were given a house for the night (like most of the houses, it consisted of one room), and were glad of a fire in the centre, not merely to cook by, but on account of the cold; for, though it was very hot in the middle of the day, there was hoar frost outside in the morning.

From this village, called Sengetong, we had a fine view of Gyala Peri, the great snow-peak across the Tsangpo, and close to the Po-Tsangpo confluence; it is a much more impressive sight from the east than from the west, by reason of its curious overhanging summit, like a monk's cowl. We descended to the Tsangpo, crossing by a rope bridge some 6km [4 miles] below the confluence, which was hidden round the corner. The river rushes furiously between sugary-white cliffs of mica-schist and is only 46m [50 yards] wide. There are three ropes of twisted bamboo, and the patient is hauled across in the usual way, within 1.8m [6ft.] of the waves. High-water mark is 9-12m [30-40ft.] above winter level, however; and in the summer this rope has to be removed and raised to a considerable height; the river is then wider also.

Meanwhile we took a boiling-point reading in the river-bed, and were elated to find that it read 95.5°C [204° F]. At the point where we left the river, just above the rainbow fall, it was 93.3°C [200°F]; and the difference in height calculated from this was 678m [2,240ft.]. That is to say, the river descended 678m [2,240ft.] in a distance which

probably did not exceed 32 km [20 miles]. If the gradient was steady, this would give an average fall of 34m [112ft.] a mile; but it seemed more likely that rapids and falls would alternate with quieter reaches. In any case, for a river of this size to descend 34m [112ft.] a mile was amazing, though alpine streams, of course, often have a much steeper gradient; and there was plenty of room for a big waterfall of 30m [100ft.] or so. Thus we were all excitement, and determined to see that part of the river which had been hidden from us. After crossing the river, we found ourselves on the long narrow spur which juts down from the north, and climbing to the summit on a long slant, reached the little Kampa village of Tsachugang, and were installed in the temple.

The village of Payi.   KSJ
The harvest is laid out to dry on a roof-top. Ward and Cawdor reached the village of Payi after a long wilderness journey through the gorge: 'Now we were in a new world. How surprising it was to see fields and houses. Nay, the surprising thing was that we were in the world at all!…And so on a sunny afternoon we marched into Payi, or Payul, amidst gardens of Cosmos and tobacco. We felt triumphant…but first we wanted to sleep, and sleep, and sleep.'

The village of Tsachu.   **KSJ**
Tsachu straddles a ridge above the confluence of the Po-Tsangpo River with the Yarlung Tsangpo. A banner of
clouds streams from the summit of Gyala Peri, on the right.

Below left: Payi with the Pome range behind.   **IB**
Fields of barley and millet spread out beneath the village of Payi; a fresh mantle of autumn snow covers the Pome range
on the opposite side of the gorge. Payi was the first human habitation which Kingdon Ward and Lord Cawdor reached
after climbing out of the gorge.

Below right: *Rhododendron scopulorum* by the Po-Tsangpo.   **KNEC**
This tender species grows at low altitudes in the Yarlung and Po-Tsangpo valleys at 2000-2500m (6,500-8,250ft.).
As a rough rule, for a plant to be hardy outdoors away from western coasts in the U.K., it should come from above
3000m (10,000ft.), so this is a plant for indoors except in very mild climates. A member of the large Maddenia
subsection, it was discovered at Gompo Ne by Kingdon Ward in 1924. At this altitude rhododendron species flower
during winter or early spring. This specimen was growing on a rock above a cliff by the Po-Tsangpo river. The
white flowers are fragrant in some forms.

CHAPTER XV

The 'Falls of the Brahmaputra'

To Gompo Ne

The view from this point, 600m [2,000ft.] above the river, almost took our breath away. The whole southern horizon was filled with the great white trunk of the Sanglung-Namcha Barwa massif which throws out dark furry limbs towards the river. To the right was a magnificent range of icebergs, rising out of a sea of forest, with the snow cornice of Gyala Peri, and the bold crags of Makandro, clear cut against the setting sun. A long saw-edged spur projects southwards from Gyala Peri, overlapping a similar spur which projects northwards from Sanglung – the one we crossed; they appear to meet, without leaving any passage. Then, when you think the gap must be sealed up, and the door bolted and barred, out of the very heart of this tomb, swinging round the spurs, leaping the rocks, comes the Tsangpo just as hard as it can go, a roaring, bouncing, bellowing flood. You see one flash of green, like jade, where the sunlight gleams on a pool far up the gorge, and after that all is white foam. On our right, almost directly below, and plainly visible, the Po-Tsangpo came galloping down from the north, while on our left the Kongbo Tsangpo came reeling up from the south, slewed sharply round a high cliff, and wriggled eastwards again.

When at last one can take one's eyes off that glittering array of snow-peaks, and the rivers crashing and grinding their way through the core, two other points stand out gablewise amongst the rafters of the world's roof. Opposite us, and facing the confluence is a huge cliff, where the Sanglung spur, which we crossed from the rainbow fall to Payi, is sliced clean off. A little farther east, another arm of the spur, which separates Payi from Gompo Ne, ends abruptly in a high pyramidal cliff, overlooking the rope bridge by which we crossed the river. Both spurs are heavily wooded above, but the cliffs below are bare.

On December 7th we set out for Gompo Ne, marching along the crest of the narrow spur, with views of the rivers on either side. After marching about 3.2km [2 miles] we

Looking towards Gyala Peri from Oscar Pukpa (Sengchen) Pemakö.   **FKW and KSJ**
Told by the villagers at Sengchen that no route lay up the river, Kingdon Ward spotted a camp fire high in the forest. Reluctantly, the villagers acknowledged that a hunter's trail ascended the ridge above the village and agreed to lead the men along the track into the upper middle rain forest dominated by great Tsuga. A day above Sengchen they 'reached a boulder, beneath which we bivouacked; water was found some distance down the hillside and brought up in bamboo tubes.' Ken Storm writes: 'This is the view from that cave, across the forested valley toward the lower ramparts of Gyala Peri, dusted in fresh snow. The tongue of the glacier reaches down between the forested slopes. In May 1996 we occupied the same campsite and looked across the valley framed by the same Tsuga tree Ward photographed in 1924. The glacier has retreated significantly in the past seventy-two years.

Opposite: Crossing the Tsangpo by rope bridge, probably at Gompo Ne.   **FKW**
The wooden slider is threaded on to rope. The passenger pulls himself along. Today a steel-cable, planked, suspension bridge spans the river on the trail between Tsachu and Payi. On the Po-Tsangpo a single cable still crosses the river. On crossing the Tsangpo below the confluence K-W wrote: 'The river rushes furiously between sugary-white cliffs of mica-schist and is only 50 yards wide. There are three ropes of twisted bamboo, and the patient is hauled across in the usual way, within 6 feet of the waves. High water mark is 30 or 40 feet above winter level, however; and in the summer this rope has to be removed and raised to a considerable height; the river is then wider also.'

descended the almost precipitous end of the spur through thick forest to the river, and turning downstream, soon reached our destination. Gompo Ne, however, is little more than a name. Amongst a wilderness of gneissic monoliths, rasped and scoured by the shock of the river, then idly cast aside, their raw wounds abandoned to the sly healing jungle, stands a tor whose shape suggests a natural stupa or pagoda; while hard by, crowning another gigantic rock, on whose face are cup-marks, is a real *chorten*. Leaning against this rock are a number of long poles, notched into steps, so finely cut that no human being could possibly climb them, and one might be puzzled to account for their presence, did

Gompo Ne.   **KSJ**

Travellers follow a pilgrimage route hung with prayer flags at this site along the Tsangpo River just below the confluence with the Po-Tsangpo River. Gompo Ne is still a popular destination for pilgrims to Pemakö.

Crossing the Po-Tsangpo River just above the confluence.   **KSJ**

Ward wrote of this crossing: 'The Po-Tsangpo is here about 50 yards wide, and flows swiftly between high cliffs of closely-banded, finely crystalline, vertically tilted schist. We underwent the usual tortures on the rope bridge, and it was dark before we were all safely lodged in a one-roomed Mönba hut, placed at our disposal by the villagers of Pingso.' Cable bridges still span the rivers in places although most have been replaced by wood-planked suspension bridges.

not one recollect that we are now in the land of *nats,* those elfish spirits which live in the trees and in the lakes, and rivers, and mountains of the twilight forest land. Strong spirits mount quickly to the head, by these ladders. There is also an open shed, where pilgrims such as ourselves, sleep the night nothing more. Once there was a monastery here, we were told, but it fell into the river; and now the great grey rocks, quarried by the river which storms by 15m [50ft.] below, lie around in confusion, while tangled mats of orchids help to conceal their bald heads, and the crawling jungle slowly buries them.

We walked upstream half a mile to the confluence, but found less turmoil here than we had expected, partly because the water was low. The Po-Tsangpo rushes in at a rather acute angle, and there is a sudden drop in the bed of the Kongbo Tsangpo at this point. The scene is a lively one, though there is not that terrific impact of opposing waters we had imagined. The altitude by boiling-point is 1650m [5,247ft.]; hence the river drops no less than 117m [388ft.] in the 6.5km [4 miles] between this point and the rope bridge, or nearly 30m [100ft.] a mile. The water of the Po-Tsangpo was amazingly blue, but that of the far bigger Kongbo Tsangpo was grey with mud, and quickly swallowed up the blue streak caused by the former.

We slept the night in the shed, and next day retraced our steps along the ridge, and

Gateway to the wild heart of the Tsangpo Gorges.   **KSJ**
Clouds hang over the village of Sengchen, situated on a long ridge that descends to the confluence. The ripening
fields in the village of Pingso can be seen below. Ward wrote 'We had only one object in coming here – to explore
that part of the gorge which had been hidden from us, between the rainbow fall and the Po-Tsangpo confluence,
where the river turns back on itself to flow north-westwards round the long jagged spur of Gyala Peri. Here if
anywhere were the 'Falls of the Brahmaputra' which had been a geographical mystery for half a century; and the
final solution – falls? Or no falls? – was now within our grasp. Ken Storm writes: 'In the spring of 1996 we followed
the same trail – the first outsiders to return since that winter of 1924.'

Prayer flags at Tsachu.   **KSJ**
Prayer flags above the Po-Tsangpo River at Tsachu, just above the confluence with the Yarlung Tsangpo.

descended to the rope bridge over the Po-Tsangpo below Tsachugang. It was not possible to march up the Po-Tsangpo itself, as the way was barred by a cliff, though only a few days later we learnt that the Mönbas had fixed a second rope bridge across, just above the confluence. The Po-Tsangpo is here about 46m [50 yards] wide, and flows swiftly between high cliffs of closely-banded, finely crystalline, vertically-tilted schist. We underwent the usual tortures on the rope bridge, and it was dark before we were all across and safely lodged in a one-roomed Mönba hut, placed at our disposal by the villagers of Pingso. Next we ascended one story from the terrace on which Pingso is built to a village called Sengchen on a spur; and then the fun began.

We had only one object in coming here – to explore that part of the gorge which had been hidden from us, between the rainbow fall and the Po-Tsangpo confluence, where the river turns back on itself to flow north-westwards round the long jagged spur of Gyala Peri. Here if anywhere were the 'Falls of the Brahmaputra' which had been a geographical mystery for half a century; and the final solution – falls? or no falls ? – was now within our grasp. Our excitement may be imagined; and the fact that the river between the rainbow fall and the confluence dropped 561m [1,851ft.] was favourable to the theory of a 30m [100ft.] waterfall somewhere.

Sengchen is a small Mönba village on a bare windy shoulder of one of the giant spurs which radiate out from Gyala Peri, and is situated just below the great forest belt. This spur is separated from the next one by a deep glen, broken by a high cliff over which the torrent drops in a fine cascade, and the next spur itself is razor-backed and wall-sided, rising from the river in a sheer precipice. The glen is filled with dense jungle, which clings to the opposite cliff. Looking at these obstacles from Sengchen, our task seemed a formidable one. We reckoned that to cut a path through that jungle, supposing that we could cross the glen and climb the wall to the top of the next ridge, would take three or four days. From the summit we might see the remaining portion of the river – or we might not; to reach the river would probably take another day, and after that there was the getting back. In trying to picture our feelings, it must be remembered that we had now been in the gorge for four weeks, on top of eight strenuous months of work in Tibet, and were feeling weary. Still, a last effort was required.

Around Gompo Ne

We were now joined by a Mönba hunter, who had been everywhere and done everything; and him we questioned closely. No, it was not possible to get along the river-bed, he informed us. No, there was no path to the summit of the next spur, and the only path which existed – a hunters' trail – went so far back towards Gyala Peri, that nothing was visible of the river. No, it was impossible to reach the river from there. He had never heard of any waterfall, but admitted that he had not seen this part of the river. The only way to see it was to return to Payi and cross the spur to the top of the cliff, whence on a clear day one could see the gorge below. So there we were, and everything looked rather hopeless for the moment; but though we felt checked, we still had a shot left in the locker. To gain time, and to test the information, we descended 364m [1,200ft.] to the river above the confluence, slithering down the steep wooded slope through a grove of huge bamboos; some of these were 12m [40ft.] high and 1m [39in.] in circumference 60cm [2ft.] from the ground, with leaves 3m [10ft.] long and 90cm [3ft.] wide. The hunters who accompanied us amused themselves by slashing through the stems with their long knives; and as the giant herbs fell the leaves split with a noise like the tearing of brown paper.

When we reached the bed of the river we turned upstream, clambering over the boulders, to the point where the cliffs drop straight into the water, and so along the wooded face of the precipice till finally brought up short by smooth rock. On the cliff here we found *Rhododendron nuttallii* in bloom, with white trumpet flowers, dyed yellow at the base, fragrant as Madonna lilies (K.W. 6333). This species, which often grows 3.6-4.5m [12-15ft.] high, with a rather lanky elegance, bore ripe capsules also, from which I collected seed. It is interesting to note that, flowering in the winter, *R.*

Rhododendron nuttallii in the Tsangpo Gorge.   **FKW**

Hoping to push up the gorge above the confluence with the Po-Tsangpo River, Kingdon Ward descended a spur from Sengchen and tried to force a route up the river. 'When we reached the bed of the river we turned upstream, clambering over the boulders, to the point where the cliffs drop straight into the water, and so along the wooded face of the precipice till finally brought up short by smooth rock. ...on the cliff here we found *Rhododendron nuttallii* in bloom, with fragrant white trumpet flowers, dyed yellow at the base, fragrant as Madonna lilies. In the *Geographical Journal*, Ward expanded on the area: '...after clambering over the boulders and along the face of a cliff till even the vegetation came to an end, we found that farther progress was only possible for creatures provided with more than the human allowance of hands and feet; not even a monkey or a cat could have clung to those walls.'

nuttallii takes nearly a year to ripen its seed, so that, unlike the wet-winter alpine Rhododendrons, it is active all the year round. At the farthest point reached in the river-bed, nearly a mile above the confluence, the altitude was 1606m [5,302ft.]; and it is at this point that the coarse-grained black mica gneiss of the upper gorge changes to the white mica schists of the confluence. From amongst the boulders on both banks issue several steam-jets, which make a slight purring noise; no water is visible, but the steam is blown out at a very high temperature. One we saw later, however, formed a miniature geyser, explosions of steam throwing up little fountains of boiling water.

That evening I climbed the hill above Sengchen, on the summit of which is perched a small *gompa,* and one or two huts. Immediately above the *gompa* the forest begins, and while looking round for a convenient theodolite station, I was surprised to see quite a

Dawn over the Tsangpo Gorge and the Namcha Barwa Massif. **KSJ**

Larch (*Larix griffithiana*) and hemlock (*Tsuga dumosa*) in the autumn in the Gorge. Kingdon Ward and Cawdor left the river above Rainbow Falls and climbed to this point on the narrow ridge before descending to the village of Payi.

The Mönba village of Sengchen, above the Tsangpo River. **KSJ**

The river flows past Gompo Ne, located just beyond the clearing on the left bank. 'Sengchen is a small Mönba village on a bare windy shoulder of one of the giant spurs which radiate out from Gyala Peri, and is situated just below the great forest belt.'

View of the Tsangpo River from a ridge above Netang. **KSJ**

Kingdon Ward and Cawdor reached a nearby vantage point for their first look into the unexplored section of river above the confluence with the Po-Tsangpo. Where they left the river at Rainbow Falls, several miles above, the river makes a sharp bend to the north-west and flows close under the east face of Gyala Peri. Here it bends back again to the east, just three to four miles above the confluence. Looking up the valley in this photograph, at the base of the snow mountains on the right is the point where the 1924 expedition left the gorge above Rainbow Falls to cross the ridge to Payi. Kingdon Ward described the view: 'Then followed a gruelling climb by a muddy snow-clad track to a notch in the ridge above, till we stood on the summit panting while great wads of snow dropped on us from the trees. We had reached our goal; and far, far below, we could see the Tsangpo for quite 2 miles, white with foam.'. From this ridge the sound of the river can be heard more than 4,000ft. below.

good path going up the ridge, in the desired direction. I followed it for a short distance, and then as it was growing dark, returned to the hill-top. The moon was shining in a clear sky, and the glacial peaks stood out hard and brilliant above the black forest. Opposite the *gompa* was the deep rent which we should have to cross, and beyond that the next ridge rose like a wall to block our way. Could we reach it? that was the great question; and again, should we see the hidden river if we did? As I gazed across the black gulf, pondering this matter, an amazing thing happened. On the opposite cliff, not far from the top, and perhaps a mile away, a red glow suddenly appeared amongst the trees, kindled brightly for a minute, and went out. I stood rooted to the spot, unable to believe my senses, and almost breathless with astonishment, raking the opposite cliff with field-glasses, waiting for the light to reappear; but never did it show again. It was just like a signal; nothing more. There was only one thing it could possibly be – a camp fire. Yet why had it disappeared? Was it, after all, imagination, or was it real? After waiting and watching for a time, I turned and raced down the hill to Sengchen, where I told my story. But the Mönbas could not or would not explain the light, and swore that the path was only a hunters' trail.

On the following day Cawdor explored the path up the ridge and followed it as far as a bivouac under a rock: but the path still went on. And in the evening we taxed the Mönbas with lying, to which they confessed quite shamelessly, and promised to take us to the top of the ridge next day! It appeared that the region which we wished to

A female monal pheasant. **KSJ**

Ralph Rynning, a member of our 1996 expedition, holds a female monal pheasant shot by the hunters. Kingdon Ward writes: 'In the forest higher up we saw several monal pheasants (*Lophophorus sclateri*), brilliant with metallic blues and greens, and a turquoise patch round the eye. At this season they are found in the Rhododendron-Tsuga forest, usually two or three together, the cocks when alarmed uttering a short mournful cry like that of a peewit, but the two notes closer together, the second one rather shrill.'

penetrate was the preserve of another hunting tribe of Pobas, with whom the Sengchen men wished to keep on good terms. Hence their anxiety to divert our attention from the forbidden land! No sooner did we call the bluff than the opposition collapsed. The Mönbas were delighted to come with us! Eight men were collected, six of whom brought their guns with them! For, they argued, they might as well be hanged for a sheep as a lamb. As these warriors were going to trespass in any case, they might as well poach; and in the five days they were away, they managed to account for three head of their neighbours' big game, and two pheasants: they then persuaded us to write a letter to the incensed Pobas, saying untruthfully that the game had been killed on our behalf!

However, these things did not matter; what did matter was that after some days of comparative inactivity we were again hot on the trail. Food for five days was taken, bedding, cameras and surveying instruments; and on the morning of December 12th we started up the mountain on our last effort to find the falls. The spell of fine weather had come to an end, the sky was overcast, and it was drizzling heavily. Following the hunters' path, we soon entered the forest, at an altitude of about 2121m [7,000ft.], and began the steep climb up the ridge. The lower jungle was now left behind, and we entered the temperate rain forest. In the sub-tropical and lower middle rain forest the trees are mixed, passing gradually from evergreen to deciduous; no tree forms forests by itself. Large-leafed Araliaceæ, with palm-like habit, two or three species of Ficus, Dalbergia, Acacia, and other Leguminosæ, and *Rhododendron nuttallii* occur. As usual in constantly wet regions, climbing plants abound – species of Clematis, Vitis, Hydrangea, and a root-climbing Ficus may be mentioned. In the undergrowth are many bamboos and the red-berried Skimmia, while on the ground, as though red spar were crystallizing out of the black earth itself, are seen clusters of gaping Curcuma fruits, like little grinning scarlet mouths lined with rows of pearl teeth. The epiphytic flora is composed mainly of orchids and Gesneraceæ.

This sub-tropical evergreen forest of the lower gorge passes gradually into the deciduous forest of the lower middle temperate belt, which is almost equally varied, but now contains maple, birch, Magnolia, and species of oak. The Rhododendrons met with as we ascend are the 'Arboreum' (*R. lanigerum*) and the scarlet-flowered 'Irroratum' (*R. ramsdenianum*). Just as some of these trees, particularly the oaks, are beginning to reach gigantic proportions, and to form forests by themselves, we pass at about 2,400m [8,000ft.] into the upper middle rain forest, or temperate rain forest, which is again evergreen. Here the species are few, but they make up in bulk what they lack in variety; for here the very largest trees are found – *Rhododendron sinogrande,* one of the largest of its kind, and a huge Tsuga (*T. dumosa*), which together make up most of the forest. In the lower gorge we saw no species of Larch or Picea; their place seems to be taken by this Tsuga, which in the upper forest is in turn replaced by Abies. In the upper middle rain forest, the only epiphytes are small Rhododendrons, of which there are at least six species found growing mostly on Tsuga trees, and a white-flowered Coelogyne; one would scarcely expect to find an epiphytic orchid growing here in the snow!

As for this Tsuga, which has the habit of a Lebanon Cedar, it is a giant, probably attaining a height of 60m [200ft.]. At intervals along the path we saw shingles and planks, cut by the woodmen and stacked for seasoning; the Tsuga planks measured 4.5 x 2.4m [15ft. by 8ft.] and were 75cm [31in.] thick! The people call it *cha,* but that seems to be a general name for Coniferous trees, or at least such as are cut for timber. The discovery of this great Tsuga may clear up a certain mystery in Assam, which has long puzzled those connected with the saw-mills in the Sadiya district.

In the year 1900 there was a great flood in the Assam Valley, the origin of which was traced to the Yigrong Lake, by Bailey and Morshead during their exploration of 1913. During that disastrous affair the swollen Dihang brought down with it besides the bodies of Pobas, logs of Coniferous wood belonging to a species unknown in the Abor Hills. This wood, which is described as strongly scented, soft and light – about 40 lb. to the cubic foot – was sawn up and used in the making of bridges, which twenty-five years later were in an excellent state of preservation; no small triumph in a hot-moist climate like that of Assam.

It was not until 1920 that this timber was heard of again. Then, on some of the densely wooded islands of the Brahmaputra, near Sadiya, a number of logs, some of them 3.6m [12ft.] in girth, were discovered half buried by sand and undergrowth, overgrown with moss, and with the heartwood destroyed; but the rest of the wood was as sound as a bell. These logs also, some of which had been cut, and others broken off, must have been brought down by the flood twenty years previously, and stranded on these low bush-clad islands when the waters retreated. They were extracted and sawn up, and a vigorous search prosecuted for more, and also for the tree itself, without success. Evidently the tree did not grow locally, though exploration was carried on for some distance. There can, I think, be little doubt that the tree brought down to Assam by the 1900 flood was this Tsuga, of which I secured some seed (K.W. 6287).

After ascending the ridge to a height of over 2,700m [9,000ft.], where the uppermost forest – Abies and Rhododendron – begins, we started on a long slanting descent towards the burn, and presently reached a boulder, beneath which we bivouacked; water was found some distance down the hillside and brought up in bamboo tubes. No sooner had we arrived than two of the hunters set down their loads, and went off into the forest with their guns. Twenty minutes later we heard a bang; but they returned at dusk rather crestfallen to report a 'magpie,' displaying a pheasant's leg in proof of their statement. The one thing we wanted now was fine weather, and we crawled under our blankets with a hopeful feeling. Alas! when we awoke on December 13th, it was snowing fast, and the forest was already draped in white. So thick was the mist that we could scarcely see across the glen; but when we started at 10.30 snow had ceased to fall. Descending steeply to the burn, which flowed from one of Gyala Peri's blunt-nosed glaciers, we crossed by a fallen tree, and turned up a rocky glen on the other side. At an immense block of stone so perched on the slope as to afford shelter to a platoon, a halt was called for lunch.

Then followed a gruelling climb by a muddy snow-clad track to a notch in the ridge above, till we stood on the summit panting while great wads of snow dropped on us from the trees. We had reached our goal; and far, far below, we could see the Tsangpo for quite 3km [2 miles], white with foam. There had been a tremendous wash-out on the other side of the ridge, and half the face of the mountain had peeled away, leaving a ragged sore. The descent down this open wound for 606m [2,000ft.] was frightful. At last we halted for the night and dug ourselves in, to avoid rolling over the edge. Consequently we presented an odd spectacle dotted about the hillside, a man under a tree stump here, two huddled under a rock there, like a lot of rabbits. For ourselves, we sat on a ledge under a rock, which gave us little enough protection from the rain.

But our indomitable hunters went off as usual, and returned an hour later having shot a foxy red goral (probably *Nemorhœdus baileyi*). In the forest higher up we saw several monal pheasants (*Lophophorus sclateri*), brilliant with metallic blues and greens, and a turquoise patch round the eye; at this season they are found in the Rhododendron-Tsuga forest, usually two or three together, the cocks when alarmed uttering a short mournful cry like that of a peewit, but the two notes closer together, the second one rather shrill.

Searching for the great falls

That night when we lay down to sleep, over 606m [2,000ft.] above the river, we were greatly agitated as to what the morrow would bring forth; for we had decided to go down and see for ourselves whether there were big falls or not; the men said there was a fall of 12-15m [40-50ft.], but their testimony was not sufficiently reliable. The day broke heavy with mist and drizzle, but about 10a.m. it began to clear up, and we made preparations to go to the bottom. Four hunters, two of whom carried guns, accompanied us. They moved with the stealth of policemen on night duty, and every now and then the leader stopped, and looked at a cliff a mile or two away, and pointed, and those behind stopped too, and looked, and nodded. The descent down the bed of the stream was unpleasant. We could see nothing of the river, but we had not gone far when we began to hear it. The noise was terrific.

Kingdon Ward's 'Falls of the Brahmaputra'. KSJ

Kingdon Ward described the anticipation as they approached the river: 'Immediately below this point, the boulder beach comes to an end at the foot of the cliff; and what happened next we could only guess, for the river, after hurtling itself through the gap, rushes headlong into a gorge so deep and narrow that one could hardly see any sky overhead; then it disappeared.'

On our left was an almost sheer cliff, but to the right (we faced south) the slopes were not quite so steep and were heavily timbered; where the burn entered, there was even a stretch of beach strewn with boulders the size of houses. It was immediately below the burn that something happened to the river, but we could see nothing – only hear the thunder of water.

At last we got down on to the beach, and all was revealed. At this point the bed of the river, which is jammed with boulders, suddenly begins to fall very steeply. A high

At the ledge above the 'Falls of the Brahmaputra'. KSJ

Ken Storm writes: 'The Tsangpo drops over a river-wide ledge about 9m (30ft.) into the wild gorge below. From my journal: 'We scramble out on this spur along the ledge that extends into the river to the brink of the falls. We move carefully now, over rock polished smooth by the waves, warned back from the edge by Phuntsok as he sees the water surge around our feet. I wedge my hands and feet deep in the cracks of the rock and feel the vibration of the thundering river through my body. My face is bathed in a fine, wind-driven spray.'

Below the 'Falls of the Brahmaputra'.

Below what Kingdon Ward called the 'Falls of the Brahmaputra'; the Tsangpo emerges from the rock-walled canyon into an area banked by dense forest. Gyala Peri rises behind as the Tsangpo flows towards its northern-most apex.

wall of rock juts diagonally across from the opposite cliff, and the loaded water has blown a hole 4.5m [15ft.] wide clean through the middle of it. Now all the water poured through the breach, but in flood an immense volume falls over the ledge, dropping down 9-12m [30-40ft.]. Immediately below this point, the boulder beach comes to an end at the foot of the cliff; and what happened next we could only guess, for the river, after hurling itself through the gap, rushes headlong into a gorge so deep and narrow that one could hardly see any sky overhead; then it disappeared. We now set to work to scale the cliff; and after felling a small tree and constructing a ladder, we mounted 30m [100ft.], hauling ourselves up through the bushes. From our vantage-point, we could see some distance down the gorge; and this was what we saw:

Below the whirlpool created by the first fall, the river flowed smoothly for about a hundred yards and was a dark jade-green colour; here it was not more than 27m [30 yards] wide, and must have been incredibly deep. Flowing more swiftly, it suddenly poured over another ledge, falling in a sleek wave about 12m [40ft.]. Scarcely had the river regained its tranquilly green colour, than it boiled over once more, and was lost to view round the corner. However, we could see it to within a mile probably of the cliff where we had found the Madonna Rhododendron in flower; and though we crawled a little farther along the cliff, till the vegetation came to an end vertically above the fall, we could see no farther.

233

Returning to the beach, we took a boiling-point observation, and found the altitude to be 1742m [5,751ft.], or 408m [1,347ft.] below our camp in the river-bed by the rainbow fall and 152m [504ft.] above the confluence. From this point to the confluence was not more than 6.45km [4 miles], and to the rainbow fall not more than 16km [10 miles]. Of the latter distance we had seen perhaps 4km [2½ miles] upstream from the pass on the previous day, and about the same distance downstream from above the rainbow fall. We are, therefore, unable to believe that there is any likelihood of a greater fall in the remaining 8km [5 miles] which we did not see. Moreover, there is a legend current amongst the Tibetans, and said to be recorded in certain sacred books kept in the monastery at Pemaköchung, that between the rainbow fall and the confluence there are no less than seventy-five of these falls, each presided over by a spirit – whether benevolent or malicious is not stated. Supposing that to be more or less true, and supposing each fall or rapid to be only 6m [20ft.] high, the difference of height is easily accounted for.

According to our map, it is 23km [14 miles] from the confluence to the rainbow fall. In the five days' journey from the Churung Chu to the rainbow fall we covered about 19.3km [12 miles], so that the distance between the point where the indomitable Bailey had to turn back and the confluence is about 38km [24 miles]. This agrees very closely with Bailey's estimated distance of 32km [20 miles], while his estimated difference of height between the Churung Chu confluence and Gompo Ne is 540m [1,780ft.], against the 713m [2,353ft.] which we actually measured. Our altitudes give an average fall of 30m [98ft.] a mile between these two points; but from the Churung Chu to the rainbow fall it is in fact less, while from the rainbow fall to the confluence it is greater, namely, 408m [1,347ft.] in 22.6km [14 miles], or 40m [132ft.] a mile. The Mönbas told us that this was the biggest fall; and as the river dropped about 30m [100ft.] in a quarter of a mile, we had no reason to disbelieve them. We had now discovered the narrowest and most profound depths of the gorge, where the river, only 27m [30 yards] in width, descends in falls and rapids over 40m [130ft.] a mile; and that was something.

While we had been exploring the falls the other two hunters had gone upstream, across a big torrent which comes down from Gyala Peri and enters the river just above the first ledge; the small geyser already referred to was in continuous eruption at this point. That night we heard that they had shot a takin. At this season it is possible to go some distance upstream along the beach, but in summer when the water is high, one must keep to the cliffs, crawling through the jungle. The hunters pointed out a notch in the great Gyala spur ahead, now buried under snow, which they said they visited in the summer; from there one could see the river on either side, including the short stretch hidden from us, though no doubt one would obtain an even better view from the right bank. But it must be remembered that only at a very few points is it possible to descend to the river. Sometimes there is a low-water beach, but it is inaccessible; sometimes one can get down the cliffs, but there is no beach. A combination of the two is exceptional; and one can never count on it.

Satisfied with the day's endeavour, we climbed up to our burrow on the hillside, and spent another rather sleepless night, and when the dawn came, we packed and prepared for the journey back to Sengchen. It was a stubborn climb from our bivouac up the wash-out; the sun tried to shine, but was driven back and the mountains played hide-and-seek with the clouds. During a halt two of the hunters decided to hold a shooting competition. A flat stone was selected and a bull's-eye painted on it by mixing a little water with some gunpowder; the stone was then set up and the marksmen nestled down amongst the rocks 18-27.5m [20-30 yards] away. The tinder rope was lighted, the gun-barrel rested on a rock, long and careful aim taken, and the fork carrying the smouldering rope slowly depressed on to the flash-pan. There was a fizz, followed immediately by a bang, bang, the two guns going off almost simultaneously. Neither hit the bull, or even the stone, but it gave one an insight into the skill and patience required of these hunters in shooting takin, goral, pheasants and other game.

A word about what we may call the gas-pipe matchlock. It is 1.2m [4ft.] long, 60cm

Steepest and narrowest part of the Tsangpo Gorge.   **FKW**
This picture was taken in December 1924 at low water, near the point where Ward found *Rhododendron nuttallii.*

[2ft.] of barrel and 60cm [2ft.] of butt, with what looks like a hay-fork hinged to the barrel – combined bayonet and agricultural implement, 'just the thing for your boy at the front'. It is not, however, a hay-fork, nor even a two-pronged bayonet, but a gun rest. The firing apparatus consists of a lever, one end of which is the trigger, while the other end carries the tinder; the fulcrum is in the middle. There is also a spring which keeps the tinder fork up and the trigger down. At rest, a small wooden chock is inserted behind the fork, to keep it down; removal of this chock depresses the trigger and releases the fork, thus cocking the gun. Pressure on the trigger, working against the spring, slowly depresses the fork, which clips the end of a tinder rope, on to the pan; a coil of tinder rope is carried in a leather pocket attached to the butt, so that prolonged aim can be taken. Also the gun can be carried ready for firing when game is sighted.

Other gadgets include a tooth-pick, tied to the pan and used for cleaning out the touch-hole; a sleeve, made of goral skin, which covers the butt and keeps the essential organs dry; and of course a powder flask, usually made from a takin's horn. The hunters make their own bullets, which are of lead and about the size of S.S.G. shot. The guns are made in Pome, and cost about 20 rupees. As for powder, saltpetre is obtained from

Kongbo, and sulphur springs abound in the gorge. Thus we see a regular gradation from the Abor jungles, where men use bows and arrows, and hunt with dogs and traps, through the gorge country, where hunting is an honourable profession carried on with primitive guns, to the Plateau of Tibet proper, where men are armed with breech-loading rifles, and do not take life.

When we were half-way up the wash-out, I halted and set up the plane table, hoping to get a good fixing; on a clear day there is a magnificent view of the snows from this point, unmasked by the stripping of the forest. But it was very cloudy, and I waited two and a half hours before anything showed up. Meanwhile I amused myself watching the antics of a goral which stood sentinel on a rock high above, while his more timid spouse hung about in the background. He stood motionless as though carved in stone, gazing steadfastly, not at us, but at the forest in front of him; occasionally he turned his head very slowly, and looked at his mate over his shoulder, as though saying, 'Yes, it's all right, you can come on now.' At last, she plucked up courage and advanced out of the shadow to join him. What they saw to beware of in the forest I do not know; but I have no doubt they kept a discreet eye on us, though they were out of rifle shot. After waiting two hours and a half Namcha Barwa showed the tip of its steeple while a man might count a score; then everything was blotted out again. I therefore packed up, and we climbed to the pass called Sumtonggongma La, 1372m [4,528ft.] above the river-bed. Slithering down the mud slide through the forest on the far side, we camped under the huge stone where we had lunched on the way up, and slept peacefully under its spacious roof.

After four days of mist and rain, December 16th turned out fine again. We crossed the burn called Ne Chu, and climbed the opposite spur, whence we had a magnificent view over the tops of the snow powdered Tsuga trees to the glaciers and seracs of Gyala Peri; there is a small glacier lake at the head of the glen. Presently, from a platform on the ridge, we had an even finer view of the Tsangpo gorge, with Sanglung beyond. By the time we reached Sengchen Gompa, just above the village, the peaks were obscured, but a couple of hours later they cleared and we were able to get our position and fix two prominent landmarks above the river.

Next day we packed up, recrossed the Po-Tsangpo, and at dusk reached Tsachugang once more. Before we started the happy Mönbas cut up one of the slain takin, and presented us with a large piece of meat; a hunter also brought in another pheasant which he had shot, a specimen of Temminck's grey-spotted tragopan (*T. temmincki*), called in Tibetan *pab*. These tragopans go about in the forest several together, and are found at lower elevations than Sclater's monal. We offered handsome rewards for any more pheasants, without result, though the hunters went off to see what they could do about it. Temminck's tragopan is known from Southern China and the Burma-Yunnan frontier, some hundreds of miles south-east of where we obtained it. It is a handsome bird, with rich red mottled plumage and blue face and horns.

We remarked several rather striking trees in the Mönba villages, some of them grown for the beauty of their flowers, others for their fruits; but as they were without leaves or flowers, it was impossible to name them. One, which resembled a Butea, and was reported to have handsome flowers, is called Singi-shing (*shing* means tree). Another which bears large bunches of small black berries, like elderberries, from which a cooking oil is expressed, is called Gya-do-gang-shing. We saw trays full of these berries drying in the sun. We also got some quite good oranges.

Before crossing the river, we descended the spur below Sengchen, in the angle between the Kongbo Tsangpo and the Po-Tsangpo, with the object of getting a photograph of the confluence. However, we found that it lay so directly beneath the cliff, that no good view could be obtained from this point. At Tsachugang our hunters left us. They were a most remarkable body of men, and had behaved splendidly. It was with real regret that we bade good-bye to the Angel (so-called because his face recalled one of those in Reynolds' picture) and his companions. They were intelligent, loyal and hard-working; once they had made up their minds to take us to the hunting preserves, they did everything they could to help us.

Chapter XVI

Christmas in Tibet

The tribes of S.E. Tibet

In the account of the gorge country I have mentioned various tribes such as Mönba, Lopa, Kampa, and Poba. It is now necessary to say a few words in explanation of who these people really are. That is soon done, because we do not know. The Mönbas came from Bhutan and from the adjoining Tibetan province of Mönyul a century ago. The Kampas are the inhabitants of Kam, a vast vaguely defined region of Eastern Tibet of which Chamdo, on the Lhasa-China road, is the principal town. The Pobas are the inhabitants of the semi-independent province of Pome, which lies to the north of the Tsangpo gorge and is watered by the Po-Tsangpo. The capital of Pome is Showa, which the Pobas call Kanam.

The Pobas are not, strictly speaking, Tibetans; at any rate they are very different in appearance to the modern Lhasa Tibetans who are the standard and dominant race. Most of the ruling classes in Tibet, the wealthy and aristocratic families, are of Lhasa extraction.

Crossing the Chimdro River by cable.   **IB**

Many rivers in the Pemakö region can only be crossed by single cables that stretch across the perilous waters. Here one of our porters crosses the Chimdro Chu River on the pilgrimage route to the sacred mountain, Kundu Dorsempotrang.

Nor is the Poba dialect easily understood in Lhasa. But clearly the term Tibetan, as we use it, is loosely applied to peoples of very different origin. To us the Kampa is a Tibetan (though no Lhasa Tibetan would admit this) just as much as the Lhasa man is; yet they are obviously unlike each other in every way, as unlike each other perhaps as Celt and Saxon. The fact is there are a number of distinct elements in the Tibetan population, as the most unobservant person can see for himself. The Pobas may have been the original inhabitants of Tibet for all we know. Here we would merely observe that the Tibeto-Burman family have moved gradually south-eastwards and southwards down the river valleys; and that the Tibetans to this day call their country Pö, and themselves Pöba; which is very like Poba. The Tibetans call all the jungle tribes of the Southern Himalayan slopes Lopa, the term including the tribes known to us as Aka, Miri, Dafla and Mishmi, as well as Abor.

The Lopas we met were undoubtedly Abors from the Dihang River of Assam; the Dihang being the lower course of the Tsangpo and the main tributary of the Brahmaputra. So far as our information and experience went the distribution of these various peoples is as follows: Kongbo Tsangpo. Right bank, Mönba and Lopa; Left bank, Mönba and Kampa. Po-Tsangpo. Right bank, Mönba; Left bank, Lopa and Kampa. Pemakö. Mostly Mönba, some Lopa and Kampa villages. Naturally there are mixtures of all degrees, but the tendency will always be for the less civilised Lopa, and possibly Poba, to disappear. For the virile Mönbas occupy the country in considerable force, and more and more Kampas migrate into Pemakö every year in order to escape the crushing burden of taxation. A similar movement is not unknown in this country.

The region down river from the confluence is called Lome or the lower Lo (Lopa) country; the region up the Po-Tsangpo from the confluence to Tongkyuk is called Lode, or the upper Lo country. But such Lopas (Abors) as still remain in this part of the gorge, and for some distance below Payi, have been more or less tibetanized, and have at least adopted the outward forms of the Tibetan Buddhist region. Nevertheless, several curious religious rites can doubtless be traced to a more primitive worship; for the Abors at least are animists pure and simple. Although no village is too small or too poor to possess a *gompa,* complete with priest, yet an eye is kept on the village spirit. Usually he lives in a hollowed tree-trunk, up-ended outside the village gate and covered with a flat lid kept down by a heavy stone, lest he should try to escape. In the grove hard by, there will be a mound of stones and broken cooking-pots, inscribed with prayers, and a tray full of wooden billets, like tent pegs, painted black, yellow and red in alternate stripes. This grove is usually surrounded by a fence made of wooden spears similarly painted.

Lilium wardii   **KNEC**
Lilium wardii was discovered by Frank Kingdon Ward on the Po Tsangpo between Tsachu and Trulung. We relocated it there again in 1996 and 1997. It grows on cliffs with narrow leaves and long shoots which poke their way out of the luxurious undergrowth. The delightful pink flowers are scented. Most of the populations we saw will have been washed away by the 2000 floods.

The Po-Tsangpo to Trulung (Pylung)

On December 18th we started northwards up the valley or rather gorge of the Po-Tsangpo. First we had to climb high above Tsachugang, and cross a big shoulder, where the river bends sharply. From a lofty scree which fell away steeply to the Po-Tsangpo, we might have had a glorious view of the snow-peaks again, but they were muffled in cloud. Five hours' marching through the forest brought us to an open shed where we spent a comfortable night. Here we were met by a fresh relay of porters from the other side of the river under the command of a jovial headman; and the Tsachugang people went back. The people we met in this valley were very different from the alert intelligent Mönba hunters of Sengchen. We had indeed some queer coolies whose characteristics were briefly summed up in their nicknames, Weary Willy, Joe Beckett, and Little Ikey, for example. Still, they made good.

On the 19th we crossed a pass called the Karma La, 2546m [8,402ft.], but again the view was spoilt by a brooding storm. However, as this was the last point from which we would be able to see the Assam Himalaya and the river confluence, we decided to wait for better weather. From the north side of the pass we had a clear view up the Po-Tsangpo, which, as Cawdor said, was as blue as a solution of copper sulphate. It was

View from the Karma La, 22 December 1924.   **FKW**
Looking north up the Po-Tsangpo River Gorge from Karma La. The trail today along the Po-Tsangpo from the highway at Trulung (Pylung) to Tsachu stays low along the river. In 1924 Kingdon Ward left the Tsangpo Gorge via a difficult trail high above the left bank of the Po-Tsangpo with superb views to the great massifs of Namcha Barwa and Gyala Peri as well as to the north, up the Po-Tsangpo. The cleared terraces above the gorge and the steep streams falling into the river are characteristic of this part of the Po-Tsangpo valley.

The path leading along the Po-Tsangpo from Gompo Ne to Trulung. **IB**
Our expedition navigates precipitous bridges and trails along the Po-Tsangpo on route to its confluence with the Tsangpo River approximately fifteen miles (24km) downstream. In Kingdon Ward's day this route did not exist. He and Cawdor climbed over a high pass on their journey from the confluence to the trailhead at Trulung (Pylung), bypassing the steep cliffs that girdle the Po-Tsangpo gorge.

Deutzia sp. (aff. *hookeriana*) **Po-Tsangpo gorge, near Trulung (Pylung).** **PC**
This species was collected by Kingdon Ward under KW 6393 in the same location. It is very close to *D. hookeriana*, differing in the non-toothed filaments (ends of the stamens). Attractive in flower, but as it occurs at 1800-2100m (6,000-7,000ft.), it has not proved to be very hardy.

The Po-Tsangpo near the confluence with the Rong Chu. KNEC
At around 1600m (5,250ft.), this is a low, hot and sticky valley, full of tender plants and leeches. The road near the village of Trulung clings to the steep cliffs and is frequently beset by landslides which render it impassable. The path from Trulung to Gompo Ne runs alongside the Po-Tsangpo for much of its length.

backed by a fine range of snow-peaks to the north.

A steep descent from the Karma La brought us out on to a cultivated terrace, where stood the small rickety village of Pongcham. Lopa houses are miserable one-roomed sheds with a paling of split logs for wall, a raised wooden floor, beneath which the pigs live, and the usual shingle roof. There is no cooking-range, not even a mud one, and the family porringer stands over three stones in the centre of a square hearth. The cooking- pots in these parts are made of stone, beautifully shaped and chipped, with lugs for handles; but they are rather brittle. When broken, prayers are scratched on the pieces, and show up white on a black ground, and these inscribed fragments are placed on religious mounds. We needed a whole house to ourselves at Pongcham, which meant that some family had to turn out of hearth and home for the night; but they did not seem to mind much.

The weather next day looked unpromising, but we decided to go on to the next village and wait there for a fine day. Accordingly we did a short march of 6.45km [4 miles], crossing two big torrents and two spurs, to the next terrace, where stood the Lopa village of Lubong. On the right bank of the river was a large village called Pemaden, connected with Lubong by a rope bridge. The weather was quite hopeless on the 21st, so we stayed where we were. December 22nd, however, was a radiant day, the temperature having fallen in the night. Leaving Lubong at 8.30, we reached the Karma La in less than three hours, and had a superb view of the Assam Himalaya, from Namcha Barwa to Sanglung; we could see a long way to the east also, but there was nothing there, except aching blue sky. Just across the Po-Tsangpo, on our right, were the glittering ice-ribs of Gyala Peri and Makandro, looking absurdly close.

We spent four hours on the pass, bathed in sunshine, photographing, mapping, and writing notes; and it was 6 o'clock when we got back to Lubong. A curious point now struck us. When we reached Gompo Ne, at the confluence of the Kongbo Tsangpo and Po-Tsangpo, we had undoubtedly passed through a great range of snow mountains. The Namcha Barwa-Gyala Peri line was behind, i.e. to the west of us. On the other hand, both Namcha Barwa and Sanglung still lay due south of us; that is to say, we were not actually on the southern slope of the Himalaya, any more than we had been at Gyala.

The question, then, was, had we or had we not crossed the Himalayan axis? If that axis turns northwards, or rather north-eastwards, from Namcha Barwa through Gyala Peri, we had crossed it; and so obviously we should have to recross it again in order to reach the plateau. But where? As a matter of fact we crossed no high pass till we crossed the Nambu La above Tongkyuk, and that was far away; the Karma La, under 2727m [9,000ft.], was too insignificant. On the other hand, if the Himalayan axis continues eastwards through Sanglung and the peaks beyond, to be cut through by the Tsangpo still farther east where that river bends to the south, then we had not crossed it. In that case, what range of mountains had we crossed, and through what range has the Tsangpo cut its deep gorge?

It has been assumed that Gyala Peri stands on the main axis of the Himalayan range; but there is no geological evidence to support the statement, while the topographical evidence is far from complete. From Gyala Peri a great range of snow mountains runs northwards, up the right bank of the Po-Tsangpo, into Pome; what becomes of them we don't know. On the left bank of the Po-Tsangpo are more snow-peaks, and the river has cut a gorge between them, just as has the Tsangpo between Namcha Barwa and Gyala Peri. But we lack all proof that this is the Himalayan connection.

From Namcha Barwa the Great Himalayan range is continued eastwards in Sanglung. So much is admitted. Beyond Sanglung is a much lower snow-peak, and then comes a group of three rocky peaks. After that the mountains sink right down; but if a direction is followed east-north-east high snow-peaks are again met with. There is no proof so far that this is not the main Himalayan range, and it is certainly a more natural direction in which to seek it. Gyala Peri, indeed, may have nothing to do with the Himalaya; it may stand on the Trans-Himalayan range. Just as the Himalayan range, east of Bhutan, sinks down to lower levels, to rise again suddenly in the great Assam peaks, so the Trans-Himalayan range, which as we have already seen crosses the line of the Tsangpo at Trap, may rise up here in the peak of Gyala Peri.

After crossing the Karma La we rapidly got into drier country. Many of the sub-tropical trees and climbing plants disappeared and instead we found forests of pine and Rhododendron. From Lubong we descended 300m [1,000ft.] to the river, and then almost immediately began to climb up again, over cliffs of crumbling white schist. Presently we reached a large village called Thongdem and halted for lunch. Pushing on again we crossed a big stream, and soon reached the Rong Chu junction, and half a mile farther on a rope bridge over the Po-Tsangpo. It was now dusk; nevertheless, we set about crossing the river, having no mind to spend the night here on the cold rocks. However, the crossing took a long time, and it was pitch-dark before the last man landed on the sandbank below the village of Trulung.

The rope bridge, which consists of two ropes, is fastened round boulders on either bank and raised up clear of the water by means of wooden tripods. In the summer it is removed from here and fixed at a much higher level. We now lit pine-wood flares and formed a torchlight procession, looking for Trulung, which we found at last – two wretched houses. On the following day we followed the right bank of the Po-Tsangpo a little way, and climbed up flights of steps over the shoulder of a high spur into the valley of the Rong Chu. It was here that the Pobas had ambushed the Chinese troops when the latter were fleeing from Pome, and killed them to a man.

The altitude of the river-bed at the rope bridge was 1960m [6,474ft.], compared with 1590m [5,247ft.] at the confluence, about 32km [20 miles] distant, giving a fall of 19m [61ft.] per mile for the Po-Tsangpo. For the next few days the weather was gloriously clear, with ground frost at night and brilliant sunshine all day. We marched through pine forest to the junction of the Tongkyuk River with the Rong Chu, and on December 26th reached Tongkyuk, much to the relief of Dick and Sunny Jim, who were on the point of sending out a search party. They had arrived seventeen days before. Here the Walrus, Shock-headed Peter, and the other Gyala folk left us to return to their homes. Their route lay up the valley of the Rong Chu to our old base at Tumbatse, and over the Nyima La; they would be back in their homes long before we reached India. They had been with us six weeks, and we were sorry to part with them. But we rewarded them for their services, and they went their way well satisfied with their treatment.

Back to the Gyamda river via the Rong

We stayed one day to repack our things and prepare for the long journey across the plateau; and then on December 28th we started, leisurely following our route of August up the Tongkyuk Valley. However, we got no farther than Paka the first day, as we had a mind to explore the big valley which comes in here from the north, as far as the village of Lumo. The Tongkyuk River splits into two at this point, and we went up the left branch a couple of miles to the village, which is a large scattered settlement; our main caravan, however, crossed the river by the bridge just below Paka, continued up the right bank for a couple of miles, and crossed over to the left bank again above the junction of the Lumo stream, just as we had done in August.

There are no villages above Lumo, but there is a trail which leads over a pass into the Yigrong Valley, though it is said not to be used nowadays. At the head of the valley we could see the snow-peaks of the Salween divide. Crossing the stream by a bridge just above Lumo, we followed the right bank back to the junction and then turned up the main valley again, rejoining our party in camp at dusk, where the four-foot Primulas grew.

December 30th was a gorgeous day, and we made fair progress, though there was much ice on the road where streams had overflowed and refrozen, and several animals came a cropper. We did not attempt to reach the *gompa,* but camped in a meadow about half-way, after stopping to collect seed of the cobalt *Cyananthus wardii* (K.W. 6082). This little plant growing on the steep granite cliffs on the sunny side of the glen was scorched and shrivelled and almost lost in the khaki-coloured grass, but we found quite a number of plants which yielded a good packet of seed. The meadows, of course, had been cut down, and against every tree a scaffolding had been reared on which hay was drying.

The temperature fell to –10°C [+15°F] during the night, and the last day of the year dawned as fresh and clear as though there were no such things as clouds. Alas! Soon after we started a cold wind sprang up, the sky became overcast, and there came that unmistakable feeling of snow in the air. We soon reached the big moraine at the junction of the two glacier valleys, and could see a high snow-peak on the Salween divide quite near. At last we were within touch of that great range we had first seen from Tsela Dzong seven months earlier. But the pastures were now brown and dead, the herds had packed up their tents and gone down to warmer regions, and the wide flat valley looked most desolate and forlorn, though there was not much snow.

Early in the afternoon we reached the little *gompa,* long since deserted, and entered into possession. Our desire was to spend the following day here fixing some peaks on the Salween divide, completing the work from the Nambu La. However, it was not to be. That night it began to snow, and the storm continued with scarcely a break for fifty hours. All through January 1st we stayed in the cold draughty little house, huddled round a fire, and so through January 2nd. That night we learnt that food was running short. So we held a council of war and decided that if January 3rd was fine we would hang on till the 4th, but if it was cloudy, whether it snowed or not, we must move. It was necessary to cross the pass before it was blocked, which might happen any day now; if we could not cross the Nambu La, we should have to return to Tsela Dzong, lengthening the journey considerably and failing to complete our map.

Accordingly on January 3rd we abandoned the fixing of our snow-peaks. The sky looked as sulky as ever, though for the moment it had ceased to snow, when we left the cold gloomy *gompa* and trudged up to the pass. Here, as already related, I tried in vain to collect seed of two dwarf Rhododendrons which were buried beneath 1.5m [5ft.] of snow. We camped in a meadow on the west side, and awoke on January 4th to find it still snowing; but by the time we reached Lo it had ceased. Nevertheless, it was a cheerless march down the long valley that grey day, all the peaks still hidden behind lowering clouds surcharged with snow, and the bleak forest so glum and still under its white mantle. In one respect we were better off than in August; the boggy meadow was now frozen hard, and we could get along anywhere without fear of being suddenly engulfed. This time we were more warmly welcomed at Lo than we had been in August, owing to the astonishing fact that we had paid for our transport. Such a concession was to be encouraged by every possible means. Accordingly, two quite decent rooms in the best house were swept and garnished for us, which was just as well, since it was a miserable night, the wind whistling down the snowy valley.

Next day we reached the lake, and halted at Je. The villagers of Je have the distinction of being the only people who fled from us on sight, or when we stared at them in reprisal for their insensate curiosity. Nor were they very solicitous about our comfort, at first refusing even to give us a fire in our room (which was also a chapel), for fear of damaging the vestments. Finally we insisted. The lake, too, shared in the general gloom – a long narrow leaden strip of water stagnant at the bottom of a big snow clad depression. It had looked less aloof in August.

On January 6th we thought it really would be fine, but after a very half-hearted attempt to clear, it stayed thick, and we lost our last chance of seeing the Salween divide, though the needle peak of Namla Karpo just pricked the clouds. We reached the end of the lake in 2½ hours, passing the pretty island monastery of Tsosang; then, crossing the stream by a dangerous-looking bridge, we halted for lunch. In the afternoon we went on down the wide stony valley, where the snow had drifted patchily

Daphne sp. **(aff. *acutiloba*) near Trulung (Pylung).**   **PC**
Not one of the most desirable Daphne species, as it has little or no scent and rather small flowers, this species occurs at fairly low altitudes. This plant was found near the confluence between the Po-Tsangpo and the Rong Chu, at around 2500m (8,200ft.).

The bridge across the Rong Chu at Trulung (Pylung). **PC**
This is the suspension bridge over the Rong Chu, a few hundred metres above where it joins the Po-Tsangpo, below
Trulung. The path across this bridge leads to Gompo Ne in the Tsangpo Gorge. Ward and Cawdor followed part of this
route at the end of their explorations of the gorge. The present-day bridge is evidently larger than the one in Ward's
day: 'The rope bridge, which consists of two ropes, is fastened round boulders on either bank and raised up clear of the
water by means of wooden tripods. In the summer it is removed from here and fixed at a much higher level.'

but was fast melting, to Shoga Dzong, reached on January 7th.

Our intention was to travel from here to Atsa and so round to Gyamda, as we had done
in August in order to complete our map; but hearing that the pass was blocked, we
decided to go up the valley only as far as Pungkar, and then if the pass was still blocked,
to return to Shoga, and so to Gyamda by the main valley. Tom, who had purchased a wild
white horse with the idea of selling it in India for more than he gave for it, had been
badly shaken by a fall the previous day, so at his request we left him behind to recover.

The weather now turned fine and cold; the wind had a venomous bite in it, but the bogs
had dried up, and in spite of the short days, we were able to get over the frozen ground at
a fair pace. Travelling leisurely we reached Drukla on the first day, only to find the monastery
almost deserted. The Labrang Lama had been summoned to Lhasa, where he was doubtless
pleading for his life; sixty monks had been locked out for misdemeanour; and a few dejected
trapa who had barely escaped the same fate, hung about the courtyards seeing red, though
probably feeling a little blue. The church, in a bold endeavour to keep up its reputation for
hospitality, sent us a hunk of butter with what looked like a question mark engraved on it;
but thanks to the cold, it was so brittle that it splintered on being struck. As we marched up
the valley the weather grew very much colder. Everywhere the people had gone into winter
clothing – long sheepskin coats, fur caps, and top-boots; but gloves they had none. From the
cliffs on either side ice hung in long stalactites, which had become joined together as they
guttered in the warm midday sun. Large grey cranes stalked over the gravel banks by the
frozen river and hundreds of pigeons oscillated their heads on the fallow. Everything was in

the grip of a ruthless winter, and between blasts an ominous silence reigned, broken only by the occasional crack of ice as it choked the gurgling river, or the rustle of babblers amongst dead leaves under the bushes. At this season a cup of hot buttered tea, the more oleaginous the better, was welcome, and the Tibetans consumed large quantities.

In Tibet one sees vast numbers of stones on which prayers are neatly carved – particularly the national prayer, *'O mani padme hum.'* These are built up into regular pyramids or walls which stand in the middle of the path, that the priests and laymen may be able to walk round them with the hope always on his right hand. We had often wondered at the almost universal skill, as we supposed, in carving these prayers; for we believed that every passer-by had added his stone to the pile. And so no doubt he has – but he did not carve it himself. There are professional stone-masons who do the carving, and are engaged by the day to carve as many 'O manis' as can be done in the time. We saw one at work at Rinchengang; he had a pile of rounded water-worn stones in front of him, and having roughed one side, he cut out the formula with the point of a small iron chisel, driving it round in the desired direction by means of a hammer. He worked with great precision and at a rapid rate, so that we marvelled at his skill. Usually the prayer is just carved on the stone without any frills, sometimes plain, sometimes coloured; but in Kongbo we saw frequently a design like a lotus flower – such a thing as would pass for a lotus flower in a wall-paper design at any rate – with one word written on each of six petals arranged in a circle. The script used is commonly Tibetan, as printed. But one sometimes sees the ancient Hinid script, engraved on the outside of prayer drums particularly.

We had an instance of Tibetan honesty here. On our way to Atsa in the summer a tin of tea had been lost; and being very short at that time, we had sent a man back to look for it, without result. Another traveller passing that way some days later, picked it up and carried it to the nearest village, where it had been kept ever since. It was now restored to us intact. At Pungkar we were greeted by a large crowd, the people being anxious to see such prodigies. Had not Cawdor cured a sick man there? Of course others now disclosed ailments real or imaginary, but we thought it best to leave well alone; it was no good overdoing a thing. After taking observations for latitude at Pungkar and Drukla we returned to Shoga Dzong, where we arrived on the 13th. Tom was better, but a difficulty now arose over his pony which we could not take with us through Bhutan, the way we proposed to return. He therefore decided to leave us at Tsetang and return direct to his home in Darjeeling, via Gyantse. This we gave him permission to do, the more readily as he had lately been giving trouble over drink, to which he was addicted; when drunk he lost his memory.

On January 14th we started for Gyamda and marched down the narrow valley to Namse Gompa, situated on a cliff in the angle where the Pasum River joins the Gyamda River. The *gompa* is falling down – has been for years by the look of it, and a fund had been opened to repair it. We were shown a list of subscribers – many of the names had been written so long ago that they were no longer legible, but nothing has been done yet. However, we paid our subscription. From Namse we had an uneventful march up the valley to Gyamda, reached on January 18th.

Our friend the *Dzongpön* of Napo, who was expecting us this time, welcomed us warmly. First he gave us dilute tea, with milk and much sugar, Indian fashion, followed by a dinner with rich meat dumplings and raw spirit. A host of servants attended, one to pour out the tea, another to pour out the wine, a third to look after the fire, and so on. For breakfast we were given a dish of chopped carrots, turnips, and meat, which we supplemented out of our own resources. Just as we were finishing our meal a troupe of dancers arrived and asked leave to perform before us. We gave our permission, and a large crowd of sightseers collected in the courtyard. There were no less than twelve in the troupe, which included children and youths, maidens and men. The men wore flat kite-shaped spotted masks which gave them a grotesque appearance. There was also a band – drum and cymbals; the girls spun on their heels till they looked like scarlet and green tops; the boys threw cart-wheels; others sang. When we had paid for the entertainment, we went on our way.

This time we did not attempt to reach Gyamda in a day. Instead we crossed the river

Winter scene on the journey home. FKW

'Winter Scene. Great snowy range north of Tsangpo. Rhododendrons, Berberis. glacier and frozen lake.' This photograph was probably taken on 6 January 1925 on the journey home when they encountered heavy snowfall along the route. 'We reached the end of the lake in 2½ hours, passing the pretty island monastery of Tsosang; then, crossing the stream by a dangerous-looking bridge, we halted for lunch. In the afternoon we went on down the wide stony valley, where the snow had drifted patchily but was fast melting, to Shoga Dzong, reached on January 7th.'

by a temporary brushwood trestle bridge – of which we saw several, and reached a place called Pangkargang, where we spent the night. The river had fallen a lot now, and was nowhere more than 46-55m [50-60 yards] wide, and 90cm [3ft.] deep; the water was crystal clear and full of floating ice. Snow still lay in patches on the slope with northern aspect, and we had severe frosts each night. Luckily there was not much wind, and in the middle of the day we could sit in the sunshine and enjoy our lunch.

On the afternoon of the 18th we reached Gyamda, crossing the almost frozen river by a temporary bridge; work on the new cantilever bridge had not yet been begun. We had wretched quarters, but were much cheered by getting our letters from the Post Office, the first mail we had received for nearly four months.

CHAPTER XVII

Winter on the Plateau

Gyamda to Tsetang

As we had been unable to make the round trip from Shoga Dzong via Atsa to Gyamda, we had to content ourselves with two converging marches towards the Salween divide. That towards the Pasum Kye La, which ended at Pungkar, has already been referred to; from Gyamda we made another up the China road as far as Gogon Gompa, two marches short of the Tro La. Though it was comparatively warm in Gyamda, at least while the sun shone, it grew rapidly colder as we ascended the narrow valley, where the snow lay deep under the trees on the northern slope. We reached Saru after seven hours' marching on the evening of January 19th, and took an observation for latitude. That night the sheltered thermometer fell to -18°C [-1°F].

On the following day we reached our objective in three hours. Gogon Gompa crowns an almost sheer isolated crag 60m [200ft.] high in the angle between two streams, the smaller from the Tro La, the larger from Trigung; a wooden bridge spans the Tro La stream, which, however, was frozen solid. A little above Gogon tree growth ceases altogether, except for a few stunted junipers clinging madly to the cliffs, for the dry cold wind can desiccate as well as freeze. However, we were able to get a little firewood at Gogon, though we had to eke it out with yak dung; and glad we were of a smoking fire, even in the tiny cell where we slept and ate, unable to turn round, when the temperature fell to -15°C [+4° F]. It would have fallen much lower only the sky became overcast.

The Tro La was probably open or would be in a day or two, for we met some pilgrims who had recently crossed the pass, and the post runners were travelling. As a matter of fact the passes on this great highway from Lhasa to Peking are open all the year round save for temporary closures after a storm. At nightfall we looked down on the twinkling fires of a large yak caravan camped on the plain below, but early next morning they were gone. They had come from the Hopa country, a month's journey distant, on the northern confines of Kam, bringing salt, and were returning with *tsamba*. There is great

---

Above. *Meconopsis integrifolia* **on the Kongbo Pa La or Mangshun La.**　　　　　**KNEC**

The 'lampshade poppy' was re-introduced to the west in the 1980s and is once again a popular plant for alpine enthusiasts. After his explorations in Tibet in 1938 with Ludlow and Sherriff, Sir George Taylor took the courageous step of becoming a pioneer super-lumper in the taxonomy of Meconopsis. Chris Grey-Wilson recently resurrected some of the 'sunk' taxa, based on field observation and extensive herbarium work. This very high altitude form, at 4900m (16,100ft.), rather defies the geography of the Grey-Wilson taxonomy, as it occurs in Tibet rather than further east. This form has exceptionally narrow leaves and may acquire some taxonomic status of its own.

traffic between the northern plains and the southern valleys of Tibet. On the Chang Tang and around the headwaters of the Salween are many salt lakes, but the country is too bleak to grow even barley, and is inhabited chiefly by wandering pastoral tribes, who take their flocks up there in the summer. In the winter these folk bring down salt to the agricultural districts of South Central Tibet, in exchange for flour. Their flocks supply them with milk, butter, cheese, meat, and clothes; tea is imported from China.

However, we had no time to cross the Tro La, and on January 21st we turned south on our tracks again, reaching Gyamda on the 22nd. Considering the long bitter winter experienced in these valleys, it was heartening to see Rhododendrons sleeping peacefully on the snowbound side of the mountain. These particular species must be of a cast-iron hardiness, seeing that without any protection whatever, they have to face temperatures well below -18°C [zero Fahrenheit]. Other plants I noticed here were *Meconopsis racemosa* (a form of *M. horridula*), *Gentiana waltonii*, *Primula alpicola* [*microdonta*], Androsace, and *Incarvillea younghusbandii*. It is often easier to see a plant in fruit standing up like a lonely skeleton, than it is to see it in flower, smothered up amongst a host of others; but of course one must needs know well what it looks like when stripped for the winter fray.

We stayed at Gyamda over the 23rd to write our last mail, and on the 24th set out for Tsetang, following the Lhasa road. This branch of the river is larger than the Tro La branch, and the path, which keeps to the left bank, is not particularly good. It is easy to see that one is approaching the plateau; the spurs flatten out towards their summits, the country becomes undulating, the houses have flat mud roofs instead of the wooden pent house

Prayer flags on the Kongbo Pa La.   **KNEC**
In Tibet, wherever a road or path reaches the top of any mountain pass, a sight such as this greets the traveller. The prayer flags brought by pilgrims, truck drivers and passers by flutter and whirr as their inscriptions are borne away as prayers on the wind. Ward and Cawdor crossed this pass on their way home in early 1925.

Travelling minstrels.   FKW

roof of Kongbo, and granite replaces the slates and schists of the lower Gyamda Valley. After passing a small monastery and crossing two big streams which roll down from the grassland country in wide shallow valleys, we reached Chinda, and found ourselves amongst a people rather different from the Kongba, in dress at any rate; for though the women still varnished their faces till they shone like Cherry Blossom Boot Polish, yet they wore on their heads the butterfly net-shaped wooden ornament, bound with scarlet cloth and studded with semi-precious stones, as turquoise, which one sees in Lhasa itself.

After a bitter night we continued up the valley, presently crossing over to the right bank by a good bridge. It was a glorious sunny day. Hour after hour we marched. The sun went down, and immediately the great cold laid its grip on the valley. Darkness fell, and the velvet cloth of night was punctured by thousands of star holes. And still we marched on. I thought we never should reach a house – the valley seemed quite deserted now, and the chances of a house or a village grew more and more remote as the stream dwindled. Suddenly we heard a faint shout. Lights appeared. We skimmed over a bridge – the river was frozen solid – and were met by men who held aloft torches of rolled birch bark, which made a delicious sound like sizzling bacon. Five minutes later we were welcomed by a crowd of people at the tight little village of Numari, having covered 27km [17 miles]. That night the temperature fell to -21°C [- 6°F] under cover; yet there were bushes by the stream – *Potentilla fruticosa,* Berberis, Hippophae and the cast-iron Rhododendrons.

If our march of the 25th had been unpleasant, that of the 26th was purgatory. We started as usual in lovely weather, continued a couple of miles up the valley, and turned sharply, following up a steep glen towards the pass. Here we met the wind. The climb to the pass was long and arduous; and yet the frozen stream was lined with all kinds of what had once

Gyamda Valley above Gyamda. Lhasa – Peking Road. FKW

Kingdon Ward wrote: 'Thousands of ponies, mules, yak and donkeys in large caravans use the road annually'. The main motorable road from China to Lhasa still follows the Gyamda River. Today, trucks haul produce, lumber, and consumer goods along this commercial artery. Pilgrims to Lhasa travel the route as well, measuring the distance by prostrating their bodies in the swirl of dust from the passing traffic.

been alpine flowers. I saw Primulas, Iris, Meconopsis, Pedicularis, Morina, Polygonum, Saxifrage, Delphinium and several others; no doubt we had found them all in flower before – there is a certain monotony about the flowers on the plateau, and you may be quite certain of finding the same things over and over again. Still, in this hell of ice it was pleasant to think that flowers had bloomed some time and would do so again. At irregular intervals we passed Chinese mile-stones, but they told us little of the real distance, though it was said to be four days' journey, or 110 Chinese miles, from Numari to Lhasa.

In the middle of the afternoon we reached the summit of the Kongbo Pa La. The sky had clouded over and the wind was raising clouds of dust; but Cawdor managed to get a boiling-point observation on the pass. For the last 3km [2 miles] the stream was a solid glacier, having guttered and solidified over and over again; the valley, which was very stony, widened out to a mile here, and the summit was a small plateau, with low ranges of barren hills on each side. Soon after 3.30 we began to descend a forbidding valley and were met by frightful gusts of wind which hurled the gravel in our faces and forced us to take shelter. After a time we saw some high rocky snow-clad peaks to the south-east, in the direction of the Lung La, and probably on the Trans-Himalayan range. Just before dark we passed a post-house, and then for more than an hour picked our way over very rough ground by the growing stream to Tsumara, the most benighted, cold, and filthy village we had yet seen; though indeed we could see nothing now and were glad to tumble into a draughty room where the atmosphere was foul with the smoke of a yak-dung fire.

Morning revealed it in all its naked horror and squalor; not even the sunshine of a Tibetan winter could gild the foul hovels and black tents which were Tsumara. A small official with an armed escort, bound from Lhasa to Chamdo, arriving early in the afternoon, had taken possession of the only decent tenement in the block, which had

Clematis tibetana ssp. *vernayi* **near the Kongbo Pa La.**   **PC**
This very common and variable species occurs in quantity over much of south and eastern Tibet. Yellow, orange, brown and dark purple/black forms often grow together, but the yellow forms are the most common. Many are unfortunately rather shy flowering in cultivation, especially as young plants, but the black and blackcurrant-purple flowered forms would create a stir if they turned out to be good garden plants.

Clematis tibetana ssp. *vernayi* **near the Kongbo Pa La.**   **KNEC**
The familiar yellow form of this species growing in hedgerows between Lhasa and Gyamda. This species differs from the well-known *C. orientalis* in its more finely cut, more glaucous leaves and more thickly-textured flowers, though many cultivated plants in the *C. tanguitica-orientalis-tibetana* group are either incorrectly named or are hybrids between the species. According to Chris Grey-Wilson, the distribution of *C. tibetana* ssp. *tibetana* is confined to northern India.

actually been prepared in advance for us; and when we arrived after dark, he, being by that time in bed, refused to give it up, despite Tom's vehement expostulation. In the morning, however, he was worried and came to us bearing the white scarf of friendship and requesting an interview; whereupon he apologised for his discourtesy of the previous night, and begged that we would not report him. Nothing was to be gained by doing so; and having told him before his inferiors that we thought him a churl, we let it go at that, though our crest was somewhat fallen. We had indeed to be content with our moral victory, for nothing could blind us to the fact that he had scored off us. Rightly or wrongly he had refused to budge, and without making a scene we were unable to compel him.

The Government party, well mounted with rifles slung on their backs, now trotted off

Stellera chamaejasmae **on the Kongbo Pa La.**   **PC**
A common plant of the Himalaya and south-west China, this Daphne relative with scented flowers is found on barren, rocky or dry hillsides, where it is often the only large flowering plant. It can be successfully cultivated in a scree or alpine house but seldom gives anything approaching the magnificent displays seen in the wild. The Chinese forms are usually yellow while the Tibetan and Himalayan are typically pink in bud, opening to white.

Euphorbia wallichii **near Kongbo Gyamda.**   **KNEC**
One of the most spectacular of the Himalayan species of Euphorbia, in south-east Tibet this occurs on barren rocky hillsides where few other plants can survive. The caustic sap prevents grazing by animals, even omnivorous goats, ensuring spectacular displays. Named after Mr Wallich who was director of the Calcutta Botanic Garden during the first half of the 19th century. Many of the plants cultivated under this name are apparently wrongly identified.

The east side of the Kongbo Pa La (Mangshun La). **KNEC**
Kingdon Ward crossed this barren pass, approximately 5000m (16,400ft.) high, on the way back to Tsetang from Gyamda. He described the ascent as 'purgatory' due to the wind which blew in their faces. The pass and its approaches are covered with an interesting range of alpine plants including *Meconopsis integrifolia* and *Incarvillea younghusbandii*.

on their 645km [400 mile] journey to Chamdo; while we left the Lhasa road and crossing the frozen river, turned due south up a wide flat valley. We had not gone far when we met a grain caravan of several hundred yak, just preparing to camp in the brown pastures. It is their custom to start very early, and when they reach grass, to camp for the day in order to allow the animals to graze. These people had come all the way from the Hopa country, bringing salt to Oga Dzong, which is a distributing centre for grain.

The valley widened out and the sluggish wandering streams had formed wide shallow lakes, now covered with ice, on which our ponies slid and fell. It would have been difficult to tell where the actual pass – called the Kamba La – was, had it not been marked with a cairn. Southwards we rejoiced to see a group of glittering snow-peaks on the north bank of the Tsangpo, close to Oga Dzong; it was the Trans-Himalayan range, which we knew for the first of the three great barriers which still separated us from India. The plateau, with its long smooth roll, seems to spread out like the ocean into the *ewigkeit;* but once you catch sight of those great ragged escarpments thrust up through the even swell, you know that you are approaching the edge; the crust breaks here, and clambering over twisted girders, you drop swiftly down from the roof of the world to the fair gardens where men dwell. But the rim was far off yet.

We saw some gazelle scampering off across the dead pastures and later put up a fat hare and a covey of partridge; so the landscape was not as entirely lifeless as it looked. The descent towards the Tsangpo was gradual at first, but we had to go down much farther than we had come up and soon found ourselves in the usual deep gravelly trench, in which a few stunted bushes began to appear. We had hoped to reach Oga Dzong and had indeed been assured that we should do so; but darkness coming on when we were still some miles away, we turned aside from the stream and took shelter in a solitary house.

Resuming our march down the valley on January 28th, we presently reached the monastery of Dzinchi, which was as clean as a new pin. They had expected us here the previous evening, so we halted and drank milk with the monks. Below Dzinchi the valley is well cultivated and there are several villages. We reached Oga Dzong in an hour, and found crowds waiting to welcome and stare at us. However, we found good quarters and a wood fire, and the night being clear were able to get an observation for latitude. The newly appointed *Dzongpön* called on us and promised us transport for next day, we being still three days' journey from Tsetang.

After our half-day's rest we continued the march, crossing the Kamba La stream by a bridge and slanting up the dry hillside to a low pass, whence we had a good view up the valley towards the Lung La; also we could see glaciers on the high peaks between Oga Dzong and Trap. Descending a funnel-shaped valley, we soon joined another stream from the north and changed transport at a village. This stream joins the Oga Dzong stream a little lower down and the combined river flows into the Tsangpo above Trap. Crossing this second stream, we again started up the mountain to a low pass and here we caught the full force of the wind. In a flying fog of grit, which rasped and stung our faces, we descended to the Tsangpo. So thick was the air here that sometimes we could not see across the river; its surface was flogged into waves by the dusty gale. We noticed that the river was higher and swifter than in April and the water more muddy.

After a tiring march in the very teeth of the wind, blinded and choked by the dust, we halted at a miserable hut. At nightfall the wind ceased abruptly and it was so still we could hear the brash ice clinking against the shore. But the fine dust cloud hung over the valley till morning and the setting moon peered redly through. Two days more we marched up the valley. By daylight the fine cloud of dust had sunk down and the sun, leaping up over the mountains, flashed its serene rays into the harsh valley. The sky was like a blue-tiled dome. It was warm and peaceful. Suddenly, without warning the wind roused itself and blew steadily and with ever-growing fury, till nightfall. It was weary work tramping over the endless sand-dunes, with the dust penetrating everywhere; by evening we felt stony all over, like a Saxifrage. The curious thing was that the wind always blew down the valley, never up. In the spring it was just the reverse.

Tsetang to Tsöna

Passing several monasteries and a large *dzong,* dust-coloured like the cliff against which it was built, we reached the ferry opposite Tsetang on January 31st, and crossed over in a barge whose bow-post was carved into the likeness of a horse's head, giving a Viking touch to the craft; but it was scarcely as swift. This was the first barrier. After the villages we had been accustomed to, Tsetang with its chortens and monasteries and houses seemed a most imposing place. It was teeming with life and trade, donkey caravans coming and going, oxen, mules, ponies and yak passing to and fro, herds of goats skipping and butting, and other signs of enthusiasm. But it suffered from the same devastating wind and powder as places farther down the valley.

We were met and fed by Atta Ulla Khan, the Ladaki trader, who, hearing of our approach, had secured rooms for us. The town was very full, as brisk business was being transacted. Atta Ulla Khan sent his son down to the willow marshes with his gun where there were thousands of birds – geese, yellow duck, mallard, teal and cranes, as well as crows, magpies and sparrows; and he returned with two fat geese, which we were to take with us on the road.

Already, after over ten months' travel, we saw ourselves in India. The worst of the journey was over – or so we thought. From Tsetang we had only to turn due south, and cross the Himalaya, and in ten days, or in a fortnight at the most, we should be in India. Happy thought! As a matter of cold fact, it took us more than three weeks to reach India. Making good marches we had done the journey from Gyamda to Tsetang in eight days, and had we not halted for half a day at Oga, might well have done it in a week. We had been enabled to do this partly because, marching westwards since leaving Tongkyuk, we had gained a little on the clock each day and thereby saved daylight – at least so long as we always started at the same hour. But from Tsetang southwards we began to lose way; and though we reached Tsöna Dzong in a week, after that we had to take things leisurely.

It was pleasant to be back by the great river, and away from the raving winds which sweep over the plateau; and to see trees again, poplar, willow and elm, row on row; most of them were standing in water now, left by the summer floods. But it was bleak enough even here, with the heavy blanket of dust lying over the valley towards the Holy City, and the bare trees and naked rocks; even sunshine and blue sky cannot, in winter, breathe life into these dead bones; for, after all, the Tsangpo Valley here is only a shallow trough in the great plateau, and Tsetang itself is nearly 3,700m [12,000ft.] above sea-level.

Atta Ulla Khan tried to persuade us to rest a day in Tsetang to see the bazaar; but we were keen to get back to India without wasting a day more than was necessary. Nor did we altogether fancy the prospect of crossing the Himalaya in the depth of winter; the sooner that ordeal was over the better we should be pleased. So on February 1st, having procured fresh transport, we started, the Ladaki riding with us as far as Netong Dzong, where he said good-bye. Tom also left us here, to return direct to Darjeeling by the way we had come, and Dick was promoted in his stead. Our road lay up the wide Yarlung Valley, which diverges from the valley by which we had approached Tsetang in April at Netong. Wide and stony, with only a small stream flowing through it, the Yarlung Valley is nevertheless well cultivated and, for Tibet, quite thickly populated. We passed through numerous villages, and saw a number of small but neat monasteries, perched on cliffs or hidden away in glens. These flat stony valleys, whose width is out of all proportion to the stream, seem to be the natural result of a climate which forbids tree growth. Every brook which comes tumbling down the mountain side opens a cavernous wound in the flank of the main valley. There is nothing to hold up the soil, or to shore up the sliding hills, which during the brief but heavy rains of summer deliquesce like sugar. The only woody plants we saw were small brushes of Hippophae and Buddleia by the stream and in the villages clumps of poplar and willow.

The houses are small, low cubes with flat roofs made of slabs of schist or slate laid on a foundation of wooden sticks which in turn are supported by the main beams. There is a low coping all round the roof with a small tower at each corner. The outer wall is usually whitewashed. Earthenware pots are much used in these parts. The fire is made

Iris lactea near the Yartö Tra La.   **KNEC**
Typically found along the edge of water courses, this attractive pale blue or pale mauve iris is widely distributed through the Himalaya and central Asia. These plants were growing near a village between Tsetang and Sanga Cholung, not far from the Yartö Tra La.

Chionocharis hookeri with *Meconopsis integrifolia*.   **KNEC**
With the dwarf form of the yellow M. integrifolia growing next to it, the outstanding blue-flowered alpine *Chionocharis* is a favourite of all who see it. It occurs on the tops of desolate and windswept passes, bursting into flower in June. There are few records of its successful cultivation, but a gritty soil similar to the one shown here would be essential. In *Assam Adventure* Kingdon Ward brings his fine powers of description to bear on this plant: 'one of the most heavenly of the Himalayan plants…each rug-headed cushion encrusted with large turquoise-blue jewels shimmering like stars in the lilac dust. These cushions grow very slowly. I think many of them must have been a century old'.

Meconopsis horridula on a pass between Tsetang and Sanga Cholung.
                                                                         KNEC
Photographed on a pass south of the Yartö Tra La, this is a wonderful deep blue form of a very widespread and variable monocarpic species which occurs all over the Sino-Himalayan region. Sir George Taylor placed a number of species in synonymy with M. horridula. These include M. prainiana, M. prattii, and M. racemosa, which Kingdon Ward treats as separate species in this book. Quite widely cultivated, though few forms match the intensity of colour of this very fine selection.

in one, grain kept in another, water drawn from a third; some of them have spouts and handles, some have perforated bottoms, some are just pots.

Making short marches, we slept the night of February 2nd at a village called Nyamoshung, and on the 3rd faced the Yartö Tra La, which crosses the Trans-Himalayan range at an altitude of 5060m [16,700ft.]. It was a long toil up to the pass, and though there was very little snow, thanks to the dryness of the climate, frozen streams sprawled and spread across the steep track, rendering it very treacherous. At the summit we came out on to a wide saddle, floored with turf; to the west rises a cluster of rock and snow-peaks, on which we observed several glaciers. Up a glen we noticed a small stone village, almost invisible against the boulders, but said to be inhabited all the year round; as it is well over 4,900m [16,000ft.], this is truly remarkable. There is a hot spring hard by; and indeed such a concession would be necessary.

From the tip-top of the pass, we gazed eastwards over a bare and gloomy scene. It was 5 o'clock on a grey February evening; nothing was visible but wide earth plains, chequered with tufts of coarse grass, and beyond that the jagged rim of snow-striped mountains; an icy wind snored over the bare gravel. There was no comfort in such a view, except the thought that somewhere out beyond the farthest mountain rim the spurs flared away to the plains of Hindustan, where flowers bloomed. Descending by a vile and ice-glazed path, we turned south again, keeping now along the foot of a lofty snow range, which divided us from the basin of the Trigu Tso, a large unexplored lake to the west. We were ourselves on unknown ground, but it was getting dark, and soon we could hardly see where we were going. We continued to march in glum silence, too tired to do more than tramp steadily on, and much too cold to ride our ponies. Daylight dwindled to dusk and dusk swiftly hardened to night. The wind still sobbed and moaned through the empty valleys and a pale moon occasionally shone through a rift in the flying clouds. But there was no sign of habitation. An hour passed. No sign yet. Two of the men lagged behind and I with them; we could hear the caravan crunching over the gravel ahead and sometimes see them against the sky as they topped a rise. Another hour passed. Suddenly a dog began to bay long and loud. 'At last!' I thought, much relieved. But nothing happened; we just went on and the baying of the dog, which came from a herd's tent, died away in the distance. By this time the caravan was swallowed up in the gloom, but we did not hasten; I felt sure that we should presently come up with them at a house.

We continued to ascend gradually, the plateau opening out in every direction, the mountains receding. We saw the red glow of a fire not far away, and again I thought we had reached our destination; but again it proved to be nothing but a herd's tent – there were yak snorting and grunting all round us now. At last we saw a house silhouetted against the sky and the men went forward joyfully shouting. A voice answered them – alas! the caravan was not there, it had gone on! The cold was sending me off to sleep and it was all I could do to stumble along; but the men said it was quite near now and that we had not stopped at the first house, because it was quite full. So we went on again and gradually, in the darkness, went right off our course. The wind now mercifully began to draw breath, the clouds were already blown to shreds, and the stars glittered like gems. We found ourselves in the midst of a vast, featureless, undulating plain, surrounded by low hills which gradually receded as we tried to approach them. Round and round we wandered looking for a trail and shouting; but to no purpose. We separated, and searched in every direction; but could not find a trail on that iron ground. We were lost on the plateau at 4600m [15,000ft.], on a winter's night.

At last, after two hours, we heard a faint cry. Whooping with joy we went after it – lost it – followed it again in another direction, like a will-o'-the-wisp, and again heard it. Next minute a man holding a torch appeared over the skyline not a quarter of a mile away. We followed him to a small stone house, hidden by a fold in the ground, and there found the rest of our party. It was 10 o'clock, and we were very cold, tired, and hungry. I could not, however, help feeling sorry for the yak and ponies; though it must have been -15°F [-26°C], they spent the night in the open yard. As for us, we had a yak-dung fire which filled the small room with vitriolic smoke ; but at least we kept warm. The place is called Tating, and consists of two stone houses, or two blocks of houses, about half a mile apart, and a few scattered tents; the altitude is over 4600m [15,000ft.]. It may be imagined that in such a place, in such a climate, cleanliness is not next to godliness. The people, muffled up in their sheepskins, are simply black. Hands and face alone are visible; but they must be nearly the same all over, only their teeth are ivory white from constant chewing of *tsamba*.

February 4th was a typical winter day on the plateau – brilliantly fine, the most distant peaks being clearly visible in the crystal atmosphere, with a knife-edge wind blowing. Immediately to the west rose two high snowy peaks, rising far above the general level of the surrounding hills. Then away to the north-north-east, in the direction of Largharyi, was another group of snow-peaks, and between these two groups is a wide gap, where the Yartö Tra La crosses the range. Far to the south we could see a long range of snow-clad mountains, the Great Himalayan range itself. Our route lay almost due south over some low gravel hills, and after a few miles we reached the highest point, the Kale La, and plunged rather steeply down into an arid valley. This ridge we had just crossed separates the streams which flow to the Largharyi River and thence to the Tsangpo, from those which flow to the Subansiri, whose head-streams we reached next day; so we were over the second barrier. Presently we came to ruins – stone walls and towers, more or less completely demolished – and still lower down to villages. At no very late hour we halted at a village called Dengshu; for a terrific wind was blowing which we found ourselves unable to face any longer. Indeed, I myself was feeling so unwell that I went straight to bed and quickly passed into a vivid stupor, throughout which my mind remained very active, though I was scarcely conscious; and so to sleep. Next day I was all right again.

Continuing down the glen, we soon entered a wide bare valley, with a stream flowing from west to east. This is called the Sikung Chu and is one of the head-water streams of the Subansiri. There was a good deal of cultivation here and we saw several villages, at one of which we halted to change transport. However, having travelled a few miles eastwards, we turned south again up a side valley, just as the wind began to blow with amazing violence. What with the force of the wind, which exploded in devastating gusts, and the flying grit, we could hardly face it and were glad to halt an hour later at Simbi.

We were warned to start early next day, as we had a long march before us, with a great range to cross; and after noon the wind would get up and rage with its usual violence till nightfall. It is this wind which makes life on the plateau for any considerable period at high altitudes so unbearable. It has a cumulative nervous effect; possibly its action is electrical, due to the constant friction of dry air. I do not know. I only know that it is slow torture; you are waging a losing fight all the time, up against something which gradually, but no less surely and ruthlessly beats you. It makes no terms; it is war *à l'outrance*.

In spite of the warning, we were too tired to start before 9. It was, as usual, a brilliantly clear morning. No stir in the air; the sun shone almost warmly; it looked as though it never could be anything but calm and peaceful – yet we had experienced the rage of the wind only a few hours before. We now left the caravan to look after itself, which of course it was well able to do, and with our guide trotted up the valley as fast as our slow-motion screws would travel. Continuing westwards for a short distance, we soon reached the junction of two streams and turned southwards again up the smaller branch, between barren mountains of black slate, studded with garnets. The stream was choked with ice and about 10 o'clock we saw a curious sight; for the hot sun had by this time melted an ice-jamb higher up, and a regular spate of water loaded with brash ice came roaring down the channel, sweeping all before it.

Painful as travel on the plateau was at this season, from our point of view, it is just the time when the Tibetans, freed from work in the fields or amongst their flocks, choose to travel, and we met several yak caravans, transporting timber from the south. But the Tibetans are wise. They travel by night when there is a moon and on into the golden morning sunshine. Before midday everything is snug in camp. The sacks of salt or flour are built into a square, the flimsy tent pitched within, and the dung fire, smoking and giving out its intense heat, is burning well. As for the yak, they wander over the plain nibbling at the scanty herbage, indifferent to wind and snow. About noon we halted under a rock and made some hot soup to brace us for the coming struggle; the wind was rising now, and this was the last shelter we should get.

The climb to the Debshi La was neither long nor difficult; but no sooner were we on the wide saddle than the wind met us full face, almost hurling us backwards. Immediately to the west rose a high snow-clad range, and as we began to descend towards the frozen Nera Yu Tso, we came into our first serious contact with the snow since leaving the Nam La in November. Marching along the lake shore for a couple of miles, we left the basin by a dry valley at its southern end; apparently no water was flowing from the lake, though it no doubt overflows here in the summer, unless indeed all the drainage is underground. But the lake, like others we had seen, is obviously shrinking, and may have shrunk below the level of its exit. The fact is, it was now snowing so heavily we could hardly see where we were going, let alone the finer points of the landscape. After riding several miles down a narrow stony glen, we came at 5 o'clock to a solitary house, glorified by a name all to itself. This was Dengshu; and a more wretched place to spend an arctic night it would be difficult to imagine. The wind fairly whistled through our cramped quarters in the passage, and no curtain would keep it out; through holes in the roof we saw the sky. The fire gave out volumes of acrid smoke, but no heat; cockerels perched on sooty beams over our heads and crowed; mules scraped and champed and pawed under them. The caravan arrived three hours after we did, and late that night we got a meal. Before turning in I went out into the yard to see the animals. Poor brutes! The wind had died down, the clouds had disappeared, the stars blazed in a clear velvet sky, and the cold of infinite space lay over the frozen, silent earth. And they stood there with their saddles still on, patiently chewing straw!

We passed an unpleasant night; the morrow would see the hardest march of all, wind and snow; but it would also see us at Tsöna Dzong, the last mile-post on the Tibetan Plateau. We arose stiff, tired, and cold on the morning of February 7th, and it was nearly 10 o'clock before we started. Immediately below Dengshu the valley widens out, and there was a stony lake-bed here, almost dry. The lake exit lay to the south-south-east, but we turned west again up a smaller valley, while the wind began to caress us with the edged touch of a razor-blade. Right above us towered a group of snow-peaks, whose short steep snowfields were truncated in walls of blue ice. We marched up the valley over deep snow, parallel to this range; there was a frozen crust on the surface, but this would bear no weight and we were soon in difficulties, sinking to our knees at each step.

We reached the summit of the Torgor La in less than four hours, and the view which greeted us was certainly one to appal us, in our present state of weariness. A wide desolate plain, over which the wind raged unceasingly; barriers of harsh mountains in every direction; and over all, filling every valley, hiding every rock, a deep pall of snow. As far as the eye could see, there was nothing but this white wilderness, with clouds like cauliflowers foaming up over the mountain ranges. What this meant we were soon to learn, for the wind was driving the surface snow before it in clouds, and it was like powdered glass. It stung; it cut; it rasped. The cold was almost unbearable, and my eyes streamed with water, and I could not read the compass bearings; but Cawdor managed to do so. For three hours we ploughed our way through the snow, gradually descending, till we climbed again to a low col, the Torgor La; and there far below in a bare little valley, lay Tsöna Dzong, snow-bound like everything else. We descended as fast as we could; but it was a weary trudge across the frozen marshes, past the hot sulphur spring, and the *dzong,* and the first clump of houses, to the residential quarter by the monastery. Luckily the transport was not far behind, for we had had nothing to eat since breakfast, and it was now 6 o'clock. But we found a comfortable room, and there was a wood fire, and hot buttered tea prepared by a friendly host. Above all was the pleasurable thought that in another two or three days we should be out of these terrifying winds, if not out of the snow, in the shelter of the forest.

CHAPTER XVIII

Through Bhutan to India

Tsöna to the Bhutan border

Tsöna may be a health resort in the summer, but it was now obviously more suitable as a centre for winter sports. The whole desolate valley slept under a deep carpet of snow, and in the village itself there seemed to be no life or movement. That, however, was deceptive. Caravans still come and go, for trade is brisk all through the long winter. For the moment the pass to Tawang was blocked and there was a lull until the yak could stamp a trail over it, that was all. An attempt had just been made in fact, but the snow was too deep, and it would be necessary to wait a few days. We therefore had to abandon the idea of going to Tawang, and decided to cross the Pö La, which is 300m [1,000ft.] lower, immediately. The *Dzongpön's* manager called, bringing us a little frozen mutton and some suspicious-looking eggs, and suggested that we wait a few days till the next yak caravan came in. But we said that we could not wait more than a day (we grudged even that), and eventually hired mules and ponies from the monastery. The people with whom we put up were engaged in the rice trade. They called themselves Government contractors and imported rice from India, which they sent on to Lhasa.

Our object all sublime now was to reach India with the least possible delay, so it can easily be imagined how that idle day dragged. The morning was brilliantly fine, but in the afternoon the usual high-velocity gale, blowing over the passes, brought up fresh snow. Still, we were better off than we had been for some time, because wood is not unknown in Tsöna, and we had a real fire. The altitude, the wind, and the cold of the last five weeks had left their mark on us. We were tired. We had lost 'that schoolgirl complexion' – and, indeed, each of us had been frost-bitten on the tip of the nose. Our eyes were sore and bloodshot from the ever-flying dust. We yearned for a change of diet. And in the evening came the authorities once more to say that they could not give us transport on the morrow! However, after further appeal from Dick, the monks decided that the thing could be done, and we turned in, feeling that we had seen the last of Tibet for some time.

February 9th was a great day. We rose early and packed. The animals came into the yard two by two, and for a long time we thought we never should get away. In the end everything went according to plan, and we started up the sparkling valley, where crowds had collected to see us off. It was only about 8km [5 miles] to the pass, with an ascent of some 750m [2,500ft.], but the snow got deeper and deeper, and the march proved troublesome, especially as we had started so late that the wind began before we reached the top. However, we reached the Pö La 4500m [14,900ft.] early in the afternoon, and what a sight greeted our tired eyes!

Behind us the dead plateau, wrapped in its dazzling white shroud, stretched out its frozen limbs to the pale porcelain mountains, all frothy with cloud. Except for the moaning wind and the swish of the driven snow blast, complete silence reigned. There was no tinkle of water, no song of birds, not even the flutter of a leaf; everything was dead, or fast asleep, or gone abroad for the winter. In front of us, the mountain dropped away steeply to the valley, the snow ceased abruptly, and the dark mysterious forests on the southern slopes of the Himalaya began! A caravan was toiling up to the pass; but we raced down anxious to see the forest again, and soon found several kinds of Rhododendron, including *R. primuliforum*, *R. phaeochrysum* and a bronze-leafed *R. arboreum*. The descent grew steeper and steeper, clearly a glacier had once forced its way through this glen; and suddenly we found ourselves in the valley of the Nyamjang Chu, which flows from the north. Perched on a shoulder 300m [1,000ft.] above the river was a small village, and here we halted. We were over the third barrier, the Himalaya, in

Mönyul, the land of the Mönbas; the last pass lay behind us! All that night it snowed, and when we awoke next morning the world looked like a Christmas card; but we had only to go down, down, down, steadily towards the fertile plains, and by evening we were out of the snow for ever.

For transport we had forty-five Mönbas, men, women, and girls; or sometimes a few yak, which can live in the upper valley, though not lower down. The path is fairly good, but too steep to ride a pony in comfort, and there are endless flights of stone steps. We therefore walked the rest of the way to India. First, we descended to the river, which is a beautifully clear stream, its steep banks thickly clothed with over hanging trees. Towering cliffs rise now on one side, now on the other, and the road dodges from bank to bank. Many of the bridges had, however, been carried away by the floods of 1924, though in some cases temporary ones have been substituted, and lower down the valley we met a whole gang of men and women rebuilding a damaged bridge. These bridges are stoutly built of timber with stone piers and revetments. The footway rests directly on the piers, and is further strengthened by struts at each end, built on the cantilever principle, and embedded in the revetment.

The Mönba porters who carried for us were a cheerful, friendly and picturesque crowd. They were somewhat quaintly dressed in thick dark red woollen clothes, with long boots to match, and wore wigs, sometimes yellow, sometimes black or brown; but these were more in the nature of a protection for their hair while carrying, like the sack a coal-heaver puts over his head, than real wigs; they had perfectly good hair underneath. The women decorate themselves lavishly. Bead necklaces, silver charm boxes, and lumps of pale amber hang round their necks; and from a knob of turquoise stuck in the ear depends a string of scarlet beads. Their houses are of stone, high and narrow, with wooden penthouse roof.

As we descended, the forest changed rapidly from pure Conifer forest to mixed forest with many species of Rhododendron. Thickets of the bushy *R. maddeni* covered the rocks by the river, and the slopes above were covered with *R. arboreum, R. triflorum, R. cinnabarinum* and *R. lepidotum*. But on February 11th the change was even more noticeable, for on that day we began to see flowers again. Clematis, Daphne and Barberry were all in bloom, and presently we found the blood-red *R. arboreum*. But on the whole the vegetation was not very unlike what we had seen in the upper part of the Tsangpo gorge. That afternoon we reached a more open part of the valley, where the stream, after flowing placidly through a wide flat meadow, plunged headlong over a rocky barrage into the glen below. Once upon a time a glacier had ploughed its way down the valley to this point; there was the terminal moraine it had left behind in its retreat, as well as the wide basin it had scooped out. All round us were lofty cliffs, above which rose the snowbound mountains; and perched on the rocks, or plastered against the walls or jammed into crevices high up, were scores of stone houses. This was Pangchen. We, however, slept in a bamboo hut in the meadow, where ponies grazed; in the summer this meadow is a lake.

Below Pangchen the sharp water has been able to cut a deep and steep-sided bed for itself. For a short distance the forest is almost tropical, with many orchids hanging from the trees. Then suddenly, without rhyme or reason apparently, everything – climate, scenery, flora – changes. The river rushes into a gorge, great overlapping spurs jut out alternately right and left, the slopes grow dry and bare-looking, with rock and grass and bracken, but few trees, and, crossing over to the left bank, we had to climb steeply some 360m [1,200ft.] by a back-aching path, to the next village. A subtle change had come over the people also; they dressed differently, and had rather different features, though the high narrow stone houses clinging tightly to the shoulders of the spurs, were much the same. But a new type of house was at least equally conspicuous, namely the bamboo house, with its bent mat roof. We spent a night in just such a hut, and because it rained we got thoroughly wet, which gave us but a poor opinion of the local Nissen hut.

Sub-tropical crops flourished here, the slopes being neatly terraced for rice and maize; but just now the fields were green with spring wheat. Bananas, pumpkins, and best of all, orange trees also make their appearance, and we were able to get the most refreshing fruit. Everywhere on the steep, dry, rocky slopes, amongst thin woods of oak and pine, glowed red-hot trees of *Rhododendron arboreum,* and for the next week's march, until we were within a few miles of the Indian frontier, this was the most vivid and virile colour in the valley. After a day's march high up on the left bank of the river, where we saw many stone and bamboo villages, we plunged down hundreds of feet, and crossed back to the right bank. The bridge shared in the change which had come over the valley and its fittings. No longer was it of the rigid cantilever type, but a flimsy thing made of twisted creepers, like a hammock, floored with bamboo matting. There was still no room to pass by the river, so we had to climb again to the level of a more ancient valley, where the slope eased off.

Back to India

We now learnt that on the following day we should cross the Tibetan frontier into Bhutan, and as we carried no passport for that State, we wondered what our reception would be. What surprised us was that we could get no information as to how far it was to railhead, or even to a cart road, or to the Indian frontier. Yet this road is used a good deal, and we met many travellers returning to Tibet, some of them driving sheep, which carried small packs on their backs. These trotting flocks of transport sheep, complete with harness, carrying a bag on each side, looked very odd. On February 14th we crossed the frontier and presently reached the first Bhutanese village, only to find it almost deserted. However, we persuaded our coolies to go on as far as the next one, where we arrived at 3 o'clock on a hot sunny afternoon, the first fine day we had had since crossing the Pö La. Opposite this point the Tawang River joins the Nyamjang Chu.

It now became necessary to declare ourselves to the Customs Authorities, so Dick went off to see the official, bearing a scarf of greeting, and presents, and honeyed words. He returned saying that all was well. Two letters were written and stamped with the official seal; one to the *Dzong* of Trashigang, who is the most powerful man in the valley; the other 'to all whom it may concern,' to be carried by us, and used whenever we required to levy transport. In fact, every one helped us, including a Bhutanese soldier who, some years previously, had been one of Lord Ronaldshay's escort when he was travelling in Bhutan; and our safe conduct through the country was arranged for in the course of an afternoon's amicable chat.

We were now informed that in six days we should reach the plains, and a road by which bullock carts travelled to railhead. The fact that it actually took us nine days was due, not so much to misinformation, as to unforeseen delays. On the following day, which was fine and hot, we were due to reach Trashigang Dzong. We started down the hill, crossed a stream by a good wooden bridge, and found ourselves by the Nyamjang Chu again, now quite a big river. Shortly after, we reached cultivated fields, and halted for lunch, but the village was away up the mountain out of sight. A fresh relay of porters was due to meet us here, but there was no sign of them. However, thinking that the transport would presently follow, as it usually did, I strolled on ahead to botanize. An hour passed, and another. I found several interesting orchids on the trees by the river, and went on very slowly. Still no sign of the transport, and I began to realize that something had gone wrong. Still, it hardly seemed worth while going back now; they would be sure to come presently and, anyhow, Cawdor was in charge of them, with Dick and Sunny Jim to assist; so on I went. Some distance ahead, perched aloft on a high spur across the river, very white against the iron grey sky, stood a fort. 'Trashigang,' I thought to myself, and set out to reach it. Trashigang was the last place shown on our large-scale map on the road to India, and therefore a very vital landmark to us.

Dusk fell swiftly and was succeeded by a peculiarly dark night. Suddenly there loomed up quite close to me the towers of a great bridge spanning the gorge, and I found the road barred by a wooden barricade. Hammering on the door, I was admitted by a surprised-looking youth, and climbing some stairs in the guard tower of the

Trashigang Dzong, Bhutan. FKW

bridge, entered a small room. Several coolies were just settling down for the night, and I was obviously not popular. However, they had to put up with me, and having tried to extract information from me in several unfamiliar tongues, they relapsed into watchful waiting. As for me, I proceeded to make myself as comfortable as my foodless and bedless situation would permit; the caravan, I decided, would not arrive till morning, and the best thing to do in the meantime was to go to sleep. However, I had underrated Cawdor's resolution. I had barely fallen into a doze on the hard wooden floor when I heard a faint shout, followed by a series of whistles; some one was banging on the guard door. Seizing a brand from the fire, I went down the ladder and opened the gate. A crowd of men stood outside, and by the fitful glare of torches, in filed a dozen coolies, and Sunny Jim, under the leadership of Cawdor. The latter was so relieved to see me that, despite the provocation he had received, he kept his thoughts about my desertion to himself, and merely said that, not knowing what had become of me, he thought it prudent to push on to the bridge with what coolies he could impress; where he arrived at 11 o'clock at night. Cawdor was like that. While we were settling into the tower he told me the story.

The first lot of coolies had refused to budge from the place where we had halted for lunch; on the other hand, they had not just dumped their loads and fled, which, as it turned out, was considerate of them. Meanwhile, Dick had gone up to the village and flushed a few coolies whom he had driven down; and between them they managed to persuade about a dozen of the other lot to go on. Having wasted five hours at this spot – it was now 6 o'clock, – they finally got under way, though several boxes had to be left behind. By this time it was already nearly dark, and after marching for two hours, half the coolies dumped their loads, pointedly lit a fire, and refused to budge till morning. Dick was therefore told off to stand by, while Cawdor and Sunny Jim, by means of threats, cajolery and other arts, persuaded the remainder to go on as far as the bridge. Strangely enough, it was the old gang, who had been carrying for us all the morning, and on whom we had no real claim, who came on; nor did we forget that when we paid them.

The coolies in the tower who, seeing me on foot and without attendants, had probably taken me for an escaped lunatic, and not worthy of attention, now bustled about, sweeping another room, lighting a fire and carrying boxes; while Sunny Jim damned them in heaps for not looking after me. After a cup of cocoa we got to bed about midnight and were abroad late next morning; indeed, while we were at breakfast (which was skimpy, because the rations had not come on), Dick rolled up with the balance of the coolies. So we had another breakfast. Meanwhile, standing under the tower across the bridge we saw two fine mules, handsomely caparisoned, in charge of an Indian *sais.*

After crossing the bridge we found that the mules had been sent down by the *Dzongpön* for us, and as the *dzong* was about 300m [1,000ft.] up the cliff, we were very glad to ride. Arrived in the great courtyard, where crowds had collected to see us, we were welcomed by the old white-bearded *Dzongpön,* who asked us to stay the day. Anxious though we were to push on, it would have been churlish to refuse such an invitation, and we were shown to charming quarters. Meanwhile, all our heavy baggage was sent on ahead, so that we could start early next morning. Trashigang Dzong, which is half fort and half monastery, straddles the extreme end of a narrow spur, whence you can look straight down 300m [1,000ft.] on to the toy bridge below. The bridge itself is the most wonderful thing we saw in Bhutan. It is of the hammock type, supported by four chains, whose links are 45cm [8in.] long; these are fastened to baulks of timber which are built into the towers. The footway is of bamboo matting, so that ponies can cross, and on each side there is a hand-rail made of four cane cables. The masonry towers are about 12m [40ft.] high, and as the bridge is 55m [60 yards] long and stands quite 15m [50ft.] above the river, it can easily be imagined what an imposing object it is.

We found several curious characters at Trashigang, including two Indian coolies. One of them claimed to have been a sepoy, but was not very convincing, and both of them had probably fled the country under urgent necessity. There was also a Bhutanese youth who had been to school at Darjeeling and spoke English quite well. He was, in fact, just starting back there to take some examination and was asked to accompany us as interpreter, an arrangement which pleased us well. The Bhutanese struck us as rather different from the Mönbas. They are a short, sturdy, round-faced people, with merry expression and bobbed hair. The women wear a long striped skirt, so tightly bound round their waists as to hobble them, and an equally tight longsleeved blue jacket. Less pleasant is their habit of chewing betel-nut. For some days now we had been able to march in 'shorts,' but at Trashigang we found the blood-blister flies very active, and our bare knees suffered badly. We were told that we should reach the plains in five days, for which I was thankful, as the mica schists of Mönyul had cut what remained of my boots to ribbons, and I was almost marching in bare feet; but it took us seven days.

On February 17th we started off again, the *Dzongpön,* to whom we had presented our excellent camp-table, lending us mules to ride. The road was surprisingly good, and we met a good deal of traffic making for Tawang. For the next four days our road lay south-east, diverging gradually from the valley of the Nyamjang Chu, and crossing a series of high spurs separated by deep glens, which discharged streams into the main river. We saw no villages, partly because the weather was dull, with low visibility, and partly because there were none, at least near our route. We slept in our tents or in bamboo shelters which we found at the end of each stage; and though we made slow progress on account of the shortness of the marches, we were getting very close to India.

And then on the 20th came a check. We had done the usual march from the bottom of one valley to the top of the next ridge, covered with the usual scented pine forest, and ablaze with the usual scarlet Rhododendrons. We found here too, in fruit, on the dry gravel slope, a lily, bearing one large solitary capsule, suggesting a very large trumpet flower. The plant itself stands 60-90cm [2-3ft.] high, having a leafy stem, and a rather small, fleshy cream-coloured bulb, growing some 15cm [6in.] below the surface. What this lily is I do not know, and one looks forward with pleasurable anticipation to seeing it flower (*L. wallichianum,* K.W. 6428).

Early in the afternoon we reached a cluster of small grass huts, evidently built for some distinguished travellers. We thought modestly they might be for us; at any rate, the coolies now set down their loads, saying they had reached the end of the stage. In the offing we noticed an irate headman, directing the operations of a gang of serfs who were cutting jungle. Here, we thought, was our man. Instead of having to wait idly till the morrow, we could change transport immediately and march on till nightfall. No one who has never wandered far out of his orbit can conceive the tremendous pull exerted by home as he approaches nearer and nearer the centre of his system. We were now deeply under the influence of this major body, being but two marches from India, and fatigue vanished; we could have marched – nay, felt compelled to march – all day and all night, drawn irresistibly towards the sun of our civilization. But we were now violently deflected by this foreign body. He was a tartar. No sooner did we mention the word 'coolies' to him than he exploded. Coolies? Who the hell were we to demand coolies! Where had we come from? Tibet? Well, then, we could go back there! We had no passport? – could impudence go further! Oh! a passport from the Trashigang *Dzongpön* indeed! And who the blazes might he be! He cut no ice here anyway!

'Nay, good sir, be not in such haste; we would speak you fair!'

'I won't listen! His Highness, the son of the Maharaja of Bhutan, is in camp below, 20 miles down the valley; write a letter to him and I will send it. If he, of his clemency, allows you, unworthy foreigners that you are, to pass, well and good. But until he sends back a letter granting you permission, here you stay.'

Diplomacy would be necessary to deal with him. Meanwhile, we tried to bribe our own coolies to go on. But no, they had done their job, and had to get back to their village, or their own headman would be unpleasant. Then we picked out half a dozen likely-looking waverers, raised the bribe, and asked them to come on with us; and they were about to accept, and risk the consequences, when the angry headman, uttering awful threats, reminded them of what might – nay, would happen if they persisted in their folly.

So they too refused, and there we were. Never in the darkest hours in Tibet had India seemed so far off and unattainable. There was nothing for it but to send the letter. We knew quite well what the answer would be, and it was that which infuriated us. His Highness would, of course, welcome us with open arms – we could never make this dull oaf understand who we were – and two good days would have been wasted for nothing. Even the certain and painful extinction of the headman could never give us back those two days.

So we sat down to write the letter, while Dick made tea. But how did one start a letter to the son-in-law of a Maharaja? Cawdor, appealed to, suggested 'Dear Bud.' I favoured the more colloquial 'Say! Bo.' In the end I compromised and wrote, 'Dear Sir.' We had been informed that His Highness understood English perfectly, and had adopted Western ideas of civilization; which was a great help. I went on to state our unfortunate position, asked for assistance, and gently but obviously insinuated the cause of all our troubles, finishing up with the usual friendly greeting, 'sent with a scarf.' We happened to possess one quite good silk scarf, and when Dick had picked the burrs out of it, and the letter was sealed, and such presents as we could muster, chosen, everything was ready. At that moment I felt a slight undulation of the grey matter. 'Why not go ourselves?' I suggested to Cawdor, 'and be our own messengers! Let us put two days' chocolate ration in our pockets, sling a blanket on our backs, and trot along to India. It will be warm enough down in the valley, and anyway it only means a night or two of discomfort.'

Needless to say, Cawdor required no persuasion, and we made instant preparations for departure; that is to say, we had a hasty meal, stowed some bars of chocolate in our pockets, got out a blanket apiece, and gave instructions to the men. Sunny Jim was to stand by the kit and bring it on when he saw an opening; Dick was to accompany us. All was now ready. We would immediately shake the dust of this perverted village from our feet and ensnare the headman. There was at any rate one indignity he could not offer us; he could not bind us, and therefore he could not prevent us departing. But no sooner did the headman learn our intention than he changed his tune entirely. It was too ludicrous. Our swift decision completely unnerved him. He was prepared for inaction, but action put him right out of his stride. We must not go, said he. The way was difficult – there were tigers, we should be eaten in the night, we should fall over the cliff in the dark, we should be frozen, we should starve. What of it? We went on with our preparations, ostentatiously taking out the gun to deal with flocks of tigers. It was only too obvious that we were winning now. 'Stop,' said he, almost beside himself with panic; 'do not go, friends. If you will stay the night I will supply porters in the morning.' That was all we wanted; we made him swear that the full number of porters should be available early the following day; we had fires put in two of the grass huts; and from that moment the headman, humbled and polite, did precisely what we told him to do.

Nevertheless, we did not start early next morning, though our nervous friend was very apologetic for the scarcity of porters. Eventually we started with half the men carrying double loads. The road – a good one – led downhill, but it was not easy. Late in the evening we came to an abrupt descent, and dropped down to the wide stony valley, lined with tropical forest. In spite of every effort, however, we did not reach His Highness's camp that night, but halted at another prepared camp. Even so, only half the porters made the stage, the rest arriving early the following morning. We had only just started down the valley on the morning of February 22nd, when we were met by servants leading two fine mules sent by His Highness for our benefit. We mounted these and soon covered the few remaining miles to the camp, which consisted of a few bamboo *pandals*. The Raja himself and his comic manager stood hand-in-hand like the babes in the wood, eyeing us shyly. Behind them were gathered clerks, grooms and servants in embarrassing numbers. All were dressed so much alike that had it not been for the grey Homburg hat worn by the Raja, we should never have recognized him for what he was, and that he removed as we rode up. He wore a long grey Chinese *makua* or close-fitting gown, top-boots, and large ear-rings like a pirate, and he chewed betel perpetually. In fact, he was a typical Bhutanese. He at once invited us into his *pandal*, which was so filled with inanimate objects that we could scarcely move; and when we had seated ourselves on cushions, he brought out from a hidden store a bottle of brandy and a tin of cream crackers. The *pandal* was hot and stuffy; just outside thousands of decomposed fish were drying in the tropical sunshine, and close alongside were the horse lines, so that it was not surprising the atmosphere was turgid with odour and humming with flies. The Raja, far from understanding English, could not even understand Hindustani, and the conversation was carried on in Tibetan through Dick!

After a short rest we rose to go. His Highness lent us mules to ride to the end of the stage. We ourselves might have reached the plains by evening, but the porters could not have done it, so we were told to go as far as a place called Godam, a few miles farther on, where there was a village and a *pandal*. One particularly useful thing the Raja did. He ordered the coolies to go on with us to the plains. As these were the conscripts of the truculent headman, we felt that we had taught him a sufficiently severe lesson in the advantage of courtesy without reporting him to the Raja, who would certainly have scalped him. We also gave the Raja, in recognition of his kindness, our electric table-lamp and a small tent, which greatly pleased him. We now set out again down the valley, and presently climbing a low spur, reached an open grassy ridge, where stood the village of Godam, or Devanguri, where we halted, though it was quite early in the afternoon.

From here the forested hills went rippling and rolling down to the plains of India, a few miles distant; but so thick was the haze that we could see nothing save here and there the gleam of a meandering river. But when night came, a great crimson glare shot up from below, where the stubble was being burnt in the cultivated fields; and the mists gathered together and lay soft and white and silvery in the moonlight along the foot of the mighty Himalaya. And with morning we rose early and raced down the rough track to the frontier and emerged suddenly from the scorched crackling hill jungle on to the plains of India. There was a market here, and hundreds of hillmen and women were coming and going. We went straight to the little white bungalow, near the Military Police lines, for our journey was over. We were now only 41km [26 miles] from the Eastern Bengal Railway at Rangiya, and to our delight we found that a car plied between this place and railhead, and was at that moment in the village waiting to return. Within two hours, the coolies having arrived with the kit, we had piled our bedding on the car and taken our seats. Dick accompanied us. Sunny Jim was left behind to bring the heavy baggage along in bullock carts, by night, and at 4 o'clock in the afternoon we bumped out on to the hot dusty plain.

There was only a dirt track, and in places that had been completely washed away and strewn with gravel for miles, where some stream had come down in spate; so progress was slow, and even uncertain. When we had covered some 35km [22 miles], a tyre burst, but seeing the lights of Rangiya railway station ahead, we pressed the driver to go on, and finally crawled into the village just after dark. Rangiya proved to be a typical up-country wayside station, and anyone who knows India will know what that means. Yet to us it seemed like paradise. We surged into the refreshment-room and from the white-robed attendant ordered tea, to be followed by dinner. We made up our beds on the stone floor of the waiting-room. We walked the length of the platform several times, looking at the red signal lights and listening to the subdued hum of life down in the small native bazaar.

How we enjoyed that meal, seated at a table with a clean white cloth! And how the ordinary Englishman, travelling in India, would have turned up his nose at the curried chicken! But to us it was manna. We retired early, but did not sleep well, because we were not yet used to the heat, though Assam is not really very hot in February! At 10 o'clock next morning the Calcutta mail came in, bound for Dibrugar. Shortly after that the bullock carts arrived with our kit, and in the middle of the afternoon the Assam mail, bound for Calcutta, arrived and we climbed aboard, sharing a carriage with two other men who were homeward bound. That night we formed a cheerful party, our new-found friends overlooking our disreputable appearance in view of our late adventures. It was nearly a year since we had set eyes on another white man. On February 25th the train steamed into Calcutta, and we were back at the place where we had started.

CHAPTER XIX

The People of South-East Tibet

This Chapter and the next are contributed by the Earl Cawdor,
who accompanied Captain Kingdon Ward throughout the journey

Kongbo, Abors and Kampas

In these short notes on the inhabitants of South-eastern Tibet it is proposed to deal mainly with the Tibetans of the Tsangpo Valley, the Mönba tribes of the jungles of the eastern extremity of the Himalaya, and the inhabitants of the province of Pemakö. Much has already been written concerning the Tibetans of the plateau. The present writer feels, therefore, that it is more within his power to discuss the character and habits of the inhabitants of the more sequestered parts of the country.

The Tibetans themselves divide the inhabitants of the Tsangpo and Po-Tsangpo Valleys into the following main divisions: Tibetans, Mönbas, and Lopas. The Mönbas appear originally to have emigrated from Bhutan, and to have settled in the dense jungle region

Above: A Lopa woman wearing a tunic of goral skin. **IB**
A Lopa woman in a tunic pieced together from the skins of two red gorals walks through a field of chillies in the village of Tsachu near the apex of the Tsangpo's 'great bend'. Lopas are generally believed to be a sub-branch of the Abor tribes in India's Arunachal Pradesh. The snow-covered peak of Gyala Peri rises behind.

A Mönba man from Sengchen. **KSJ**

Mönbas from a village in the lower Tsangpo gorge.   **IB**
Mönbas – whose name means 'people from the southern forests' – migrated into the Tsangpo gorge region from
eastern Bhutan and adjacent areas in the 17th century and afterwards.

south of the main axis of the Himalaya in the province of Pemakö. They are also to be
found in the valley of the Po-Tsangpo, and south of Tsöna Dzong on the marches of
Tibet and Bhutan. The Lopas appear to be Abors: the aboriginal inhabitants of this part
of the Himalaya. The term 'Lopa' seems to be loosely applied by the Tibetans, and really
means any kind of jungle people. It is equivalent to our word 'jungly'. The Tibetans, no
doubt, would classify Abors, Mishmis, and Daphlas impartially under the name of 'Lopa'.

There are no noticeable racial changes in the Tibetans as one goes east along the Tsangpo
Valley. Rather, as one leaves the barren plateau country farther behind, and penetrates
deeper into the warmer, wetter, and more fertile parts approaching the Tsangpo gorge, one
realizes an almost imperceptible change in the people: they begin to have more the
appearance of a jungle race. Fewer clothes are worn by the natives, proclaiming a more
genial climate, and sloping wooden roofs on the houses suggest a heavier rainfall. Nearly
all the Tibetans of the plateau wear their hair in a pigtail which is usually twisted round
their heads; farther east there appears to be no fixed rule for hairdressing. One sees some
men with hair reaching to their shoulders, some with 'bobbed' hair, some with their hair
cut short, and some with pigtails. Most of the men carry swords, but these are, for the most

part, short and well suited for use in the jungle. One sometimes sees men with very long swords, but these are most common amongst the Pobas. Swords are always carried horizontally at the waist; and the length of a sword is supposed to be regulated by the length of the man's arm, so that it may be drawn out of the scabbard without difficulty.

Throughout Kongbo a characteristic garment is worn by both sexes; this is what might be described as a 'double apron' of leather. It is generally made of the skins of cows or goats roughly tanned, though the skins of goral, takin, and bear are also used. It is an oblong piece of leather some 1.8m [6ft.] long and 60cm [2ft.] wide, with a hole in the middle. The wearer puts his (or her) head through the hole, and allows the two aprons to hang down back and front. The ends of the aprons are pulled up till they reach about the level of the knees, and the whole, when secured by a leather thong round the waist, forms an excellent weatherproof garment. In wet weather the hairy side is worn outermost. This seems to be a Tibetan garment, though it is worn by some Mönba tribes.

In the provinces of Takpo, Kongbo, and U it is the fashion for the women to paint their faces black. There is a legend to the effect that one of the Dalai Lamas found difficulties in keeping his vows of perpetual celibacy unless the ladies took this precaution; but whether there is any truth in it one cannot say. Certainly a woman does not look her best with her face polished like a black-leaded stove. None of the Mönbas or Lopa tribes seem to have recourse to these aids to beauty; one often sees very fair-complexioned women amongst them.

All along the Himalaya, salt is responsible for periodical migration of jungle folk across the range. In Kongbo it is the Mönbas and Abors who carry on this traffic; farther west the Daphlas are responsible. Salt is brought into Kongbo from the north-east by Horbas and other nomadic tribes inhabiting the north-eastern boundaries of Kam. They exchange salt for *tsamba* at Gyamda, whence the salt is distributed throughout the province. The Mönbas and Abors in turn bring rice in exchange for salt. The chief centre of exchange with the jungle people is Pe, a village on the Tsangpo at the northern end of the Himalayan pass known as the Doshong La. This pass is open from about the middle of August till the middle of November, and during the months of September and October there is a never-ending procession of Mönbas up and down the road. Besides rice, they bring chilis, ginger and other spices, bamboo baskets, rattan cane (used by the Tibetans for whip-handles), embroidered cloth, and other merchandise. A Tibetan agent at Pe values the loads, and hands over salt in exchange, in the course of which transaction the unfortunate junglies are, no doubt, done in the eye.

During these busy months Pe has the appearance of a centre of vast mercantile activity. The bulk of the trade is done by Mönbas from villages round about Yortong, but a good many Abors and Kampas trade too. We met only one party of Abors in Pe; they had come twenty-five days' march, and stopped only one night. Evidently they had no relish for stopping in the enemy's camp longer than was absolutely necessary. The Tibetans regarded them as a huge joke; the fact that they spoke a strange language – not unlike the growling of dogs, on first acquaintance – was considered extremely humorous. In fact, the Abor contingent were as good as a circus for Pe. We found it none too easy to get information out of the Abors, for they knew nothing except their own language; even when we found a Mönba linguist who knew the Abor language as well as Tibetan, they did not prove very forthcoming.

All the Abors we met wore a garment not unlike the Tibetan *chupa,* but very short, and reaching only a short way below the waist. A strip of cloth hanging from a thong fastened round the waist completed their costume. They were bareheaded and barefooted, though some of them wore fringed puttees round their legs while they were in the village. They all carried a short heavy knife, not unlike a meat-cleaver, with a blade about 30cm [1ft.] long by 7.5cm [3in.] deep, and with a blunt end. This was carried not in the Tibetan fashion but in a basket slung about their necks. Some had bamboo bows about 1.5m [5ft.] long fitted with bamboo strings, and iron-tipped arrows poisoned with aconite, and notched through about 7.5cm [3in.] from the point. These Abor bows and arrows are exactly the same as those used by the Mönbas: one end of the bow is shod with iron and serves as a combined alpenstock and ice-axe, as well as a weapon of offence. Most of the Abor men wear ear-rings consisting of a silver disc more than 2.5cm [1in.] in diameter. The ornament is decorated with a sun disc with radiating beams. The hole in the lobe of the ear is gradually enlarged by means of a strip of bamboo coiled like a watch-spring. A small knife in a skin sheath is attached to the girdle; the blade is curved and sharpened on the outside of the bend. The Mönbas use a knife of the same type, and I understood that it was made in this fashion for cutting thin strips of bamboo for making ropes and baskets. For, like all jungle folk, the Mönbas and Abors depend on bamboo for many of the necessities of life.

The loads of rice and salt are carried in strong bamboo baskets about 90cm [3ft.] deep. Bamboo leaves are usually woven into the sides of the baskets to make them waterproof, and they are provided with covers of bamboo matting to go over the top. The usual load is from 36-45kg [80-100lb.]. These are heavy loads when one considers the roads over which they are carried. Cliffs, snowfields, bogs, ladders, log-bridges, and fords are some of the obstacles that have to be negotiated on the Doshong La. All along the road there are camping places: hollow trees and overhanging rocks are the most sought-after refuges, and judging by the usual condition of these popular hostels the guests are not too particular in their habits.

The Doshong La is not a high pass as Himalayan passes go: the summit is about 4100m [13,500ft.]. But one is forced to admire the hardiness of these half-naked junglies, who, having overcome the difficulties incident to the earlier part of the journey from their villages, tackle the steep snow slopes with their ponderous burdens and descend into a strange country. It is to be wondered at that there is not a heavy death-rate amongst these salt-traders, for the weather on the pass is uncommonly vile, and they are but ill-equipped for the encounter. We did hear dreadful stories on another pass of a party of Mönbas who walked to their doom up the wrong glacier in a blizzard; but accidents seem to be infrequent on the Doshong La, where, every year, these hardy, cheerful little folk cross in their thousands.

The Kampas (natives of the province of Kam), a certain number of whom join in the salt traffic of the Doshong La, seem to be fairly recent settlers in Pemakö. We were told that owing to the heavy expenses in connection with the formation of an army at Lhasa, rates and taxes in Kam had increased enormously. A number of Kampas have therefore emigrated to Pemakö, which appears to be a happy hunting-ground for those who are anxious to escape the avaricious grasp of the Chancellor of the Exchequer. It is a good example of the measures that men will adopt in order to avoid taxation – always supposing the story is true. It is hardly probable that there can be several villages in Pemakö inhabited by escaped criminals from Kam. Yet most of the Kampas we met in course of our travels seemed to be 'wanted by the police.' At all events, whatever the reason for their emigration, the Kampa settlers seem to be getting on well enough in Pemakö. One would not expect them to take kindly to the change of air; for it must be a very different climate from that of their own country, and, as a rule, Tibetans regard jungle country as an abomination.

Mönbas, Lopas and bridges in Tibet

In Pemakö and in Pome we found very considerable differences in the conditions of life of neighbouring Mönba communities. At Payül on the Tsangpo we found a most miserable tribe of Mönbas. Practically all of them suffered from goitre – a very common disease in these parts – and there was a high percentage of cretins amongst the inhabitants. The altitude of the villages hereabouts is from 1500-1800m [5,000-6,000ft.]. Most of the men possessed but one garment apiece, hardly any of them had boots, and their only weapons were swords and bows and arrows. They lived entirely on millet, which is boiled until it forms a thick paste. They usually mixed bear's fat with it to make it more palatable. They were reputed to hunt takin with dogs and bows and arrows. They certainly were successful in snaring game, for on a spur above the river we found a dead takin in a snare made of bamboo rope. They also set snares for musk deer.

At Sengchen, a Mönba village close to the confluence of the Po-Tsangpo and the

A Kampa at his home at Payul (Bayu). **IB**

A Kampa pilgrim who married a Mönba woman and settled in Pemakö sits outside his home in Payul (Bayu) with his grandson who is dressed in a tunic fashioned from a monkey skin (Assamese Macacque).

Tsangpo, we met with a much more highly-developed type of Mönba. The men were all well developed and very muscular; some of them stood over 1.8m [6ft.] in height. They were well clothed and provided with takin and goral skins, and almost all wore Tibetan boots. The men seemed to be either hunters or woodmen, the former all being provided with matchlocks with which they did great execution amongst takin and goral. We found this tribe extremely friendly and most intelligent; goitre was not so common, nor were there so many cretins.

In Pemakö and the southern part of Pome different crops are harvested almost all the year round: maize, millet, wheat, barley, rice, and potatoes are the main crops. Besides these they grow chilis and white turnips. The chilis, when gathered, are dried in the sun upon the roofs of the houses. It is quite a feature of the landscape in this country to see brilliant scarlet patches on the roofs of houses where the chilis are put out to dry. This is quite an important crop to the Mönbas, since they pay tribute to the King of Pome in the form of chilis, huge baskets of which are sent up to Showa each year. Red chilis are very popular in Tibet, for the Tibetan uses them to flavour his otherwise rather uninteresting fare of barley-meal. No doubt the King of Pome makes quite a good thing out of his 'line' in chilis.

The Mönbas are nominally Tibetan Buddhists, but the restrictions as to killing game prescribed by that religion does not appear to cause them the smallest uneasiness, for they indulge in the chase with the utmost spirit and cheerfulness. There are Buddhist temples in most of the villages, and close beside them one often sees a tree surrounded with wooden spears where birds have been sacrificed to propitiate the spirits of the forest. It is a common thing to see a hollow tree-trunk placed upright in the middle of a field in which the spirit guarding the crop is supposed to dwell. A flat stone is generally placed on the top of the log, but whether it is to keep the rain out or the spirit in I cannot say. There are plentiful signs of Phallic worship in this part of the country; one frequently sees a wooden phallus driven into the ground outside a village. (In parts of Bhutan almost every house has one of these ornaments suspended from the ridge of the roof.) We used even to see a phallus carved on a tree-stump in the forest beside a hunters' shelter.

Farther north, up the Po-Tsangpo Valley, we encountered Lopa villages. The inhabitants, although they called themselves Lopas, did not resemble Abors in the slightest degree. They were rather more like Mönbas, but in some ways different from any other people we met. The men were short and sturdy, with curly hair cut fairly short. They wore the ordinary Tibetan clothes, and seemed to be well supplied with gear. They were particularly cheerful and friendly, but inclined to be idle as porters. Once we had left the Mönba villages of the lower part of the Po-Tsangpo, we passed through villages inhabited by so-called Lopas until we got into Kongbo. We met very few Pobas. These seem to be a sturdy and warlike tribe, judging by the way they dealt with the Chinese soldiers some years ago. Our porters pointed out one narrow defile on the road by the river where about a hundred of the Chinese transport were enfiladed and cut up by Poba warriors.

Near Tongjuk, at the entrance to a village, were a couple of wooden figures of men about 2.7m [9ft.] high – grotesque faces were carved on them, and the heads and bodies had at one time been painted. Inquiries from local inhabitants failed to elicit more than that they were 'wooden men' – we might have guessed as much ourselves. They professed a total ignorance of when the figures were put up or why. We saw a single wooden figure outside another village near by, and one at a village on the Nyang Chu between Gyamda and Tsela Dzong; but in no case were we able to discover anything concerning their

Opposite: A Mönba woman near the village of Medog.   **IB**

Taken at Medog in the lower Tsangpo, this Mönba woman carries freshly brewed *chang* (a form of beer made from barley) in dried gourds. Hospitality in Pemakö demands that villagers offer their potent brew to anyone who passes through the village.

history. We never saw anything like them in any other part of Tibet, nor had we ever heard of such things. It is possible that they were erected by the Chinese; for we know that they came through Tongjuk. But in that case one would have expected the local people to have remembered something about them. In actual fact the local wits knew, or pretended to know, no more about their origin than if they had fallen from heaven.

No account of this country, however short and however vague, could be considered complete without reference to the bridges built by its inhabitants. The Tibetan seems a bridge-builder by nature. He has, of course, to adapt his plans to the material obtainable, but the results are very commendable. On the plateau the usual method of crossing a stream is to walk through it in the summer and in the winter to slide across on the ice. A convoy of heavily-laden mules skidding about on a frozen stream provides a most exhilarating form of winter sport. On the Tsangpo, opposite Tsetang, is the remains of what was once an iron chain bridge supported by masonry piers. To-day too little of it remains for one to see exactly how it was arranged. The piers seem to have been built on a mass of loose rubble which was used to make an artificial island in the middle of the river. This alone must have been no mean undertaking. It is possible, however, that this bridge was engineered by the Chinese. Since this bridge was destroyed, the passage of the river is made in a wooden barge, not unlike a four-poster bed, and not much more seaworthy. When we went across in the winter it was in better condition than usual, the leaks in the bottom having frozen solid. A little farther down crossing is effected by skin boats; these are about 2.4m [8ft.] long, with a beam of 1.2m [4ft.]. The frame is of withies, and is covered with yak skins. On other parts of the river dug-out canoes are employed. These are made from logs 10-12m [35-40ft.] long and 75cm [30in.] in diameter; they are hollowed out to a depth of 60cm [2ft.]. In order to make the craft sufficiently stable for the transport of ponies, two canoes are often lashed together side by side.

On rivers where timber is plentiful, and the span is not too great, cantilever bridges are built. This appears to be the type of bridge in which the Tibetans and Bhutanese are particularly expert. Masonry foundations are built in which the ends of the beams are anchored. The beams are keyed together and each projects a little farther than the one below; there may be from six to eight beams. The central section is usually a flimsy platform fitted with side rails. In the event of one end of the bridge being attacked, it is an easy job to lift out the central section, and drop it into the river. These bridges are often provided with gate-houses. The finest specimen of a cantilever bridge that we saw was over a tributary of the Manas in Bhutan.

A type of bridge common in Tibet where long spans are encountered is the rope bridge, or monkey bridge. The ropes are made from long strips of bamboo twisted up, and are usually from 10-12.5cm [4-5in.] in diameter. The rope bridge at Gyala consists of two of these ropes with a span of 91m [300ft.]. The intending passenger ties a rope to one arm of a bullock yoke, hitches the yoke over the ropes of the bridge, passes the other end of the small rope round his waist, and secures it to the other arm of the yoke. He then launches himself into space, and, having slid to the bottom of the sag – the yoke taking his weight and acting as a slider – he has to haul himself up the other side with hands and feet. The process is both slow and laborious, but not nearly so painful as the alternative, which is to be hauled across by means of a line attached to the yoke. To get loads across, a party on either side of the river have a long line made fast to the yoke on which the loads are slung, and haul it back and fore.

A rather more advanced type of suspension bridge is the hammock bridge. Here cables either of bamboo or rattan are used. Two or more cables make the floor of the bridge, and other cables, slung rather higher, make the sides. The cables are secured to trees, stakes, or rocks on the bank. Bamboo or rattan ropes are looped round the cables forming a network on which bamboo matting is laid as a roadway. This kind of bridge is common in Bhutan; one, at Trashigang Dzong, had a span of 60m [65 yards] and was about 15m [50ft.] above the water. In this case the weight was taken by iron cables, and the bridge was so rigid that mules could cross it.

Entrance to a village
in Pome.   FKW

CHAPTER XX

House and Home in South-East Tibet

Houses, clothes and furniture

Among the Tibetan women of the plateau of Southern Tibet the chief variation in ornament is in regard to their head-dress. Round about Gyantse the hair is stretched out on huge frames of wood and wire, which project some 20cm [8in.] on either side. These frames, also, are generally decorated with red and blue beads, and the wooden and wire parts are covered with red cloth. The women of Lhasa and the province of U wear a smaller cloth-covered wooden frame and attach long tails of false hair at either side of it. These tails, I fancy, are only used on high-days and holidays. All these ladies when travelling wear a red cloth covering over their head-dresses. In this part of Tibet the women generally wear aprons of striped cloth. These are made in narrow strips sewn together. It seems to be a Lhasa fashion, but has spread all over Southern Tibet. In Lhasa, as in Paris, fashions are set, the chief difference being that they are a good deal cheaper and much less diaphanous.

As regards the clothes worn by men in this part of Tibet, there are no very marked variations. The *chupa* is worn in all parts of the country, and resembles a dressing-gown girded up round the hips, leaving a large bag in front in which provisions for the immediate future are commonly stored. It is an accommodating form of dress; if it is cold, another *chupa* is added; if warm, one or more is discarded. It is a common sight to see muleteers, having arrived at the lower altitudes of a sheltered valley, marching with their *chupas* hanging down and tied by the sleeves about their waists. In winter the

275

dwellers on the plateau usually wear *chupas* made of sheepskins, with the wool inside. These notes on dress apply only to the rank and file of the men; the aristocracy and higher official classes nearly all wear Chinese clothes. The wealthy ladies, however, all seem to favour the costume of their own country.

The rainfall being slight in this part of Tibet, the houses are all built with flat mud roofs. The walls are of stone, built like a dry stone dyke, and in larger buildings of several stories are very thick through at the base, making a batter up the outside of the wall. The ground floor of the house usually serves as a byre; the weary wayfarer, finding his way to the foot of the rickety ladder that serves for a staircase, has, like Agag, to 'tread delicately.' In most houses – even those inhabited by the wealthier people – a hetero-geneous collection of pigs, sheep, goats, cows, and sometimes ponies are driven into the byre at night and the door is barred. Sometimes there is an enclosed yard as well, and in this case stables are often made along one wall of the yard.

Doors are generally made with the hinge-pin on the door itself and the socket on the jamb; in old doors in England it is usual to find the order reversed. Doors are secured, as a rule, with wooden bolts of generous dimensions, or sometimes by Chinese iron padlocks. There were in the province of Kongbo some most ingenious hollow bolts which were locked by wooden pins held in the door-jamb. When the bolt was pushed home the pins fell into holes in the wooden bolt and held it secure. To unfasten the bolt a key made of a specially-shaped piece of wood had to be inserted into the bolt to lift up the pins; the bolt could then be withdrawn. Windows, as a rule, are fitted with wooden shutters which are secured by a wooden latch. In some of the better-class houses the window-frames are fitted with wooden lattice frames over which paper is pasted. This is evidently an introduction from China. We met one magnate who was so far in advance of the times as to import glass from India for the centres of his paper-covered windows, which were protected outside by wire-netting.

When the primitive nature of the tools used by carpenters in Tibet is considered, the work is found to be of quite a high order. The saw is unknown, so that all trees are felled by the use of the axe alone. The logs are split up with axes and wooden wedges, and the shaping of beams or planks is done with the axe or the adze. The latter implement is largely used, as in India. In the forest we used to see planks cut from Tsuga wood (*Cha* in Tibetan) measuring 2.5m x 0.42m x 10cm [8ft. x 17in. x 4in.], and well squared up.

As one travels farther into the more rainy parts of South-eastern Tibet one finds that the flat mud roofs are replaced by sloping roofs made with wooden shingles. These shingles generally measure about 45 x 15cm [18 x 6in.], and are cleft from Coniferous timber. Over the beams of the roof a framework of laths is spread, on which the shingles are laid, the upper rows overlapping those beneath. A line of laths is put along each row of shingles, and large stones are placed on them to prevent the roof blowing off in windy weather. These roofs are, on the whole, pretty water-tight, but leaks are not unknown during the rainy season. When the inhabitants climb upon the roof, armed with long poles with which to move the wooden slabs, the last state is, not infrequently, worse than the first.

Interior fittings in Tibetan houses are not very numerous; they comprise nothing much besides necessities. The most common form of fireplace is of the open-hearth variety, and consists of a square fireplace on a flat stone slab surrounded with either a stone or wooden curb. Iron dogs are placed upright in the fireplace to support cooking-pots. We could never discover where these dogs are made; they appear to be cast, and are common throughout South-eastern Tibet. One sometimes finds a more elaborate form of fireplace which is in the nature of a kitchen-range reduced to its simplest terms. The range is built of stone and clay and has round holes in the top upon which pots are placed. The position of the fireplace would appear to be quite immaterial; sometimes it is in the middle of the room, and sometimes against one wall. Chimneys are not supplied; the smoke finds its way out by the line of least resistance.

This about exhausts the furniture of the average Tibetan house. Chairs are not required, for it is the custom of the country to sit on the floor. The very great, for whom

Child with a milk churn.
AC

This picture was taken near the village of Temo on the south side of the Temo La. These wooden churns are found in every Tibetan house and are used to make the famous salty yak butter tea, which, as Cawdor says, is probably best considered as a kind of soup. Cawdor succinctly describes how to make Tibetan tea: 'The leaf from which Tibetan tea is made is in the form of brick tea imported from China. A handful or so is broken up and dropped into a wooden churn, the leaves are scalded with boiling water, a good-sized lump of butter and a handful of salt are added, and the whole concoction is churned up and down with a wooden piston. This action emulsifies the butter, and the liquid can be strained off into a teapot'.

the floor is too hard, sit upon cushions. Beds consist of a few hard cushions made like carriage cushions, and bed-clothes are provided by spare clothing. Chairs and tables are rare, except in the houses of the wealthy. They are usually of Chinese origin or copies of Chinese articles. The same applies to cupboards and chests; the only things to be found of native origin are *yakdahns,* which are probably common to all parts of Central Asia.

Cooking and food

Cooking-pots and household utensils vary greatly; those most characteristic of the country are the teapots. These are made either of copper, brass, or earthenware. The metal pots are made largely at Shigatse, and also, I believe, at Darghi. The earthenware teapots are made the same shape as those of metal, but I could never discover their place of manufacture. A certain number of kettles and teapots of enamelled iron are beginning to be seen in Tibet; these are made in Japan and probably imported by way of India. It is noticeable that the Japanese copy exactly the Tibetan designs for the shape of their reproductions. The ordinary pot used for cooking and for boiling water is of brass, and is made with shoulders as well as lips. These are made in various sizes; we used to see pots sometimes measuring as much as 1m [3ft.] in diameter. The larger pots are used for parching barley and for fermenting grain.

In the province of Kongbo stone pots are used to a large extent. These are of local manufacture and are very well made. They are wider at the bottom than at the top, and are made with small lugs to serve as handles. Brass-bound wooden teapots and jugs are often to be seen on shelves in Tibetan kitchens. They are of fine workmanship and the brass-work is frequently chased. I never saw any of these in use; they appear to be kept as ornaments. Stone mortars and pestles are very common. The mortars are made from a block of hard stone hollowed out and smoothed by constant use. The pestles are generally any stone of a convenient shape. Mortars vary in size according to the purposes for which they are required. A small mortar is usually kept in the kitchen for grinding up chilis and spices for culinary operations, while larger ones are kept for mixing dyes. In the jungle country of the Tsangpo gorge and in Bhutan one sees the type of mortar and pestle common over a large part of Asia. The mortar is made from the trunk of a tree, and the pestle is a ponderous double-ended affair of wood. We never met with this type in Tibet proper.

Hand-mills are found in some villages, but it is more common to find mills worked by water-power. The ordinary type of hand-mill consists of an upper and nether millstone supported on battens over a hollowed-out tree-trunk. The grain is put into a hole in the middle of the upper stone, which is revolved by means of a wooden handle. The flour falls into the tree-trunk which forms a horizontal trough. The water-mills work on the same principle, the wheel being placed horizontally and the shaft vertically. Water-wheels are used all over the country for turning prayer-drums. In South-eastern Tibet the corn is threshed by hand, and not by the method, so common in many parts of Asia, of letting oxen trample the grain out of the ear. Threshing-floors are provided in every village – often the flat mud roofs of byres are used. Flails are made without a leather joint between the two parts; the movable part of the flail is bound to a wooden pin which fits into a hole at the top of the handle. The movable part of the flail is usually made of a willow stick about as thick as a man's forefinger and about 1.5m [5ft.] long. Threshing is done both by men and women, to the accompaniment of singing.

After threshing, the grain is winnowed from the chaff by being poured out of one basket into another. Large shallow trays, about 1.2m [4ft.] square, are used to receive the grain, which is poured from a smaller basket held up high by the operator. This process is repeated until the chaff is all blown away. The grain is stored in baskets about 90cm [3ft.] deep, or else in sacks. *Tsamba*, or parched barley-meal, which is the staple food of the country, is made by parching the grain over a fire before milling it. All classes live chiefly on *tsamba;* sometimes it is eaten raw, sometimes mixed with hot water or tea into a kind of gruel, and sometimes it is eaten with red chilis. The great advantage of this diet is that it requires little or no cooking. Tea, *tsamba,* and butter are the chief staples of the country. Tibetan tea, as is well known, possesses certain peculiarities of its own. But its unpleasantness has, to my mind, been greatly exaggerated. When drinking native tea the great thing to do is to look upon it as soup rather than tea as we understand it; if this is done it will be found to go down like nectar. It is certainly an excellent beverage in a cold climate, and particularly good when made into a sort of broth with *tsamba.* The leaf from which Tibetan tea is made is in the form of brick tea imported from China. A handful or so is broken up and dropped into a wooden churn, the leaves are scalded with boiling water, a good-sized lump of butter and a handful of salt are added, and the whole concoction is churned up and down with a wooden piston. This action emulsifies the butter, and the liquid can be strained off into a teapot. Earthenware jars filled with glowing charcoal are often used as stands for teapots, to keep the tea warm.

The plough used in south-eastern Tibet does little more than scratch the surface of the ground. It consists of only two parts: the beam and the share. The beam is about 2m [7ft.] long and is usually made from a bough of evergreen oak along with part of the trunk. This provides the necessary elbow in the beam. The short arm is mortised into the share, which is also made of oak. Wedges are driven into the mortise and the share is further secured by a lashing of thongs to the bend of the beam. A yoke of oxen are attached to the end of the ploughshare, and the ploughman leans his weight on a handle on the upper end of the share in order to encourage the point to go deeper into the ground. Since the ploughshares are not iron-shod nor hardened in any way, they last only a short time in stony ground.

Besides the plough there are not many agricultural implements in use: such as there are resemble those that the men of prehistoric times might have used. The most usual form of mattock is a conveniently-shaped branch with a handle about 90cm [3ft.] long, and with the point hardened in the fire. These are used indifferently for hoeing or as a mallet for breaking-up clods. In a few places iron-headed mattocks are used, but they are not very common. Clods in the fields are sometimes broken up by pulling a log of wood over a field with oxen; the driver usually helps by balancing on the log. We used to see reaping-hooks in some of the villages, but I think these are used only for cutting grass. Barley and wheat crops seem always to be pulled up by the roots. The method used for making hay – harvest coming during the wet season – is to put big wooden ladders against trees and to festoon them with hay. This method is not unlike that prevailing in some parts of the west coast of Scotland, where the hay-crop is hung on the fence to dry.

In Kongbo, besides barley and wheat, oats are sometimes grown along with tares; this crop is usually cut green and fed to stock. Potatoes are obtainable at times, also carrots and white turnips. In a few places in the Tsangpo Valley we used to get green peas as a great luxury. The only vegetable one can apparently always be sure of obtaining is onions. These are small, but may be described as 'full-flavoured'. About the only fruit trees regarded in any degree of economic significance are walnuts and peaches. Kongbo, it appears, has always been famous for its walnuts; they are certainly large, and provided with phenomenally thick shells. The natives cannot be said to pay much attention to the 'care and maintenance' of the peach-trees, unless the ruthless pollarding to which they are subjected is calculated to improve their fruit-bearing qualities. Peaches are collected in the autumn by the simple expedient of stoning the trees, and gathering up the fruit that falls to the ground. The fruit is dried in the sun on the roofs of the houses, and is subsequently chewed during the winter by the inhabitants. It is certainly a sound investment, for, sucked conscientiously, a sun-dried peach lasts a long time.

Textiles in South-eastern Tibet are of local manufacture, and of only one quality: presumably 'the best'. Cloths of fine texture are probably imported: the jungle tribes (Mönbas, etc.) make their cloth for their own clothes. Wool is collected and spun into yarn by men and women by means of wooden spindle whorls. The yarn is wound on to spools which are fitted into the shuttle as required. The loom has a strong wooden frame, the warp is horizontal, and the threads are attached to the frame at one end. The finished cloth is rolled up round the cloth beam as it is made. There are four heddles which are worked by wooden treadles placed below the loom. Looms vary slightly in different parts of the country, but only in detail: they all work on the same principle. The cloth is usually made about 60cm [2ft.] in width and is thick and soft in texture. As a rule it is left the natural grey colour, but sometimes it is dyed red. We never saw any native vegetable dyes: they all seemed to be imported from India.

The province of Pome appears to specialize in the manufacture of weapons of offence and defence. The best swords are said to come from thence; though swords are made in the village of Lunang in Kongbo. This same village is also famous for the manufacture of metal plates for belts. These plates are of iron or brass or sometimes a combination of the two. They are carved in very coarse sort of filigree patterns, but the workmanship is excellent. They are worn by every woman in Kongbo. Matchlocks are made in Pome and there is said to be a very good gunsmith in Showa – the capital of the province. Fire-arms are not very common in Kongbo, though one sees plenty of them in Pome. This is probably because in the latter province shooting game is considered quite a legitimate pursuit. How sport is reconciled with the Buddhist doctrine is not explained. One industry which appears to be peculiar to Kongbo is the making of hats. These are of a coarse kind of felt made from yak hair and are in the shape of a parson's wideawake hat. They are made both black and white, and are a very suitable form of head-gear in a country where the rainfall is considerable. They are worn alike by men and women during the monsoon.

This ends some rather haphazard notes on the buildings, furniture, ornaments, and articles and implements in common use in part of South-eastern Tibet. The writer has attempted only to deal with part of the provinces of Takpo, Kongbo, and Pome, and the list has no pretensions to being a complete inventory of domestic and agricultural appliances; but it is hoped that it may give some slight idea of the conditions and state of civilization in this part of the country.

iv

Exploration of the Tsangpo Gorges region from 1925
The Attempts to Explore Pome

Kenneth Cox

For hundreds of years, the Tibet-China border area was disputed territory. From time to time one side or the other would launch a concerted attack, exerting authority over a town or village, or claiming an area of land. More often than not this would be later reclaimed by the other side and the cycle of violence would continue. To complicate matters, on the Tibetan side of the border lived the fearsome Kampa warriors, feared by either side, who had a reputation for rustling and thieving and killing. The early years of the twentieth century were particularly unstable with an almost constant guerrilla war being waged between the two sides. Unsurprisingly, the European missionaries and plant hunters who operated here did so at considerable risk. The French missionary and intrepid plant collector Abbé Soulié travelled in disguise deep into Tibet, then a country still virtually closed to foreigners. In 1905, refusing to heed warnings to flee the border area, Soulié was caught by lamas at Batang, tortured and shot. His friend, the Scottish plant collector George Forrest who was also in the area, narrowly escaped a similar fate.

The Pome range above the Tsangpo Gorge.   **IB**

The Pome range and the region of the Su La pass emerge from the clouds from a ridge high above the Tsangpo gorge (Sechen La). This picture was taken in May 1993. The Tsangpo flows southward through the area concealed by dense mist.

View of Jhu Long from below the Dokar La.   **PC**
The view of the mountain range which divides Pome from the Salween is an extraordinary sight in clear visibility.
Ward twice had a view of the range from further north, describing it as 'the mysterious snowy range of Pome…a
glittering skyway'.

Sixteen out of his seventeen mainly Chinese staff lost their lives and Forrest was forced
to flee south towards safety, travelling for nine days. His diary describes the events of his
journey: he discarded his boots 'to avoid leaving distinctive trails' and:

> Another day I had to wade waist deep for a full mile upstream to evade a party
> who were close at my heel: once a few of them came upon me suddenly and I was
> shot at, two of the poisoned arrows passing through my hat…

Things went from bad to worse:

> At the end of eight days I had ceased to care if I lived or died: my feet swollen out
> of all shape, my hands and face torn with thorns, and my whole person caked with
> mud I knew the end was near and determined to made one more bid for life.

Starving and unable to walk any further, Forrest gave himself up at a small village where
fortunately the friendly Lissu inhabitants gave him protection, and eventually smuggled
him back to safety in Yunnan.

    To the south-west of the area where Abbé Soulié was captured lies the area of Tibet
known as Pome. In 1913 Kingdon Ward, now working for Forrest's former sponsor
A.K. Bulley, mounted his third expedition with the aim of reaching this virtually

Omphalogramma tibetica **below the Dokar La.**   **KNEC**
Discovered by Tsongpen, one of Ludlow and Sherriff's collectors in 1947, but never introduced, due to permit
problems in the Pome area, this may be the first time this plant has been photographed. We found the plant during
our 1996 expedition on the eastern slopes of the Dokar or Showa La. Like many of the Omphalogramma species,
which are closely related to Primula, this one has never been cultivated, but its near relative *O. delavayi* from Yunnan
is proving to be quite amenable in gardens, and this species may prove equally good.

unexplored area. A.K. Pandit and Bailey had both passed through Pome, but neither had paid much attention to the plants in the mountains surrounding it. Ward had read the accounts of the earlier explorers and he was aware that Morshead and Bailey were already in Tibet attempting to explore the Tsangpo Gorges, to the west. The plant collector George Forrest had made it clear to Ward that he regarded Yunnan as 'his territory', out of bounds to other collectors. Ward was therefore forced to look further afield for unexplored areas likely to yield interesting plants. He wrote to the president of the Royal Geographical Society, Dr. Scott Keltie in 1913, explaining that he had decided to attempt to reach Pome:

> I have heard something of the Province of Pomed [*sic*], which I am particularly aiming for -of warm valleys, big lakes, big rivers and high mountains…if all goes well I will attempt to reach Lhasa by the southern road….

Ward set out from Zhongdian (Chungtien) in Yunnan, China, eventually reaching the Salween from where he intended to continue west into Pome itself. There was particularly severe unrest in the Tibet-Yunnan border area at the time and the Chinese tried to stop Ward going any further by preventing him from recruiting porters. The Englishman was determined to carry on but was forced to proceed up the Salween with minimum supplies. After three days of appalling weather, he was struck with fever and his few remaining staff went on strike. In *The Mystery Rivers of Tibet,* Ward recounts the disappointing news he received from his guides, when he felt he was within reach of his objective:

> There is a great deal of trouble in Tibet this year. The Chinese are trying to get into Tibet and there is much fighting. The roads through Pome and Zayul are crowded with soldiers…they have killed the Chinese Garrison at Menkung and Rima…the chief has received strict orders from Lhasa to allow no one to proceed without a passport.

Though frustrated, Ward finally had the good sense to admit defeat and he returned south where the Chinese, fearful for his wellbeing, insisted he return immediately to safer parts of Yunnan. The unrest of 1913 was of a similar magnitude to that which Forrest encountered eight years earlier, and it is more than likely that Ward would have been murdered had he continued this journey. Once back in safer parts of Yunnan, he had to inform his employer Bulley of the failure of the expedition. Bulley was not impressed by the recklessness which had yielded a poor plant haul and cost him a great deal of time and money, but luckily decided to give him another chance. Ward, not one to give up easily, was still firmly set on reaching Pome at some time in the future, writing:

> …of this I am sure, Pomed is a country where we shall find some wonderful things and solve some of the Indo-China puzzles, and I will go there if I die for it, some day.

The 1924-25 expedition covered in *The Riddle of the Tsangpo Gorges* did reach the northern edge of Pome but did not venture south of the confluence of the Po and Yigrong rivers. During the 1924 expedition, Ward describes Pome's 'great range of snow-clad peaks' which he glimpsed to the south-east while crossing the Nambu La.

In 1933, Ward crossed from India into the southernmost part of Tibet not far from the Burmese border and explored the area to the south of the Tsangpo Gorges. He reached the monastery of Shugden Gompa which lies on a hill overlooking the lakes which are the source of the Nagong Chu (Po-Tsangpo) which runs north through the Pome valley, eventually joining the Yarlung Tsangpo in the gorge. In *A Plant Hunter in Tibet* Ward again states his wish to reach Pome:

> There is an unexplored stretch between my camp on the Nagong Chu and Showa (capital of Pome) which would be interesting to a botanist…I would have liked to

follow the Nagong river further, but was unable to do so as I had promised the Tsongpön that I would not go into Poba territory…the word 'Poba' means no more than an inhabitant of Pome.

It is surprising, given Ward's determination to reach Pome in 1913, that he did not try harder to persuade the Tsongpön to let him go.

Ward's final attempt to explore Pome was in 1935, his 'illegal' trip to Tibet, when he did not realise the 'permit' he could not read was in fact a refusal of entry. Ward intended to head for Showa, capital of Pome from the north, following the Po-Tsangpo. In *Assam Adventure*, the record of this 1935 expedition, Ward recounts that on his way to Pome, at the village of Tongkyuk, he met Colonel Yuri of the Lhasa police force. Apparently the police chief mistook Ward for Urush Marpo, a Bolshevik spy whom he was hunting at the time. It took Ward some time to convince Yuri that he had found the wrong man. Yuri quizzed Ward what route he was intending to take:

Showa (in Pome) was still on the agenda; but when I suggested it, the Colonel received it with disfavour. Pome in the rainy season was intolerable, he said, and strongly advised me not to go there. Since it was not, so far as I knew, essential to my plan of discovering the great snowy range, I withdrew the motion…but I was sorry to give up Showa.

Instead Ward retraced part of his 1924 journey north towards Pasum Tso. From the Shobe La, he again glimpsed the magnificent mountain range to the east of Pome which he had first hoped to reach in 1913:

The lost range was found! The enormous flight of bergs which Cawdor and I had seen far off eleven years earlier…a glittering skyway joining east and west…No wonder I felt uplifted.

From the Shobe La, Ward completed a circular trip north-west to Gyamda as he had done in 1924-25. By the time he returned to India, he had covered well over 1600km (1,000 miles).

Inspired by the expeditions of Morshead and Bailey, and Kingdon Ward, the first Frank Ludlow and George Sherriff expedition to south-east Tibet took place in 1938. The two British collectors were accompanied by Sir George Taylor, later the author of a monograph on Meconopsis and director of the Royal Botanic Gardens at Kew. In 1947 Ludlow, George and his wife, Betty Sherriff and their friend Colonel Elliot set out on a further expedition to explore the area around Pemaköchung in the Tsangpo Gorges and to reach the mountains of Pome. To cover as much territory as possible, the collectors split up to botanize different areas simultaneously. On arriving at Trulung in January, Ludlow was struck with poisoning after eating locally produced honey; rhododendron flowers were thought to be the cause. Such poisoning was not uncommon; Kingdon Ward also suffered from a bout of honey poisoning in Burma. To add insult to injury, a swarm of bees attacked Ludlow's dog, a Labrador called 'Joker', so severely he was paralysed for a time. When the two were sufficiently recovered, they made a brief reconnaissance to Showa in February, but it was too early in the season. Ludlow comments in his diary:

The range near Showa looks promising for flowers…2 passes cross the Sü La range (into the gorge) near Showa…the Showa or Dokar La (and) the Sü La, similarly the Dashing La further up the valley.

Ludlow sent two Tibetan members of the team to reconnoitre the mountains in June while he went north to Pasum Tso. Word was received that the two Tibetans had been forced to leave the Showa district and were refused assistance in obtaining food, water and transport until the Dzongpön had seen the expedition passport which at the time

***Arisaema consanguineum* with two leeches near Trulung (Pylung).**   **AC**
A fine example of flora and fauna combined, this slide was taken in the humid low-lying area where the Yigrong, Po-Tsangpo and Rong Chu rivers merge. Leeches can survive for months or even years in a state of suspended animation. They sense the approach of a potential meal from a considerable distance and start to extend and wave, trying to locate it. The photographer, Anne Chambers, an Arisaema enthusiast, was the anticipated prey. *A. consanguineum* is distinguished by the narrow leaflets and the long tails on both the leaflets and spathe.

was in Ludlow's keeping. Ludlow was irked, writing:

> There is only one passport and this cannot be split amongst 4 parties. We did ask for a duplicate passport but it was not customary to grant duplicates...The Dzongpön has now ruined our plans for collecting on the Sü La range.

It was especially galling because from their brief reconnaissance in the mountains Ludlow's collector Tsongpen had brought back a quantity of fascinating plant specimens, two of which were a curious small red-flowered lily and what turned out to be a new species of Omphalogramma. (*O. tibetica*).

China and Tibet closed their doors to foreign exploration in the 1950s and so it was that Pome still remained a largely unexplored area, all the more enticing for future generations of explorers and plant-hunters.

***Rodgersia pinnata* near Showa.**   **KNEC**
This well-known hardy perennial has distinctive, large chestnut-like leaves and white or pink flowers in summer. It requires plenty of moisture during the growing season. Here near the foot of the Dokar/Showa La, it is growing in fairly deep shade.

Exploring Pome 1996-97

Kenneth Cox

My first expedition to Tibet in 1995 (led by myself and David Burlinson) explored three passes: the Doshong La, Nyima La and Temo La. These passes were fairly thoroughly explored by Kingdon Ward and Ludlow and Sherriff, though some of the plants from this area had not previously been introduced or had been lost to cultivation. Once access to this part of Tibet had finally been achieved, we were curious to return to explore further afield. Not surprisingly, Kingdon Ward's unsuccessful attempts to reach Pome and the specimens collected near Showa on the Ludlow and Sherriff expedition inspired us to try to reach Pome ourselves. Thanks to the well-documented history of the previous expeditions, we knew where to look for interesting plants. What Ludlow calls the 'Sü La range' forms the eastern flank of the inner Tsangpo Gorge and lies west of the Po Yigrong, running from Tangme south to the Dashing La and beyond. It seemed straightforward enough, provided we managed to acquire the relevant permits, to penetrate at last areas where even the determination of Kingdon Ward and Ludlow had not prevailed.

The permits acquired, our 1996 party split into two groups. David Burlinson and He Hai (our Chinese leader and friend) drove off towards Pome to check the notoriously

---

Mahonia pomensis. **PC**
Discovered by Ludlow and Sherriff at Trulung (Pylung) in 1947, this magnificent but tender species appears never to have been introduced to cultivation. The flowers are reported to be yellow with red tinting. It would make a handsome garden plant for very mild climates.

bad road and to try arrange porters for our expedition to the Dokar or Showa La. Meanwhile, I led the remainder of the party (including my father Peter Cox) over the Doshong La in appalling weather, wading through deep snow. We had arranged to meet up with David and He Hai approximately six days later at Lin-chih on the Gyamda Chu. There was no sign of David and He Hai when we arrived at Lin-chih and the local police (the infamous Public Security Bureau) were not impressed that we were not in possession of our group passport. This passport was in Pome with David and He Hai, in an ironic reversal of fifty years earlier. We were held under house arrest at the local hotel until our papers arrived. This delay led to our chance meeting that evening, in a restaurant near our hotel, with Ken Storm and Ian Baker, returning from one of their expeditions in the Gorges. The beer flowed and stories were exchanged. We soon discovered we were all fully signed-up members of an unofficial Frank Kingdon Ward appreciation society. We were not grounded for too long, as David and He Hai arrived that evening with the missing papers. The following morning the two groups headed off in opposite directions.

The drive to Pome was to take the best part of two days. Having driven over the 4560m (15,000ft.) Sirchem La, we made our first interesting discovery. By the roadside above the Rong Chu valley, we found a single small plant of *Rhododendron lanatoides* with its distinctive silvery leaves and yellowish-green indumentum. Herbarium specimens of this species were collected by both Kingdon Ward and Ludlow and Sherriff, but taxonomists failed to identify them as anything new or significant until mature plants (still bearing their collectors' numbers) were discovered in several British gardens during the 1980s. Dr David Chamberlain, responsible for the classification of rhododendrons at the Royal Botanic Garden, Edinburgh, recognised a new species and the taxon was duly named *R. lanatoides*. Despite searching the previous year (particularly by Stephen Fox, the unofficial historian of this species), we failed to locate any *R. lanatoides* and suspected it might simply be a natural hybrid. In 1997, a few days after finding the single plant, we located a forest of the species at the foot of the Tra La, at the east end of the rong, and any doubts about it being a 'true' species were cast aside.

The drive from Tumbatse in the rong to Trulung (now called Pylung), where the path to Gompo Ne and the Tsangpo Gorges begins, is a long and winding descent from 3,500m (11,500ft.) to the confluence of the Po-Tsangpo and Yigrong rivers at 2000m (6,500ft.). Here the climate is sticky and humid and the plants take on a tropical appearance. Leeches hang expectantly from branches and leaves seeking the movements of any warm-blooded creature passing by. The plants from such low-lying areas are tender and need greenhouse cultivation in all but the mildest areas. As well as rhododendrons such as *R. nuttallii* and *R. scopulorum,* we located plants of *Mahonia pomensis* (discovered by Ludlow and Sherriff but never previously introduced), the long trailing stems of *Lilium wardii*, not yet in flower, and a Rubus (bramble) with delicious sweet orange fruit which would be a sensation in gourmet circles.

The road into Pome from the bottom of the valley around Trulung to Tangme, north of Showa, is treacherous, said to be the most dangerous in the whole of this part of China and Tibet. Blasted and cut out of steep hillsides, the road is frequently washed away by land and mudslides. The broken corpses of trucks lying at the bottom of the cliffs are evidence of lives lost on the road every year. The glistening muddy surface is the consistency of wet cement or discarded potters clay, and the Japanese-designed jeeps slither treacherously, only inches from the precipice, as the drivers go as fast as they can to maintain traction and to avoid falling rocks. All along the roadside were gangs of men and women breaking rocks; some of these workers were prisoners, we were informed, while others were migrant Muslim Uigurs from the Tibet-Pakistan border region, recognisable by their distinctive headgear. Along the same road, a year later in 1997, we were surprised to find the road gangs in much larger numbers. On enquiry we were informed that they were digging a ditch along the whole length of the road to lay fibre optic cables. Whether these will remain operational for long in an area so prone to landslides is doubtful.

Our aim was to reach, and perhaps cross, the Dokar La which straddles the mountain

Kenneth Cox with *R. campylocarpum* on the Doshong La. **PC**

range lying to the east of the Tsangpo Gorge. We hoped to be able to see into the gorge itself from the top of the pass and, weather permitting, to see impressive views of Namcha Barwa on the far side of the river. We had a copy of the Ludlow and Sherriff field notes listing the plants their collector Tsongpen had found, so we knew there were some very interesting and unusual things to seek out. The nearest village to the start of the trail, Showa, lies on the west side of the Yigrong Tsangpo, across a very narrow bridge only passable on horseback or by 'iron horse'. The 'iron horse' is an go-anywhere, bone-shaking motor-cycle-tractor hybrid which sustains much of Chinese and Tibetan agriculture. From our camp site, situated between the two parts of the village, looking south beyond a bend in the river we could see a stately, pointed, snow-capped peak appearing and disappearing in the clouds and mist. With the whirr of vibrating strings of prayer flags releasing the words printed on them into the wind, we negotiated terms for porters with the headman and determined to head off the next morning. Things looked less than promising when a small number of teenage boys and girls arrived at breakfast time to carry the heavy loads. Used to the professional Doshong La porters, and seeing large loads heaved on to the small shoulders of the youngsters, we feared the worst. When many of them sat down for a rest a few hundred yards along the flat road, I was convinced we were not going to see our luggage again that day, and that a cold and hungry night on the mountain side might be in prospect. The headman assured us everything would be fine.

So we set out through the village walking south, the first few miles parallel to the river. The sun was out, and at this relatively low altitude, it was very warm. In places, the forest floor was a carpet of chestnut-leaved *Rodgersia*; here and there clumps of the orchid *Callanthe tricarinata* poked their slender flower heads up through the vegetation. There

287

Callanthe species near Showa, Pome.   KNEC
This white species which may be *C. chloroleuca* was growing with the well-known and widely distributed *Callanthe tricarinata* in mixed woodland on slopes west of the Po-Tsangpo south of Showa. We thought at first that it was an albino version of the yellow species, but the floral parts were very different.

was also a second white Callanthe species. At first we thought it was an albino form of the yellow species but the corolla shape was quite different (probably *C. chlorantha*). Further on was a fine display of ferns and, between them, the stems of *Cardiocrinum giganteum* (the giant Himalayan lily) were starting to elongate, probably still a good month away from opening their stack of sweetly fragrant white flowers. Here too was a much smaller member of the lily family, *Streptopus simplex,* with narrow leaves and tiny white flowers. From time to time the path descended to cross stream beds which, in a month or so, would overflow with monsoon rainwater. We found a few remaining flowers on the rather tender *Rhododendron virgatum,* a species Kingdon Ward had found in the gorge. A waist-high shrub with mahogany-coloured exfoliating bark turned out to be *Deutzia compacta* with its green buds just starting to show the colour of its white flowers. After two to three hours the path began to ascend and pine forest gave way to *Tsuga dumosa* and then to spruce. Peter Cox located a tree of a red-flowered Sorbus (*S. microphyllus* or *S. filipes*). This was a really important find, as it proved the earlier collectors had not been dreaming: conventional wisdom dictated that Sorbus had white or pale pink flowers and yet red-flowered Sorbus had been reported in the wild. This was the first time one had been located in recent years. Other finds included *Xanthoxylum artmatum,* a shrub whose wood is used to make walking sticks and whose fruit is used in the Himalayas to cure toothache. Above us were enormous old trees of *Pieris formosa* var. *forrestii* (the source of the well-known 'Forest Flame') rising up to 6m (20ft.) or more.

We made camp at the relatively low altitude of 3000m (9,900ft.) because we were worried the luggage might not arrive. As usual, the keen bridge players in the party soon had a game underway; we sat next to the frame of the yak herders' summer shelter. These shelters are dismantled in winter to protect the roofs from breaking under the weight of snow. Our porters arrived, one or two at a time, and soon the walls of the shelter began to appear and the young men hauled up roofing planks and slats to lay across the rafters. In the event, the young Tibetans had done us proud, bringing huge loads up the hill which their professional rivals on the Doshong La would have refused, unless press-ganged by the Chinese military. The mess tent erected and the cooking underway, it was apparent the villagers were treating our expedition as a holiday. The girls collected rhododendron flowers to put in their hair and built a fire beside the hut. They were to sing and dance the night away.

As the sun started to set, an astonishing sight was revealed. Opposite, to the east across the river far below, a jagged, snow-covered mountain range appeared through the dissipating cloud, stretching as far as we could see to north and south. This was obviously the very range that had so excited Kingdon Ward from the Nambu La: 'the mysterious snowy range of Pome… a glittering skyway'. The main peak, known as Jhu Long, well over 6100m (20,000ft.), is as steep and stark as the north slope of Namche Barwa to the west. We realised we were probably the first westerners to enjoy this view and much film was expended trying to capture it. The next day the view was just as spectacular, this time with a delightful pink and yellow morning light. We moved camp a little higher to 3275m (10,800ft.), on the way passing some impressively tall, stately yellow lampshade poppies, *Meconopsis pseudointegrifolia*. Arriving before lunchtime, we decided to take advantage of the fine weather to climb as high as possible as we wanted to find a route to the pass known as the Dokar La. Through a spruce and birch forest, where the small white flowered *Berneuxia thibetica* grew in damp shady spots, we soon reached the treeline and were treated to views of snow-fringed, bowl-shaped valleys, with purple *Rhododendron calostrotum* and yellow *R. wardii* in the foreground. We sat down for a rest in the warm sunshine in this extraordinary setting, surrounded by flowers, distant mountains and blue sky. We felt a similar sense of exhilaration to that which Kingdon Ward described time and time again, when high in the mountains of Tibet and China. We could have sat and drunk the view for the rest of the day but a few members of the group with energy to spare continued onwards and upwards. It was not clear where exactly the pass was. The ridge was still deep in snow and with precarious cornices making approach dangerous in case avalanches were set off.

It was only then we learned from the villagers that the Dokar La is seldom open and virtually never used. Reluctantly accepting we were not going to be able to cross the pass, we set about exploring the alpine meadows high above the treeline. Here the plants, with their branches still flattened by the weight of months of snow, their leaves brown and forlorn, were just waking up after their winter hibernation. Within a few days of the snow melting, the plants spring back to life and flower buds begin to swell. In hollows there were patches of fine deep red *Rhododendron sanguineum*; this is as far west as this species has been recorded. Where it grew with *R. wardii* were obvious natural hybrids with fine rich reddish-pink flowers. Compact forms of the normally rather leggy *R. primuliflorum* were spotted, with outstanding deep pink, daphne-like flowers. Beneath the rhododendrons we found plants of the Primula relative *Omphalogramma tibetica* (found by Ludlow's collectors in 1947) with its curious purple flowers with fine hairs in the throat. Here too was *Rhododendron pemakoense*, a low

***Sorbus* sp. (*filipes?*) with red flowers.**   **PC**
Sorbus species show a huge variation in colour of fruit, but the flowers are invariably white or pale pink. There are a few herbarium specimens which describe the flowers as red, but this is almost certainly the first example to be found by western collectors for many years. It was located by Peter Cox on the eastern slopes leading up to the Dokar or Showa La in 1996.

carpeting plant with a mass of purplish-pink flowers. This species was discovered by Kingdon Ward in the Gorge above Pemaköchung and this is only the second time this species has been recorded by western collectors. It was now late in the afternoon and we were getting hungry as we'd skipped lunch, so we headed back to camp, satisfied with a wonderful day's plant-hunting. We had ticked off many of the plants on the Ludlow and Sherriff field notes. The one great disappointment was that there had been no sign of the red lily, though we were close to where it was originally found.

The next day it was agreed that, as the pass was no longer a realistic objective, the party would spend the morning in further exploration of the area around the camp and return in the afternoon and evening to our starting point at the village of Showa, way below by the river. Our teenagers were most disappointed to have to return to their village a day early as their paid holiday was proving so much fun and romance had blossomed between one of our guides and one of the porters. A very friendly and inquisitive yak, whose face was covered in ticks, was determined to investigate every tent as it was dismantled, despite being shooed away by the porters. Meanwhile my father, exploring above the treeline, got involved in an altercation with a more bad-tempered yak. It charged him and in the usual manner, in return, he sent back a volley of rocks in its direction. I set out on the long walk back downhill at a leisurely pace, enjoying the views and hunting for plants such as the red-flowered Sorbus which I had missed during the ascent. Back at Showa, later in the day, the inevitable bridge game was underway. One of the last to arrive back at the river was June Ross, an experienced mountaineer and intrepid member of the party. She was clutching a little bundle. On a treacherous scree, she had spotted a flash of red. Carefully clambering over to investigate, she'd photographed the flower and picked a single bloom for identification purposes when the unstable scree caused her to make a faster and less comfortable descent than she intended. I unwrapped June's specimen, and there it was. Unmistakably, this was the red lily. We were now several hours' climb below its habitat, with no prospect of seeing it for ourselves. I determined to return and search for it again another year. The red-flowered *Lilium paradoxum* is so named as it was the only known lily species with a distinct whorl of leaves, and puzzled botanists considered placing it in another genus. It was described from Tsongpen's specimen from the 1938 Ludlow and Sherriff expedition. It grows 30–50cm (1–2ft.) and has rich dark red flowers. It has considerable potential as a parent of fine dwarf lily hybrids and is certainly a plant that any lily enthusiast would love to grow.

Back in Britain I recounted the saga of the red lily to a friend who worked as a journalist for a national newspaper. Claire had always wanted to go to Tibet and this looked an interesting story. Her editor loved the idea of this elusive plant, still living undisturbed in the Tibetan mountains. 'Don't you dare come back without finding the red Lily' he warned her as he signed the commission for the article.

So Claire joined us for the 1997 expedition. As well as seeking out the red lily, we wanted to explore the area near Zayul, south of the Tsangpo Gorges. We knew this was a sensitive area as far as the Chinese army were concerned but none the less we were given permission to explore fairly close to the Burmese border. We visited Shugden Gompa, visited by Bailey in 1911 and Kingdon Ward in 1933, to find that part of the monastery building had been painstakingly reconstructed following its destruction during the Cultural Revolution. Only one monk had survived from that era. He explained that he had lived in the forest to escape the Chinese but was eventually captured and imprisoned for many years. He was delighted when we gave him a copy of Kingdon Ward's photograph of the Gompa taken in 1933 and he said that we were the first foreigners to visit the rebuilt monastery. It was indeed an honour to know this, and everyone agreed this place had a strange but magical atmosphere. No one will forget the view from the monastery, looking out over a glacial lake up to the Zo La pass in the south-east and towards the Ata Kang Glacier in the west. The town at the lakeside below looks primeval, hewn from local rocks in the same colour as the surrounding mountains and the flat roofs of the houses are covered with timber racks

A stunning display of *R. wardii* and *R. calostrotum*.   **PC**
The snow-covered peaks and carpets of several species of rhododendrons in the mountains above Showa, provided some stunning vistas. This is the hillside where Tsongpen collected specimens for Ludlow and Sherriff, before being ejected from the area because he was not carrying the expedition passport.

Reconstructing a herders' hut east of the Dokar La. KNEC
Huts like this one are found high up in meadows on many of the passes of south-east Tibet. Most are dismantled in the autumn to avoid damage to roof and walls from winter snows, and are quickly re constructed in spring by porters crossing the passes above and by herdsmen who take their animals up to high pasture in summer.

This valley lies just below the Dashing La, on the east (Pome) side of the pass. There are several glaciers in this impressive mountain range which forms the eastern boundary of the Tsangpo Gorge. Many species of alpine plants are bursting into flower in the areas where the snow has already melted.

where crops are laid out to dry. The air was cold, the sky clear and the small brazier burnt juniper and rhododendron, the spicy scents wafting towards us as we sat inspired by the view. The landscape is described in detail in Kingdon Ward's *A Plant Hunter in Tibet* and little appears to have changed in the intervening years.

Our next objectives were the Dashing La, and then the Sü La, as both were likely habitats for the red lily. The track leading to the Dashing La branches off the Pome road a few miles south of the town. Passing huge piles of *mani* stones, we found a suitable camp site, enlisted porters and next morning headed up the valley on a very long walk, very gradually gaining altitude. In a forest of *Rhododendron beesianum* and *R. uvariifolium*, Claire and I were sitting eating lunch in silence when she gestured to me. Moving through the undergrowth was a red panda: about the size of an average dog but with a characteristic long striped tail. These rather timid animals are a rare sight. Around our camp site, by a chilly fast-flowing river, we found an old favourite *Enkianthus chinensis* in full flower, with its pendent cream bells with red stripes.

The next day we decided to try to reach the pass. Unfortunately, but not unusually, the morning weather was foul: low cloud, wind, rain, hail and sleet. After an hour or so of

The Sü La pass, the home of the red lily.   **IB**
Porters climb towards the top of the Sü La, the glaciated peaks of the Pome range rising behind. The red lily was
located in the steep ravines leading towards this snow-covered pass.

Lilium paradoxum, **below the Dokar La.**   **JR**
This picture shows *Lilium paradoxum* found by June Ross in 1996, below
the Dokar La on a steep scree-covered slope. This was probably the first
time this plant had ever been seen by a western plant hunter.

Enkianthus chinensis **east of the Dashing La.**   **KNEC**
The genus *Enkianthus* is closely related to the rhododendrons, and the two
genera enjoy similar woodland conditions in the wild and in the garden. A
deciduous shrub, growing to 4m (13ft.), with pendulous racemes of creamy
yellow, bell-shaped flowers with pink stripes in spring. Enkianthus can have
amongst the finest autumn colour of any shrubs. This specimen was
photographed on the east side of the Dashing La, south-east of the Tsangpo
Gorge.

293

trekking in driving rain, several people headed back to camp. But as so often happens, the weather began to clear shortly after midday, as we were sheltering in a herder's hut, and at last we were able to see where we were – at the bottom of a huge bowl surrounded by glaciated slopes, becoming steeper as they rose higher and higher. The slopes were a curious mixture of snow glaciers, black rock and pale yellow mud, and looked as if they had only recently been scarred and scraped by moving ice. At the top the cliffs were almost vertical with increasing amounts of snow as they rose higher and higher. Overhanging cornices gave way from time to time with a puff of white, followed a few seconds later by a crack and then the roar of avalanche. Gingerly crossing a steep snow field, we found a spectacular carpet of *Rhododendron forrestii* as good as anything on the Doshong La, with multicoloured *Diapensia purpurea* keeping it company. The pass was at least 300m (1,000ft.) above us to the left, but the risk of avalanche forced us reluctantly back to camp, where an unpleasant surprise awaited us. Several armed Chinese soldiers had arrived in camp while we were absent. Amy Denton, an American member of the party, had been sunbathing and was horrified to open her eyes to find rifles pointing at her. The Chinese ordered the party to descend immediately but our Chinese leader managed to convince the army to allow us to remain at camp until the following day. We promised to report to the police headquarters in Pome on our descent.

Once again, it was the *Dzongpön* of Pome, or at least his modern day equivalent who, unhappy with our presence, was determined to expel us from his district. Ostensibly our crime was to have hired porters without his permission, but we later learned from the Abbot of the local monastery (then in exile in Kathmandu) that the headman had a reputation for intransigence and cruelty and a great dislike for foreigners. Unusually for Tibet, where powerful positions are generally held by Chinese, this headman was Tibetan. He was not interested in any permits, valid or otherwise, and we were ordered to leave the district within twenty-four hours. It was almost certainly the end of the red lily search as there was no reason to believe that it occurred anywhere outside Pome. We spent the night at a camp site by a shrine decorated with hundreds of prayer flags. Here a miserable Claire had to contemplate the consequences of returning the Britain without her story.

This story does, however, have a happy ending. Back in Kathmandu, we met up with Ian Baker, about to embark on another Tibet expedition to the Tsangpo Gorges and Pemakö with his friend, Kenneth Storm. And, yes, they were intending to cross the Sü La, home of the red lily. Claire was invited to join the expedition and it was not long before she was heading back to Tibet.

Kenneth Storm, Jr. takes up the story:

We planned to travel south from the Pome Valley via the Sü La, a 3960m (13,000ft.) pass on the mountain range bounding the Gorge to the north and east. We had long anticipated this historic crossing, reversing the route taken by F.M. Bailey and Henry Morshead on their epic exploration in search of the legendary falls of the Tsangpo Gorge in 1913. I knew nothing about the 'Red Lily' until Claire told us the story – and from then on I could think of little else.

On the morning of 15 August I left our camp in the forest and ascended a small stream flowing through a broad meadow flanked by steep and rugged mountain walls. Long slender waterfalls streaked the mountains to the south and at the head of the valley the clouds hung low over the dirty, blue-grey snout of a glacier. The winter snows had withdrawn from the steep slopes and in its wake it was Spring. Primulas blossomed near patches of snow and along small brooks. The route to Sü La ascends abruptly from the valley up a narrow rock-strewn gully. As I climbed higher I saw large snow fields lying close above. I was journeying back into winter. A breeze freshened and clouds rolled overhead and spilled down the slope. The vegetation soon thinned out, replaced by a loose scree, and my hopes of finding the red lily faded. Perhaps the Tibetan collector

***Lilium paradoxum* from the Sü La, Pome.**   **IB**
A villager from Pome reveals the roots of a Red Lily, which Tibetans prize as a potent medicine against fever and other diverse ailments. The silver amulet box slung across his shoulders contains sacred relics including dried plants believed to be not only curative but spiritually elevating.

had wandered somewhere beyond the trail to find his precious lily – it could be anywhere in this vast landscape. Maybe it was not yet in flower in this narrow threshold between winter and spring. Still, I examined the ground, probed every plant, and scanned the slopes for a flash of red. I felt an exhilaration that comes with attending closely to a wild landscape and delighted in the search.

Then I saw them – not one but several blooms, nodding in the breeze on a steep slope beyond the track I was climbing. The deep burgundy of the corollas burned brightly into the grey day as I carefully made my way to the plants, dug my feet into the side of the slope, and lowered myself to eye-level with them. How delicate they seemed, spotted with drops of rain. I feared my breath might scatter the petals. I lay there a long time admiring the arc of the veined stems, the whorls of narrow leaves, and the dance of the bell-shaped corollas framing the valley far below. Soon Claire appeared, scrambling up the steep slope. 'I found it,' I called to her, and she soon joined me on the hillside to share the beauty and the goal of her own personal quest. A story had led me on a search for a flower on a mountain in Tibet, but I had found much more. I awoke to unexpected wonder and delicate beauty that cast an aura of enchantment over the days that followed – and that lingers still.

The newspaper published Claire's article. And the red lily is still out there and, as far as we know, no one has yet managed to collect it. It is somehow curiously satisfying to know that, early in the twenty-first century, there are still a few plants out there in the mountains which have still managed to avoid being tamed, domesticated and preened, plants which only a tiny handful of explorers have ever seen. Despite the determination of Kingdon Ward, Ludlow and ourselves to explore the Pome area, the various Dzongpöns and other officials of Pome and surrounding districts have always treated potential foreign visitors with equal disdain and guarded their red lily from almost everyone who has tried to find it.

Exploration of the Tsangpo Gorges from 1925
Kenneth Storm, Jr.

On a late afternoon in May 1993, Ian Baker and I scrambled atop a large boulder along the margin of the Tsangpo River. Spray exploded high into the air at the base of furious rapids upstream and dissolved in a mist illuminated by sunlight slanting through the gorge. At our feet, the river surged around the boulder where we stood and flowed off to the east a short distance and ran up against a great silvery cliff rising sheer for more than 600m (2,000ft.). At the base of the cliff, where a lovely side stream spilled into the Tsangpo in a waterfall, the river turned abruptly to the north and disappeared from view.

Only twice before had western explorers reached this point – F.M. Bailey in 1913 and Frank Kingdon Ward and Lord Cawdor in December of 1924. For Bailey, this was the end of his desperate dash deep into the gorge below Pemaköchung. The Mönbas who promised to guide him through abandoned him here, throwing down his gear from the cliffs above and hurrying on to their homes in Lugu by a route only they knew. Frank Kingdon Ward and Lord Cawdor had slightly better luck. They surmounted lower cliffs along the river above the bend and reached the base of the great wall. A short distance downstream a horizon-line spanned the river. Beyond, in a burst of December sunlight, a rainbow arced through the veil of rising mist. 'The Falls at last,' Kingdon Ward speculated. Clinging to the river-polished sides of the gorge they climbed as high as they dared and strained for a view. It was indeed a waterfall – the largest they had yet seen – 12m (40ft.) perhaps – but not the 30m (100ft.) fall they hoped to find. One thing was clear, their journey along the river ended here. Beyond the drop they named 'Rainbow Falls' the river slipped out of sight between the narrowing walls and rugged, forested spurs plunging into the gorge. They had no choice but to retreat upstream and find another way out.

For more than two weeks Ian and I had worked our way downriver from Gyala to this point, travelling with our companions Jill Biewlawski, Eric Manthey, Geng Zuanru, and a small group of Tibetan porters. Our journey took us along the steep flanks of the gorge, often cutting our way through dense forest following the elusive trace of takin. Sometimes we scrambled over slick boulders along the river's edge or bridged swift side streams spilling from the tongues of glaciers hidden up the wild valleys below Namcha Barwa. I carried a dog-eared photocopy of Frank Kingdon Ward's *Riddle of the Tsangpo Gorges* as our guidebook. At camp each night we would read aloud from its pages, Ian translating for the porters gathered around the fire who were eager to hear of the travails of those explorers of long ago and anxious for some clue to the passage ahead. None of them had travelled this far into the gorges before. We marked our progress by the plants Kingdon Ward described – the first appearance of the lovely weeping pine, a large magnolia – and by the sudden twists and turns in the river. Now, with supplies of food running low and confronted by the same terrain that defeated Bailey and turned back Kingdon Ward and Cawdor, our thoughts raced ahead to the daunting thought of scaling that awful cliff.

In the years following 1924, few travellers penetrated deep into the Tsangpo gorges. The 1950s brought a surge of refugees fleeing down the lower gorges to India, but the upper gorge traversed by Kingdon Ward and Cawdor in 1924 remained largely untravelled, the old routes forgotten. The monastery at Pemaköchung melted back into the jungle, perhaps destroyed by the Assam Earthquake of 1950. Today, just a handful of pilgrims make the arduous journey to the ruins there, and few venture beyond.

The only western expeditions to reach the gorges after Kingdon Ward and Lord Cawdor were those of Frank Ludlow and George Sherriff. In the years leading up to the Second World War and immediately after, this intrepid pair mounted several collecting expeditions with the goal to explore systematically all of South-east Tibet. In February 1947 Sherriff and his wife Betty reached Gompo Ne at the top of the Great Bend where the Po-Tsangpo River joins the Yarlung Tsangpo. Later that spring Ludlow, along with Henry Elliot, returned to

Pemaköchung, collecting dozens of species of rhododendron and other plants. They were eager to return the following season and complete their explorations deeper into the upper gorges but the Tibetans, worried over the recent Chinese advances, would not extend them permits. The window of opportunity for western exploration in the Tsangpo gorges slammed shut. It would be more than forty-five years before western explorers would set foot there again.

Chinese scientists began exploring portions of the Tsangpo gorges – primarily the lower, tropical sections near Medog – in the 1970s and 1980s. Beginning in 1994, Chinese scientists were joined by Swiss geologist Jean-Pierre Burg and his colleagues in a study of the geological history of the region. In 1992 a Japanese climbing team reached the summit of Namcha Barwa, then the highest unclimbed peak in the world. In April 1993 an American team of David Breashears and Gordon Wiltsie turned back just beyond Pemaköchung on an unsuccessful attempt to traverse the upper gorges. When we arrived at the gorge later that month as part of another American expedition we found the same untrammelled wilderness beyond Pemaköchung that Bailey, Morshead, Kingdon Ward and Cawdor experienced in the early part of the twentieth century.

The day after Ian and I contemplated the journey ahead from atop the boulder along the Tsangpo River, the weather changed. Clouds filled the gorge, sealing off the upper mountain ramparts from view. Under a driving rain we ascended a knife-edged ridge, setting ropes where landslides had peeled away the forest along our track. To the north, through rents in the clouds, we looked down the narrowing corridor where Frank Kingdon Ward and Lord Cawdor once clung to the walls of the gorge, straining for a view into the unknown. It was a scene of wild grandeur. On the right, waterfalls spilled out of the clouds in long silver threads cascading down the rocky flanks of the gorge, a thousand feet to the river. To the left, a long sinuous ridge, set with ghostly cloud-raked hemlock, descended into the gorge. Pressed tightly between, the river raged around a bend and out of sight. We could

At the top of the Great Bend.   **KSJ**

Clouds play in the gorge as the river bends to the south below the village of Tsachu. Beyond this point, just below the confluence with the Po-Tsangpo River, the course of the river is south toward India and a tropical world. KW reached here on 4 December 1924. Kintup probably followed the river downstream past here in 1882 after being held captive for several months at a village north of the gorge.

The Tsechu.   **IB**

Porters from lower Kongbo attempt to bridge the Tsechu, a tributary stream which flows into the Tsangpo below the village of Payi (Payu, Payul, Bayi, Bayu or Bayul) . This was taken on an expedition in May 1993. For days we had travelled on meagre rations without any sign of a trail.

see little more than Kingdon Ward and Cawdor saw from along the river years before.

We now had more immediate worries on our minds. With our supply of food running low, we sheltered from the rain for two days in a boulder-cave high above the Great Bend, hoping for a break in the weather. When it didn't come, we made a desperate dash into the clouds and crossed a pass only to find ourselves morassed in an uninhabited, subtropical wilderness growing wilder with each step. It took two days to throw a bridge across a raging glacier stream. Then we stumbled into a surprised group of hunters from a village on the other side – Lugu – the same village Bailey hoped to reach years before. The hunters guided us out.

It would be several years before our explorations took us back toward the 'gap' beyond Rainbow Falls. After 1993, Hamid Sardar, an American of Iranian descent – and a Tibetan scholar – joined our core group of travellers. In the years that followed, we travelled more as pilgrims than western explorers. In 1994 we followed in the footsteps of Kintup, Bailey, and Morshead in a traverse of the lower gorge. In 1995 Ian and Hamid led a pilgrimage to the same sacred mountain, Kundu Dorsempotrang, visited by Kintup more than one hundred years before. In 1996 Ralph Rynning inventoried the birds of the gorge on an expedition with Ian and me. That year we explored deep into the 'gap' along the left bank of the Tsangpo above the confluence with the Po-Tsangpo River. We also completed our historical 'pilgrimage' along the Kingdon Ward/Lord Cawdor route by reaching their 'Falls of the Brahmaputra', guided by Dungle Phuntsok, the grandson of Kingdon Ward's guide in 1924.

In August of 1997 we crossed from Pome into the lower gorge over Sü La, along the route Bailey and Morshead used in 1913, rediscovering the 'red lily' along the way. Near the village of Lagung, where Bailey and Morshead met with the *Nyerpa* of Pome, our expedition split. Ian and Hamid led a group down the Tsangpo and out via Doshong La, while brothers Gil and Troy Gillenwater and I went north, hoping to return to the upper gorge in the vicinity of Rainbow Falls. It had been more than four years since Ian and I and the others had lost our way in the clouds above the 'gap' left unexplored by Kingdon Ward and Cawdor. Now, several days of clear weather and the fortuitous meeting with a Tibetan hunter, Jyang, opened the way. Jyang led us down a steep gully to the edge of a cliff. There our route ended where the stream we followed plunged over a thousand feet to the Tsangpo in the same slender cascade I saw streaking the walls of the gorge down the cloud-decked corridor four years before. At our feet was Rainbow Falls, clouds of mist wrapping the trees overhanging the river on the left bank. Just below, hidden beyond a

Ian Baker, Dungle Phuntsok, and Ken Storm, Jr.   **RR**

Mönba guide, Dungle Phuntsok, points out Ward's route.   **KSJ**

Ken Storm writes: Our Mönba guide, Dungle Phuntsok, points out the place where his grandfather led Frank Kingdon Ward and Lord Cawdor, 'two Ingles', into the gorge in search of the 'Falls of the Brahmaputra' in 1924.

My journal entry describes the moment: 'At one point, high on a traverse, the clouds open to reveal the Tsangpo River tearing wildly into the gorge toward the east and the confluence with the Po-Tsangpo River. Ian Baker and I have been descending with Dungle Phuntsok, at 55 our oldest Mönba guide. He stops now, teetering under his basket loaded with takin meat and hides, and points with his walking stick to a long slope that drops down from the back of the ridge in the direction of Sengchen. Ian and he are engaged in excited conversation. 'Look there!' he points. 'My grandfather led two 'Ingles' down to the river there many years ago.' What a remarkable moment! Usually silent, often fingering his prayer beads alone in the cave at night, this is the first time he has spoken to us about that expedition. We had assumed the memory of that distant journey had long ago been forgotten – we had not even asked. Now, out of the gloom and tedious labour of our descent we reach out across the years. I half expect to see Frank and Cawdor and their line of porters emerge from the mist on that distant hillside. I think of Jean (Frank's widow) far away in England and long to tell her of this wonderful moment!

hairpin bend, the river pooled, then darted to the left and exploded over another great drop – a 'new' waterfall. It was clear from our higher vantage point, and from the photographs Kingdon Ward and Cawdor took looking downstream beyond Rainbow Falls, that they could not see this waterfall – a spur blocked their view. They retreated up the river and climbed out of the gorge with no more views of the river beyond. Hopes of finding a Niagara-sized waterfall in the Tsangpo gorges had been given up long ago, but Kingdon Ward still held out the possibility of finding a spectacular waterfall in the range 'of 100 feet or so'. He never found that 'big waterfall'. Could this indeed be the waterfall western explorers sought long ago and gave up as legend? I realised that until we actually reached it and documented its height we could not be certain. That final journey to the waterfall, a joint quest involving Ian, Hamid, and myself, would be the goal of our 1998 expedition.

Before then, in the spring of 1998, Ian and Hamid, along with Ned Johnston, made a reconnaissance into the 'gap' below Rainbow Falls, learning of additional Tibetan hunter trails into the area, in preparation for our joint journey in the autumn. They also viewed the waterfalls for themselves from high on the cliffs and, for the first time, the Tibetans revealed tantalising stories of their sacred waterfalls – a rich glimpse into the mystical world of Pemakö.

Dungle Phuntsok, Mönba guide.   **KSJ**

The next day we climbed out of the gorge and rested for tea in a small cave 2,000ft. above the river. Dungle Phuntsok was talking again about the 'Ingles' as we huddled together out of the rain. 'They stayed here for the night,' he said, motioning to the back of the cave. His grandfather told him they had a small dog that had been trained to fetch things from their packs. How many times since 1924, I wondered, had these Mönba hunters from Sengchen stopped in this same cave on their seasonal hunting expeditions. Each time was perhaps an occasion to tell again, father to son, grandfather to grandson, that story of those strange 'Ingles' travellers they had guided here in search of a waterfall. Not for the first time in my travels through the Tsangpo Gorge, we had the uncanny sensation that Frank Kingdon Ward and Lord Cawdor had passed only moments before. The world here seemed timeless.

Beyond Rainbow Falls: A Photographic Journey
Kenneth Storm Jr.

Waterfall on the Tsangpo   **FKW**

This is Kingdon Ward's famous 'Rainbow Falls'. In 1924 Kingdon Ward and Lord Cawdor were forced to leave the river here, in a harrowing ascent up the steep walls of the gorge. In a letter he wrote to Arthur Hinks of the Royal Geographic Society, he described the scene: 'Exploring round the bend from our bivouac that evening, I turned the corner and saw the gorge filled with spray, and the river dropping vertically over a ledge. "The falls at last," thought I. However, it wasn't. We couldn't get within six hundred yards of the fall, but estimated a vertical drop of about forty feet from the spray and noise and the level of the river below.'

The massif of Namcha Barwa.   **IB**

Taken on a clear day in November, the massif of Namcha Barwa ('Blazing Meteorite')
and the sacred pyramid of Dorje Pagmo are framed by conifers on a ridge high above
the gorge. To the left of this rock buttress the Tsangpo begins its legendary curve to the
north-west and disappears into the 'five to ten mile gap' which Kingdon Ward never
explored.

Kingdon Ward stated that he was looking for 'a big waterfall of 100 feet or so' (page
220 of this edition). Little did he realise that his 'big waterfall' was just a quarter mile
below, hidden from view around a tight hairpin bend of the river. On 7 November
1998, while Hamid Sardar explored farther down the gorge, Ian Baker and I,
accompanied by National Geographic filmmaker Bryan Harvey, our Sherpa porters and
Tibetan guides, descended the forested ridge seen on the right of the photograph on
page 300. Viewed from the ridge below, 'Rainbow Falls' is a beautiful, river-wide
cascade split by the huge boulder seen in Kingdon Ward's photograph. With a
clinometer and laser range finder we measured the falls at 21.3m (70ft.), nearly twice
Kingdon Ward's estimate. (The volume of the river was higher during our visit in 1998
than in December 1924.) We camped that night amid the pines on the ridge,
marvelling at the spray and mist rising from below Rainbow Falls and wrapping the
conifers on the rocky cliffs above. It was easy to imagine Kingdon Ward and Cawdor
scrambling up the cliffs above the falls so many years before, straining for a view into
the unknown gorge below, where we were now camped.

Ken Storm rappels down towards the Hidden Falls of Dorje Pagmo.   IB
Only a quarter mile below Rainbow Falls, this 30m (100ft.) cataract was concealed by a gneissic spur descending from the monolithic peak of Dorje Pagmo, the Tantric goddess whose sacred energy is said to suffuse the entire region of the Tsangpo gorges. Some Tibetans believe that this long-sought waterfall conceals the entry to a hidden paradise.

The next day we continued down the ridge and rappelled the last 23m (75ft.) to a ledge above the brink of the 'new' falls we had first glimpsed from high above a year earlier. The river pooled above the brink, narrowed, and thundered over a drop we measured at over 30.5m (100ft.) – the 'big waterfall' at last! We named the falls 'Hidden Falls of Dorje Pagmo' in honour of the Tibetan goddess whose mountain rises above the cataract. At over 70 and 100ft. high respectively, and only a quarter of a mile apart, these two waterfalls are the highest yet recorded on a major Himalayan river. For our Tibetan guides the waterfall was a sacred, mystical place. What had once been spoken of in Tibetan myth and searched for in the West lay before us in its sublime splendour!
    When I returned home and telephoned Frank's widow, Jean, with the news, she remarked: 'I am glad Frank left something for you to find.'

Rainbow Falls from our camp on the ridge downstream **KSJ**

Mönba hunters Jyang and Bullock look at Rainbow Falls.

Ward described the view as he approached the area from upstream: 'A quarter mile ahead a blank cliff, striped by two silver threads of water, towered a thousand feet into the air…Cliffs towered up on both sides, so close together that it seemed one could almost leap from crag to crag; and the cliffs were *smooth* as well as sheer. Only high up against the skyline did a few trees cling like fur to the worn rock surface. Obviously we could get no further down the gorge; to scale the cliff seemed equally impossible' (page 214 of this edition). In 1924 Ward and Cawdor scrambled up the walls of the gorge on the right bank a short distance above the falls and looked beyond to see mist rising from below and a rainbow arcing across the brink. They estimated the height of Rainbow Falls to be about 12m (40ft.) – not the large, 30.5m (100ft.) falls they hoped to find.

Hidden Falls of Dorje Pagmo from below. **(KSJ)**

Confined in a narrow chasm, the river explodes over the drop in a spray of mist. Situated a little more than a quarter mile below Rainbow Falls, this 30.5m (100ft.) drop cannot be seen from the point where Ward and Cawdor left the river in 1924. Visible above Hidden Falls can be seen one of the small streams Kingdon Ward describes falling into the river at Rainbow Falls.

The Tsangpo Gorge downstream from Hidden Falls. KSJ

Sheer walls and a raging river stop the traveller from following the river in the gorge. Although Ward never reached this point, he wrote earlier: 'The river continued to advance by jerks in a general north–east direction, with fierce rapids which ate hungrily into the core of the mountains. Already we seemed to be far below the level of the ground, going down, down, into the interior of the earth; and as though to emphasise the fact, the temperature grew steadily warmer. And the gorge was growing ever narrower, the gradient steeper, till the power behind the maddened river was terrific. Its blows fell on rock and cliff with frightful force; and at every turn a huge cavernous mouth seemed to open, and gulp it down faster and faster' (pages 210-211 of this edition).

The raging Tsangpo River in the gorge below Hidden Falls. KSJ

Autumn blazes on the slopes of the gorge above the sharp bend of the Tsangpo where the river virtually turns back on itself. Ian and I explored the gorge from the steep, forested flanks above the river, working our way downstream where we eventually met up with Hamid. [The panorama above was made looking downsteam from the point where the river emerges at the left in this photograph.]

Namcha Barwa and Gyala Peri   **KSJ**

The Namcha Barwa Massif (to the left) and Gyala Peri (on the right) stand sentinel over the wild heart of the Tsangpo Gorge. The Tsangpo River burrows deep within the forested folds of the inner gorge, more than three miles below the mountain summits.

'The Falls at Last'
Documenting the 'Hidden Falls'
Kenneth Storm, Jr.

The history of exploration has often been filled with dispute. From the discovery of America by Europeans, to the race to find the source of the Nile, there have sometimes been conflicting versions, claims and counter claims, often ignoring the fact that the local inhabitants had of course been there all along. The 'discovery' and measurement of 'Hidden Falls' is, unfortunately, no exception.

Our expedition to document these falls began in late October 1998. When we entered the gorge we learned that the Chinese were already in the field with a large expedition of their own comprised of three separate groups. One Chinese group crossed the Doshong La to explore the lower gorge up-river from Medog. A second focused on the area around the confluence of the Tsangpo with the Po-Tsangpo Rivers. A third group began at Gyala and followed the river downstream into the upper gorges. Even before the Chinese took to the field, an American expedition led by Wickliffe Walker attempted a kayak descent of the Tsangpo River through the upper gorges. A short distance below Gyala one of the boaters, Doug Gordon, was swept to his death and the expedition members left the river well short of their goal. We met the grieving party as they were leaving the area, offered our condolences, and promised to look for any sign of Gordon or his equipment. Nothing was found.

When we descended beyond Rainbow Falls and reached 'Hidden Falls' on 8 November 1998, the Chinese group was still some distance up-river. We learned this a few days later when a runner from their expedition reached the village of Payi to resupply. When our expedition ended in late November we expected an announcement forthcoming from the Chinese expedition. Meanwhile, the National Geographic Society announced the results of our expedition in a press release from Washington, D.C. on 7 January 1999. The story was reported in the national and world press, prompting a Chinese response in *China Daily* on 29 January. The headline of that article, 'Chinese Explorers get to the Falls First', is not quite accurate. Although they report seeing and photographing the waterfalls from a helicopter in 1987 they acknowledge that they never actually reached the 'core section' of the gorge until late 1998 – after our expedition. Later, we would also learn that David Breashears had observed the same waterfall from a point high on the ridge above Payi in 1993 but did not attempt to reach it. Here are some extended excerpts from the article in *China Daily*.

Chinese Explorers get to the Falls First   *China Daily* 29 January 1999
Although Chinese scientists are surely not short of bravery, rigour and a desire for perfection, they sometimes may be slow to communicate their findings. After ending a pathbreaking 36-day scientific expedition to the Yarlung Zangbo Grand Canyon in the Tibet Autonomous Region last December, a team of Chinese scientists spent their time sorting out data and writing reports.

But they did not reveal details of their trip until hearing about the findings of another group. The National Geographic Society of the United States announced on January 8 that four Americans, Ian Baker, Hamid Sardar, Ken Storm, Jr., and Bryan Harvey, discovered a waterfall in an unexplored section of a Tibetan canyon, which they called 'Tsangpo Gorge'. *The Washington Post* published a story and pictures about the so-called 'Hidden Waterfall' the next day. Although the report on the Society-funded expedition was certainly newsworthy, the area has been no mystery to Chinese explorers.

Dawn over Gyala Peri. **IB**
Gyala Peri (syn. Pelri), the 'sow's head' of the goddess Dorje Pagmo, is illuminated in the first light of dawn as seen from the small village of Ganglam above the Po-Tsangpo confluence.

'The four Americans might be the first group of Westerners to catch sight of the waterfall,' Yang Yichou, a geologist with the Chinese Academy of Sciences (CAS) and one of the four organizers of the expedition, told *China Daily* in an interview. 'But we Chinese were the first to make the actual discovery of the waterfall,' Yang said. Yang, 63, has been to the world's deepest gorge eight times since China started to explore it in 1973. According to Yang, Che Fu, a Chinese photographer with the People's Liberation Army (PLA) Pictorial, was the first person from outside Tibet to find and record the waterfall on film. While flying across the canyon in an army helicopter, he caught bird's-eye views of two waterfalls on the Yarlung Zangbo River, which roars through the canyon and becomes the Brahmaputra River after crossing into India.

He took some pictures and showed them to Professor Yang after returning to Beijing. It was the first time Yang obtained concrete evidence of the existence of waterfalls on the main part of the river. 'One of the two waterfalls is what the American adventurers call 'Hidden Waterfall' [actually, 'Hidden Falls of Dorje Pagmo'], Yang said. 'We named it No. 1 Zangbo Badong Falls.' In the following years, Yang, along with professors Gao Dengyi, Li Bosheng and Guan Zhihua, also

311

with CAS, trekked into parts of the canyon several times on scientific surveys. It was Yang, Gao and Li who determined in 1994 that the canyon is the deepest of the world, being 5,000 meters deep on average and 496.3 kilometres long. They were not able to explore the core section of the canyon until last October…they found not only the two waterfalls, No. 1 and No. 2 Zangbo Badong Falls, but also two other groups of multilevel waterfalls which were unknown to the world. They were named Rongzha Falls and Quigu Dulong Falls.

…According to Professor Gao, head of the expedition, the well-preserved biodiversity inside the impressive canyon has stirred Westerner's desire to explore it since the beginning of this century. In 1924, British botanist Frank Kingdon Ward discovered the famous 'Rainbow Falls.' During last year's expedition, the Chinese explorers arrived at the site where Kingdon Ward described where he found the falls, but failed to find it. 'We think it was destroyed by an earthquake of magnitude 8.5 (on the Richter Scale) that took place on August 15, 1950,:' Yang said.'

The Chinese speculation that Frank Kingdon Ward's Rainbow Falls may have been destroyed in the Assam Earthquake of 1950 is incorrect. What they call 'No. 1 Zangbo Badong Falls' is undoubtedly the same as 'Rainbow Falls' although the height given, 33 metres (108ft.), is too high. 'No. 2 Zangbo Badong Falls' is almost certainly our 'Hidden Falls of Dorje Pagmo'. Their measured height of 35 metres (115ft.) corresponds closely to our own results.

The article describes two other groups of 'multi-level' waterfalls in the section between Rainbow Falls/Hidden Falls and the confluence with the Po-Tsangpo River – 'Quingu Dulong Falls' (which we did not reach) and 'Rongzha Falls'. 'Rongsha Falls', described as a waterfall of 'seven levels', is the same waterfall Frank Kingdon Ward and Lord Cawdor reached in 1924 and described in the 'Falls of the Brahmaputra' chapter of *The Riddle of the Tsangpo Gorges*. We visited the area in 1996, guided by the grandson of Kingdon Ward's 1924 guide.

We look forward to hearing more from the Chinese about their explorations in the gorges.

Geological Note
Jean-Pierre Burg

The eastern termination of the Himalayas in the Namcha Barwa region is considered symmetrical to the western termination of the mountain range in the Nanga Parbat region, in northern Pakistan. Both Namcha Barwa Peak and Nanga Parbat Mountain seem to mark the vertical axis of a 180 degree bend of the Himalaya chain giving rise to the hair-pin bends of the Yarlung Tsangpo (Brahmaputra) River in the east and the Indus River in the west. The legendary Namcha Barwa area remains the least known of these two regions, owing to its remote location in a nearly uninhabited region. The steep and unstable topography prevents safe settlement and the local Tibetans do not dare challenge the 'standing mountain-goddess'.

It is only in recent years, after a geographical and geological survey by Chinese earth scientists, that one question that bothered Frank Kingdon Ward could be answered. Kingdon Ward could not account for the sudden termination of the great snow-mountains he had passed through on his traverse of the gorge from Gyala to the Po-Tsangpo River. Did the Himalayas end here or did they continue to the east? Now we know. The Himalayan axis turns abruptly northwards from Namcha Barwa to abut imperceptibly against the Trans-Himalayan Range along the eastern bank on the Po-Tsangpo.

As the first western earth scientists to have access within the Great Bend of the Tsangpo, geologists from the Swiss Federal Institute of Technology (ETH) began investigating this end of the Himalaya in September 1994, along with collaborators from the Chengdu Institute of Geology and Mineral Resources. Their work concluded that Namcha Barwa Peak is one of the fastest growing mountains in the world. Its twin peak, Gyala Peri, belongs to the same mountain system incised by the Yarlung Tsangpo. A combination of the fast rising topography with the rapid incising of the mighty Yarlung Tsangpo River has produced the world's deepest canyon.

The geological history began nearly sixty million years ago when the Indian continent collided with Asia. The Tethys Ocean, which had separated these two continents for nearly 150 million years, left a scar which the Yarlung Tsangpo River follows eastward from its source nearly 1550km (970 miles) to the west in the sacred Kailas region. This 'scar' is the geological suture between the ancient continents and loops around Namcha Barwa Peak. Almost everywhere along its course the Yarlung Tsangpo parallels the suture, which is identified by serpentinites, the soft, green rocks quarried by the local population to make cooking pots. Rocks characteristic of the Trans-Himalayan Ranges rim the suture in the Namcha Barwa area.

Namcha Barwa Peak is comprised of rocks pertaining to the Indian continent. These rocks were strongly deformed and recrystallised during continental collision and the subsequent formation of the Himalayan Range. About fifteen million years ago they were still buried at a depth of nearly 30km (19 miles). They remained at this level until about four million years ago when the exhumation and the associated uplift of Namcha Barwa began. Continuing compression between India and Asia produced a large fold, up-arching the Indian continent. Namcha Barwa Peak stands on the eroded crest of this fold, which still rises by three to five millimetres (about ⅔in.) per year and explains the steep slopes and singularly high elevation of the mountain with respect to the surrounding mountains. Rapid erosion due to nearly permanent rains and glaciers flowing down into tropical forests since the Ice Age, about one million years ago, is still decapitating the growing fold. Impressive landslides and an average gradient of the Yarlung Tsangpo River of nearly 30 metres/km (160ft./mile) from Gyala to Medog, around the Great Bend, indicate that uplift and erosion in the area is extreme.

Ongoing compression and folding is expressed by active seismicity, including some of the biggest earthquakes recorded during the twentieth century. A local hunter described to me the sudden creation 'of a one-house high wall striated as if someone had scratched it' during an earthquake in 1959. The same quake destroyed a mountain monastery that was never rebuilt. It is probable that the fabled waterfalls are on one of these active faults. Faults that offset the topography along the Yarlung Tsangpo abound and hot springs along the fault zones demonstrate their recent activity.

It is remarkable that the Namcha Barwa and Nanga Parbat areas, at both extremities of the Himalayan Range, have recorded similar geological histories over the last four million years, although they are nearly 2500km (1,500 miles) apart. Both result from mountain building processes typical of the pin-ends of the range. Under these geological conditions, the East-Himalaya 'goddess', Namcha Barwa, is destined to stand higher than Nanga Parbat in the future.

V

The Tsangpo Gorges in the 21st Century
Flooding, Dams and Conservation in the Tsangpo–Siang region
Kenneth Cox

The early morning of 10 June 2000 on the banks of the Siang (the Indian name for the Yarlung Tsangpo) was typically damp and sticky at the beginning of the summer rainy season. Villagers and farmers were working in their fields and crossing the river on the many suspension bridges which line the Siang valley between Tuting and Pasighat. Locals were startled by a low rumbling sound up river from the direction of the Chinese border. Within minutes the noise had increased in volume to a roar and, as more people poured out of their houses to ascertain what the racket was, a foaming white wall of water and spray, rocks, mud, trees and other debris, almost 20m (65ft.) high, poured down the river carrying everything before it: buildings, bridges and animals. Purung village and the engineering camp near Geling were completely washed away (*The Assam Tribune,* 13 June 2000). Army radio officials ran to their offices

The Po–Tsangpo after the 2000 flood   **KSJ**
Walking on the debris carried downriver by the dam burst. A flat gravel-boulder plain has replaced the dense forested margin.

314

The Po Yigrong   **WK**
The devastation on the Po Yigrong following the 10 June 2000 dam burst. This picture was taken two years after the floods in June 2002 by geologist William Kidd.

(Opposite top) The Po-Tsangpo below Pelung   **KSJ**
The Po-Tsangpo is confined on the right bank by fluted vertical walls set with a tapestry of vegetation. During the floods of 2000, a landslide momentarily dammed the river here, below Pelung. The fury of the debris loaded surge blasted away one of the spurs and scoured the banks, dramatically changing the character of the valley. The pre-flood photograph on page 240 was taken in this vicinity.)

to radio downstream to warn of the danger, but failed to make contact. Further down river, in the narrowest part of the lower gorge, the wall of water reached a height of 30m (nearly 100ft.), *The Assam Tribune* later reported. People not quick enough or unable to run away from the banks were washed into the roaring water; at least fifty people were drowned. We interviewed one man who, with a friend, had climbed up an electricity pylon to escape the rising flood, before it too toppled into the water throwing him into the deluge: he survived but his friend was drowned. The flood surge lasted for several hours. In Arunachal Pradesh over twenty bridges were destroyed and more than fifty villages reported damaged, with up to fifty thousand people left homeless. In addition valuable farmland was washed away with a large number of livestock. The Arunachal Pradesh government estimated the loss at more than 22.9 million U.S. dollars (*Indian Express*, Bombay, 11 July 2000).

Members of Arunachal's government and legislature vented their fury at the events. It was clear that a dam had burst up river in Tibet, but there had been no warning from officials in China that the floods were coming. Inter-governmental relations in this part of India have always been strained because the whole state of Arunachal is disputed territory between the two countries, but this lack of warning was interpreted by India as deliberate and wilful negligence. In the spirit of suspicion and mistrust, *The Assam Tribune* pointed the finger firmly at China:

> Officials suspect that the People's Liberation Army of China may have blasted the dam to experiment the impact of the flash floods in the sensitive North-East and to study the potential such a flood may have to cause damage on the Indian side… the Arunachal Pradesh Government too has drawn the attention of the Central Government to the sudden floods that left the State devastated, urging it to take up the issue with China… When the Ministry of External Affairs contacted China it was conveyed that there were no floods on the Chinese side on the river Brahmaputra and instead attributed the occurrence of floods on the Indian side to natural causes, revealed the Minister of State for External Affairs, Ajit Panja in the Parliament last week.   *The Assam Tribune,* 21 August 2000

At first the Indian Ministry for External affairs received denials from China that any floods had taken place. It was a full month before the Chinese were prepared to admit what they knew about the flood. An official of China's Water Resources Department of the Tibet Autonomous Region government in Lhasa admitted to the Agence France Press agency that the cause was not a man-made hydroelectric dam but a natural one 60m (200ft.) high and 2.5km wide (1½ mile), formed by a major landslide of the Zhamolong Gully of Gonglharongbabo Mountain that occurred on 9 April:

> 'That landslide, the biggest ever seen in Asia and the third biggest in the world, created a dam in a matter of eight minutes,' said the official, who declined to be identified. The Xinhau news agency (Beijing) reported that 'Nearly 500 million cubic meters of mud and stone rolled down the mountain slope and blocked the Yigrong river'.

The Chinese officials in Tibet had known for at least a month that the dam would break and that the flood would take place. Indeed it had been quite widely reported in the Chinese press:

> Engineers and rescuers at the scene of a landslide in eastern Tibet will dig a ditch to move water from a blocked river and all residents in the potential flood area will be evacuated.   *China Daily,* 5 April 2000

> The water level of the river-turned-lake continued to rise and may flood the area before June 5th according to a team of engineers.   *People's Daily,* 10 May 2000

Chinese officials had carefully evacuated everyone from the potential flooding areas of the Tsangpo river bank, yet neglected to advise Indian officials of these precautions. Due to advanced warnings, no one was reported killed on the Tibet side of the border, but it was nevertheless a terrifying experience for the villagers who lived in the Tsangpo Gorge. Ken Storm returned to the Tsangpo Gorge as a member of the 2002 international kayak expedition, led by American Scott Lindgren, in which seven boaters made a successful descent of the river from Pe to a point just above Rainbow Falls. The expedition arrived in Tsachu in early March 2002 at the end of a traverse of the Upper Tsangpo Gorges, as Ken Storm records:

> At the village of Tsachu, situated on a spur overlooking the Po-Tsangpo River, we learned of the terrifying events of that night in early June 2000. Pema, a Mönba villager, was awakened in the middle of the night (10 June) by an unusual odour carried on a sudden, strong wind blowing down the gorge from the North. Soon the ground began shaking violently. Fearing an earthquake, Pema spread the alarm to the village and climbed to the ridge overlooking the Po-Tsangpo River to check on the strange wind, now carrying an ominous roar. Below, in the darkness, he could see the river rising fast, eating away at the base of the spur below the village. Fearing that the river might tear away the entire spur and carry the village away he ordered everyone to higher ground. At dawn of the first morning, the river level fell dramatically and Pema thought the danger had passed. But then the fury was unleashed again. A fresh landslide just upstream from Tsachu had created a new dam across the Po-Tsangpo which had then burst. For three days the terrified villagers lived in the open in the forest, until it was safe to return.

The breaking of the dam on the Yigrong has altered the landscape of the lower Yigrong and lower Yarlung Tsangpo gorge dramatically as Ken Storm describes:

> In those earlier days, the trail from Tsachu up the Po-Tsangpo traversed the forested slopes of the valley or followed the course of the river, often hidden beyond a screen of trees and only glimpsed at intervals, its sound muted by dense foliage. Now and then the trail crossed the river on high, swaying plank bridges where I had paused to marvel at the raging rapids below. Now, all traces of the bridges were gone, replaced by makeshift cables anchored to great boulders. Porters roped me into a harness with a small pulley and I zipped across the river at a frightening speed. Beyond, I walked wide plains bounded by vast grey slopes ripped from the forest above. Everywhere I found a world of sharp, splintered stone and gravel blasted from the great spurs that once confined the river. Light flooded the valley. Gone were those intimate passages through green glens splashed with the spray of cascading waterfalls. Silence replaced the remembered birdsong and hum of insects, dazzle of butterflies and forest flowers which delighted me along the way. Gone too was the familiar smell of damp tropical vegetation and the hot sulphur pools where I had bathed my body after so many long, hard days in the gorges below. I travelled with the realisation that the wonderful vegetation that had drawn Frank Kingdon Ward here and so enchanted me was but the thin veneer on a hard-edged earth. I was at once saddened and thrilled by the transformation that had taken place here – the shaping of a new world.

The devastating 2000 flood was far from a one-off. There is evidence that the Tsangpo Gorge itself was partly formed by what are known as 'megafloods' formed by the bursting of huge glacial lakes (Montgomery et al., 2004). The unstable, extremely steep terrain and regular torrential rain of the region leads to regular landslides, sometimes on a massive scale, some of which dam the river for a time before being broken by the weight of water built up behind them. The photograph on page 205 of this book clearly shows the site of a huge landslide which fell into the main Tsangpo at some

The Po-Tsangpo below Tsachu, 1996
Prayer flags frame the Po-Tsangpo below the village of Tsachu, looking north, in the spring of 1996.

point in the past. Plant hunters Ludlow and Sherriff reported a serious dam burst in the 1930s and another flood took place in the upper Tsangpo valley in 1954 which damaged the cities of Gyantse and Xigaze 120km and 200km (75 and 125 miles) downstream as well as affecting the gorge itself.

There is reason for hope that the witholding of early warnings for the Indians of the 2000 flood will not be repeated in the future. *China Daily* 28 April 2002 reported:

> Three hydrological stations in southwest China's Tibet Autonomous Region will offer hydrological data to India during the flood season. China's Ministry of Water Resources announced on Thursday that the Chinese and Indian water authorities had signed an agreement on this issue in New Delhi, capital of India on April 24, 2002. According to the agreement, the three hydrological stations, all located along the Yarlung Zangbo [Tsangpo] River, will offer hydrological forecasts to India from June 1 to October 15. The forecasts will help India with flood prevention and cutting losses caused by floods.

We have been informed that Indian officials are now studying satellite imagery for tell-tale signs of floods to come. Such monitoring led to serious alerts in late summer 2004, due to reports and rumours of a landslide dam near Pe and of a breach in the Sango Dam in western Tibet. Thankfully both turned out to be false alarms. But the 2000 floods have left a legacy of nervousness and mistrust; perhaps unsurprisingly, Indian officials tend to turn to the west for information rather than relying on the Chinese to warn them.

The process of natural reforestation after major natural disasters such as floods and volcanoes is always fascinating to observe. I had a chance to see the recovery of Mt St

The Po-Tsangpo below Tsachu, 2002   **KSJ**
The same view in March 2002 showing the extreme damage caused by the 2000 floods. Perhaps no vantage point
was more dramatic than the view of the flood from the Tsachu Spur that straddles the Po-Tsangpo and *Yarlung*
Tsangpo rivers at their confluence. The earth shaking terror of that event is remembered by Pema and the other
villagers. Gone is the wild tangle of jungle that spilled down the flanks of the gorge to river level. In its place is a
harsh world of rock and gravel and landslide-stripped walls. In just hours the flood moved mountains of rock that,
under the more genial, gradual effects of seasonal erosion, might have taken thousands of years to achieve. The Po-
Tsangpo on the right flows toward the base of the Tsachu Spur and is deflected to the left (west) toward the
confluence with the Yarlung Tsangpo at Gompo Ne, three miles (5km) below.

Helens in Washington, USA after the early 1980s volcanic eruptions. While in
Arunachal, Ken Storm and I have watched the remarkably swift regeneration of plants
in the Indian portion of the gorge since 2000. The mud and stone banks, bared by the
ferocious onslaught of raging rock and debris-filled water, are already green again; seed
has dropped from the trees and other plants higher up the bank and now there is a mass
of germinating seedlings already jostling for space. The river has an inspiring ability to
heal itself.

Plans for hydro-electric dams on the Tsangpo/Siang

Like every other major river in the region, the Tsangpo-Siang is being carefully
evaluated for its hydroelectric potential by both India and China. A grandiose and
frightening Chinese scheme was reported widely in the world's press in October 2000:

> Chinese leaders are drawing up plans to use nuclear explosions, in breach of the
> international test-ban treaty, to blast a tunnel through the Himalayas for the world's
> biggest hydroelectric plant. The proposed power station is forecast to produce more
> than twice as much electricity as the controversial Three Gorges Dam being built on
> the Yangtze river. …Last week, China's state-run media reported that the project
> would form part of a national strategy to divert water from rivers in the south and

The lower Siang river near Boleng, Arunachal Pradesh, 2001   KNEC
A new cable suspension bridge replacing the one washed away the previous year in the 2000 floods. The scars left
on the river banks by the tidal wave of water can clearly be seen. This is close to one of the putative dam sites
identified on the river.

west to drought-stricken northern areas. The reports said that a 38 million kilowatt
power station at Muotuo on the Yarlung Zangbo [Tsangpo] river in Tibet would
harness the force of a 9,840ft [3,000m] drop in terrain over only a few miles. The
capacity of the station would make it the world's largest power generation facility,
much bigger than the 18 million kilowatt plant at the Three Gorges. The cost of
drilling the tunnel through Mount Namcha Barwa has not yet been announced, but
appears likely to surpass £10 billion. At the bottom of the tunnel, the water will flow
into a new reservoir and then be diverted along more than 500 miles [800km] of the
Tibetan plateau to the vast, arid areas of Xinjiang region and Gansu province. Beijing
wants to use large quantities of the plentiful waters of the south-west to top up the
Yellow River basin and assuage mounting discontent over water shortages in 600
cities in northern China.

Damien Mcelroy for The Daily Telegraph, London 22 October 2000

The scale and potential of this project can be seen from the raw statistics:

A dam built across the Great Yalungzangbo [Yarlung Tsangpo] Canyon, the world's
deepest, could take advantage of a drop of a staggering 2,340 meters [7,677ft.] and a
flow that averages 1,900 cubic meters [67,100cu.ft.] per second throughout the year.
Its theoretical capacity would be 68,000 MW – with an installed capacity of 38,000
MW, twice that of the [Yangtze] Three Gorges and therefore by far the greatest
installed power in the world.

Gavan McCormack, 2001

320

It is clear that the whole eco-system of the greater Namche Barwa region would be under threat if any of this plan were put into practice. The Chinese have already built a major dam in Tibet on the Lhasa river, the Zhikung Hydroelectric Power Station, to the north-east of Lhasa. Nicknamed 'The Three Gorges of Tibet', it is shortly to supply power to Tibet's major cities and to the Qinghai-Tibet Railway (*China Daily*, December 27, 2005). As far as we can ascertain, so far there has been no further development of the Muotuo Tsangpo bend scheme, but there is no doubt that the Chinese government are investing substantial effort into evaluating hydro power potential from the Tsangpo Gorges. Another scheme which has been mooted and which would be less devastating to the environment is to divert some of the flow of the Tsangpo through a tunnel under the Doshong La and build turbines to exploit the fall of over 2,000m (6,500ft.) on the south side of the range.

Further south, on the Indian portion of the Tsangpo/Siang river and its major tributaries, three alternative dam sites were being investigated. We noted dam surveying activities from 2001 to 2003 in the region. One of the drawbacks to large-scale dams in the Tsangpo-Siang area is the distance to a major population centre and the difficulty and expense (up to $400,000 per km) in building long-distance power transmission lines. Perhaps more importantly, the S.E. Tibet/Arunachal Pradesh region is extremely unstable geologically, threatened by floods as described above, but more significantly by major earthquakes. According to seismologist Roger Bilham, University of Colorado, the two most significant were the 1897 earthquake in Shillong, a 8.1 magnitude shock which caused part of the overlying Shillong Plateau to shoot up 10-15m (33-60ft.) in just three seconds, and the 8.6 magnitude Rima earthquake of 1950 witnessed first-hand and documented by Frank and Jean Kingdon Ward. These were two of the largest earthquakes ever recorded. It is unlikely that any large-scale dam would be able to withstand an earthquake of this intensity, and geologists believe that that another such quake is inevitable at some point. There have been legal challenges in India brought against the proposed dams. We have communicated with several Arunachal government officials in an attempt to ascertain whether any of the schemes are going ahead and it seems that on the main Siang all projects are on hold for the time being. Local officials are keen to build more micro-schemes on side rivers to provide local electricity, but most are opposed to large scale hydro-projects. However, it is clear that, as far as Delhi is concerned, the dam proposals are still 'live'. MP Rahul Gandhi, grandson of Indira, inaugurated the Siang River Festival in December 2005 at Tuting and said in his opening speech:

> Arunachal Pradesh has vast hydro power and tourism potentials, which if harnessed scientifically could accelerate the process of development of the state as well as meet the country's ever growing hydro power requirement

suggesting that further dam plans, particularly on the Subansiri, are still in the government's reckoning. The huge volume of water flowing down Arunachal's rivers has caused it to be called the potential 'Powerhouse of India'.

Recent Exploration in Arunachal Pradesh

Even as Ken Storm and I were exploring the Tibetan Tsangpo Gorges region on our various expeditions during the 1990s, we always had one eye on the area to the south, over the border in the Indian state of Arunachal Pradesh. We first gained access to Arunachal Pradesh in 2000 and have since mounted four expeditions in several of its mountain ranges. Few foreigners have been allowed to penetrate the hidden valleys and mountain ranges of Arunachal and we have been privileged to be the first non-Indians into several areas. Our Arunachal explorations will hopefully appear one day, in another book.

Arunachal is over 500km (300 miles) wide, from its borders with Bhutan in the west to Burma/Myanmar in the east, covering 83,743 sq. km (32,325 sq. miles), about the same size as Austria. This untamed mountainous region, still 80% covered in jungle, rises to the north of the Assam plains where the mighty Brahmaputra drains the mountain rains down into Bangladesh. From the plains the mountains gradually rise to a ridge, part of the main Himalayan range, which ranges in height from 4,000-6,000m (13,100-19,685ft.), along which lies the border between Tibet and India. The fearsome reputation of local tribes such as the Adi and Tagin and the impenetrable terrain had largely thwarted nineteenth and twentieth century British attempts to explore what is now Arunachal and consequently the British Raj government placed the mountain border area outside a declared 'outer line'. The area was designated 'The North East Frontier Agency' (N.E.F.A.) and it remained more or less unsubdued and unexplored. After Indian independence, following advice from anthropologist and champion of India's scheduled tribes, Verrier Elwin, Nehru's government declared that N.E.F.A. was to remain out of bounds to all, Indian and foreigner alike. To retain an almost impenetrable buffer zone along the disputed frontier with Tibet suited the 1950s political situation well. The border, known as the McMahon, line had been drawn on the map at the Simla treaty of 1911 by Henry McMahon, then Governor-General of India. The Chinese have since claimed that their representative and signatory at Simla was unauthorised and that they therefore do not recognise the extant border, which they call 'the line of control'. The Chinese claim on the territory, which they call *Zàngnán* or 'South Tibet', led to a temporary invasion in 1962 when red army troops overran much of the state. International pressure forced a retreat. The Chinese have not renounced their claim and large numbers of troops are still posted in many areas on both sides of the border, but, despite occasional heated rhetoric, the political situation is now relatively calm. For Chinese conscripts from far-away provinces, the steamy, leech-infested, monsoon drenched Pemakö border posting must be every soldier's worst nightmare; we have met many a forlorn Chinese soldier struggling over the windswept, snow-clad passes which lead into this magical but hostile land.

Cross border considerations: the Flora and Fauna of Greater Pemakö

Politically we have to accept that the Tsangpo/Siang region divides down the middle into two countries, not always on speaking terms. But Pemakö, as a Buddhist sacred land, recognises no frontier. Yang Sang is simultaneously an idealised earthly paradise and a valley on the map which Ken Storm and I have spent two expeditions exploring. Just south of the Indian border, it links into the kora (pilgrimage circuit) of Kundo Dorsempotrang which lies just to the north. These two pilgrimages are amongst the most significant in all of Pemakö; pilgrims long to be able to cross the frontier to travel through the whole of this sacred landscape.

Even more important, the Greater Pemakö/Tsangpo Gorges area, which straddles the India-Tibet border, is a single natural wilderness region of almost unparalleled richness in mountain landscapes, near virgin forests, and endemic flora and fauna. After remaining largely unknown and unchanged for generations, the last ten years have seen significant – both worrying and encouraging – changes in both countries; we have seen these take place almost year on year as we return again and again to explore this part of the world that has so captivated us. Though there are encouraging moves towards environmental protection, the whole area is under threat from over-population and the resulting pressure on cultivated land, poaching of larger mammals and logging. In addition, there are plans for increased tourism and major hydroelectric dams. All or any of these factors could have a drastic detrimental effect on the whole region.

Chinese scientists, often with help from their foreign counterparts, have made thorough surveys of the geology, flora and fauna of the Tibetan Pemakö region and, in consequence, in 1999 the Chinese government established The Yarlung Tsangpo Grand Canyon National Reserve, which covers over 9,000 sq.km (3,474 sq. miles). The Indian and Arunachal State government have, in turn, inaugurated the Dihang-Dibang

Adi tribesmen at the village of Damro   KNEC
Adi tribesmen in locally woven costumes and hats and helmets made out of bamboo performing traditional
dances. Damro is one of the oldest villages in the upper Siang district, with its origins going back at least 500 years.
Many of Arunachal's government members trace their lineage back to this village.

Biosphere Reserve. This consists of 5,112 sq.km in the districts of west Siang, Upper
Siang and Dibang valley of Arunachal Pradesh. An area of 4,095 sq.km constitutes the
core zone, with 1,017 sq.km of buffer zone. As a comparison, the US state of New
Jersey and the country of Wales are both just over 20,000 sq.km.

Eminent naturalist George Schaller, Director for Science of the International Pro-
gram of the Wildlife Conservation Society in New York, and world-recognised expert
on lions, gorillas, snow leopards and other larger mammals, made thorough surveys of
the wildlife and conservation issues of the Pemakö region in 1998 and 2000 on both
sides of the border. On the Chinese side, within the reserve area, George Schaller
reports (2000) a permanent indigenous population of over 14,000 plus large numbers
of Han Chinese army personnel and migrant workers. It is clear that the relatively large
population in the limited areas where cultivation is possible has had a detrimental effect
on the ecology of the area through over rotation of slash and burn agriculture and
particularly through hunting. The establishment of the reserve in 1999 outlawed
hunting but there is still a significant illegal trade in valuable animal bi-products such
as muskdeer pods and bear gall bladders, used in traditional Chinese medicine. Slash
and burn agriculture, known as *jhum* in Arunachal Pradesh, is now being controlled on
both sides of the border, due to excess deforestation in some areas and the resulting
erosion caused by cultivating very steep slopes.

Chinese surveys (including Ni and Cheng 1992) give an indication of the species
richness of the region, reporting 64 mammal species, 232 birds, 44 reptiles and
amphibians, and almost 4,000 species of vascular plants. What is more significant is that
many of these species are endemic to this region. Some of the many alpine endemic
plants include: *Rhododendron pemakoense, R. leucaspis, R. parmulatum, R. venator, Primula
falcifolia,* and *P. baileyana,* while Sun Hang and Zhou Zhekun (2001) report 117
endemics in the tropical and subtropical regions of Medog (Pemakö), below 2,500m
(8,200ft.). The extreme mountain terrain covers a vast range of climatic zones from
permanent snow and ice though alpine meadow, conifer forest, broad-leaved forest and
the world's most northerly wet tropical evergreen forest. Locally occurring plants are
used extensively in Tibetan medicine and modern Chinese medicine. Two examples are
Cephlotaxus, used to treat leukaemia, and *Curuma aromatica,* used in the treatment of

Unnamed species of Rhododendron KNEC
An as yet unnamed (new to science) species of Rhododendron discovered by Kenneth Cox in 2001 in the mountains surrounding the Yang Sang valley, Arunachal Pradesh. This species appears to be endemic to this area.

cervical cancer. It is very likely that there are other plants whose medical potential has not yet been discovered.

Medog is almost certainly the last viable tiger (*Panthera tigris*) population in China but this population is severely under threat of hunting as tigers have killed significant numbers of domesticated and semi-domesticated animals such as the buffalo-like Mithun (*Bos frontalis*). George Schaller (2000) estimates that the population of tigers may be as small as fifteen. Over 50% of the villagers he interviewed in Medog had never seen a tiger. The region is also home to many other rare and threatened mammal species. Some of these include two species of macaque (*Macaca assamensis, M. mulata*), red panda (*Ailurus fulgens*, one of which we observed on the Dashing La), Asiatic black bear (*Ursus thibetanus*), leopard, clouded leopard and snow leopard (*Panthera pardus, Neofelis nebulosa, Uncia uncia*), and Asiatic wild dogs (*Cuon alpinus*). Wild pigs (*Sus scrofa*), goral and red goral (*Nemorhaedus goral & N. baileyi*), muskdeer (*Moschus Moschiferus*) and takin (*Budorcas taxicolor*) are some of the most significant hoofed animals. Amongst amphibians, one of the most notable is *Rhacophorus translineatus*, a species of gliding frog. Up to 1997, 195 species of birds had been recorded in the Dihang-Dibang reserve area. Of these the rare Sclater's Monal (*Lophophorus sclateri*), Blyth's Tragopan (*Tragopan blythi*) and Temminck's tragopan (*Tragopan temminckii*) are amongst the most notable.

This book should be evidence enough of the extremely rich flora of Pemakö, on the Chinese side of the border. The Arunachal flora is less well recorded and, due to the greater range in altitude, probably even richer. Ashish Paul et al. (2005) report that Arunachal Pradesh harbours around 50% of the total number of plant species in India. Although many plant species occur on both sides of the border, it is surprising how different the taxa on the Indian side of the border are. Looking at Rhododendrons as an example, on one short expedition in the upper Siang area in 2003 I discovered what appear to be at least three rhododendron species new to science. I'm sure there must be several more in adjoining valleys. It is apparent that most Survey of India botanical work in Arunachal has so far concentrated largely on the accessible areas such as Tawang in the west of Arunachal and on the low altitude flora. Much of the mountain flora appears as yet undocumented.

Depopulation

One of the processes which does seem to be aiding the recovery of wildlife in the areas isolated from roads is the reduction of population levels. In India this process appears to be happening on a voluntary basis. Our 2003 expedition though Mishmi villages of the upper Dibang revealed the recent depopulation of valleys more than a few hours' walk from the road. It was clear to us that already in the remote Mishmi villages only the old remained and soon they too would have to move as there would be no young to care for them, their crops or livestock. The young tribesmen move down the valley for education and medical support and are reluctant to return to the subsistence farming of their parents, settling permanently instead in the villages and towns by the roads. Another consequence of the depopulation process is the deterioration or disappearance of trails and bridges; it seems likely that in the foreseeable future some valleys may become impenetrable to humans and therefore wildlife populations should increase. On the Chinese side of the border a similar process is occurring, but here the

Mishmi villagers at Atali
Near the Dibang valley, Arunachal Pradesh.

KNEC

local populations have been ordered to move out from the Tsangpo Gorges to towns such as Bai. With the removal of the Mönba and Lopa from their homelands in the gorge, a whole culture will be lost; the knowledge of the sacred geography, the hunter trails and the sources of medical plants will probably die out within a single generation. What life these resettled gorge dwellers, many of whom have helped on our expeditions, will have in the incongruous glitter of Bai, one of the ugliest and most unpleasant towns in Tibet, is of some concern.

Conservation: differing approaches

As an outsider to the complex world of conservation, and at risk of some opprobrium, it seems to me that there are two broad philosophical or ideological approaches being advocated by different bodies. These could be characterised as 'carrot' and 'stick'. The 'stick' approach of guarding the resources and punishing wrongdoers (for illegal logging, for example) is deemed more appropriate when both the environment and the wildlife are degraded. In the case of Pemakö, the environment is largely in pristine condition and only the wildlife is in immediate danger. In this situation, a 'carrot' approach of working with the local people in education is considered more appropriate. It would be fair to argue that the Chinese err towards the 'stick' approach to conservation, and the Indians towards the 'carrot'. Daniel Taylor from Future Generations explains this latter approach:

> The earlier model of separating conservation from people has worked on a modest scale where it was well funded and where supervision could be provided. But the model is not viable for very large and geographically fractured regions. The community-based approach has a much lower operating cost and provides clear evidence of being more effective. Rather than pushing people outside the process, it engages them as partners.

Daniel Taylor sums this up as 'it depends if you see the people as the problem, or the solution'. Actually they are, of course, both of these simultaneously, but there is no doubt that unless the local people and their leaders and politicians are involved in, and supportive of, the conservation effort, there is little chance of long term success.

The Indian protected area is known as Dihang-Dibang Biosphere Reserve, within the framework of UNESCO's Man and Biosphere (MAB) programme. Biosphere reserves should fulfil the following three objectives:

In situ conservation of biodiversity of natural and semi-natural ecosystems and landscapes

Contribution to sustainable economic development of the human population living within and around the Biosphere Reserve

Provide facilities for long term ecological studies, environmental education and training and research and monitoring.

The key player in the establishment of the reserve has been Pekyom Ringu, until recently the Director of the Biosphere Reserve, who has worked tirelessly to ensure the support of both the Arunachal and Delhi Governments.

George Schaller reports that most tribesmen have to travel days from their villages in order to find animals to hunt, as the areas near to significant population have been hunted to near extinction. There is a significant amount of poaching from outsiders, even cross-border poaching. The nominal protection of the new park is not always enforced and the possession of large numbers of guns by tribesmen has the result that large numbers of animals are still being killed. On the Indian side, most of the Adi and Mishmi houses are adorned with animal skulls and skins. Our experience accompanying Adi and Mishmi hunters, as we have done on three occasions, is that they shoot (with guns, bows and blow-pipes) almost any bird or animal that they spot, and most of the time they are reduced to trapping squirrels and other small animals with snares as most larger animals and birds have retreated far from human range. This has been referred to by conservationists as 'empty-jungle syndrome' where smaller and smaller animals and birds are killed by increasing populations until there is nothing left at all; even the small songbirds, bats and rats are killed.

An Adi villager from Kuging   **OT**
Cutting up a takin which had been caught in a snare, at Titapuri, north of the Yang Sang valley, Arunachal Pradesh.

Rainbow Falls   **KSJ**
Canadian climber Andrew Shepperd, a member of the 2002 international kayaking expedition led by Scott
Lindgren, at the brink of Rainbow Falls.

One encouraging initiative has been started by a respected local official in Tuting:
Dorjee Tensing has founded the Yang Sang Pemakö society with some Japanese
donations of money. The aims are to encourage the clearing of litter from the
pilgrimage trails and, more importantly, to cut down hunting by trying to convince the
Adi and Mishmi villagers to reduce the use of snares used for catching takin and other
large mammals, to institute a seasonal rather than year-round hunt and to refrain from
hunting in certain areas (by mutual consent and compensation) in order to create
reserves. This small-scale, local initiative may be as effective as state government and
NGO activities.

The extreme inaccessibility of most of the Tsangpo Gorges/greater Pemakö area to
vehicles has probably saved it from any major logging and timber extraction. It is easy
to predict the impact that a permanent road into Medog would have. One was constructed from Pome in the 1980s but was not maintained and remains impassable to
vehicles most of the time. Evidence of what can happen with heavy vehicle access is
the Rong Chu valley, which lies on the Bayi-Pome road to the north of the Tsangpo
Gorges and which has seen significant deforestation in recent years. All the old-growth
timber in this valley looks under threat, despite the national park which has been
declared. Yang Yichou (2000) reports:

> …with the construction of the Sichuan-Tibet Highway, there has been a sharp
> increase in the area's population. From the 1960s to the 1980s, the area suffered from

random tree-felling. Soil erosion was serious and landslides and mud-stone flows occurred more frequently.

Our observations are that the most extensive logging is very much more contemporary than this Chinese report admits and that recent logging is a major cause of frequent erosion and landslides.

Another significant contributor to the isolation of Medog is the tense relationship with India to the south. It would be relatively easy to connect Medog to India via Tuting, but the border remains firmly closed and the road access across the border is not complete. George Schaller concludes that the construction of a road into Medog would seriously threaten the viability of the national park.

Tourism to Tsangpo Gorges and Pemakö

Both the Chinese and Indian governments seem keen, in theory, to open up this region for tourism. While undoubtedly there is considerable potential for trekking and for spiritual tourism for people interested in Buddhism (following the model of the popular treks to Mt Kailas), the extreme terrain, the fickle and often appalling weather which can render trails too dangerous to use, and the abundant blood-sucking, biting and stinging creatures will restrict the popularity of the area as a significant tourism destination. As much of the wildlife is confined to areas far from villages and roads, perhaps the flowers are the greatest accessible attraction. In Tibet the roadside from Pylung to Bayi, which climbs over a 4,000+m (13,000+ft.) pass, is a mass of rhododendrons and other plants. Perhaps the Indian sector of Pemakö has the greatest tourism potential. Trekking along the Yang Sang Valley though Adi, Mönba/Tibetan and Mishmi villages to the rhododendron clad Abroka mountain range is a great attraction for keen walkers, though the weather can be severe, and therefore the route dangerous, at any time of year. There is also rafting potential on the Siang south from Tuting. As is clear, the biggest drawback to this area for tourism is undoubtedly the weather. In the many expeditions we have made around the area of the Tsangpo Gorges, the great mountains have appeared out from behind the clouds only intermittently and we have put up with appalling weather on most of our trips, not surprising in a region with an average annual rainfall of over 5,700mm. (220in.).

The infrastructure of transport, accommodation or trekking guides does not yet in any way match what is available in Nepal or Bhutan, where the mountain views are clearer and more dependable, the trails well maintained and where local people have many years' experience looking after tourists. The sensitive political situation on both sides of the border means that obtaining the necessary tourism permits is never easy. In Tibet huge sums are now demanded for anyone who wishes to explore the Tsangpo Gorge and, even when such sums are forthcoming, officials place further obstacles in the way, the removal of which usually involves the lining of their pockets. I know of several recent planned expeditions which have had to pull out due to such difficulties.

What is clear from all of the conservation issues − from dam building, erosion and flooding, logging, population, hunting and tourism − is that the greater Pemakö region which straddles the Tibet/India border should be viewed as a single entity with cross-border co-operation in all areas. Encouragingly, the NGO Future Generations has facilitated preliminary cross-border discussions on these complex issues. The government of the ironically named Tibet Autonomous Region (as it is, of course, ruled largely without autonomy for the ethnic Tibetans) has appointed a task force under the Department of Science and Technology which is preparing a formal management proposal for the proposed Four Great Rivers Nature Preserve. This is an even more ambitious and wholly commendable project to extend environmental protection to a much wider area, covering the Yangtze, Mekong, Salween and Tsangpo rivers which rise on the Tibetan plateau and for a time run parallel through China and Tibet into India and Burma. The first three rivers flow within 30 to 50km (20-30 miles) of each other for

Tuting, Arunachal Pradesh, India   **KNEC**
This bamboo and steel suspension bridge was brand new in 2001, replacing the one washed away by the 2000 floods. It leads from Tuting to the Yang Sang valley.

nearly 300km (190 miles). This plan has already been partly implemented: in 2003 when UNESCO designated the Three Rivers Region (which excludes the Tsangpo) as a World Heritage Site because of the area's 'unique and diverse geology, topography, and biology'. UNESCO lists the criteria for inscription for the three rivers region which would equally well apply to the extension which would include the Tsangpo:

> This area may be the most biologically diverse temperate region on earth…its location at the juncture of the East Asia, South-east Asia, and Tibetan Plateau biogeographical realms and its function as a N-S corridor for the movement of plants and animals (especially during the ice ages), marks it as a truly unique landscape, which still retains a high degree of natural character despite thousands of years of human habitation. As the last remaining stronghold for an extensive suite of rare and endangered plants and animals, the site is of outstanding universal value.

Whatever the future brings, it will require an enormous amount of domestic political will in China and India, as well as international pressure, to preserve one of the world's foremost mountain and wilderness areas for generations to come. Our sincere wish is that this book can, through documenting the wealth of natural riches of the Tsangpo Gorges region, bring it to the attention of the world, and contribute in some way to its conservation for generations to come.

Author Biographies

Ian Baker studied literature and comparative religion at Oxford and Columbia Universities and has written extensively on the art and culture of Tibet and the Himalayas. Since 1993 he has made eight expeditions into the region of the Tsangpo gorges following pilgrimage routes described in ancient Tibetan texts. In 1998 he was the leader of a National Geographic Society expedition which documented the Hidden Falls of Dorje Pagmo in the deepest section of the Tsangpo gorge. He is the author of *Celestial Gallery* (New York*: Callaway Editions, 2000), The Tibetan Art of Healing* (London: Thames & Hudson, 1997)*, Tibet: Reflections from the Wheel of Life* (New York: Abbeville, 1993) as well as *The Heart of the World, A Journey to the Last Secret Place, Secrets of the Tsangpo* (New York: Random House, 2004). For the past sixteen years he has lived in Kathmandu, Nepal, and the USA.

Kenneth R. Storm, Jr. graduated with a BA in Anthropology and Journalism from the University of Minnesota in 1975. For more than a year he explored, on foot, the length of the Sierra Madre Mountains in Mexico, living for a time among the Tarahumara Indians in their home deep in the great gorges of north-western Mexico. In 1982 he began a series of explorations and travels on the Colorado Plateau in the American South-west. On one journey he retraced the route of the 1869 Powell Expedition by boat down the Green and Colorado Rivers. Ken has travelled extensively in the western Himalayan region of Ladakh in northern India. He has co-authored two books on the area*: Ladakh: Between Earth and Sky* (with Siddiq Wahid, W.W. Norton & Co., 1981) and *Ladakh: The Secret Land Beyond the Himalayas* (Lustre Press, 1989).

From 1993 to 1998 he made five journeys to the Tsangpo gorges in South-east Tibet. In 1993 he was a member of the first Western expedition to traverse the Upper Tsangpo Gorge since the 1924 expedition of British explorer Frank Kingdon Ward. In November 1998 Ken and fellow explorer Ian Baker descended deep into the gorge beyond where any Westerner had travelled. They reached and measured a thundering 100ft. (30.5m) high waterfall – the highest yet documented on a major Himalayan river. From 2000-2005 Ken Storm and Kenneth Cox have made a series of expeditions in Arunachal Pradesh, which included the lower Siang and Yang Sang valleys and surrounding mountains.

Kenneth Cox is grandson of the writer, plant hunter and nurseryman Euan Cox, V.M.M., and son of nurseryman, writer and plant hunter Peter Cox, V.M.H. All three generations were and are considered world experts on the genus *Rhododendron*. Kenneth is married with two sons and lives and works at Glendoick, Perth, Scotland where he runs the family horticultural business, breeds rhododendrons and plays music. He has travelled extensively and has led two plant hunting expeditions to Yunnan, China, five to Tibet and made four expeditions to Arunachal Pradesh with explorer and contributor to this book Ken Storm Jr. Kenneth is author of *The Encyclopedia of Rhododendron Hybrids* (with Peter A. Cox, Batsford 1988), *A Plantsman's Guide to Rhododendrons* (Ward Lock 1989), *Cox's Guide to Choosing Rhododendrons* (with Peter A. Cox, Batsford 1990), *The Encyclopedia of Rhododendron Species* (with Peter A. Cox, Glendoick Publishing 1997), *Rhododendrons, A Hamlyn Care Manual* (Hamlyn 1998) and *Rhododendrons and Azalea, A Colour Guide* (Crowood 2005).

Bibliography

Allen, Charles, *A Mountain in Tibet*, London 1982.

Bailey, F.M., *Report on an Exploration on the North-East Frontier 1913*, Simla 1914.

Bailey, F.M., 'The Story of Kintup', *Geographical Magazine* 15 (1943): 426-431.

Bailey, F.M., *China–Tibet–Assam: A Journey, 1911*, London 1945.

Bailey, F.M., *No Passport to Tibet*, Rupert Hart-Davis, London 1957.

Baker, Ian, *The Heart of the World, A Journey to the Last Secret Place*, Penguin 2004.

Bean, W.J., *Trees and Shrubs hardy in the British Isles*, 8th edition, John Murray 1970.

Bentinck, A., 'The Abor Expedition: Geographical Results', *Geographical Journal* 41 (1913): 97-114.

Bilham, R., 'Earthquakes in India and the Himalaya: tectonics, geodesy and history' (2004), *Annals of Geophysics*, 47(2), 839-858.

Coates, Alice M., *The Quest for Plants*, Studio Vista 1969.

Cox, Peter A. & Cox, Kenneth N.E., *The Encyclopedia of Rhododendron Species*, Glendoick Publishing 1997.

Cox, Peter A., *The Smaller Rhododendrons*, B.T. Batsford 1985.

Cox, E.H.M., *Plant Hunting in China*, Collins 1945.

Davidian, H.H., *The Rhododendron Species Vol. I, II, III*. Timber Press 1982, 1989, 1992.

Dunbar, George, *Frontiers*, London 1932.

Fletcher, Harold R., *A Quest of Flowers*, Edinburgh University Press 1975.

Gordon, Robert, 'The Irawadi River', P.R.G.S. n.s. 7 (1885): 292-331.

Grey-Wilson, Christopher, '*Meconopsis integrifolia* the yellow Poppywort and its allies' in *The New Plantsman* Vol. 3 part 1, March 1996.

Grey-Wilson, Christopher, *Poppies,* B.T. Batsford 1993.

Fox, Stephen, 'The Forgotten Treasure of Nam La' in *Rhododendrons with Magnolias and Camellias* R.H.S. 1993**.**

Halda, Josef J., *The Genus Primula,* Tethys 1992.

Hang, Sun, Zhekun, Zhou, *Seed Plants of the Big Bend Gorge of Yalu Tsangpo in SE Tibet, E Himalayas,* Yunnan Science and Technology Press 2001.

Holdich, T.H., *Tibet the Mysterious,* London 1906.

Hopkirk, Peter, *Trespassers on the Roof of the World: The Race for Lhasa,* London 1982.

Huxley, Aldous, *Heaven and Hell,* Harper & Row, New York 1955.

Kaulback, R., *Tibetan Trek,* Hodder & Stoughton 1934.

Kingdon Ward, Frank, *A Plant Hunter in Tibet,* Jonathan Cape 1934.

Kingdon Ward, Frank, *Assam Adventure,* Jonathan Cape 1941.

Kingdon Ward, Frank, *Himalayan Enchantment,* edited by John Whitehead, London 1990.

Kingdon Ward, Frank, *In the Land of the Blue Poppy: Travels of a naturalist in Eastern Tibet,* London 1913.

Kingdon Ward, Frank, *Pilgrimage for Plants,* Harrap 1960.

Kingdon Ward, Frank, *Plant Hunting on the Edge of the World,* London 1930.

Kingdon Ward, Frank, *Plant Hunter in Manipur,* Jonathan Cape 1952.

Kingdon Ward, Frank, *The Mystery Rivers of Tibet,* London 1923.

Kingdon Ward, Frank, *The Romance of Gardening,* Harrap 1960.

Kingdon Ward, Frank, Field notes from 1924–25 expedition to S.E. Tibet.

Kingdon Ward, Frank, Letters to F.M. Bailey, 6 February 1923 to 24 May 1928, private collection.

Kingdon Ward, Jean, *My Hill so Strong,* Jonathan Cape 1952.

Lancaster, R. *Travels in China, A Plantsman's Paradise,* Antique Collectors' Club 1989.

Lyte, Charles, *Frank Kingdon-Ward: The Last of the Great Plant Hunters,* London 1989.

McCormack, Gavan, 'Water Margins, Competing Paradigms in China', *Critical Asian Studies,* Vol. 33, No. 1, 1 March 2001, Routledge

McKay, Alex, *Tibet and the British Raj: The Frontier Cadre 1904-1947,* Surrey 1997.

McLean, Brenda, *A Pioneering Plantsman, A.K. Bulley and the Great Plant Hunters,* H.M.S.O. 1997.

Meyer, Karl E. & Brysac, Shareen Blair, *Tournament of Shadows: The Great Game and The Race for Empire in Central Asia,* Washington 1999.

Michell, John F., *Report (Topographical, Political, and Military) on the North-East Frontier of India,* Calcutta 1883.

Montgomery, David R., et al., *Evidence for Holocene Megafloods down The Tsangpo River Gorge, S.E. Tibet,* Quaternary Research Center, University of Washington, Seattle, 2004

Morshead, H.T., *Report on an Exploration on the North East Frontier 1913,* Dehra Dun 1914.

Morshead, Ian, *The Life and Murder of Henry Morshead,* Cambridge 1982.

Mundy, Talbot, *Om: The Secret of the Ahbor Valley,* Carroll & Graf Publishers, Inc. New York 1984, pp. 340, 391.

Musgrave, T. Gardner, C. & Musgrave, W., *The Plant Hunters,* Ward Lock 1998.

Paul, Ashish, Khan, M. L., Arunachalam A., & Arunachalam K., 'Biodiversity and conservation of rhododendrons in Arunachal Pradesh in the Indo-Burma biodiversity hotspot', *Current Science* Vol. 89, No. 4, 25 August 2005.

Polunin, O. & Stainton, A., *Flowers of the Himalaya,* Oxford University Press 1984.

Postan, C. ed., *The Rhododendron Story,* Royal Horticultural Society 1996.

Qiu, Ming Jiang & Bleisch, William V., 'Preliminary Assessment of large mammals in the Namcha Barwa region of south-eastern Tibet, in *Oryx* Vol 30, 1 January 1996.

Reid, Sir Robert, *History of the Frontier Areas Bordering on Assam from 1883-1941,* Shillong 1942.

Richards, John, *Primula,* B.T. Batsford 1993.

Rushforth, K.R. & McAllister, H., Field notes.

Schaller, George B., Zhang, Endi, Zhi, Lu, An Ecological Survey of the Medog Area in the Yarlung Tsangpo Great Canyon National Reserve, Tibet. Report of the Tibet Forestry Department, 2000.

Schweinfurth, U., *Exploration in the Eastern Himalayas and the River Gorge Country of South eastern Tibet: Francis (Frank) Kingdon Ward (1885-1958): an annotated bibliography with a map of the area of his expeditions* (Geo-ecological research).

Scobie, C. *Last Seen in Lhasa,* Ebury 2006.

Shakespear, L.W., *History of Upper Assam, Upper Burmah and North-Eastern Frontier, London* 1914.

Swinson, Arthur, *Beyond the Frontiers,* London 1971.

Taylor, George, with Cox, Euan H.M., *The Genus Meconopsis,* New Flora and Silva 1934.

Taylor, George, unpublished diaries.

Trungpa, Chögyam, *Born in Tibet,* George Allen & Unwin UK 1966, pp. 208, 238, 241.

Van Geldern, D. & Van Geldern C., *Maples of the World,* Timber Press 1999.

Waddell, L.A., *Lhasa and Its Mysteries,* London 1905.

Waller, Derek, *The Pundits: British Exploration of Tibet and Central Asia,* Kentucky 1988.

Wordsworth, William, *The Prelude.*

Yichou, Yang, 'Yi'ong mud-stone flow' in *China's Tibet,* No. 6, 2000.

Flora of Bhutan, Royal Botanic Garden, Edinburgh.

Guidebook to Pemakö: Dispelling Clouds and Increasing Faith, discovered by Dondrul Pawo Dorje.

'Kintup's Report'. Report on the Explorations…Explorer K-P, 1880-84…in *Sikkim, Bhutan and Tibet. Survey of India,* Dehra Dun 1889.

Official Account of the Abor Expedition 1911-1912, General Staff India, Simla 1913.

Unesco World Heritage website, 'Three Parallel Rivers of Yunnan, Protected Areas, Criteria for inscription'.

Index

Page numbers in bold type refer to illustrations and captions

Aberconway, Lord, 18
Abies chayluensis, **131**
Abies forrestii, **131**
Abor Country, **36**
Abor Expedition, 38-40, 43-44
Abor Hills, 27, 35
Abor tribe, 28, 34, 35, **35, 39,** 146, 194, 238, 268-271
Abroka mountain range, 328
Abu Lashu, **55**
Acer caesium ssp. *giraldii,* **135**
Adi tribe, 322, **323, 326, 326,** 327, 328
Agapetes sp., 211
Agence France Press agency, 316
Ailurus fulgens, 324
Amdo, 174
Amitabha, Buddha, 62
Ammo Chu, 75
Androsace bisulca var *bramaputrae,* **188**
Anemone obtusiloba, **154**
Arisaema consanguineum, **284**
Arisaema elephas, 149, **155**
Arisaema flavum, **93**
Arisaema nepenthoides, **155**
Arunachal Pradesh, 314-329, **320, 324, 325, 326**
Assam earthquake (1950), 21, 296, 310
Assam Tribune, 314, 316
Aster albescens, **172**
Ata Kang Glacier, 290
Atali, **325**
Atsa, 185
    Tso, 186
Atunse, 20

Bai, 325
Bailey, F.M., **27, 29,** 36-48, **37,** 74, 78, 82, **98,** 104, 163, 167, 203, 206, 281, 282, 283, 290, 296, 299
Baker, Ian, 294, 296-300, **299, 300,** 310
    biography, 330
    narrative, 48-63
Balfour, Professor Bailey, 20
Banda La, 185
Bangladesh, 322
Bayi/Bayu(l) – *see* Payi
Beijing, 316, 320
Bentinck, Captain, 40
Berberis calliantha, **107,** 211
Berberis temolaica, 106, **107**
Bergenia purpurescens, **136**
Berneuxia thibetica, 289
Betula szechuanica, 130
Betula utilis, **135**
beyul, 50
bharal, 78
Bhutan, 75, 262, 321, 328
Biewlawski, Jill, 296
Bilham, Roger, 321

Blyth's Tragopan, 324
Boleng, **320**
Born in Tibet, 48
Bosheng, Li, 311-312
Bower, General, 40
Brahmaputra, 27, 69, 316, 322
    Falls of the, **58-59, 232,** 299
        existence of, 206
        searching for, 231
Breashears, David, 297, 310
brewing barley beer – *see chang*
bridges, **224,** 230, **240,** 246, 261, 262, 264, 274, **298,** 299, 314
    cable, **237,** 317
    rope, 22, 23, 162-163, 219-220, **222-224,** 226, 242-243, **245,** 274
    suspension, **320, 329**
Buchu Sengyi Lhakhang, 54
Buddhism, 328
Buddleja agathosma, 187
Bulley, A.K., 18, 19, 20, 281
Bullock, **304**
Burlinson, David, **172,** 285
Burg, Jean-Pierre, 297, 312-313
Burma (Myanmar), 321, 328

Calcutta, 73, 267
Callanthe, **288**
Callanthe chlorantha, 288
Callanthe tricarinata, 287
Cambridge, 19
Cape, Jonathan, 20
Caragana, 167
Cardiocrinum giganteum, 288
Cassiope fastigata, **124**
Cassiope selaginoides, **102, 103,** 152
Cassiope wardii, **124**
Cawdor, Lord, 23-25, **23, 24,** 48, 59, *passim*
    chapters by, 268-279
Cephlotaxus, 323
Chake, 87
Chamberlain, Dr David, 154, 286
Chambers, Anne, **284**
chang, 218, **273**
Changu, 75
Chimdro, 42-43, 145
    Chu, 237
China, 314-329
China Daily, 310, 316, 318, 321
Chinese exploration of Tsangpo Gorges, 310-311
Chionocharis hookeri, **85, 256**
Chomo, 94, 95
Chongyechen, 79
Chongyeshö, 80
Chökorchye monastery, 83
Chomodadzong, 179
Chumbi, Sonam, 42
Chumbi Valley, 75
Chumolarhi, 76

Chunyima, 172
chupa, 275
Churung Chu, 210, 234
Cirrhopetalum emarginatum, 216
Clematis barbellata, **135**
Clematis montana, 100
    'Burlinson's Blush', 172
    (*C. gracilifolia*), 83
    f. *grandiflora,* **102**
Clematis tibetana ssp. *vernayi,* **252**
clothes, **97, 199,** 245, 250, 261, 266, 275-276
Clutterbuck, H.M., 23
Cobbett, Captain, 78
Codonopsis, 167
Codonopsis convolvulacea, 60, 162
Coelogyne, 230
Coelogyne cristata, 75
cooking, 277-278
Cotoneaster conspicuus, **188**
Cox, Euan, 20, **110,** 330
Cox, Kenneth, **287, 324**
    biography, 330
    narrative, 10-13, 17-26, 285-295, 314-329
Cox, Peter, 286, 288, **289,** 330
Crawfurdia, 219
Cremanthodium, 167
Cremanthodium palmatum, 167, **168**
crops, 279
Cultural Revolution, 290
Cuon alpinus, 324
Cupressus gigantea, **85**
Curuma aromatica, 323
Cyananthus lobatus, 119, **119**
Cyananthus wardii, 175
Cynoglossum amabile, 180, 188
Cypripedium tibeticum, **131**

Daily Telegraph, 320
Dali, 20
Damro, **323**
Daphne sp. (aff. *acutiloba*), **244**
Daphla tribe, 269
Darjeeling, 73
Das, Sarat Chandra, 37
Dashing La, 285, 292, **292, 293,** 324
David, Abbé Jean Pierre, 17, 18
Davidia involucrata, 18
Debshi La, 259
Delavay, Abbé Jean Marie, 17, 18
Delphinium sp., 185
Dengyi, Gao, 311-312
Deqin, 20
Deutzia compacta, 288
Diapensia purpurea, **142,** 196, 294
Dibang, 27, 323, 324, **325**
Dihang, 27, 38, 40, 135, 157
Dihang-Dibang Biosphere Reserve, 322-323, 324, 326
Dokar La, **281,** 283-290, **289, 291**
doors, 276

Dorje Pagmo, 45, 54, 55, **56, 57,** 59, 60
    Hidden Falls of, **27, 303, 305, 306-307,** 310-311
Dorje Traktsen, **55,** 59
Doshong La, **21,** 48, 49, 89, **64, 102,** 104, 130ff., **130ff.,** 286, **287,** 321
    crossing, 148-149, **146-147**
    autumn, 152-160, **150ff., 195-197**
    south side, **155**
    summit, **147**
Drakpuk Kawasum, 59
Drokpa, **67**
Drukla Chu, 180
Drukla Gompa/Monastery, **179,** 180, 182-183, **183,** 245
Dunbar, Captain Sir George, 35, 38
Dundas, Captain, 43, 44

Elaeagnus umbellata var. *parvifolia,* 216
Elliot, Henry, **85,** 283, 296
Elwin, Verrier, 322
Enkianthus chinensis, 292, **293**
Eriophyton wallichianum, 186
Euphorbia wallichii, **252**
Everest, Mt., 26, 75

'Falls of the Tsangpo' (sketch), **27**
Farrer, Reginald, 20
Ficus, 230
fireplaces, 276
First World War, 20
fleas, 144, 162, 169, 173, **199**
flower colour, 108-109
food, 73, 277-278
Forrest, George, 17, 18, 20, **201,** 280-282
Fortnum & Mason, 73
Fortune, Robert, 17
Four Great Rivers Nature Preserve, 328
Fox, Stephen, 286
Fritillaria cirrhosa, **129**
Fu, Che, 311
furniture, 276-277

Gallipoli, 47
Gandhi, Rahul, 321
Gangtok, 47, 74
Gansu, 320
Gautsa, 75
gazelle, 76
Geling, 314
Gentiana filistyla, **185**
Gentiana waltonii, 194, 249
geology, 312-313
Geranium donianum, **184**
Gobshi, **77**

Gompo Ne, **50, 51, 53, 61, 62-63,** 218, **221,** 222, 223, **222-224,** 226, **228, 240,** 296, **319**
Gonglharongbabo Mountain, 316
goral, 231, 236
Gordon, Doug, 310
'gushuk', 95, **97**
Graham, Dr., 74
grain, 278
Great *Yalungzangbo* Canyon, 320
Grey-Wilson, Chris, **248, 252**
Griffith, Dr. William, 17
Gyala, 30, 31, 45, 46, 47, 53, 163, 169, 198, **198,** 200, 310, 312-313
Depa of, 163
outskirts, **197**
Gyala Peri, 30, 32, 45, 54, 192, 214, 219, **220,** 226, **233,** 234, 242, **268, 308-309, 311,** 312
Gyamda, 186, 246-247, **251**
Chu (River), 89, **89, 91,** 94, 187, 286
Valley, 90, **251**
Gyamtso, 40-43
Gyantse, 37, 75, 76, 78-81, 275
Gyantze, 318
Gyatsa Dzong, 84

Hai, He, 285-286
Hang, Sun, 323
Harmon, Captain, 30, 34
Harvey, Bryan, 302, 310
Henry, Augustine, 18
Hilton, James, 50
Himalaya, 17, *passim,* 312-313
Holdich, Thomas, 39
Hooker, Joseph, 17, 75
houses, 276-277
Huxley, Aldous, 62
Hydrangea, 230
Hyslop, Major, 78

Incarvillea longiracemosa, 83, **84**
Incarvillea younghusbandii, **184,** 185, 249
India, 314-329
Indian army, 20
Indian Express, 316
Iris chrysographes, 112, **113, 136**
Iris decora, 90, **92, 171**
Iris lactea, 256
Irrawaddy, 27, 30, 69
Isopyrum grandiflorum, 167, 175

Jasminum humile, **164**
Jaypo, Mt., 20
Je, 244
Jhu Long, **281,** 289
Johnston, Ned, 300
Juniperus squamata/fargesii, 110
Jyang, 299, **304**

Kacharis, 172
Kailas, Mt., 26, 37, 328
Kalimpong, 74
Kampa tribe, 146-147, 194, 237-238, 268-271, **272,** 280
Kanam Raja, 172
Kangla Karpo, 54
Karma La, 239, **239,** 242
Karo La, 78
Kashmir, 69

Kaulback, Ronald, 24
Khan, Atta Ulla, 80, 255
Kidd, William, **315**
Kingdon Ward, Frank, 17, 19, **19, 22,** *passim*
daughters, 20
publications, 20
    A Plant Hunter in Tibet, 282, 292
    Assam Adventure, **256,** 283
    In the Land of the Blue Poppy, 20
    Pilgrimage for Plants, 20, 22, 24
    The Mystery Rivers of Tibet, 282
    The Romance of Gardening, 150
relations with Cawdor, 23-25
Kingdon Ward, Florinda (née Norma-Thompson, 20, 23
Kingdon Ward, Jean (née Macklin, later Rasmussen), 21, 321
Kintup, **27-28,** 29-35, **32,** 37, 43, 45-47, **47,** 52, 59, 203, 206, 299
first journey, 29-30
second journey, 30-35
Kintup's falls, 206, 207
Kongba tribe, 146, **198-199,** 268-270
Kongbo, 54, 91, 94, 95, **97,** 180, 187, 270, 277, **298**
Gyamda, 252
Nga La, 86
Pa La, **249,** 251, **252, 253**
Peri, 94
towers, **179, 189**
Kuging, **326**
Kundu Dorsempotrang, 33, **237,** 299, 322
kyang, 76
Kyikar, 165, 169, 199-200

Lagung, 43, 45, 46, 299
Lamas, **56, 58-59**
Dalai, 42, 43, 47, 55, 59, 75, 86, 171, 190, **193**
Dorje, Rigzin Düdrul, 48
Gyatso, Serap, 31, 168
Gyatso, Lopsang Den, **193**
Labrang, 182, 183
Rinpoche, Kanjur, 56
Samdup, Tsiang, 52
Tashi, 42, 43
Trungpa, Chögyam, 48-49
Wangpo, Konchok, 53
Larix griffithiana, 130, **130, 228**
leeches, **284**
Leptocodon gracile, 174
Leptodermis microphyllus, **88**
Lhasa, 26, 80, 190, 275, 316, 321
Lijiang, 20
Lilium lophophorum, 126
Lilium mackliniae, 21, 22
Lilium nanum, **115,** 126, 160
Lilium paradoxum, 61, 290, **293, 295**
Lilium tigrinum, 187
Lilium wallichianum, 265
Lilium wardii, 174, **238,** 286
Lilung, 87
Lin-chih, 286
Lindgren, Scott, 317, **327**
Lissu, **215**

Litiping, 20
Llagyari Dzong, 82
Lobaria pulmonaria, 124
Lohit, 27, 38
Londonderry, Lady, 20
Lonicera cyanocarpa, 106, 191
    var. *porphyrantha,* 122
Lonicera hispida, 122, 167, 192
    var. *bracteata,* 164
    var. *setosa,* 122, 167
Lonicera setifera, 99
Lonicera webbiana, 120, **121,** 128
Lopa (Abor) tribe, 87, 194, 219, 237-238, **268,** 271-272, 325
dress, 194, **268**
Lophophorus sclateri, **229,** 231, 324
Lubong, 242
Luculia gratissima, 219
Ludlow, Frank, 25, 78, **85, 98, 115, 119, 132, 143, 204, 248, 281,** 283-287, **285, 291,** 290, 296, 318
Lugu, 46, 296, 298
Lunang, 47, **111,** 112, 171, **172**
Lung La, 82, 83, 254
Lusha, 94
Lyte, Charles, 24

Macaca assamensis, 324
Macaca mulata, 324
McAllister, Hugh, **84**
McCormack, Gavan, 320
MacDonald, Mr., 75, 76, 78
Mcelroy, Damien, 320
Macklin, Jean – *see* Kingdon Ward, Jean
McMahon, Henry, 322
Magnolia campbellii, 75
Magnolia rostrata, 211
Mahonia pomensis, **285,** 286
mail to and from Tibet, 95, 105, 144, 190, 246
Makandro, 242
Mandalting, 169
Mandragora caulescens, 168
mani, **71**
Manthey, Eric, 296
Marpung, **32,** 33-35
Meade, Captain H.R., 78
Meconopsis aculeata, 104
Meconopsis baileyi, 45, 47, 104, 114
Meconopsis betonicifolia, 22, 100, 104, **106,** 114, **115,** 165
Meconopsis florindæ, 160
Meconopsis horridula, 76, 125, **127,** 185, 186, **256**
    [*M. prainiana*], 104, 125, 161
Meconopsis impedita, 104, 127, 167
Meconopsis integrifolia, **256**
Meconopsis latifolia, 104
Meconopsis lyrata, 160
Meconopsis pseudointegrifolia, **103,** 104, **106,** 114, **125,** 127, 186, 289
    [var. *brevistyla*], 104
Meconopsis (*horridula* var.) *racemosa,* 249
Meconopsis simplicifolia, **103,** 104, **106,** 114, 126-127, 149
Meconopsis speciosa, 104, **125,** 127
    [*M. cawdoriana*], 127
Meconopsis x *harleyana,* **106, 114**

Medog, 33, **273,** 296, 310, 313, 323, 324, 327, 328
Mekong, 27, 69, 70, 328
minstrels, **250**
Mipi, 40-45
Miri Padam, 34
Mishmi Hills, 38, 41
Mishmi tribe, 28, 269, 324, **325,** 326, 327, 328
Mithun *(Bos frontalis),* 324
Mönba tribe, 46, 60, **64, 141,** 146-147, 219, 226, 229, 237-238, 261, **268, 269,** 271-272, **273,** 296, **297, 300, 304,** 324, 327
dress, 197, 261
Morina coulteriana, **84**
Morina longifolia, **84**
Morshead, Henry, **29, 37,** 41-47, 82, 163, 203, 206, 282, 283, 294, 299
Moschus Moschiferus, 324
Mundy, Talbot, 50-52
Muotuo, 320, 321
Myanmar – *see* Burma

Naga tribe, 39
Nagong Chu (Po-Tsangpo), 282
Nam La, 104, **124,** 163, 165-170, 199
ascent, 168
in November, **170**
Nam Tso (Lake), 176
Nambu Gompa, **173,** 175
Nambu La, 101, 176, **177,** 243, 282
Namcha Barwa, **29,** 30, 31, 32, 45, 48, 54, 69, 70, 90, **93,** 93-94, 163, **165,** 191-192, 203, **205, 213, 228, 302, 308-309,** 312-313, 320-321
Namgye, *Nyerpa,* 43
Namla Karpo, 179
Nang Dzong, **84,** 86
Nanga Parbat, 312, 313
Nanking, Treaty of, 17
Napo Dzong, 187
Napo, *Dzongpön of,* 246
Nathu La, 74, 75
National Geographic Society, 310
nats, 224
Nemœrhœdus baileyi, 231, 324
Nemorhaedus goral, 324
Neofelis nebulosa, 324
Nepal, 328
Netong Dzong, 80
Nevill, Captain, 41
New Delhi, 317
Ni and Cheng, 323
Norbu Linka, **193**
Norma-Thompson, Florinda, 20
North East Frontier Agency, 322
Nyemong Kunchog, 60
Nyima La, **99, 103, 113, 114,** 122, **123, 124, 126,** 126-129, 193, 285

Oga Dzong, 254
Omphalogramma delavayi, **281**
Omphalogramma tibetica, **281,** 284, 289
Onosma sp., 180
Onosma hookeri, **181**
Orchis latifolia, 100

Pa La, 122
Pab Ri, 91, 93
Pachakshiri, 87
Padmasambhava, 48, **52**, 60
Paeonia lutea var. *ludlowii*, 95, **98**
Pamirs, the, 69
Panja, Ajit, 316
Panthera pardus, 324
Panthera tigris, 324
Pasighat, 314
Pasum Kye La, 184
Pasum Tso, **67**, 177-180, **178, 181,** 283
    watch tower, **189**
Paul, Ashish, 324
Payi (Payu, Payul, Bayi, Bayu, Bayul), 46, **62-63**, 216, **220, 221,** 222, 310, 327, 328
Pe, **128**, 129-130, 133-135, 144, 194, **196,** 198, 317, 318
    Depa of, 198
Pelung, **314-315**
Pema, 317, **319**
Pemakö, 30, 41, 43, 46, 48-63, **55, 64,** 144-160, **151, 154,** 322-329
Pemaköchung, 29, 31, 32, 35, 46, 47, 59, 60, 163, 203-209, **208, 211, 213,** 283, 296, 297
Pemashelri, 60
Pemberton, Major, 125, 149
People's Daily, 316
pestle and mortar, 278
Phari, 73, 76
pheasants, **229,** 231, 236
Phuntsok, Dungle, **49, 195, 232,** 299, **299, 300**
picahares, 76
Picea likiangensis, 130
Pieris formosa var. *forrestii*, 288
pilgrims, 30-31, 33, 48ff., **51, 54, 61-63,** 174, 178, **224, 249, 251**
Pingso, 226
Pinus armandii, 130, **130**
Pinus bhutanica, 210
plant hunters of China and the Himalaya, 17
    routiner, 109-110
Pleione scopulorum, **208**
ploughs, 278
Po-Tsangpo, 45, 219, 224, **224, 225,** 226, 236, 238-242, **239-241, 244,** 282, 283, **284,** 286, 310, 312, **314-315,** 317, **318, 319**
    confluence, **298,** 299
Po Yigrong, 285, **315**
Poba tribe, 94, **97,** 146, 171ff., 219, 230, 237-238
    dress, **97**
Podophyllum aurantiocaule, **159, 160**
Podophyllum hexandrum, **159**
Podrang La, **122**
Pome, 38, 43, 44, 48, 89, 100, 145, 148, 171ff., **275,** 279, 280-295, **280,** 326
    Dzongpön of, 294
    Nyerpa of, 46, 299
    range, **221**
    Valley, 294
Populus alba, 90
Populus rotundifolia, 130
porters, **141,** 194, **195, 196,** 200,

213-214, **237,** 261, 271, 287-288, **291, 293, 297, 298**
Potala palace, Lhasa, **93**
Potentilla arbuscula, 167
Potentilla fruticosa, 78, 82-83, **124,** 167
Primula advena var. *advena*, 128, 166, **166, 169**
    var *euprepes*, 128, **128,** 166
Primula alpicola, **111,** 116, 127, 133, 165, 176, 249
    var. *alpicola,* **184**
    var. *luna,* 112
    var. *violacea,* **113,** 162
Primula atrodentata, 83, **84,** 91, 100, 112
Primula baileyana, 167, **169,** 323
Primula bellidifolia (ssp. *hyacinthina*), 114, **114**
Primula calderiana [*P. roylei*], 94, 114, **122,** 123
Primula cawdoriana, 25, **25**
Primula chionantha ssp. *brevicula* [*P. rigida*], 126
Primula chionata, 149, 152
Primula chungensis, 100, 111, 115, **115**
Primula cockburniana, 115
Primula denticulata, 75, 83, **84**
Primula dickieana, , 149, **150, 154**
Primula doshongensis, **99**
Primula dryadifolia ssp. *philoresia,* 125, 143
Primula falcifolia, 114, **142,** 143, 152, **159,** 195, 323
Primula florindae, 23, 115, 116, 127, 133, **173,** 175
Primula glabra, **99,** 143
    ssp. *kongboensis,* 94
Primula kongboensis, **99**
Primula latisecta, 128, 178, 179, **180**
Primula littledalei, 167
Primula macrophylla var. *ninguida,* 106, **107,** 124
Primula maximowiczii, 128
    var. *euprepes,* **128**
Primula microphylla var. *microphylla,* **124**
Primula morsheadiana, 114, 143, 152, 195
Primula petiolaris, 75
Primula pseudocapitata, 192
Primula pulchella [*P. pulchelloides*], 94, 129, 175, 179
Primula pumilio [*P. pygmæorum*], 77, 83
Primula rhodochroa, 143
Primula sikkimensis var. *pudibunda,* 112, 125, 161-162, 167
Primula sinopurpurea, 106, 124 [*P. rigida*], 124
Primula szechuanica, 128
Primula tibetica, 83, 100, 112, **113, 184**
Primula valentiniana, 114, 143, 149, 152
Primula walshii, 123
Primula waltonii, 78, 83, 176
Prunus serrula, 111
Public Security Bureau, 286
Pundits, 28-29, 46
    A.K., 38, 282
    U.G., Lama Ugyen Gyatso, 37

Pung, Rinchen Riwoche Jedung, 62
Pungkat, 184
Puparang, 169
Purung, 314
Putrang La, 82, **85**
Pylung – *see* Trulung
Pyrola forrestii, 130

Quercus semecarpifolia, **128,** 129

Rainbow Falls, **26, 217, 229,** 296, 299, 300, **301,** 302, **304,** 310, 312, 317, **327**
Red Lily, 290-295, **295**
Rhacophorus translineatus, 324
Rheum alexandrae, 124
Rheum nobile, **123,** 124
Rhodiola himalayensis?, 125, **125**
Rhododendrons, hardiness of, 153
Rhododendron aganniphum, **136, 146,** 153
    Doshongense gp., 132
Rhododendron arboreum, 75, **216,** 260, 261
    ssp. *delavayi,* **216**
Rhododendron arizelum, 215
    aff., 149, **154**
Rhododendron auritum, 207
Rhododendron barbatum, 75
Rhododendron beesianum, 292
Rhododendron bulu, 87, 91, **96,** 110
Rhododendron calostrotum, 134, 289, **291**
    ssp. *riparium,* 134, **134,** 137, **146,** 196
Rhododendron campylocarpum, **21, 106, 136,** 137, **137,** 140, **146,** 153, 195, **287**
    x *cerasinum,* **106**
Rhododendron campylogynum, **146,** 176
Rhododendron cephalanthum, Nmaiense gp., 142, **144, 146**
Rhododendron cerasinum, **106, 131, 132,** 149, 157
Rhododendron chamaethomsonii, 139, 153
Rhododendron charitopes ssp. *tsangpoense,* **136,** 140, **146,** 148, 153, **154**
    Curvistylum gp., 140
Rhododendron cinnabarinum, 75, 148, 202, 261
    ssp. *xanthocodon* Purpurellum gp., **129**
    ssp. *xanthocodon* Concatenans gp., 148, **150, 154**
Rhododendron coryanum, 166
    R. coryanum, aff., 202
Rhododendron dalhousiae var. *rhabdotum,* 209
Rhododendron dignabile, 105, **107,** 110, **131,** 153, 166
Rhododendron doshongense, 140, 143, 195
    (*R. aganniphum*), 137
Rhododendron edgeworthii, 207
Rhododendron exasperatum, 157, **204,** 207, **208**
Rhododendron falconeri, 75
Rhododendron faucium, 100, **102,** 110, 130, 162, 202

Rhododendron forrestii, 139, **139, 142, 146, 147,** 176, 195, 294
    Repens gp., 137, 138, **138**
    Tumescens gp., **138,** 140
    x *R. aganniphum (R. chamaethomsonii),* **136**
Rhododendron fragariflorum, 101, **102,** 103, **103,** 110, 153, 162
Rhododendron fulvum ssp. *fulvoides,* **155**
Rhododendron glaucophyllum, 75, 140
Rhododendron glischrum ssp. *rude,* **201,** 202, 215
Rhododendron grande, 75
Rhododendron headfortianum, 209, **209**
Rhododendron hirtipes, 91, **96,** 105, 110, 130, 153, 165, 196, 202
Rhododendron imperator, **158**
Rhododendron keysii, **145,** 157, **159**
Rhododendron kongboense, **110,** 141, **146**
Rhododendron lanatoides, 153, **164,** 286
Rhododendron lanigerum, **155,** 157, **204,** 215, **216,** 230
Rhododendron laudandum, 110, 153, 162
    var. *temoense,* 101, **103,** 142, **146**
Rhododendron lepidotum, 110, **119,** 120, 161, 175, 261
    [*R. elægnoides*], 153, 167
Rhododendron leucapsis, **209,** 323
Rhododendron lindleyi, 209
Rhododendron maddenii, 202, 203, 210, 216, 261
Rhododendron megacalyx, 202, **204**
Rhododendron megeratum, 157, **158**
Rhododendron mekongense, **134,** 142, **144**
    var. *rubrolineatum,* **144**
Rhododendron micromeres, 157
Rhododendron montroseanum, 202, **204,** 215
Rhododendron neriiflorum, 139
Rhododendron nivale, 86, **88,** 93, 94, 101, 110, 111, **111,** 124, 140, **146,** 153, 162, 188
Rhododendron nuttallii, 226, **227,** 230, 286
Rhododendron oreotrephes, 110, 120, **121, 128, 129,** 191, 202
Rhododendron parmulatum, **136,** 148, **150,** 323
    x *R. forrestii,* **150, 154**
Rhododendron pemakoense, 207, **209,** 289, 323
Rhododendron phaeochrysum, 25, 86, 90, 91, **99,** 110, 153, 260
    ssp. *agglutinatum,* 91, 93, 166
Rhododendron primuliflorum, 80, 86, 93, 101, 110, **110,** 142, 166, 260, 289
Rhododendron principis, 110, **111,** 129, 130, 161, 166, 188
    [*R. vellereum*], **111**
Rhododendron pumilum, 142, **146**
Rhododendron ramsdenianum, 202, 203, 230
Rhododendron sanguineum, 289
Rhododendron scopulorum, 216, **221,** 286

Rhododendron setosum, **102**
Rhododendron sinogrande, **155, 159,**
  166, 203, **204,** 207, 210, 215,
  230
  [*grande*], 157
Rhododendron strigillosum, 157
Rhododendron taggianum, **209**
Rhododendron tephropeplum, 207
Rhododendron thomsonii, 75
Rhododendron trichocladum, **144,**
  149, 152
Rhododendron triflorum, 87, 91, 94,
  100, 110, 130, 161, 166, 188, 261
  Mahogani gp., **88**
Rhododendron uniflorum, 149
  (*R. imperator*), 152, **158**
Rhododendron, unnamed, 324,
  324
Rhododendron uvariifolium, 91, 110,
  130, 153, 162, 165, **201, 202,**
  292
  var *griseum,* **201**
Rhododendron vaccinioides, 202, 210
Rhododendron venator, 202, 203, **204,**
  323
Rhododendron virgatum, 174, 188,
  203, 210, 212, 288
Rhododendron viridescens, **131,** 157
Rhododendron wardii, **21,** 22, 93,
  100, 105, 110, 128, 130, **131,**
  132, 133, 153, 165, 289, **291**
  x *phaeochrysum,* 105
Rhododendron wightii, 75
Rima, 22, 321
Rinchenpung, 33, 43, 60
Ringu, Pekyom, 326
Rinpoche, Khamtrul, 53-55
Rinpoche, Kanjur, 59
Riudechen, 80
Robinson, William, 18
Rock, Joseph, 17
Rodgersia, 287
Rodgersia pinnata, **284**
Rong, 112ff., **113,** 171
  flowers of the, 119-122
Rong Chu, 32, 45, 47, 98, 101,
  105, 112, **115, 241, 244, 245,**
  284, 286, 327
Rongchakar, 82
rooves, 276
Rosa macrophylla, **121,** 122
Rosa moyesii, 122
Rosa sericea, 78, **81,** 90, 95, 100,
  149, 152
  forma. *pteracantha,* **98**
  var. *omeiensis,* **81**
Rosa wardii, **121,** 122
Ross, June, **293**
Rothschild, Lionel de, 18
Royal Botanic Garden, Edinburgh,
  20
Royal Geographical Society, 22, 30,
  47, 282
Rubus, 286
Rubus lineatus, 211
Rungpo, 74
Rushforth, Keith, **84, 131, 177**
Ryder, Captain, 36
Rynning, Ralph, **229,** 299

Sadiya, 35, 38, 39
Salween, 27, 69, 282, 328

Samding monastery, 55
Sang La, 105, **113**
Sanglung, 207, 210, 212, 214, 217
  spur, 215
Sango Dam, 318
Sardar, Hamid, 299-300, 302, 310
Saxifrages, 167
scent in flowers, 108-109
Schaller, George, 323, 324, 326, 328
Schisandra neglecta, **164**
Scottish Royal Geographical
  Society, 22
seed collecting, 190-198
Sengchen, **215, 223, 225,** 226,
  227, 230, 271, **297, 300**
  Gompa, 236
  La, 215
Sengdam Pu, 169
Sengetong, 219
Shamda La, 79
Shanghai, 19
Shangri-La, 49-50
Shelkarlungpa, 59
Shepperd, Andrew, **327**
Sherriff, George, 25, **85, 98, 115,**
  119, 132, 143, 204, 248, 281,
  283, 285-286, **285,** 290, **291,**
  296, 318
Shillong, 321
Shingche Chögye (Sinji-Chogyal),
  32, 46, 47, 53, 55, 162, 170, 203
Shobe La, **283**
Shoga Dzong, 245, 247
Shoga, *Dzonpong* of, 179, 182
Showa, 44, 45, 282-294
  La, **289**
Shugden Gompa, 38, 43, 282, 290
  Kingdon Ward at, 290
Siang, 314, **320,** 321-323, 328
Sichuan-Tibet Highway, 327
Sikkim, 47
  Maharajah of, 75
Simla, 46, 322
Singh, Kishen, 38
Singh, Nem, 29, 30, 34
Sinji-Chogyal – *see* Shingche
  Chögye
Sinopodophyllum hexandrum, **159**
Sirchem La, **84, 99, 124, 164, 169,**
  286
Skimmia, 230
Sophora davidii [*viciifolia*], 78, **81,**
  83, 90
Sophora moorcroftiana, **81**
Sorbus filipes, **176,** 288, **289**
Sorbus microphyllus, 288
Sorbus rehderiana, **84**
Soulié, Abbé, 280, 281
Spiraea sp. (*S. arcuata*), **88**
Stellera chamaejasmae, **252**
Storm, Kenneth, **195,** 294, **299,**
  303, 310, 317, 319, 321, 322
  biography, 330
  narrative 294-312
Streptopus simplex, 288
Strobilanthes, 219
Sü La, 44, 217, 285, 292-295, **293,**
  295
Subansiri, 87, 321
Sur La, **98**
Survey of India, 30, 34
Sus scrofa, 324

Swiss Federal Institute of Technology, 313
Szechuan, 69

Tagin tribe, 322
takin *(Budorcas taxicolor),* 46, 210,
  212-215, **212-213, 215, 297,**
  324, **326**
  skin, **97**
Tang La, 76, 122, 161
Tangme, 285, 286
Tantric Buddhism, **52, 56, 57**
Tashi Jong, **56**
Tawang, 324
Taylor, Daniel, 325
Taylor, (Sir) George, **114, 248, 283**
taxation, 194
Temo, **93,** 94, 98-104, 110-111, **277**
  Dzongpön of, 105, 112
Temo Gompa, 98, 100
Temo La, 25, **25,** 98-104, **102,** 110-
  111, **113, 114, 119,** 122, **161,**
  191, 285
Tensing, Dorjee, 327
textiles, 279
Thalictrum diffusiflorum, 119, **120**
Thalictrum dipterocarpum, 120, **120**
Thermopsis barbata, **171**
Thogme, Dorje, 50, 54
Three Gorges Dam, 319-320
Three Rivers Region, 329
Tibet
  Autonomous Region, 318, 328
  dances, 198
  dress, 95
  floral zones of, 97-98
  geography of, 66-70
  mastiffs, 47, 97, **98**
  poodles, 97
  people of South-east, 237, 268-
  273
  'Three Gorges of', 321
Tista Valley, 74
Titapuri, **326**
Tongkyuk, 33, 45, 101, 174, 283
  Dzong, 174
Tra La, **115,** 122, 170, 286
Tragopan blythi, 324
Tragopan temmincki, 236, 324
Trap, 82, 254
Trashigang Dzong, 262, **263,** 264
Tratsa, 79
Trenchard, Major, 126, 149
Tro La, 186
Trube (Tripe), **111,** 162, 163, **165**
Trulung (Pylung), **216, 238,** 239,
  240, 245, 283, **285,** 286, 328
Trungsashö, 86
Tsachu, **220-221, 225, 238, 298,**
  316, 317, **318, 319**
Tsachugang, 226, 236
Tsakuntuzangpo, 60
tsamba, 201, 270, 278
Tsangpo – *see* Yarlung Tsangpo
Tsari, 34, 87, **107**
Tsechu, 298
Tsela Dzong, 86, 89-97, **91-93**
Tsetang, 29, 78-82, **79, 81,** 255
Tsöna, 255, 260
  Dzong, 259, 269
Tsongpen, **281, 284,** 287, 290, **291**
Tsosang Gompa, 179, 244, **247**

Tsuga dumosa, **228,** 230, 288
Tumbatse, 33, **96,** 101, 105, 111,
  116-118, **117-118, 120,** 126,
  171, 286
Tuna, 76
Tuting, 314, 321, 327, 328, **329**

Ulmus pumila, 80
Uncia uncia, 324
UNESCO, 326, 329
Ursus thibetanus, 324
Usnea longissima, **124**

Vaccinium sikkimense aff. **141**
Vaccinium nummularia aff., **158**
Vajra Yogini, 57
Veitch, Sir Harry, 18
Viburnum mullaha, **158**
Vitis, 230

Waddell, L.A., **27**
Wallich, Nathaniel, 17, **252**
Washington Post, The, 310
weapons, 279
Walker, Wickcliffe, 310
Wildlife Conservation Society, 323
Williams, J.C., 18, 19
Williamson, Noel, 35, 38
Wilson, Ernest, 17, 18
Wiltsie, Gordon, 297
Wordsworth, William, 62
World Heritage Site, 329

Xanthoxylum artmatum, 288
Xigaze, 318
Xinhau news agency, 316
Xinjiang, 320

yak butter tea, **277**
Yamdrok Tso, 55, 78. 79
Yang Sang, 322, **324, 326,** 327,
  328, **328**
  Pemakö Society, 327
Yangtze, 27, 69, 70, 320, 328
Yarlung Tsangpo (Yarlung
  Zangbo), 26, **83, 89, 92-93,**
  196, 225, 313, 314, 317. **318,**
  319, 320
  Grand Canyon National
  Reserve, 322
Yarlung-Siang 319, 321
Yartö Tra La, **256,** 257
Yatung, 75
Yellow River, 320
Yichou, Yang, 311, 327
Yigrong, 94, **284,** 286, 316, 317
  Tsangpo, 287
Younghusband, F., 36, 37, **184**
Yunnan Plateau, 69
Yuri, Colonel, 283

Zàngnán (South Tibet), 322
Zayul, **98,** 282
Zhamolong Gully, 316
Zhekun, Zhou, 323
Zhihua, Guan, 311-312
Zhikung Hydroelectric Power
  Station, 321
Zhongdian (Chungtien), 282
Zo La, **98**
Zuanru, Geng, 296

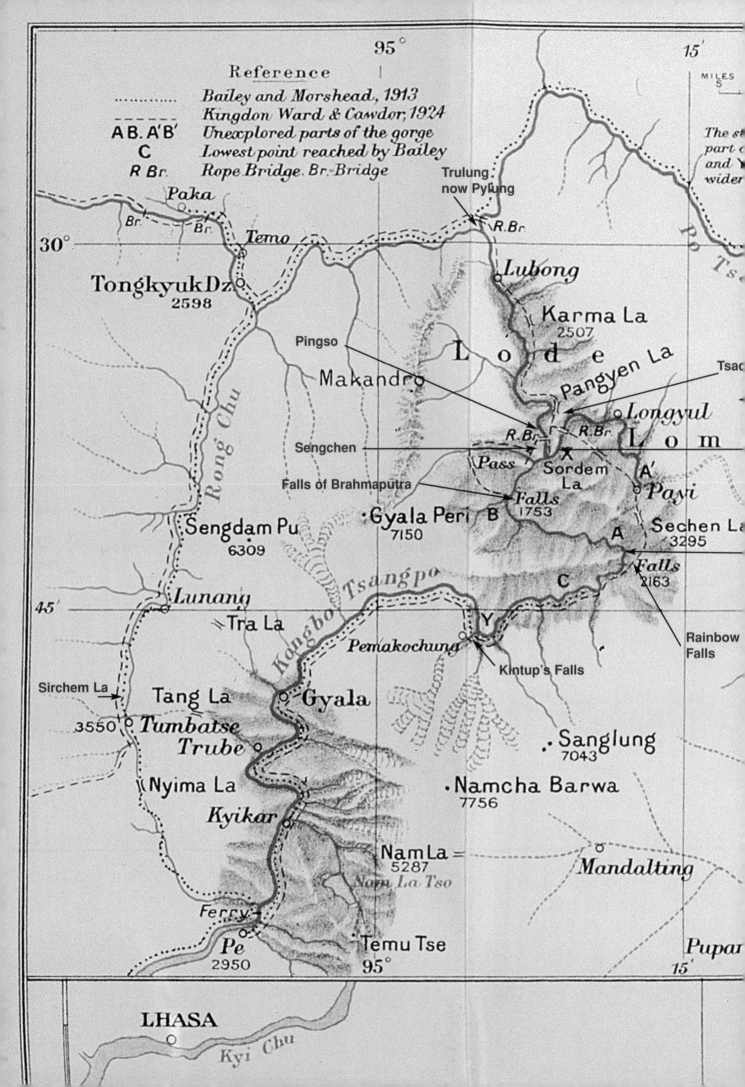

Reference
.... Bailey and Morshead, 1913
– – – Kingdon Ward & Cawdor, 1924
A B. A'B' Unexplored parts of the gorge
C Lowest point reached by Bailey
R Br. Rope Bridge. Br. Bridge

95°

15'

MILES
5

The st...
part o...
and Y...
wider...

Paka

Br.

Br.

Temo

Trulung
now Pylung

R.Br.

Po Ts...

30°

Lubong

TongkyukDz.
2598

Karma La
2507

Pangyen La

L o d e

Rong Chu

Pingso

Makandro

Tsad...

Longyul

Lom

R.Br.

R.Br.

Sengchen

Pass

Sordem
La

A'

Falls of Brahmaputra

Falls
1753

Pavi

B

Sengdam Pu
6309

Gyala Peri
7150

A

Sechen La
3295

Falls
2163

C

Lunang

Kongbo Tsangpo

45'

Rainbow
Falls

Tra La

Pemakochung

Y

Sirchem La

Kintup's Falls

Tang La

Tumbatse
3550 Trube

Gyala

Sanglung
7043

Nyima La

Namcha Barwa
7756

Kyikar

Nam La
5287

Mandalting

Nam La Tso

Ferry

Temu Tse

Pupar...

Pe
2950

95°

15'

LHASA

Kyi Chu